P9-CLF-838

DISCARDED

The Evolution of American Electoral Systems

Recent titles in
Contributions in American History
Series Editor: Jon L. Wakelyn

Alcohol, Reform, and Society: The Liquor Issue in Social Context
Jack S. Blocker, Jr.

War and Welfare: Social Engineering in America, 1890-1925
John F. McClymer

The Divided Metropolis: Social and Spatial Dimensions of Philadelphia, 1800-1975
William W. Cutler, III, and Howard Gillette, Jr.

The Southern Common People: Studies in Nineteenth-Century Social History
Edward Magdol and Jon L. Wakelyn

Northern Schools, Southern Blacks, and Reconstruction: Freedmen's Education, 1862-1875
Ronald E. Butchart

John Eliot's Indian Dialogues: A Study in Cultural Interaction
Henry W. Bowden and James P. Ronda

The XYZ Affair
William Stinchcombe

American Foreign Relations: A Historiographical Review
Gerald K. Haines and Samuel J. Walker, editors

Communism, Anticommunism, and the CIO
Harvey A. Levenstein

Fellow Workers and Friends: I.W.W. Free-Speech Fights As Told by Participants
Philip S. Foner, editor

From the Old South to the New: Essays on the Transitional South
Walter J. Fraser Jr. and Winfred B. Moore Jr.

American Political Trials
Michal R. Belknap, editor

The Evolution of American Electoral Systems

Paul Kleppner,
Walter Dean Burnham,
Ronald P. Formisano
Samuel P. Hays,
Richard Jensen,
and William G. Shade

Contributions in American History, Number 95

Greenwood Press
WESTPORT, CONNECTICUT • LONDON, ENGLAND

Library of Congress Cataloging in Publication Data

Main entry under title:

The Evolution of American electoral systems.

(Contributions in American history; no. 95
ISSN 0084-9219)
Includes index.
1. Elections—United States—History—Addresses, essays, lectures. 2. Political parties—United States—History—Addresses, essays, lectures.
I. Kleppner, Paul.
JK1965.E96 324'.0973 80-24632
ISBN 0-313-21379-8 (lib. bdg.)

Library of Congress Catalog Card Number: 80-24632
ISBN: 0-313-21379-8
ISSN: 0084-9219

First published in 1981

Greenwood Press
A division of Congressional Information Service, Inc.
88 Post Road West, Westport, Connecticut 06881

Printed in the United States of America

10 9 8 7 6 5 4 3 2 1

CONTENTS

Preface xi

1. Critical Realignments and Electoral Systems
PAUL KLEPPNER 3

2. Federalists and Republicans: Parties, Yes—System, No
RONALD P. FORMISANO 33

3. Political Pluralism and Party Development:
The Creation of a Modern Party System, 1815-1852
WILLIAM G. SHADE 77

4. Partisanship and Ethnoreligious Conflict:
The Third Electoral System, 1853-1892
PAUL KLEPPNER 113

5. The System of 1896: An Analysis
WALTER DEAN BURNHAM 147

6. The Last Party System: Decay of Consensus, 1932-1980
RICHARD JENSEN 203

7. Politics and Society: Beyond the Political Party
SAMUEL P. HAYS 243

Index 269

FIGURES

3.1 Correlations between Adjacent Presidential Elections, The United States: Jackson-Democratic Vote 83

3.2 Correlations between Adjacent Presidential Elections, Mississippi and Pennsylvania: Jackson-Democratic Vote 85

3.3 Correlations between Adjacent Presidential Elections, New Jersey and New Hampshire: Jackson-Democratic Vote 86

3.4 Correlations between Adjacent Presidential Elections, Illinois and Virginia: Jackson-Democratic Vote 87

TABLES

1.1	Political System Discontinuity: Measures for Selected Midpoint Years	15
1.2	Democratic Longitudinal Means	19
1.3	Longitudinal Partisan Competitiveness	21
1.4	Longitudinal Standard Deviations of the Democratic Vote	23
1.5	Voter Turnout by Time Periods	25
1.6	Estimates of the Components of the National Electorate	27
2.1	Presidential Electoral Votes by Section, 1800-1816	39
2.2	Party Development in New England, 1800-1824	44
2.3	Party Development in the Midatlantic States, 1800-1820	52
2.4	Federalist Percentage of the Vote in Congressional Elections, New Jersey, 1796-1822	53
2.5	Party Development in Maryland and Delaware, 1796-1820	55
2.6	Number of Contested Counties in Maryland Presidential and Congressional Elections, 1796-1816	57
3.1	Sectionalism and Presidential Elections: Jackson-Democratic Vote	83
3.2	Correlations between Adjacent Gubernatorial Elections: Jackson-Democratic Vote	90
3.3	Correlations between Adjacent Presidential and State Elections: Jackson-Democratic Vote	92
4.1	Partisan Autocorrelations by States and by Counties	115

4.2	Distribution of Partisan Presidential Vote by States	117
4.3	Empirical Characteristics of the 1876-1892 Stable Phase	125
4.4	Estimates of Partisan Stability, 1876-1892	130
5.1	The Geographical Base of Political Dissent: Greenback (1878) and Populist (1894) Strength	155
5.2	Votes on Financial Planks: 1896 Democratic and Republican Conventions	159
5.3	Nonsouthern and Southern States Stratified by Party Lead and Major Office, 1874-1950	172
5.4	Nonsouthern and Southern States Stratified by Partisan Lead, Lower House of State Legislature, 1874-1950	177
5.5	Location of Individual States on State-Legislative Partisan Lead Continuum, 1874-1950	178
5.6	Major Party Leads by Selected Region and Metropolitan Status: Presidential Elections, 1876-1940	184
5.7	A Summary History of Competitiveness in Congressional Elections: North and West by Period, 1834-1978	186
5.8	Aggregate Competitiveness in Congressional Elections, North and West, 1880-1940	187
5.9	Turnout in Congressional Elections, by Region, 1880-1940	193
5.10	Turnout and Partisan Distribution of the Presidential Vote in Ward 6 (Pittsburgh) and Edgewood, 1920-1948	194
6.1	Labor Vote, 1936-1948, Democratic Percentage	207
6.2	Correlates of the Vote, 1940-1944: Catholics and Total Population	208
6.3	Denominational Effects, 1940-1944	209
6.4	Democratic Vote by Size of Place, 1932-1948	210
6.5	Turnout in 1940 and 1942 by Socioeconomic Status	211
6.6	1936 Roosevelt Vote by 1932 Vote and Opinion of Social Security	213
6.7	Liberalism in 1936, by Socioeconomic Status and Vote	213
6.8	Party Identification in 1948	217
6.9	Republican Share of Elected Officers, 1948-1980	221
6.10	Ethnocultural and Socioeconomic Correlates of Party Identification by State, 1968	231

PREFACE

Elections are important events. To earlier generations of Americans they were probably social happenings as much as they were contests for public office. Today, election campaigns lack the excitement and the capacity to fire public enthusiasm that typified the process a century ago. That change signals an immensely significant transformation in mass attitudes toward the electoral process. But it was never the hoopla and histrionics that gave elections their important character. Rather, they were—and are—important because they constitute those occasions on which the governed selects its public decision makers. They provide institutionalized opportunities for the governed to influence the shaping of public policy.

To suggest that there is a link between electoral politics and public policymaking is not equivalent to arguing that "the system works." Public officeholders do not automatically respond in positive ways to citizen demands. The relationship among citizen interests, voting, and public policymaking must be conceived as problematic. It is an "unknown" to be investigated and not a "given" to be assumed. Moreover, it is an "unknown" whose properties most likely have been variable across space and over time in the American past (and present).

Yet the suggestion is useful because it draws attention to the limitations of electoral analysis. It does that by bringing into focus the relationship between the electoral subsystem and the larger political system. Through elections citizens select executive and legislative officeholders, the personnel of the polity's legitimized rules-making institutions. In theory at least, the potential for citizen influence within the electoral process seems both high and direct. But theory and reality are not always automatically and wholly congruent. It would be naive to assume that the *vox populi* expressed on election day is the only source of influence on the shaping of public policy. Equally erroneous is the assumption that elections offer the only opportunities for citizens to influence policy, or that they always provide the most efficacious channels for the expression of public sentiment. Other channels certainly exist; other sources of influence surely impinge upon the decision-making process. A complete analysis of public decision making must sort out and weigh the relative strengths of all possible determinants. To classify, analyze, and explain election results and electoral behavior will not, in other words, produce generalizations that explain the specifics of the policy-making process. Such an explanation requires a wholly different research design, but one that explicitly takes into account the elective position of public policy makers.

To analyze electoral politics, then, is not to cover the entire political system, but to deal with a single, specific, vitally important dimension of it. It is to focus on a single channel of citizen influence, but one that differs in kind from other modes of influence, such as lobbying activities and petition campaigns. For in the final analysis public officeholders depend on the voters' ballots for their positions. An analysis of electoral politics should be seen as the first step toward the development of a dynamic theory of politics, one that is capable of integrating electoral change with other dimensions of change within the larger political system.

By focusing primarily on electoral politics, the essays presented here aim at accomplishing that initial step. To be sure, they touch upon other aspects of party and political activity, but largely to illuminate the electoral connection. The "party system" conception serves as a periodizing and integrating device. The sweep of American electoral history has been conceived here as being divisible analytically into a series of discrete party or electoral systems. That overarching conception is delineated in the initial essay. Each of the next five essays treats a single electoral system, demarcating its chronological boundaries, its systemic properties, and its sociopolitical cleavage lines. Taken collectively, these essays constitute an analytic whole that provides insight into the evolution of American electoral politics.

The final essay transcends the electoral system conception, and, indeed, the conception of party as the exclusive or primary agent for the articulation of political demands. It draws attention to the dynamic quality of the interrelations between society and party and to the ways in which larger societal contexts have shaped the channels available for the expression of political impulses. It does not celebrate the accomplishments of the "new political history" so much as it challenges political historians to take up a larger agenda of research concerns. For if the practice of political history has changed considerably over the past two decades, if it is no longer characterized by preoccupation with presidential administrations and presentation of the biographies of justifiably obscure second- and third-rank leaders, it has not yet fully matured. It is not only that many topics dealing with party politics remain inadequately researched—topics such as the social contours of voter participation, the social character of grass roots party leadership, the nature of the linkages among the separate sectors of party, and the policy consequences of electorally induced elite turnover—but also that critical topics have remained unarticulated, especially those dealing with the ways in which changing sociopolitical contexts have conditioned the operations of the political system.

To move beyond party and electoral history, while integrating those findings into a more inclusive analytical conception of the relations between "politics and society," is the new challenge confronting American political historians. That such a challenge can be perceived and articulated more clearly now than two decades ago is itself a positive comment on the changed character of American political history. But even more so it is a stark reminder of the "unfinished business" that needs to be tackled.

Paul Kleppner

The Evolution of American Electoral Systems

*Paul Kleppner**

CRITICAL REALIGNMENTS AND ELECTORAL SYSTEMS 1

Le plus ça change, le plus c'est la même. Or so it appears in the case of American electoral politics. Although the United States has felt the impact of enormous territorial expansion and population growth, wholesale transformations in economic and social structures, and drastic shifts in its international role, the nation's political parties seem to have remained impervious to change. At least since the mid-1850s, party battles have been waged between the same major combatants, neither of which has effectively challenged, or even attempted to challenge, the dominant ideological and cultural hegemony of corporate capitalism.

Nevertheless, continuity of party labels and consensus on the parameters of political economy should not be construed as an absolute and immutable identity of party contents. When viewed across space, any single party label encompasses a wide range of character traits and associated party practices. When viewed over time, the unchanged identity of party labels masks significant longitudinal transformations in party characters and social coalitions.

The dominant American political parties have never been internally homogeneous—socially, ideologically, or in any other important way. They have instead been constituent, or coalitional, parties, entities that have united a wide variety of disparate groups into single, but limited, systems of action.[1] This coalitional characteristic of American parties is an organizational response to their legal and socioeconomic milieux. It emerges from the fact that parties operate both within the

*The research for this chapter derives from a larger project supported by grants from the National Endowment for the Humanities and the National Science Foundation. These grants are being administered by NSF as grant SOC77-14155. I gratefully acknowledge this assistance.

constitutional context of a federalized governmental structure and within a nation of continental size characterized by a spatially asymmetrical distribution of social and economic groups.

The constituent character of American parties has had significant implications for the electoral process. First, the problems of building and maintaining electoral coalitions have been in the forefront of party concerns. Uniting diverse and sometimes latently antagonistic population subgroups into a single and successful voting coalition has required subordinating intergroup tensions to party objectives. Developing a " 'joint preference ordering' of organizational objectives," while simultaneously communicating to each subgroup that the party "represents" its values, has never been a simple task.[2] And at times it has required delicate orchestration. This preoccupation with the tasks of subgroup integration and coalition management has virtually excluded any sustained concern by parties for policy articulation. Second, the dynamics inherent in the constituent nature of American parties have given rise periodically to large-scale and enduring transformations in the aggregate shape of the electoral universe. Each such transformation can be thought of as having involved the breakdown of one mode of subgroup integration and its displacement by another. What results is an electorally significant and durable change in the composition of party social coalitions and in the character of party opposition. Thus, while party labels may have remained the same, periodic electoral realignments have significantly altered party contents.

CONCEPT AND THEORY

Critical realignments, or sequences of elections that transform the electoral subsystem, are of considerable substantive and analytical significance. Therefore, it is useful to specify precisely what they involve and how they differ from other types of elections.

Election returns "merely record periodic readings of the relative magnitudes of streams of attitudes that are undergoing steady expansion or contraction."[3] A series of election returns can be studied to gauge the comparative sizes of these attitudinal streams. Some elections involve large and durable shifts; others give evidence of narrow and temporary swings; and still others exhibit different combinations of these possibilities. These distinctions underlie efforts to construct a typology of elections.

The classification of elections, as so much else in electoral research, owes a great deal to the work of V. O. Key, Jr. As a step toward what he hoped would become "a more general theory of elections," Key isolated a type that differed in important respects from most other elections. Using aggregate data for towns and cities in the six New England states, Key defined a *critical election* as one that reveals "a sharp alteration of the pre-existing cleavage within the electorate . . . [that] seems to persist for several succeeding elections."[4] To isolate and time the occurrence of such elections, he graphed the Democratic percentage for a number of socially distinctive voting units across a time-series of presidential contests. His graphs typically showed a clear break in the series, a point at which the party's proportionate share of the vote changed abruptly compared to an earlier level. Moreover, the change was not temporary; for in subsequent elections Democratic strength stabilized around its new level. Such breakpoints provided empirical evidence that critical elections existed in fact as well as in concept.

Key's definition implicitly subsumed another important concept. While he did not employ the term, his analysis assumed the existence and the capacity to measure a normal party vote.[5] It assumed that over a specified sequence of elections certain social types of voting units can be expected regularly, or normally, to return particular levels of partisan support; and that sharp and persisting departures from that norm draw attention to durable reshufflings of party coalitions. At least in a general way, Key's before-and-after comparisons of party percentages pointed to the possibility of using aggregate data to measure a pre- and post-realignment normal party vote. Thus, we can restate Key's conception: a critical election is one that substantially alters the normal partisan division of the vote.

Key's concept of a critical election has been broadened into a general classification scheme by the work of the Michigan Survey Research Center. Using nationwide survey data and applying concepts derived from small-group research in social psychology, the SRC group for nearly two decades has tackled the problem of explaining individual voting behavior. Their collective work forms the expository base of the paradigm that continues to dominate the field of voting behavior studies, and their election typology is a corollary of that paradigm.[6]

Central to the SRC group's explanatory scheme is the proposition that most individuals possess relatively stable sets of attitudes and predispositions that they use to interpret their political worlds. These emerge from early socialization experiences, are reinforced by subsequent group involvements, and therefore are quite resistant to change. Chief among these stable predispositions is the individual's "affective orientation" to a political party.[7] It is that underlying sense of psychological identification with a particular party, that internalized sense of "being" a Democrat or a Republican, that imparts long-term consistency to the individual's voting decision. Summed across individuals within the electorate, it also accounts for the long-term stability in voting patterns at the aggregate level.

If we knew the underlying distribution of partisan loyalties among the electorate, and if elections pivoted exclusively on these standing attachments, then we would be able to predict outcomes with complete accuracy. But current events and the relative attractiveness of candidates vary from one election to another. However resistant they are to change and however much they induce selective inattention to new and counter-disposing information, partisan loyalties are neither immutable nor automatically operative. Thus, an individual's voting decision in any election is the result of the interaction between his stable partisan identification and his current evaluations of parties, candidates, and issues. Summed across individuals, the collective decision of the electorate can be conceived as a vector of the interaction of long-term forces (underlying party loyalties) with short-term influences. Since the relative strengths of these components are not constants, an analysis of their valences across a series of elections constitutes the SRC group's basis for developing its taxonomy.[8]

The original typology itemized three categories of elections. That was subsequently emended to take into account a fourth category, the logical opposite of one of the original types. In developing their classification scheme, however, the SRC group used two criteria that are not axiomatically related. Election categorization depends both upon the relative strength of long-term partisan attachments in producing the outcome and upon whether the majority or the minority party wins the election. Yet it is possible for voting behavior to satisfy the long-term—short-term valence criterion associated with a particular election type without producing the outcome that the SRC scheme necessarily predicts. This emphasis on election victories, however substantively significant they might be, unnecessarily limits the general applicability of the typology.[9] We can surmount the difficulty by dropping that emphasis. If we do so, but otherwise apply the SRC conceptions summed across individuals in the electorate, we can use a classification scheme that itemizes two broad categories of elections that differ from each other in kind and three subcategories.

On the one hand, in general contrast with Key's critical elections, there are elections in which the underlying distribution of party loyalties is not permanently changed. In such cases the collective electoral decision reflects a mix of traditional party identifications and short-term influences. By taking into account the relative weights of the long- and short-term components, we can distinguish three subtypes of this general category of *system-sustaining elections*. First, there are simple *maintaining elections*, ones in which existing partisan identifications serve as the primary attitude influences that shape the collective voting decision. Second, there are *deviating elections*, ones in which short-term attitude influences produce a partisan division that differs significantly from the underlying distribution of party loyalties. Third, there are *reinstating elections*, or counter-deviating elections, ones in which the underlying balance of partisan attachments reasserts itself following the expiration of some set of deviation-producing attitude factors. None of these subtypes of elections permanently alters the coalitional bases of mass politics. The "standing decision" that structured the normal partisan division of the vote among the mass electorate remains essentially intact.

On the other hand, some elections produce a repudiation of that "standing decision." These are *realigning elections*, or critical elections, ones in which the partisan decisions of electorally significant proportions of voters are permanently altered. Such elections bring about a persisting net change in the normal partisan division of the vote. Whatever factors influence such change, and however it occurs, realigning elections—unlike other types of elections—exhibit aggregate properties that indicate a durable reshuffling of the coalitional bases of partisanship. These coalitional adjustments may not occur within a single election but may extend over several successive elections. Thus, it is appropriate to speak of a realigning sequence, or realigning phase.[10]

The SRC's treatment of the phenomenon of critical realignment necessarily has been constrained by the fact that none of the elections for which nationwide survey data are available were of that type. Except for an effort to integrate their theory of individual motivation into the conception, the SRC analysis does not move much beyond Key's original formulation. Fortunately, Walter Dean Burnham's brilliant work has helped to fill much of the theoretical and operational void.[11] In certain respects Burnham's analysis followed and developed leads originally suggested by Key. In other important respects it moved beyond those leads to an insightful and important elaboration of the critical realignment concept.

Key originally raised a general question concerning the temporal frequency of realignments and the implications for the political system. While he did not present an extended time-series of election data, it is clear that he believed that such massive changes did not occur often. Following that lead, but applying more precise and systematic measurement techniques to a series of presidential data extending from 1828 through 1968, Burnham isolated three national-level break points—one each in the mid-1850s, the mid-1890s, and the early 1930s.[12] Realigning elections have been indeed relatively rare events.

To be more precise, of the thirty-three presidential elections between 1844 and 1968, only eight (or 25 percent) could reasonably be categorized as realigning.[13] Given the infrequent occurrence of massive transformations in the aggregate shape of the electoral universe, the predominant rhythm of mass politics over the past century and a half could be described as one of long periods of relative electoral stability punctuated by infrequent, short, and intense bursts of electoral reorganization.

As Key recognized, these periods of massive coalitional reshuffling exhibited unusual intensity. They involved elections in which "voters are . . . unusually deeply concerned, in which the extent of electoral involvement is relatively quite high."[14] Pursuing and developing that lead, Burnham suggested that the intensity extends beyond high rates of voter mobilization to other important elements of the electoral process. It spills over, for example, into the nominating processes of the parties, and it may produce shifts in the locus of power within one or both major parties. Thus, instead of performing their normal integrative function, under conditions conducive to critical realignments, the candidate selection processes contribute to polarization.

The rise in intensity is also reflected in the fact that the level of issue polarization between the parties is much greater than customary in American politics. The parties come to be associated with highly salient issue clusters and their positions on issues become—given the American norm—unusually unambiguous. Thus, critical realignments can be thought of as issue-oriented phenomena that are marked by atypically high levels of ideological polarization extending from the nominating through the campaigning process.

In general, what are the conditions conducive to realignments? Key did not deal with the matter in any specific way, and the SRC group simply associated realignments "with great national crises."[15] That association is clear enough (and in the correct causal direction) in the cases of the depressions and realignments of the 1890s and the 1930s. However, merely to point to that association provides neither an adequate explanation nor reasonable grounds for theory development. Furthermore, in the case of the 1850s even the causal direction imputed to the association is suspect. It is by no means incontrovertible that the realignment of the 1850s *resulted from* the crisis engendered by the debate over slavery that ultimately produced the Civil War. It is more plausible to reverse the causal direction and to suggest that the realignment of the 1850s *created* a set of crisis conditions at the level of the political system that ultimately culminated in the Civil War. In any event, simply invoking the phrase "great national crises" does not tell us much that is analytically useful concerning the conditions that underlie realignments.

Burnham's analysis does. Realignments are not systemic aberrations, but emerge directly from the dynamics inherent in the predominantly constituent nature of American parties. They arise "from emergent tensions in society which, not adequately controlled by the organization or outputs of party politics as usual, escalate to a flash point."[16] When such tensions are both broadly diffused and intensely felt by the mass public, and when they are not adequately integrated and aggregated by the party system as then constituted, they serve to shatter the existing coalitional arrangements by providing new bases for electoral mobilization. Realignments, then, emerge from the basically constituent nature of American political parties and are in themselves constituent acts.

This conception of realignments as constituent acts serves the important function of linking the study of electoral behavior with the analysis of political systems. It has been often overlooked that Burnham's conceptual framework integrates changes in the shape of the electoral universe with subsequent transformations in the contours of public policy. Since they are constituent acts, critical realignments serve to "determine the outer boundaries of policy in general, though not necessarily policy in detail."[17] To be sure, Burnham is not specific about how that linkage is effected in practice. While those specifics must await detailed historical research designed to explore the operation of that process in a variety of contexts and time periods, it seems plausible to suggest a causal sequence that flows in the following direction. Realigning elections produce durable net change in the partisan division of the vote. By doing that they induce swings in the partisan balance in a relatively large number of legislative districts. The effect of such swings is to accelerate partisan turnover among legislative officeholders, to alter the processes of their recruitment, to modify the size and shape of legislative coalitions, and thus to create the conditions necessary for a change in the general shape of legislative outputs.[18]

This linkage between transformation in the electoral subsystem and change in the larger political system underpins the concept of an electoral era, or party system. Each brief but intense burst of electoral reorganization has produced its own distinctive patterns of voting behavior as well as its own "characteristic patterns . . . of elite and institutional relationships, and of broad system-dominant decisions."[19] Realignments emerge from the incapacity of "politics as usual" to aggregate or control emergent tensions. When these tensions burst into electoral politics, they produce coalitional reshufflings that durably alter the existing partisan balance and that redefine the meaning of party oppositions. The parties which emerge from this process are electorally and socially reconstituted entities; in tangible and symbolic ways they "represent" antipodal positions on the policy issues associated with the tensions that set realigning change in motion. The resulting new partisan cleavage is structured to produce policy outputs that mirror those tensions. Alignments forged under conditions of great intensity and sharp issue polarization tend to endure.

To say that the coalitional arrangements and partisan balance produced by a realigning sequence remain stable over a long period of time does not mean that they remain static. From election to election there may be wide fluctuation in party strengths and/or considerable movement into and from the electorate. And some subareas (and, by implication, subgroups of voters) may even permanently change their collective partisan selections. However significant these changes, it is important to realize that they do not involve a net change in the division of partisan strength at the system level. Nor are they necessarily associated with a subsequent restructuring of the general shape of policy outputs. In their effects, then, such movements fall short of the criteria of critical realignments. Even more obviously they lack the requisite intensity associated with realigning elections. Thus, regardless of their specific consequences, we can think of the elections that occur between realignments as being ones that sustain the partisan structure inaugurated by the realigning sequence that shaped it. And we can define an *electoral system*, or electoral era, as a set of adjacent maintaining, deviating, and reinstating elections bounded on both temporal ends by realigning sequences.[20] The first realignment creates the partisan structure that predominates during the era, and the second displaces that structure and inaugurates a new electoral system.

To recapitulate, critical realignments are infrequent occurrences. They involve intense bursts of electoral reorganization extending over a relatively short sequence of adjacent elections. The intensity that typifies a realigning sequence is manifest in unusually high levels of voter participation, the incapacity of the nominating process to perform its normal integrating function, and an atypically sharp issue polarization between the dominant parties. Realignments produce significant and durable changes in the aggregate shape of mass partisanship. Because they arise from the inherent dynamics of the constituent nature of American politics and are themselves constituent acts, critical realignments have enduring consequences on the roles played by institutional elites and on the general shape of public policy. Thus, critical realignments constitute a unique type of change in the electoral subsystem because they entail redefinitions of the social and ideological bases of party oppositions.

While these characteristics and consequences of realignments are clear, there are at least two relevant matters that require some elucidation. First, critical realignment theory addresses itself in the first instance to macrolevel change, to a transformation in the shape of the electoral universe. That does not mean that the change extends to all subparts of the universe at the same time and to the same extent. Some of the subparts—and it does not matter whether these are conceived as states, counties, or voter groups—may withstand the initial shock and only later give signs of a partisan swing that can best be thought of analytically as an aftereffect. And other subparts may give no signs of realigning change.

Thus, it is not axiomatic that realignments must give evidence of severe and durable partisan changes that are also geographically extensive. Some realignments may have been broad as well as deep; others may not; and at least one—that in the 1850s—involved geographically extensive change in one region of the country while elsewhere the change was quite limited spatially. It may be intuitively appealing to assume that "massive coalitional reshufflings" imply change that extends to all or most voting units or voting groups. But amplitude as a dimension of change is distinct from magnitude, and it is a dimension that is not essential to the conception.[21]

Of course, whether some subpart of the electoral universe (e.g., state, city, county or particular voter group) experienced realignment is of substantive importance. Forests, after all, are composed of individual trees, and sometimes it can be interesting as well as useful to examine them individually. But when we do that, and especially in the electoral case in point, two factors should be kept in mind. First, only macrolevel data are relevant in testing the credibility of propositions bearing on macrolevel behavior. Whether a particular state (or county or voter group), for example, realigned in the mid-1890s reveals nothing that has direct bearing on whether the electoral universe as an electoral universe experienced realignment. Only data describing the behavior of the macrolevel universe as such is useful for such tests. Second, analyses of behavior within a subpart of the electoral universe should not lose sight of the larger whole. The voting behavior of a state or voter group, for example, never occurs, and therefore can never be explained, in isolation. It occurs as an integral part of a larger system of action and can only be analyzed within that framework.[22] Indeed, the most important questions confronting voting behavior analysis are those that bear on the interrelationships between microlevel behaviors and macrolevel contexts.

There is another matter relevant to the concept of critical realignment that needs to be clarified. The course of late twentieth century American politics has raised questions concerning the general applicability of the theory.[23] Elections since 1960 have been marked by extraordinary volatility in voting behavior and by declining turnout. Whether viewed in the aggregate or through survey data, what has occurred since 1960 hardly resembles the "politics as usual" state of the 1950s. Fundamental and presumably enduring change seems to have occurred, and it has come about through some process other than a critical realignment of the classical type.

If this reasonably describes the recent operation of the electoral system (and it probably does), then should we not discard realignment theory and seek out some other theory that can cover contemporary as well as past system-transforming changes? To do that would be akin to throwing out the baby with the bath water. Realignment theory cannot account for the type of change that has occurred recently for two related reasons. First, classical style realignments required partisanship as an intermediary between citizens and their voting selections. The theory assumes that parties serve as effective conduits of voting decisions. Second, the most important dynamic operating within the electoral subsystem since the beginning of this century has been the progressive erosion of partisan linkages. And the speed at which partisan decomposition has occurred has increased over the past decade.[24] As a consequence parties no longer play their traditional roles as intermediaries. Taken together these considerations lead to an obvious conclusion that can be stated succinctly: no parties as intermediaries, no realignments of the classical type.

That contemporary conditions do not allow for classical style realignments does not mean that transforming change is impossible through some other process. Nor does it mean that realignment theory is analytically inadequate to explain such change when parties do serve as intermediaries. Thus, the fact that realignment theory cannot account for contemporary transformations should not be construed as evidence of the general inapplicability of that theory. Instead it should be viewed as the most powerful evidence yet adduced of the political system consequences of partisan decomposition.

DATA AND DESCRIPTION

Theoretical discussions resemble the bones of a skeleton. They provide the necessary outline but lack a great deal that is essential. An application of critical realignment theory to the longitudinal context of American politics can help to supply some of the missing flesh and blood.

The purpose of this application, however, is a limited one. It does not intend to summarize, or even to preview, the contents of the essays on discrete electoral systems that constitute the core of this book. Instead, the objective is to paint a picture of the evolution of those systems with very broad strokes. Thus, while each of the essays treats in detail with a single electoral system, the focus here will be on a comparison of empirical characteristics across systems. That will create a context within which to locate each electoral system and thus aid in perceiving its relation to the longitudinal whole. And by providing a basis for comparing discrete systems, it will facilitate descriptions of long-term electoral dynamics.

In practice the effort here will be even more circumscribed than the preceding description implies. Classical style realignments presume the operation of parties. In our own day, parties exist and party labels are regularly employed, even though the quality of the underlying linkages is quite different from that of a century ago. But in a much earlier day—from the beginning of the nation through about the mid-1820s—clear-cut party labels were not consistently used. It is meaningful to speak of the period through the mid-1820s as an "electoral era" only in a restricted sense of that term. The designation can be applied to indicate that elections were conducted and that in some important respects aggregate electoral behavior seems to have differed in kind from that characterizing the electoral universe after the mid-1820s. But in the absence of durable and identifiable organizational structures (i.e., political parties) that aggregated citizen demands and channeled vote decisions, it is inappropriate to identify the period as involving a "party system."

Preparty, or late-colonial, politics does not lend itself readily to empirical descriptions at the macrolevel. Without a series of consistently designed microlevel studies, it is extremely difficult, for example, even to construct a consistent time-series of "partisan" strengths. Difficulties of this sort at the operational level reveal a great deal, at least by implication, about the nature of predominant political practices and of citizen orientations toward the electoral process. But they inhibit the collection and ordering of the data required to compare the resulting behavior with that of later electoral eras. As a consequence, the discussion and comparisons here will be confined to the time encompassed by the nation's second through its latest (or fifth) electoral system.

We can begin by dealing with the periodicity of critical realignments and electoral systems. Since realigning elections differ in kind from other types of elections, it is possible to pinpoint their occurrences empirically. Several analysts have done that by examining time-series voting percentages. Their efforts have not resulted in exact agreement on the timing of the breakpoints. Partially that reflects differences in the measures used to construct the time series and differences in the aggregate levels at which the data have been examined. But it also results from the fact that no single election has ever been a pure type and that realignment can extend over several adjacent elections. However, the relevant findings do provide a consensual basis for at least a general timing of realignments. Such transforming electoral upheavals occurred in the 1850s, the 1890s, and the 1930s.

Since critical realignments are macrolevel, or system, phenomena, analysis of time-series data at that level seems most relevant to timing them more exactly. Burnham presented the most extensive and rigorous analysis of those data, and we can initially make use of the breakpoint years that he isolated. Using the Democratic percentage of the two-party national vote as the unit of measurement, Burnham took sequences of ten successive presidential elections and statistically compared the first-five with the second-five elections to "identify 'cutting points' of transition between one system of electoral politics and another." He calculated t tests and discontinuity coefficients and identified three "knife-edged" cutting points that gave evidence of critical realignment. These occurred in association with the following midpoint years: 1854, which separated the 1836–1852 and 1856–1872 presidential sequences; 1894, dividing the 1876–1892 from the 1896–1912 presidential elections; and 1930, setting off the 1912–1928 presidential sequence from that of the 1932–1948 period.[25]

We can adopt Burnham's logic and apply it to a time series that includes both presidential and congressional election returns at the national level and that uses the partisan percentages of the total vote cast as the basic units of measurement. If we percentagize by the total vote cast, rather than by the two-party vote, then the series for the two dominant parties will not be mirror images of each other and it will be necessary to examine each separately. That is an unfortunate but necessary complication.[26]

We can apply the same reasoning and operational procedures to time series of other relevant data. Critical realignments are causally associated with changes in the general contours of policy. It is most plausible to assume that it is electorally induced change in partisan control over policy-making institutions that links these two sets of transformations. Thus, if we examine a time series measuring the partisan division among legislative officeholders, we should find cutting points that correspond in their magnitudes and timing to those in the election series.[27] Two such time series have been analyzed for this purpose. The first is a series measuring the percentage of Democrats and of their major party opponents among all members of the U.S. House of Representatives. The second is a similarly constructed series of the partisan divisions in the lower houses of state legislatures.

For each series the data have been aggregated to the national level and calculated for biennial sequences. Longitudinal t tests and discontinuity coefficients (r_d) have been calculated for each of these two series and for the vote series; Table 1.1 presents the relevant discontinuity indicators for midpoint years corresponding to the ones Burnham isolated.[28]

Table 1.1 Political System Discontinuity: Measures for Selected Midpoint Years

	DEMOCRAT		WHIG/REPUBLICAN	
	t	r_d	t	r_d
Midpoint Year 1853				
Vote	.794	.298	1.934	.579
U.S. House	3.395	.786	1.798	.562
State Legislatures	4.274	.843	.853	.345
Midpoint Year 1893				
Vote	1.986	.606	2.759	.669
U.S. House	3.612	.813	3.176	.765
State Legislatures	4.227	.857	3.890	.844
Midpoint Year 1931				
Vote	4.663	.851	4.625	.861
U.S. House	6.338	.901	6.114	.900
State Legislatures	5.535	.876	5.533	.873

With the exceptions of some of the indicators associated with midpoint year 1853, the data generally confirm Burnham's periodization. They provide clear evidence that the breaks were not limited to presidential voting but extended as well to the selection of federal and state legislators. Since these officeholders were directly responsible for enacting policy, these durable shifts in the partisan composition of legislatures help delineate the link between realigning electoral change and subsequent transformations in the broad contours of policy.

The data for midpoint year 1853 require further notice. On impressionistic grounds alone, the developments of that decade point to fundamental political changes. The decade witnessed the expiration of one of the major parties, the Whigs; the sudden emergence and success of a party whose roots were in a secret society, the Know-Nothings or Native American party; the eventual emergence of the Republicans as the major party opposition to the Democrats; the sectional rupture occasioned by the nominating process within the Democratic party in 1860; and, of course, the ultimate breakdown of the political process that culminated in secession and the Civil War. Either individually or collectively, these were developments that surely were beyond the bounds of "politics as usual." Yet the techniques applied to the time-series data do not seem to have captured their significance. While the Whig/Republican vote series exhibits a break that reaches the lower bounds of statistical significance at midpoint year 1853, the Democratic vote series does not. Furthermore, both Democratic legislative series, but neither of the Whig/Republican ones, show statistically significant cutting points.

These apparent anomalies, however, do accurately tap some of the unusual aspects of the political change that marked the decade. The Whig party did not expire immediately after the 1852 election. It persisted and continued to nominate candidates in some locales until nearly the end of the decade. In some places, too, the Know-Nothings remained in the field as an anti-Democratic alternative that competed for voters with the developing "Republican" party. And the rise of the Republicans was gradual, sometimes agonizing, and nearly everywhere complicated by the need to displace existing anti-Democratic alternatives and to attract still higher levels of support either by mobilizing nonvoters or by converting Democrats. The problem of coalition development prompted local anti-Democratic party builders to adopt designations that symbolized the encompassing nature of their effort. They used a variety of labels—most commonly, People's, Fusion, and Independent. Thus, the development of a consolidated anti-Democratic opposition—whether in the electorate or in legislatures—was a slow process that extended over several elections before and after the 1853 breakpoint.

The Democratic vote series fails to exhibit a sharp break at midpoint year 1853 for similar reasons. The party's vote losses extended over several elections on both sides of that midpoint year. Outside New England those losses, while severe and durable, were geographically limited. And from 1850 until its sectional rupture a decade later, the Democrats gained strength in the South. These currents and countercurrents when aggregated to the national level tended to balance out statistically.

Table 1.1 presents only three snapshots of much longer and larger statistical arrays. The full longitudinal series exhibits one important difference when compared to Burnham's presidential series. When data from off-year elections are included in the series, the cutting points are not so knife-edged as they are when only presidential data are used.[29] The biennial series brings into view the fact that periodically several adjacent elections show higher-than-usual discontinuity indicators. Each of these relatively short series of elections is then followed by a longer series that on the whole exhibits much lower levels of longitudinal discontinuity.[30] That pattern empirically supports two observations. First, we can best think of critical realignment as a process extending over a short sequence of elections rather than as an event occurring at a single point. Second, since these brief series characterized by high discontinuity are followed by longer ones marked by relative electoral inertia, we can distinguish between realigning phases and stable phases of electoral eras.

The realigning phase that inaugurated the third electoral era (1853-1892) was unusually protracted. Secession, Civil War, and Reconstruction were the developments that underlay its extended duration. While the broad contours of the emerging party oppositions were generally in place—at least throughout the North—before 1860, system-level realignment continued from its inception in 1853-1854 to the 1874-1876 reinstating sequence. In turn, that sequence began a stable phase that lasted through Grover Cleveland's second election to the presidency in 1892.

In comparison, the dissolution of the third party system was a temporally compressed process. The convulsions that marked election contests in the West, and to a lesser extent the South, in 1890 and 1892 presaged its breakup. Systemic realignment commenced only in 1893-1894 and was completed by 1900. The fourth system's stable phase extended from that point through 1930. To be sure, the 1918-1920 sequence had a pro-Republican reinstating effect as behaviorally and systemically significant as was a similar pro-Democratic electoral movement over the 1874-1876 sequence. But neither these shifts, nor a broadening of the franchise, nor minor party candidacies originating in bolts from the majority party (in 1912 and 1924), nor the presidential candidacy of an Irish Catholic produced systemic realignment.

The Great Depression did that. Even under the impact of that economic catastrophe, realignment began slowly. Once it commenced in 1932 its velocity increased sharply through the 1936 election.[31] At that point that fifth electoral era lapsed into a stable phase. Whether or not that still endures is arguable. No classical style realignment has occurred since 1960, and on that basis we might extend the duration of the stable phase beyond the Kennedy-Nixon contest. Yet it is also clear that the electoral universe has experienced a series of upheavals since the mid-1960s. The increasing magnitude of election-to-election fluctuations in party percentages provides ample evidence of that. More important, the decay of partisan linkages makes impossible classical realignments that require parties as intermediaries between citizens and their voting decisions. Such considerations render problematic the claim that we are still living through the "stable" phase of the New Deal electoral system.

Each of these electoral systems has displayed its own characteristic patterns of partisan competitiveness, electoral behavior, and voter mobilization. Table 1.2 presents an overview of Democratic voting strength for each discrete electoral system and for two subsegments of the fifth era.[32]

The data contain no great surprises. They show the extraordinarily even regional distribution of party strength that was a hallmark of the second electoral system. That contrasts with the strong regional polarities that characterized the third and fourth systems. Over the 1854-1892 period those regional conflicts involved enormous value and interest clashes that united the South and Border states against the rest of the country. The sectional polarities that dominated the 1894-1930 period pitted the country's colonial outposts, the South and the mountain West, against its urban-industrial metropole. The strength of this periphery-core conflict was drastically muted by the realignment of the 1930s. The electoral system forged during the depression showed much lower levels of regional variance (σ^2) than its predecessor. And the distribution of the Democratic vote over the most recent sequence (1962-1972) exhibits a regional uniformity that more nearly approximates the second electoral system than any other.

Evidence of strong sectional imbalances in the vote distributions typically suggests a corresponding decline in partisan competitiveness within regions. Partisan cleavages structured around regional polarities are ones in which each party attains nearly hegemonic dominance within one or more geographic sections. That has clearly been the case in the American past.

Over the 1832-1852 electoral era neither party was dominant in any region. The widest Whig mean partisan lead was 3.5 percentage points in the New England states, while the Democratic high was a mean lead of 3.9 percentage points in the East North Central area.[33] Thus the relatively close balance between the two parties at the national level—a mean Democratic lead of 2.1 percentage points—resulted from geographically widespread competition.

The even narrower national lead over the 1854-1892 period—1.2 percentage points in favor of the Democrats—was produced by entirely different conditions. It resulted from very wide Democratic leads in the South and Border areas and equally strong Republican ones in New England and the West North Central states. The smaller Republican leads in the Midatlantic, East North Central, and Pacific regions were still within a competitive range. They fell from that category with the realignment of the 1890s. That transformation created virtual partisan hegemony for the Republicans in the New England, the Midatlantic, the East North Central, the West North Central, and the Pacific regions. Their dominance in these areas more than offset the enormous Democratic lead in the South (44.3 percentage points) and the increased competitiveness that marked the Border and Mountain

Table 1.2 Democratic Longitudinal Means (in percentages)

	1836-1852	1854-1892	1894-1930	1932-1972	1932-1960	1962-1972
United States	47.4	45.8	41.4	50.2	50.5	49.4
Nonsouth	47.6	43.8	38.5	48.9	48.7	49.6
New England	42.3	37.6	38.3	51.0	48.7	56.8
Middle Atlantic	46.8	45.0	37.0	49.3	48.9	50.5
East North Central	49.3	45.0	38.9	48.1	48.2	48.1
West North Central	-	34.8	33.3	44.7	44.2	46.2
South	46.2	56.3	69.1	66.5	73.0	50.0
Border	46.1	51.6	49.3	54.2	55.5	51.1
Mountain	-	42.9	42.5	50.3	52.3	45.5
Pacific	-	46.1	28.7	46.7	45.7	49.1
Measures of Central Tendency (By Regions):						
Mean	46.1	44.9	42.1	51.3	52.0	49.6
σ^2	5.03	41.95	136.08	39.93	73.59	10.73
σ	2.24	6.47	11.66	6.31	8.57	3.27

areas. The result at the national level was a mean Republican lead of 7.5 percentage points, and an even wider lead of 12.8 percentage points for the nonsouthern portions of the country.

Republican hegemony was shattered by the realignment of the 1930s. That electoral transformation restored partisan competition to at least the nonsouthern sectors of the electoral subsystem. The swings to the Democrats were large and produced wide partisan leads in all regions during the 1932-1936 realigning sequence. As the system stabilized those leads contracted and party battles in most regions and states were waged within competitive contexts. Table 1.3 provides a longitudinal overview of the competitive contours of the nation's electoral past.

Most voters (55.1 percent) lived in strongly competitive contexts during the 1836-1852 period, and relatively few (3.4 percent) lived in highly noncompetitive ones.[34] The sectional imbalances in party strengths that typified the third electoral system reduced somewhat the relative electoral weight of the highly competitive categories. More important, these imbalances produced a large increase in the proportions of states and voting population in the noncompetitive range. The sizes of those extremely noncompetitive categories were further increased with the realignment of the 1890s; and, at the same time, there was a sharp decrease in the relative size of the electorate in highly competitive states. As a result, while only 11.4 percent of the electorate lived in highly competitive states, 45.1 percent lived in virtually noncompetitive ones.

The electoral system created in the 1930s broadened the size of the electorate in highly competitive contexts to a level just below that of the second electoral era. At the same time it continued to reflect (through about 1960) the partisan impress of long-standing sectional polarities. These took the form of noncompetitive and pro-Democratic margins in the Solid South. Dissolution of that Democratic hegemony in the states of the former Confederacy underlies the observable post-1960 contraction in the size of the extremely pro-Democratic category.

Widespread and viable competition between the major parties has usually been taken for granted. Analysts, of course, have long recognized that the emergence of one-party control and the consequent breakdown of the integrative and aggregative functions of party conflict were characteristics of the post-1900 South. They have been somewhat slower to notice that the hegemonic conditions underpinning a kind of "no-party" politics existed as well in a large and electorally important number of nonsouthern states.[35] Although that partisan dominance was never legally institutionalized as it was in the South, its behavioral consequences were not dissimilar. Virtual partisan hegemony precluded the possibility that election contests *between*

Table 1.3 Longitudinal Partisan Competitiveness

		VOTING POPULATION by STATES (in percentages)					
Partisan Lead		1836-1852	1854-1892	1894-1930	1932-1972	1932-1960	1962-1972
20.0%+	DEM.	3.4	15.8	22.7	22.4	22.1	10.6
10-19.9%	DEM.	10.0	12.9	-	7.2	8.9	5.3
5- 9.9%	DEM.	14.3	1.6	4.1	9.6	9.6	21.8
0- 4.9%	DEM.	30.9	-	6.6	28.8	21.3	35.3
0- 4.9%	REP.	24.2	43.7	4.8	21.3	30.4	13.2
5- 9.9%	REP.	5.8	8.5	17.3	7.5	2.5	9.0
10-19.9%	REP.	11.1	7.7	21.8	2.5	4.5	3.8
20.0%+	REP.	-	9.5	22.4	0.2	0.2	0.7

parties could serve as mechanisms for resolving social and policy contention. Such struggles instead had to be waged *within* the dominant party. Groups not integrated by that party became bystanders to the process. The diffusion of such conditions early in this century causally underlay the enormous decline in mass electoral participation and the widespread demand for the direct primary as an institutionalized means of resolving conflict within the dominant party.

Intervening changes of this order in behavioral and legal contexts served to mute the systemic consequences of the increased competition between parties that resulted from the realignment of the 1930s. Thus, while the fifth system's level of competitiveness nearly approximated that of the second, its impact on electoral behavior has proven to be quite dissimilar. Important dimensions of that difference will become clear from an examination of two additional characteristics of American electoral systems, their levels of longitudinal partisan stability and their rates of voter mobilization.

When standing party identifications guide individual voting choices, we expect considerable consistency over a series of separate selections. If we consider collective voting decisions as the summations of individual voting choices, then under conditions of party-cued selections the aggregate data should show little fluctuation from one election to the next. We can measure the amount of fluctuation by calculating two indicators: a mean of each party's percentage of the total vote across a series of elections and the standard deviation (σ) about that mean. The larger the standard deviation, the greater the amount of dispersion about the mean.[36] In the substantive case in point, the higher the standard deviation, the greater the amount of election-to-election fluctuation or volatility across the time series. Since realigning sequences, by definition, involve high rates of fluctuation, we can confine the inquiry to the stable phases of the nation's electoral systems. Means and their associated standard deviations have been calculated across biennial sequences, for both parties, and for each state. Table 1.4 uses the relevant Democratic indicators to provide a panoramic view of the long-term trends in longitudinal partisan stability.[37]

During the stable phase of the second and third electoral eras most election outcomes fluctuated within fairly narrow ranges. Most states, encompassing majorities of the voting population, had longitudinal standard deviations below 5.0 percent. High rates of competition combined with longitudinal stability in the partisan division of the vote are compelling signs of party-structured outcomes. The post-1900 period manifest symptoms of a strong and long-term trend toward the destabilization of partisan outcomes. That trend began in the 1900-1930 period and only temporarily abated during the 1938-1960 se-

Table 1.4 Longitudinal Standard Deviations of the Democratic Vote

σ =	1836-1852	1876-1892	1900-1930	1938-1972	1938-1960	1962-1972
A. Percentage of States:						
0- 2.4	26.6	18.4	-	-	-	-
2.5- 4.9	30.0	26.3	14.5	2.0	25.0	-
5.0- 7.4	16.6	18.4	35.4	37.5	31.2	8.3
7.5- 9.9	10.0	18.4	20.8	20.8	14.5	45.8
10.0-14.9	3.3	15.7	18.7	20.8	12.5	27.1
15.0 and over	13.3	2.6	10.4	18.7	16.6	18.7
B. Percentage of Voting Population by States:						
0- 2.4	33.0	19.0	-	-	-	-
2.5- 4.9	23.8	32.2	11.3	5.5	44.6	-
5.0- 7.4	10.4	18.2	50.9	42.5	20.7	19.5
7.5- 9.9	19.2	20.6	13.4	10.2	7.2	47.9
10.0-14.9	5.7	8.8	13.8	21.6	12.0	14.1
15.0 and over	7.5	1.0	10.4	20.0	15.1	18.3

quence. Since 1960 it has resumed and with accelerated velocity. Wide partisan swings, landslides followed by counter-landslides, are now a dominating characteristic of the electoral system. The competitive structure of the contemporary period, unlike that of the nineteenth century electoral eras, is not the product of longitudinally stable, party-cued outcomes. It results instead from geographically widespread and massive partisan swings from one election to the next. Such swings are symptomatic of the accelerating incapacity of parties to structure the collective voting decision.

These longitudinal changes in the structure of competition and the levels of partisan stability have been paralleled by another trend of considerable importance: declining rates of mass participation in the electoral process. High rates of voter mobilization were widespread hallmarks of the second and third electoral eras. Over the presidential and off-year elections of the stable phase of the second system, national turnout averaged 61.7 percent; and that increased to 71.3 percent over the 1876-1892 period.[38] These high participation levels and the positive linear trend toward increased turnout associated with them changed by the end of the nineteenth century. Even before the enfranchisement of women, turnout sagged; it averaged only 62.0 percent over the 1896-1916 sequence. When the franchise was broadened, it dropped further; the 1896-1930 mean was 54.9 percent. Even these abysmal rates of participation suggest too roseate a picture; they include the high intensity, high turnout, realigning sequence of the mid-1890s. If that is excluded, turnout between 1900 and 1916 averaged 60.3 percent, and 53.0 percent between 1900 and 1930; in contrast with the earlier periods, the linear trends for these sequences were steeply negative.[39] The New Deal realignment reversed the direction of the linear trends, and mildly boosted turnout over the low levels of the 1920s. Between 1938 and 1960 it averaged 50.1 percent; and the slight improvement (to 52.9 percent) evident over the 1962-1972 sequence was due exclusively to the removal of legal obstacles to participation by black voters in the South.[40] The data in Table 1.5 summarize these changes in the shape of voter turnout.

The long-term decline in citizen participation is apparent. The apex of mass mobilization occurred during the third electoral era; 52.5 percent of the states, with 66.5 percent of the voting population, had turnout means of 65.0 percent or higher. As the data for both post-1900 segments suggest, the conditions underlying electoral demobilization were widespread. Furthermore, despite the intensity associated with the realignment of the 1930s and the increased competitiveness that it produced, the resurgence in voter turnout was neither powerful nor enduring.

The most recent period has been one marked by a somewhat less

Table 1.5. Voter Turnout by Time Periods

Turnout Categories	1836-1852	1876-1892	1900-1916	1900-1930	1938-1972	1938-1960	1962-1972
A. PERCENTAGE OF STATES:							
80.0+	-	2.6	2.0	-	-	-	-
70-79.9	13.3	23.6	4.1	2.0	-	-	2.1
65-69.9	23.3	26.3	12.5	4.1	10.4	10.4	10.6
60-64.9	23.3	13.1	4.1	6.2	20.8	22.9	19.1
50-59.9	23.3	15.7	37.5	39.5	35.4	33.3	38.2
Below 50.0	16.6	18.4	39.5	47.9	33.3	33.3	29.7
B. PERCENTAGE OF VOTING POPULATION BY STATES:							
80.0+	-	3.6	3.0	-	-	-	-
70-79.9	8.6	24.8	1.4	2.8	-	-	0.4
65-69.9	23.5	38.1	17.0	1.4	5.1	5.1	3.0
60-64.9	30.5	10.6	1.1	10.1	13.8	16.2	12.4
50-59.9	22.5	11.4	43.8	35.2	50.4	50.1	54.6
Below 50.0	14.8	11.2	33.4	50.1	30.5	28.5	29.4

skewed structure of longitudinal competition. But that pattern results from historically wide partisan swings between elections and involves the mobilization of relatively low proportions of voters. While it may bear surface similarities to earlier periods, its distinctive shape is the product of strong and secular trends toward partisan decomposition and electoral demobilization.

Comparisons of the aggregate rates of electoral mobilization across time and space point to a long-term and broad trend toward lower levels of citizen involvement. Other aggregate indicators point in the same direction and collectively suggest an electorate whose orientations toward the electoral process have changed considerably over time. We can pursue that lead and inquire into whether there have been changes in the underlying distributions of citizen orientation toward electoral politics.

The orientations in question are those bearing on the individual's psychological sense of involvement in politics. The findings of voting behavior research underscore the role of this orientation in shaping the citizen's outlook on the relevance of electoral politics and on the value of voting. While the degree of psychological involvement varies widely among individuals at any time, it exhibits considerable stability within individuals over time. Generally, the stronger the individual's psychological involvement in politics the greater the likelihood of voting. Yet psychological involvement alone does not determine that likelihood; it plays a mediating role between current campaign events and the citizen's decision; and some campaigns provide a higher stimulus to turnout than others.[41]

Based on psychological involvement as a stable orientation and elections as unstable generators of stimuli, three categories of voters can be posited.[42] First, we can speak of *core voters*, those whose levels of interest and involvement are more-or-less uniformly high. Voters of this type can be expected to vote in successive elections regardless of variations in the amount of political stimulation produced by current campaigns and candidates. Second, there are *peripheral voters*, those whose levels of involvement are lower than the ones that characterize core voters. These citizens go to the polls when current political events provide sufficient stimulation to activate their sense of involvement and to motivate them to vote. Since the amount of stimulation produced by campaigns varies, these voters can be expected to vote in some elections but not in others. Third, there are *nonvoters*, those whose levels of psychological involvement are uniformly low. Even in the face of high stimulus elections, these citizens do not participate.

Since it can be presumed that the degree of psychological involvement in politics has always varied among individuals, we can plausibly assume that each electoral era has been characterized by groups of core, peripheral, and nonvoting citizens. Thus, the question is not whether such groups have always existed but what their relative sizes have been and how those relations have changed over time. What is at issue is the size of the core group compared to the sizes of the other categories.

We can use aggregate voting data at the county level and regression procedures to estimate the size of each of these categories.[43] In the case in point, that involved regressing the proportion of the total electorate (across a set of counties within a region) who voted in one election on the proportion who voted in the preceding election. From that procedure estimates were derived of the probability of voters casting ballots at both elections or at only one of the two. Since the total turnout for the entire set of counties was known, these estimated probabilities were then translated into proportions of the eligible electorate that behaved in the specified ways. For the estimates given here, regressions were calculated within each region for each presidential election pair during the stable phase of each electoral era. These estimates were then weighted by the relative size of each region's voting population to the national total. The weighted estimates for each election pair were then summed across all election pairs and divided by the number of pairs that occurred within each electoral era.[44]

The estimates also depend upon a particular operational definition of each of the categories of voters. There are potentially a number of ways to develop such a definition. For present purposes, *core* voters were defined as those who repeated their turnout in two successive presidential elections. *Peripheral* voters were those who voted in one or the other of the two. And *nonvoters,* of course, were those who abstained in both. Table 1.6 presents estimates of the sizes of each of these categories of voters across the stable phases of the second through fifth electoral systems.

Table 1.6. Estimates of the Components of the National Electorate (in percentages)

	Core	Peripheral	Nonvoters
1840/1844-1848/1852	62.1	12.6	25.2
1868/1872-1888/1892	64.2	13.8	21.9
1900/1904-1920/1924	49.5	11.6	38.8
1940/1944-1960/1964	56.5	7.5	35.9

From the second to the third systems there was not much difference in the relative sizes of the categories. Each era showed a large group of core voters, a much smaller number of peripheral voters, and a nonvoting group that was about one-third the size of the core group. During the fourth electoral era the size relations changed drastically. The core contracted by 14.7 percentage points (compared to the third system), and the size of the nonvoting group increased by 16.9 percentage points. While the relative size of the peripheral group did not change much, the changes in the core and nonvoting groups meant that the latter was more than three-fourths the size of the former. The New Deal era increased the rates of voter mobilization and the size of the core voting group. But most of the gain in the core seems to have come at the expense of the peripheral category. The result is a more clearly bimodal distribution than that of any of the earlier electoral eras. Clearly, it is not only the gross indicators of citizen participation in electoral politics that have changed over the past hundred years and more. Those indicators mirrored an even more important change in the underlying distribution of degrees of psychological involvement among the electorate.

Electoral systems, no less than individual voting decisions, are vectors of long- and short-term forces. Their aggregate shapes result from an interaction between electoral statics and electoral dynamics. Analysis of any electoral era must recognize that interaction. While it is true that "men make their own history," it is equally true that they do so *only* "under circumstances directly encountered, given, and transmitted from the past."[45] Understanding any aspect of that history requires taking into account the ways in which historically conditioned contexts influenced current behaviors. Explaining the electoral dimension of that history requires bringing into analytical focus the long-term processes underlying the evolution of American electoral systems.

NOTES

1. Samuel J. Eldersveld, *Political Parties: A Behavioral Analysis* (Chicago, 1964), especially pp. 47-97, offers an excellent analysis of party as an "alliance of subcoalitions."

2. Ibid., p. 7; Murray Edelman, *The Symbolic Uses of Politics* (Urbana, Ill., 1964), p. 188.

3. V. O. Key, Jr., "Secular Realignment and the Party System," *Journal of Politics* 21 (May 1959): 198.

4. V. O. Key, Jr., "A Theory of Critical Elections," *Journal of Politics* 17 (February 1955): 3-18, and the quotations, respectively, are on pp. 3-4.

5. For the conception, see Philip E. Converse, "The Concept of a Normal Vote," in *Elections and the Political Order*, by Angus Campbell et al. (New York, 1966), pp. 9-39.

6. The major works of the SRC group include Angus Campbell et al., *The American Voter* (New York, 1960); and Campbell et al., *Elections and the Political Order*.

7. Campbell et al., *The American Voter*, p. 121.

8. The original typology is presented in ibid., pp. 531-38; and is elaborated by Angus Campbell, "A Classification of Presidential Elections," in *Elections*

and the Political Order, by Campbell et al., pp. 63-77. For another elaboration, one that introduces the category of "converting" elections, see Gerald Pomper, "Classification of Presidential Elections," *Journal of Politics* 29 (August 1967): 535-66.

9. Nancy Hill Zingale, "Electoral Stability and Change: The Case of Minnesota, 1857-1966" (Ph.D. dissertation, University of Minnesota, 1971), pp. 10-12.

10. Duncan MacRae, Jr. and James A. Meldrum, "Critical Elections in Illinois: 1888-1958," *American Political Science Review* 44 (September 1960): 669-83; and for the application of the techniques to other states, see MacRae and Meldrum, "Factor Analysis of Aggregate Voting Statistics," in *Quantitative Ecological Analysis in the Social Sciences*, ed. Mattei Dogan and Stein Rokkan (Cambridge, Mass., 1969), pp. 487-506.

11. Walter Dean Burnham, *Critical Elections and the Mainsprings of American Politics* (New York, 1970); and "The United States: The Politics of Heterogeneity," in *Electoral Behavior: A Comparative Handbook*, ed. Richard Rose (New York, 1974), pp. 653-725.

12. On the reinstating character of the breakpoint in the mid-1870s, see Burnham, "The United States," pp. 666; and Paul Kleppner, *The Third Electoral System, 1853-1892; Parties, Voters and Political Cultures* (Chapel Hill, 1979), ch. 2.

13. And that generously classified the 1964 and 1968 elections as realigning; see Burnham, "The United States," table 4, p. 666.

14. Key, "Theory of Critical Elections," p. 4; and for Burnham's elaboration, see *Critical Elections*, pp. 6-8.

15. Campbell et al., *The American Voter*, p. 534.

16. Burnham, *Critical Elections*, p. 10.

17. Ibid., p. 10. Forging the link between voting and the larger political system was one of the purposes that Key itemized in urging the development of a typology of elections; see Key, "Theory of Critical Elections," p. 17. The SRC group's approach is especially vulnerable on the problem of developing links between micropolitical behavior and the macropolitical system; see Walter Dean Burnham, "The Politics of Crisis," *Journal of Interdisciplinary History* 8 (Spring 1978): 747-63.

18. For a slightly more extended discussion, see Kleppner, *Third Electoral System*, ch. 9.

19. Walter Dean Burnham, "Party Systems and the Political Process," in *The American Party Systems: Stages of Political Development*, ed. William Nisbet Chambers and Burnham, 2d ed. (New York, 1975), p. 289, and the characterization of each party system on pp. 289-304.

20. Thomas P. Jahnige, "Critical Elections and Social Change: Towards a Dynamic Explanation of National Party Competition in the United States," *Polity* 3 (September 1971): 468.

21. By defining a voting cycle as "a recurrent pattern of fluctuation in county party percentages," Benson fuses these two dimensions together; see Lee Benson, *The Concept of Jacksonian Democracy: New York as a Test Case* (Princeton, 1961), pp. 126-30. That conceptual error has been replicated by other scholars who have too uncritically borrowed from Benson; for example, see

Paul Kleppner, *The Cross of Culture: A Social Analysis of Midwestern Politics 1850-1900* (New York, 1970), pp. 9-10. And the same error inheres in the critique of realignment theory by Lee Benson and Joel H. Silbey, "The American Voter, 1854-1860 and 1948-1984" (Paper presented at the Convention of the Organization of American Historians, New York, April 1978).

22. Critical realignment theory has ample flexibility to integrate findings that point to subsystem variations; see Burnham, *Critical Elections*, pp. 20-26. For the opposite view, see Lee Benson, Joel H. Silbey, and Phyllis F. Field, "Toward a Theory of Stability and Change in American Voting Patterns: New York State, 1792-1970," in *The History of American Electoral Behavior*, ed. Joel H. Silbey, Allan G. Bogue, and William H. Flanigan (Princeton, 1978), pp. 78-105.

23. Benson and Silbey, "The American Voter."

24. Burnham, *Critical Elections*, pp. 91-174; and Walter Dean Burnham, "American Politics in the 1970's: Beyond Party?" in *American Party Systems*, ed. Chambers and Burnham, pp. 308-57.

25. Burnham, *Critical Elections*, pp. 13–18. For other approaches, see William H. Flanigan and Nancy H. Zingale, "The Measurement of Electoral Change," *Political Methodology* 1 (Summer 1974): 49-82; and Gerald M. Pomper, *Elections in America: Control and Influence in Democratic Politics* (New York, 1973), pp. 99-125, 267-69.

26. Flanigan and Zingale, "Measurement of Electoral Change," pp. 54-55.

27. Walter Dean Burnham, Jerome M. Clubb, and William H. Flanigan, "Partisan Realignment: A Systemic Perspective," in *The History of American Electoral Behavior*, ed. by Silbey, Bogue, and Flanigan, pp. 45-77.

28. These series and the other data arrays in this chapter are based upon data provided by the Inter-University Consortium for Political and Social Research. The Consortium bears no responsibility for the interpretations offered here.

29. That is also clear from Burnham's state-level discontinuity indicators which are based upon biennial ten-election sequences; see Burnham, *Critical Elections*, pp. 22-23 and 63-65.

30. The following data illustrate the point. Over the 1891-1893 midpoint years (N=3), the Democratic vote series shows a mean t value of 1.550; but across the 1895-1919 midpoint years (N=13), it has a mean t value of 0.907. Over the 1927-1931 midpoint years (N=3), the mean t value for the Democratic vote series is 3.928; and over the 1933 to 1957 midpoints (N=13) the mean t value is 1.227. Concerning the realignment of the 1930s, it is worth noticing that the peak t value in all Democratic series and all Republican series occurs at midpoint year 1931.

31. One can support the case that realignment began on the Republican side—but not the Democratic—with the 1930 election. That seems to be the case in Minnesota; see Zingale, "Electoral Stability and Change," pp. 151-55. What occurred in the first depression election in 1930 was that support for the party in power eroded, but that did not translate directly and immediately into new voting support for the major opposition party. The same behavioral pattern is evident in the 1894 election, the first one held during the depression of that decade. But there seems to be an important difference between the

collective voter responses in 1894 and 1930. A comparison of the 1892-1894 and 1928-1930 drop-off patterns is revealing. In 1894 the size of the Democratic vote declined in every state from its 1892 level. In twenty-nine states (or 65.9 percent of the total) the absolute size of the Republican vote was greater than it had been in 1892. By way of contrast, while the size of the Republican vote dropped off in every state between 1929 and 1930, the Democratic vote increased in only sixteen states (or 33.3 percent of the total states), and six of these were in the South or Border regions where the candidacy of an Irish Catholic had reduced the Democratic vote in 1928. That suggests that Democratic percentage strength gains in 1930 reflected disproportionate Republican drop-off more so than the Republican gains in 1894 reflected Democratic drop-off.

32. The Democratic percentage of the total vote for presidential and congressional elections is the basic unit of measurement. The actual figures, but neither the distributional pattern nor the general tendencies, would differ somewhat if gubernatorial data were used for the states that conducted such elections in off years.

33. The observation has to be qualified slightly if one subdivides the South into two areas. In that case, the largest Democratic lead, 6.1 percentage points, was in the Deep South. But elsewhere below the Mason-Dixon line the Democrats were less successful during the second electoral system. In the Outer South the Whig lead was 2.4 percentage points, and it was 3.4 percentage points in the Border states.

34. The most competitive categories are those in which neither party held a mean lead of 5.0 percentage points; the most noncompetitive are at the other extreme—mean leads of 20.0 percentage points or more.

35. The major exception is Burnham, "The United States," pp. 672, 679-80, and "Party Systems and the Political Process," pp. 298-301. Over the course of the third electoral system, 13.5 percent of the nonsouthern states (with 12. 1 percent of the nonsouthern voting population) had partisan leads of 20.0 percentage points or more; the proportions over the 1894-1930 period were 29.7 percent of the nonsouthern states and 29.3 percent of the nonsouthern voting population.

36. That statement oversimplifies considerably, but it is adequate for present purposes since an array of the requisite measures of relative dispersion (coefficients of variability) shows the same pattern as the standard deviations. To calculate σ : take the mean Democratic percentage across a set of elections; subtract the Democratic percentage at each election from that mean and square each difference; sum these squares; divide by the number of elections in the series; and extract the square root.

37. The Republican indicators are not mirror images of those in Table 1.4, but they reveal the same trends.

38. The averages reported here are arithmetic means. Over the entire 1836-1900 period, the national turnout mean was 65.6 percent. Turnout calculations here and in chapter 4 are based on estimates of the size of the legally qualified voting population. These estimates take into account variations across states, and over time within states, in the enfranchisement of aliens and of women. The procedures used to develop the estimates at the state and county levels are

outlined in Paul Kleppner and Stephen C. Baker, "The Impact of Voter Registration Requirements on Electoral Turnout, 1900-16" (Paper presented at the Annual Meeting of the American Political Science Association, Washington, D.C., September 1979), Appendix A.

39. For example, the regression-line trends for both the 1836-1900 and the 1854-1892 biennial sequences were mildly positive; respectively, b = +.38 and b = +.68. While that for the 1896-1916 period was much steeper and in a negative direction, b = −1.38.

40. At the national level the linear trend between 1928 and 1972 was positive but modest, b = +.25. Turnout in the former Confederate states had a mean of 21.2 percent over the 1938-1960 period, and 37.4 percent from 1962 to 1972. The corresponding means for nonsouthern turnout were 58.9 percent and 57.8 percent. It goes without saying that since the 1870s turnout in the nonsouth has been considerably higher than in the South. But even if the nonsouthern electorate is considered separately, its pattern follows that described here. The relevant means for the nation outside the South: 1836-1900 = 67.8 percent, 1876-1892 = 75.5 percent; 1896-1916 = 70.4 percent; 1896-1928 = 64.1 percent; and 1928-1972 = 59.0 percent. In short, the post-1900 decay in turnout that is apparent at the national level was not due exclusively to the legal contraction of the electorate in the South.

41. Campbell et al., *The American Voter*, pp. 101-2; Ray M. Shortridge, "Voter Turnout in the Midwest, 1840-1872," *Social Science Quarterly* 60 (March 1980): 617-18.

42. Angus Campbell, "Surge and Decline: A Study of Electoral Change," in *Elections and the Political Order*, by Campbell et al., pp. 40-62.

43. The approach here replicates that used by Shortridge, "Voter Turnout in the Midwest." For a more technical discussion of the use of regression estimation, see Laura Irwin Langbein and Allan J. Lichtman, *Ecological Inference* (Sage Univerity Paper Series on Quantitative Applications in the Social Sciences; Beverly Hills and London, 1978). And for an illustration of its applications to historical voting data, see Peyton McCrary, Clark Miller, and Dale Baum, "Class and Party in the Secession Crisis: Voting Behavior in the Deep South, 1856-1861," *Journal of Interdisciplinary History* 8 (Winter 1978): 429-57.

44. For the second electoral era, the number of pairs is three; for the other eras, the number of pairs is six. The estimates presented here should be seen as first approximations dependent upon particular operational definitions of the specified categories. One improvement would involve calculating the estimates by counties within states and then weighting those to generate the national estimates. In work that is currently in progress, I am pursuing this and other approaches to the problem.

45. Karl Marx, "The Eighteenth Brumaire of Louis Bonaparte," in *Marx and Engels: Basic Writings on Politics and Philosophy*, ed. Lewis S. Feuer, (Garden City, N.Y.: Anchor Books ed., 1959), p. 320.

Ronald P. Formisano

FEDERALISTS AND REPUBLICANS: PARTIES, YES—SYSTEM, NO

2

Marc Bloch in his reflections on historical understanding pointed to the "idol of origins" which besets so many historical processes. In looking for the origins of an institution, scholars often find the beginnings of something that developed over time; they then exaggerate the actual presence of the thing itself during its time of hatching, so that what was only a period of preparation becomes commanded by the phenomenon in all its glory. Such a fallacy preoccupies historians of the first political parties in the United States, parties which arose sometime after 1789 and disappeared by the 1820s.

Until recently, the fallacy flourished under cover of loose or unstated definitions of the term "party." Few bothered to define it, and most simply asserted that parties began during Washington's presidency, precipitated by the original falling out of his cabinet ministers, Alexander Hamilton and Thomas Jefferson. It was enough to know that sharp divisions arose in cabinet and Congress over Treasury Secretary Hamilton's financial policy and then over foreign policy toward England and France, that partisan epithets entered political discourse even before Washington left office, and that under John Adams (1797-1801) they flew as thickly as "wild geese in a storm." And when the challenger Jefferson led his Republicans into the presidential contest of 1800 and defeated Adams, and, even more vitally when Adams and the defeated Federalists turned over national office to the opposition, the American two-party system had arrived in a triumph of moderation, majority rule, and democratic procedures.

The "revolution of 1800," as Jefferson called it, did establish a precedent priceless to the resolution of conflict in a heterogeneous Union. But despite the fact that historians readily translated the political dramas of the 1790s and after into political parties, they never made the case that parties' degree of institutional development in the 1795-

1820 period was comparable to the fully formed parties of the 1840s. If the Whigs and Democrats of the 1830s and 1840s are taken as models of developed electoral machines, legislative organizations, and patronage distributors in a symbiotic relation, then there is doubt that the Federalists and Republicans attained a comparable degree of maturation.

In recent times historians' approaches to political parties have become much less semantically casual. They began to define their terms and to describe organizational activities, legislative behavior, and mass electorates. In a period when computer technology invaded and reshaped whole areas of the social sciences, it was no surprise that the word "system" held increasing attraction as a conceptual framework for understanding political parties. The writings of Joseph Charles and William N. Chambers were especially influential in making the case for the Federalists and Republicans as "modern" parties and in moving other researchers to more vigorous and careful definitions of party.[1]

Yet even as some historians continue to find full-grown parties throughout the early republic, others have taken a more limited view. Different judgments about the parties' scope and their time of arrival seem closely related to what scholars have chosen to study. At the risk of oversimplifying, those who have taken a national approach have tended to make the most extensive claims for the existence of a national party system performing a variety of functions such as national integration and policymaking. Scholars studying particular states have tended to emphasize the local origins of parties and their arrested development.[2]. Whatever their disagreements, however, many historians do not hesitate to label Federalist-Republican competition a "system." If recent scholarship increasingly has attained conceptual clarity, its least helpful tendency has been an almost unthinking adoption of this ahistorical term.

In the precomputer age, "machine" preceded "system" as the favorite metaphor for political organization. But neither word adequately describes the transitional character of politics still deeply rooted in preparty attitudes and behavior. Applied to early national parties the "system" metaphor obliterates the essential character of a period filled with contradictions in behavior and attitudes toward political organization. It hides the persistence of older ways of managing things in politics and obscures the continuing influence of social elites in a society still hierarchical amidst common people still deferential.

It must be admitted that Federalists and Republicans did engage in extensive efforts to get out the vote with often spectacular results. Historians have been rightly impressed with the flourishing of participation (voting), but they have been misled by the bitter partisan invective of the time and have confused partisan emotion—passionate to be sure—with party structure. Federalist and Republican political culture was a deferential-participant phase in the longer development of modern parties through the period from the 1790s to the 1840s. The early parties—or "interests"—were more like factions or stable coalitions of limited duration than the highly articulated organizations of Democrats and Whigs.[3] Above all, Federalist and Republican political parties acquired neither legitimacy nor an institutional life as entities apart from particular political crises.

If thinking of early national politics as a system causes a misreading of social structure and the relations between classes, it even more erroneously minimizes the importance of the political environment.[4] Events are always important, but especially so when system is weak. This was the case during the period 1796 to 1816. Then, far more than later, organized competition rose and fell almost wholly in response to issues, most of which arose in foreign policy and affected most states, but some of which were peculiar to individual states. Thus, organized competition was primarily a dependent variable. Recently, historians have tended to stress the relationship between party competition and voter turnout as if the former were an independent cause operating in a vacuum. Organization and turnout did go together, of course, with both being stimulated by the political context. Disenthralling ourselves of the "system" concept is the first step toward returning political events to their primacy in this period.

A foreigner contemplating United States political history for the first time might well ask: given that many countries have experienced multiparty rivalries, why have there been *two* parties? For most of American history the answer would entail describing rules-of-the-game, winner-take-all elections, a liberal-capitalist political economy, and a tradition of pragmatic consensus. In the early national period the answer would also emphasize several critical issues which inescapably confronted and deeply divided the young republic in the uncertain world of the 1790s.

Three major questions dominated public life from the formation of the new national government in 1789 to the end of the War of 1812. Divisions over these questions created Federalists and Republicans, and the positions men took on each were strongly influenced by geography, cultural heritage, state pride, occupation and economic relations, religion, and other social attributes.

Above all, relations with England dominated American politics for the last third of the eighteenth century. From the mid-1760s to the end of the Revolutionary War the issue created violent upheaval until it was temporarily resolved in Independence. All this is well known, as is the weakness of the Confederation which followed. The withdrawal of Britain's central control from the American states and the need felt by influential men for some form of central government led to the second major question of late 18th century American politics: how much government, or even, should there be an effective central government? During 1787-1789 two broad coalitions struggled over this question, and the strong government supporters, advantageously misnamed "federalists," were the winners. Neither the federalists nor their opponents, misnamed anti-federalists, came to form anything like organized parties, and after the fight over ratification of the new constitution ended, the coalitions collapsed. When parties arose later, some who had been federalists became "Federalists" and some Anti-Federalists became Jeffersonian Republicans, but there was also enough realignment to make generalizations hazardous.

Still, the question "how much government?" remained. In the 1790s as the new nation became entangled in a war between the British and French empires for world supremacy, the problem of relations with England revived, now complicated additionally by diverse American reactions to the French Revolution and its stormy aftermath. The United States was a new nation; indeed, it might be said simply that it was an attempt to make a nation or at least a Union. The Confederation of the 1780s, an attempt at a limited Union, had been found wanting and scrapped. No one knew how long or if the experiment of 1787 would last. Disagreement about "how much government?" remained; and as the new government took action, its policies were bound to please some and alienate others.

In the 1790s the European wars fused the problems of union and government with those of foreign policy and England. Relations with a mother country are bound to be sensitive; and when a revolution has provided the means of separation, working out a new relationship can be fraught with tension. As citizens of a nominally independent country, American merchants saw no reason why their ships could not work a neutral and highly profitable trade with both Britain and France. England seemed disposed, however, even without war to treat the United States as an inferior, and imposed restrictions on American trade with her empire. France, as a former ally, expected the United States to give her preferential treatment or, at the very least, not to be reintegrated into the British commercial nexus on England's terms. From 1795 to 1815, as the struggle between the two European superpowers continued, the United States maneuvered to maintain its interests, neutral rights, and status as a nation. Throughout, relations with England threw firebrands into American politics until the United States fought a second war with England, and until, luckily, the European wars came to an end with Napolean's defeat.

The coalition of federalists that had fought for the 1787 constitution took charge of the new government headed by Washington. As fresh lines of cleavage developed over domestic and foreign policy, the coalition reconstituted itself behind the policies of the Washington and Adams administrations and, until 1800, the congressional majority. By the late 1790s a heterogeneous faction known as Federalists led by Alexander Hamilton and others had superseded the old, looser "federal" coalition which had been defined by broad attitudes rather than several specific issues. Especially after Washington's administration threw its support behind the pro-English Jay Treaty, Federalists sorted out to be those who favored good relations with England, because of commercial ties or strong cultural affinities, even if that meant accepting England's terms. Increasingly, Federalists also favored an energetic and vigorous government. They wanted a government that would act in the general interest—an interest determined by the wise, respectable, and virtuous—despite opposition from large minorities. They favored government action to discourage opposition because they tended to equate opposition to or criticism of their administration with opposition to government itself. Thus, even the legitimacy of opposition and by extension of "party" was itself a question over which Federalists and Republicans fell out. (When in power, however, the Republican attitude tended more toward the initial Federalist posture of undermining the legitimacy of opposition.) As is well known, former "federalist" James Madison led the opposition in Congress to what he saw as pro-English policies and anti-republican excesses of government, while the Republican "interests" gradually adopted another Virginian, Thomas Jefferson, as their chief. The men who had made the Revolution were essentially those who, with minority defections and objections, also made the Constitution. In the 1790s, however, that generation and the cohorts who followed immediately on its heels split deeply over the great questions of how much government and how to deal with England. As those divisions came to be grounded in sectional and other social variables, they turned naturally into a third question: who would govern?

Frequently that question meant which section would govern? The political coalitions which formed in the early national period, like many of those which came later, had a pronounced sectional basis. Though the Federalists acquired some supporters in the South and more strength in the Middle States, their heartland lay in New England. The Jeffersonian Republicans drew much strength from the Middle States and eventually made substantial inroads in New England. But a Republican national administration was first of all a southern, even a Virginian, led government.

In the 1790s New Englanders enjoyed great influence in the national councils of the Federalists. That section enjoyed highly favorable government policies toward its maritime commerce and industries, and there was no political opposition to speak of in New England. In 1800, Federalist New Englanders lost national power and opponents of customary elites within the section grew increasingly able to contest and even to win elections and take power. The tendency of the South, however, was just the reverse. In the 1790s a Federalist interest arose in various parts of the South and by 1800 seemed to be on the verge of creating competitive politics. But the Republican ascendancy after 1800 buried Southern Federalism and cut off competitive politics just as it began to bloom.[5]

A look at the sectional distribution of electoral votes from 1800 to 1816 (Table 2.1) starkly shows the geographic polarization of the Federalist and Republican coalitions. This index, however, misleads in several ways: the electoral vote is a poor guide to the relative strength of parties in the states because few voters took part in presidential elections (few could do so directly); consequently it underestimates the growth of organized opposition in New England and the Middle States; and, most importantly, this mode of measurement presents an artificial picture of two organized parties competing on the national level throughout the period. This was not the case.

In the 1790s the Republicans went furthest along the path of creating a national organization to contest the election of 1800, in part for the obvious reason of being out of office and needing extralegal machinery. The Federalists, in contrast, "thought of themselves as a government, not a party; their history in the 1790s would be the history of alignments within the government, rather than of external alignments which sought to influence the machinery of government."[6] In the late 1790s the Federalists presented the ironic spectacle of a group reaching extremes of partisanship—the Alien and Sedition Acts aimed at nothing less than silencing Jeffersonian opposition—and falling simultaneously into incoherence as a party with the Adams and Hamilton factions bitter enemies by 1800.[7]

The election of 1800 did not establish "a system of competing national parties," not, at any rate, one that lasted. No formal and public nominating process operated, no political platforms addressed the voters, and no such mechanisms came into being. Federalist organization in particular remained stubbornly ad hoc, arising from networks of "old friends, comrades in arms in the Revolution or battles over the Constitution, or . . . birth, marriage or business connections. . . ."[8] Republicans on the other hand kept developing as an organization after 1800, though that development relied heavily on the congressional caucus and communication through congressional networks. How-

Table 2.1 Presidential Electoral Votes by Section, 1800-1816

	1800		1804		1808			1812			1816	
	Fed.	*Rep.*	*Fed.*	*Rep.*	*Fed.*	*Rep.*	*Clinton*	*Fed.*	*Rep.*	*Clin.- Fed.*	*Fed.*	*Rep.*
New England	39	0	9	36	39	6	0	0	8	43	31	12
Midatlantic	20	7	0	47	0	41	6	0	25	37	0	62
Maryland, Delaware	8	5	5	9	5	9	0	0	6	9	3[d]	8[e]
West[a]	0	7	0	16	0	15[b]	0	0	27[c]	0	0	31
South	0	41	0	54	3	51	0	0	62	0	0	62

a - Kentucky, Tennessee, Ohio

b - 1 Kentucky abstention

c - 1 Ohio abstention

d - 1 Delaware abstention

e - 3 Maryland abstentions

ever, since no historian pretends that Federalists developed in the same way, there can be no ground for arguing that a national system was established in 1800. If it had existed then, is it not reasonable to expect that it would be continued beyond a single election?[9]

Another sign that parties did not exist lies in the office-specific electoral coalitions for state and federal offices in 1800. Voters who elected a Republican congressman in a particular state or district were frequently not the same ones who elected a Republican governor or who cast votes for Republican electors. Consider three of the five states which chose presidential electors by popular vote. North Carolina split its electoral vote eight to four while choosing five Republican and five Federalist congressmen. Maryland divided its electoral votes evenly (five-five) while this so-called "Federalist" state elected five Republican and only three Federalist congressmen in 1800. Rhode Island gave Adams all four of its electoral votes while electing two "Republican" congressmen.[10]

Subsequent presidential elections displayed similar patterns and advanced little beyond 1800 in developing national organizations. As in 1800, historians have discerned varying levels of organization-as-effort, or organization-as-campaign-activity, which should not be confused with organization-as-system. That semantic escalation turns history into anachronism.

After 1800 Jefferson's presidency, which incurred displeasure only among Federalist elites and in New England, led to the withering of any Federalist national activity by 1804. While Republicans used their incumbency to full advantage in working informally and in concert to a degree to reelect Jefferson, the Federalist effort was nonexistent.[11]

In 1808, according to Irving Brant, "neither the Republicans nor the Federalists possessed a systematic, organized structure." The caucus of Republican congressmen nominated James Madison for President, but this method excluded states with no Republican representation in the national legislature. Meanwhile, "Federalist candidates for President and Vice-President popped out of a shadowy no-man's-land—the product, apparently, of a self-assembled conclave of party leaders from various states."[12] Indeed, Republicans concerned themselves less with any Federalist opposition and more with a possible challenge to Madison from within Republican ranks, specifically from Vice-President George Clinton, former governor of New York and leading claimant of New York's place in the sun. Madison's backers, in short, spent far more time worrying about the health of the Virginia-New York alliance than about a Federalist "ticket" that was "put forward early in September with no public statement about the who, when, or where of the nominating gathering."[13]

Between 1808 and 1812, under the lash of an intensifying foreign policy crisis, political competition in several states reached new heights and pushed some states far down the road toward party modes. But the 1812 presidential contest did not display a party system functioning on a national level. The main anomaly of the election sprang from the fact that the two major presidential candidates were nominally of the same party—Republican. Their rivalry originated primarily in New York's desire to share "the sceptre" with "arrogant" Virginia. George Clinton had been the object of New York's hopes in 1804 and 1808, and when he died in April 1812, the banner of the Empire State passed quickly to his nephew DeWitt Clinton. Clinton's bid sought to capitalize on Federalist resurgence in state elections from 1810 to 1812 and the Federalists' willingness to back Clinton as a "peace" candidate to maximize their opposition to the War of 1812. The result was that Clinton came to be seen in some areas as a "Federalist" candidate, but he was also seen as a "Republican," or as a "Peace," or "Coalition" candidate. As Norman Risjord observed, "party labels were fluid in 1812."[14]

As in 1808, a group of Federalist leaders in 1812 held a secret meeting in New York City where they attempted to assemble delegates to decide on election strategy. Sixty-four men, many appointed by corresponding committees, showed up from eleven (of eighteen) states. Some historians continue to find in this gathering an important step toward the national nominating conventions of a later period, if not the later thing in embryo. The meeting was not a convention, however, least of all because it fell short of being national, but because representatives to it were self-selected, because it nominated no candidate (leaving Federalists able to back Clinton), and above all because it was a secret meeting, conspiratorial in conduct and tone.[15]

Whatever impetus existed toward national organization in 1812, it could not outlast the foreign policy crisis and war which had produced such movements. Federalism died nationally with the war's end in 1815 and in the outburst of nationalism following Jackson's victory at New Orleans. The Presidential election of 1816 was a noncontest. The Republican caucus nominated James Monroe who won in a cakewalk. The Federalists nominated no one—Federalist leader, Rufus King, who received thirty-four electoral votes, did not even think of himself as a presidential candidate.[16]

The collapse of the divisive foreign policy dispute, especially the restoration of amicable relations with England, were the most powerful but not the only forces removing partisanship. As John Adams remarked in 1813, "Our two great parties have crossed over the valley and taken possession of each other's mountain." Under pressure of war, the Republicans adopted the strong government attitudes, or at any rate some specific national policies, of the Federalists; by 1816 they also favored a national bank, a protective tariff, federal internal improvements, and a strong navy.

In 1816, now that it no longer mattered, ten of nineteen states possessed some form of popular election of presidential electors. The first burst of partisanship in the new nation had thrown the election of presidents into fewer hands. In 1800, for example, Virginia passed an act changing the mode of election from one by districts to a general ticket to prevent Federalists from gaining electors in even one or two districts. Massachusetts took the choice away from districts, too, but gave it to the state legislature to insure the complete shutting out of any opposition. In 1800 eleven of sixteen state legislatures, more than in 1796, were responsible for choosing electors. In contrast, the collapse of partisanship in 1816 opened the way for the popular election of electors, and in the near unanimous election of Monroe in 1820, fifteen of twenty-four states chose electors by popular vote.[17]

If the traditional image of Federalists and Republicans as national parties and the newer notion of them as a national party system must be discarded, there is substance to the claim that Federalists and Republicans in the national Congress behaved as parties-in-the legislature. As in other arenas, however, party voting in Congress from 1796 to 1816 rose and fell in response to events. Incipient legislative parties can be discerned particularly during the period 1808 to 1815, and those dates signal immediately the parties' sensitivity to the foreign policy crisis. In addition, regional and sectional loyalties also influenced legislative behavior, notably roll call voting, and the institutionalization of the legislature itself and of partisan groups within it remained at a very low level compared to later periods.[18]

The problem of executive patronage must be viewed in a similar way. National administrations from Washington on appointed men they knew to share their political philosophy and who would work—or had worked—for their cause in elections.[19] But governments throughout the world had behaved in similar fashion for centuries. Was it a novel situation because officeholders were expected to repay their chiefs and retain their positions by "exerting influence" in elections and mobilizing an ever-expanding electorate? Yes, in part, but this too differed only slightly from political practices that had prevailed in England at times for at least in excess of one hundred years.[20] In the early national period the rewarding of friends and the punishing of enemies were deliberate means to an end, pursued sometimes systematically, sometimes erratically. To the victors went the spoils, especially during the flurries of partisan competition between the late 1790s and 1816. While for many individuals officeholding was an end in itself, the republic had not yet reached the point where men simply pursued political careers within party organizations with office-seeking their consuming motivation, thus making the party organization's major reason for being the winning of spoils.

PARTIES IN THE STATES

Since Federalists and Republicans did not really exist as nationally competitive parties, the case for "party" must rest on an assessment of party development in the states. This does not imply that a top-down approach is irrelevant to a full understanding of the first parties, since national issues did help to form limited interstate and intersectional coalitions and to shape party identities within the states, but for purposes of measurement one must turn largely to the states to test whether or how much parties grew as institutions. State elections brought far more voters to the polls than did federal elections, and some state parties achieved a degree of explicitness, elaboration, and continuity not at all present on the national scene. Neither the available space nor the state of scholarship permits a full or accurate summary of the extent of party development in each state; nor is it possible to give a satisfactory description of the variety of political cultures present in different sections and regions.

Ideally, it would be desirable to assemble for every state for the period 1795 to 1820 or 1825 data indicating the presence of 1) party-as-organization (as nominator, voter mobilizer, fund raiser); 2) party-in-office (as executive party and especially as party-in-the-legislature); and 3) party-in-the-electorate (as loyalist voters consistently casting ballots for the party's nominees). The quantity and quality of this information vary greatly, but it is possible to give rough estimates of relative degrees of development and to observe the relationship between partisan competition and the political environment, especially foreign policy crises. The estimates will rely heavily on electoral data, in part because historians have attached great importance to surges of voter participation in the era and in part because such data are available and comparable. The states in the Union by 1816 will be considered in five sectional groups: New England (Massachusetts, Vermont, Connecticut, New Hampshire, Rhode Island); Midatlantic (New Jersey, New York, Pennsylvania); Border (Delaware, Maryland); South (Virginia, North Carolina, South Carolina, Georgia, Louisiana); and West (Ohio, Tennessee, Kentucky).

In New England, Massachusetts ranked first in overall party development. There the Federalists held on to state power longer than elsewhere, and gubernatorial contests of some scope and intensity occurred in 1823 and 1824. By contrast, competitive electoral politics was sporadic and short-lived in New Hampshire and Rhode Island (see Table 2.2).

Table 2.2 Party Development in New England, 1800-1824

A. Estimated Levels of Party Activity

	Electorate	*Office (legis.)*	*Organization*	*Overall*
Mass.	High	(Medium)	(low-Med)	low-HIGH
Vt.	High	(med-Low)	(med-Low)	low-MED
Conn.	Med	(med-Low)	(med-Low)	high-LOW
N.H.	Low	(med-Low)	(med-Low)	med-LOW
R.I.	Low	(low-Low)	(low-Low)	low-LOW

B. Years of High Electoral Competition, Gubernatorial Elections

Mass.	1800 ———— 1824
Vt.	1801 ———— 1816
Conn.	1803 ———— 1817
N.H.	1802-1805 —— 1809 ———— 1817
R.I.	1811 ———— 1818

Very little is known about the legislatures of these states and the degree or duration of party organization and voting in legislatures, so all of the ratings in that sphere are estimates (indicated by parenthesis in the tables) based on impressionistic or even indirect evidence. If patronage distribution on party grounds were to be considered as the chief indicator of party-in-office, these ratings might be higher, but it seems unlikely that any state experienced a purely partisan office distribution system throughout this period. Patronage distribution also was a variable over time and place.

In Massachusetts Federalism as a statewide competitive force lasted longer than anywhere else in the country. Despite (or because of) annual gubernatorial elections, a Federalist sat in the governor's chair from the start of the War of 1812 to the election of 1823. The Federalists made one last state campaign in 1824; and though they lost in 1823 and 1824 by decisive but not wide margins, the end then came swiftly and totally. Still, it had been a remarkable "Indian summer" for Federalism (as Samuel E. Morison once called it), considering that the opposition had been fairly well organized since about 1804-1805, and had managed to win several elections between 1805 and 1812. The mass electorate displayed levels of partisan voting as high or higher than anywhere else in the Union, and while party organization in the legislature was probably less well developed, patronage also seems to have been ruled at times to a heavy degree by party considerations.[21]

In Vermont competitive politics was considerably more short-lived than in Massachusetts, getting underway between 1800 and 1805 and ending abruptly after 1815. Federalists controlled the state in the 1790s and in 1800 an opposition candidate for governor managed to get only a third of the popular vote. A Republican interest gradually organized and increased its share of the vote until it finally won the governorship in 1807. Federalists regained the seat in 1808, lost it for the next four years (1809-1812), won it again in 1813 and 1814, and then lost it for good thereafter. Partisanship seems to have been at its most intense during the War of 1812—certainly electoral turnout peaked in elections from 1812 through 1815. The Federalists, surging because of opposition to the war, organized a Washington Benevolent Society in 1812, and in 1813, calling themselves "the friends of peace, commerce, and liberty," held a rare state convention to nominate their gubernatorial candidate. Though the latter polled slightly fewer votes than the Republican candidate, neither had a majority. While Republicans carried the Council, Federalists won the Assembly which, after rejecting the votes of a town for improper voting, elected the Federalist candidate as governor by a vote of 112 to 111.[22]

While Federalists and Republicans in the two branches of the legislature fought tooth and nail for control of the state from 1812 to 1815, party voting seems to have existed in the legislature during the period 1800 to 1812 at least with reference to national issues, governors' messages, and speaker elections.[23] The governor's message, whose acceptance by the legislature was largely symbolic, constituted a particular bone of contention especially during the war years. In 1816 with the decline of partisanship the legislature ended the practice of discussing and voting on the message as it took too much time in "violent party contention."[24]

Patronage in Vermont also followed a similar pattern of varying intensity between the years 1798 and 1815. Here too evidence is impressionistic, but an early historian chronicled the beginnings of "prescription" in 1798, its decline, its revival in 1803 under Republicans, and its acme or "highest pitch" during the Federalist ascendancy of 1813. Yet even in this realm there is evidence that "good feelings" began early in Vermont.[25]

Closer scrutiny of even the most intense years of Federalist-Republican struggle in Vermont indicates the limited growth of institutionalized parties. Election outcomes were frequently office-specific, with different results obtained in gubernatorial, assembly, and congressional races. The Federalists seldom if ever held an out-and-out party convention. More importantly, Federalist organizing efforts (and success) in 1808 and 1813-1814 depended heavily on issues and political events. In 1808 the Federalist campaign drew life from opposition to the Embargo but was "uncoordinated" and weakened by "intraparty squabbles at the local level, and by sufficient ticket-splitting to preserve Democratic-Republican control of the assembly." Many Vermonters had economic ties with Canada and hated the War of 1812, so by 1814 the war had created more support for Federalists than ever before, but this was "an artificial unity based on hostility to the war [and] the Federalists could not expect to stay in power." Springing from reactions to political events after 1807, Federalist strength had no long-term basis.[26]

At first glance Connecticut appears to have resembled Massachusetts in possessing a strong Federalist party and a competitive minority which eventually won control of the state even several years earlier than the Republicans had in Massachusetts. Before then, however, Connecticut Federalism seemed almost impregnable and highly unified. According to one early nineteenth century observer, "There can be no divisions among the ruling party in Connecticut; because the leaders act as one head; divulge no minor disagreements . . . and lose all subordinate differences of opinion, in the one point upon which they cannot but constantly agree;—the preservation of the party."[27] This gave rise to a minority opposition which historians have seen as "superbly organized under state, county, township, and district managers." Indeed, there is evidence of intense partisan competition in the electorate from shortly after 1800 to about 1820.[28]

In 1800 Republicans first began to persuade voters to unify behind opposition tickets and as a result ticket voting and turnout climbed rapidly in the early years of the century. This was all the more remarkable because Connecticut held two general elections every year, and in 1801 the Federalists passed a "Stand Up" election law requiring an open standing vote by freemen. In April, the governor and lieutenant governor were chosen as well as representatives to the General Assembly. In the fall freemen again chose representatives and also "nominated" twelve assistants who represented the state at-large on the Council. The twenty nominees with the greatest number of votes were then submitted to the freemen in the next April election, with the incumbent assistants or any ex-assistants heading the list no matter how many votes they had won the previous fall. This system naturally favored the reelection of the traditional elite, especially under the complex and protracted mode of open voting. Long terms of service characterized officeholders at all levels of government in Connecticut.[29]

With voting conducted under the gaze of local officers, gentry, and Congregational ministers, any opposition would need to be brave, deliberate, persevering, and careful to shield its plans with as much secrecy as possible. But other considerations also prompted both

Republicans and Federalists to prepare for elections covertly and to deny that they acted as parties. Connecticut's traditions all inhibited electioneering; overt political organization ran against the grain of accepted behavior and smacked of conspiracy. The idea of party was not accepted and competition was regarded as temporary. "Both parties felt that they were in competition to win a decisive victory and that the end must be the destruction of their opponents and the complete triumph of their principles." Thus, by 1803 both Federalists and Republicans had a "grand caucus" and a "general committee" which organized their supporters from the top down in highly centralized fashion, and both did their best to disguise the fact.[30]

In 1801 after a public rally Republican candidates for governor and lieutenant governor first appeared, with the former attracting only 1,056 votes to the Federalist incumbent's 11,156. Meanwhile a Jeffersonian congressional candidate did much better, losing 7,397 to 3,256, and Republicans won about a sixth of the legislature (33 seats). In 1803 a spirited effort by Republicans raised their gubernatorial total to 7,848, but the Federalists countered with all the weight of their influence and reelected Governor Jonathan Trumbull with 14,375 votes. Indeed, during the rest of the period the Federalists never lost a straight-out contest to the Republicans: Federalism ended, or began to end, when Federalists faltered and finally fell because of divisions in their own ranks.

Still, it could be said that the Republicans established something of a party. Jefferson's victory in 1800 gave them the powerful New Haven collectorship and eventually some one hundred and twenty postmasterships and one hundred other appointed federal officials throughout the state.[31] Much of this "influence" would be brought to bear in elections. Historians have found party caucuses in the legislature acting throughout the periods before and after the Federalist ascendancy.[32] Most important, some Republicans seem to have had a more positive attitude toward political organization and even to "party" than Federalists, as indeed circumstances dictated.[33]

On the other hand, the Federalists' refusal to acknowledge that they were a party sprang from something more substantial than hypocrisy, and encompassed something more than self-preservation. When the Federalists said that they were the "government" and not a party, they had reason. They could throw the entire weight of most of Connecticut's institutions into the political fray. Aside from the top state officers, legislators and their friends, every county had a sheriff with deputies. There were judges at all levels, and all towns had an average of about seven justices of the peace, appointed, like the sheriff, by the legislature, and the senior justice had charge of local elections. According to Purcell, "Every parish had a 'standing agent' whose anathemas were said to convince at least ten voting deacons. Militia officers, state's attorneys, lawyers, professors and school-teachers were in the van of this 'conscript army.' In all, about a thousand or eleven hundred dependent office-holders were . . . the inner ring which could always be depended upon for their own and enough more votes within their control to decide an election. This was the Federal machine." And it included Yale University, its professors and networks, and the Congregational clergy and a powerful array of benevolent societies which Republicans said spread more Federalism than gospel.[34] Thus, Federalism was an establishment and not a party. To say that all institutions (charitable, literary, religious, educational) were "made to serve party purposes" is to stand the Standing Order on its head.[35] A Federalist political party as an institution separate from existing institutions had no life at all; political power flowed instead from social control, from the unity of the social, religions, economic, and political elite. The "ruling party" might have been called a ruling class. The proof that Federalism had no separate being as a party lies in the fact that when the Federalist establishment ended, when the Stand Up law was repealed and church and state made separate, Federalism came quickly to an end. There was no party to keep it going.

From 1801 to 1810 the Republicans usually conducted vigorous campaigns for governor, assistants and state representatives. Their goal became a well organized and highly centralized chain of command that would extend quietly down from a state committee through counties to towns where canvasses would be made in local districts of the exact numbers of Federalist, Republican, and neutral voters.[36] Nonetheless, in 1808 the Republican cause slowly began to decline with the revulsion against national commercial policies. Republican representation in the General Assembly had reached a high of seventy-five in the fall of 1807: thereafter it fell steadily to sixty-one and fifty in 1808, to forty-four in the spring of 1810, and still lower during the war. By 1810 the vote for Republican assistants had fallen to just above the 1801 level, so the Republicans nominated no candidates for the Council again until 1815. In 1810 an unprecendented split had occurred in Federalist ranks during the gubernatorial election, and although the regular Federalist candidate had beaten the Republican easily by 10,265 to 7,185, a second Federalist attracted 3,110 votes. That insurgent was Roger Griswold, a lifelong Federalist of impeccable politics and a wealthy Episcopalian who was not a "professor of religion." Griswold represented the lawyers, secularists and Episcopalians who had grown restless under the dominance of the Congregational clergy within the Federalist establishment. In the next year Griswold again appeared at the head of a "Toleration" ticket in opposition to the in-house Federalist, Jonathan Trumbull. The Republicans decided to make no nomination and to back Griswold, who won with 10,148 votes to Trumbull's 8,727. Griswold's moderation as governor brought harmony to Federalist ranks and he appeared as the only Federalist candidate in 1812. The Republicans, however, could not abide Griswold's opposition to the war, so they turned to another wealthy Episcopalian in their own ranks, Elijah Boardman. The result was a landslide for Griswold—11,725 to 1,487. In 1813 the Federalists united once again on a traditionalist representative of the Standing Order, John Cotton Smith, and this raised Boardman and the Republicans to a significant showing while losing in the gubernatorial race again (11, 893-7,201), but in 1814 the Federalists romped as the Republican vote fell sharply—the leading Republican vote getter for Congress received only 104 votes. While elsewhere in the country political competition had revivied during the foreign policy crisis of 1808-1814, in Connecticut it was dying.[37]

Ironically, Republicanism in Connecticut seems to have been weakest just before Federalism's sudden collapse. While Republicanism did revive with the war's end in 1815, Federalism's fall owed less to Republican success as a party and more to the division and transformation of the old establishment.

Once again Connecticut defied all patterns. In Massachusetts and many other states political activity and voter turnout fell rapidly in the good spirits induced by the war's end. In Connecticut voter turnout would climb to its greatest height—but while "parties" there were, "party" could not claim the credit.

The Republicans nominated their own men for governor and Council in 1815 and won only about half as many votes as did the Federalists. In 1816, however, the Republicans merged behind a ticket resembling Griswold's coalition of 1811. For years the Republicans had been trying to break off the Episcopalian minority from its alliance with the establishment; and this now began to happen under the aegis of an "American ticket" or "American Toleration and Reform ticket," which was known generally—as Griswold's had been—as the Toleration ticket. Heading it was a banker and manufacturer, Oliver Wolcott, a Hamiltonian Federalist of the 1790s, who appealed to Republicans and moderate Federalists because he supported the 1812 War and was liberal in religion. For lieutenant governor the Tolerationists offered Judge Jonathan Ingersoll, a wealthy New Haven lawyer and Episcopalian. The Federalists countered with the incumbent champion of the ancient politico-religious order, Governor John Cotton Smith, and named for the second place a former member of the Hartford Convention. The chief issue was reform of church-state relations and a lessening of the clergy's power. Other issues usually agitated by Republicans also received Tolerationist attention: the need for a new constitution; election procedures and suffrage; finances and taxation; monied corporations; and the militia. The Federalists narrowly held the governorship but lost the second place, while Tolerationists won eighty-five seats in the General Assembly, more than Republicans ever had. In the fall the Tolerationists arranged a mixed list of assistants, throwing their support to moderate Federalists; by the same strategy also they caused new men to be elected to Congress.

In the spring of 1817, with church and state and related issues still paramount, Wolcott received 13,655 votes to Smith's 13,119—Purcell estimated that probably "nearly every freeman voted." In the fall the Tolerationists continued their tactic of mixed tickets and broke the Federalists' grip on the Council and in 1818 the Federalists departed from the gubernatorial contest. Wolcott, widely perceived as above party, breezed in with over 16,000 votes, and retained the office through most of the next decade. Federalist assistants still attracted a customary vote, and Federalists contested seats for the 1818 constitutional convention; but Tolerationists now held a majority in the General Assembly as well and party lines there became increasingly blurred.[38]

Federalist-Republican competition had not yet run its course. In 1817 the Stand Up law was repealed. In 1819 and 1820 assistants became state senators under the new constitution, and in elections of very high turnout Republicans and Federalists waged spirited contests. Though ballots now replaced standing to vote, the Federalists had fought tenaciously to require that the new mode of balloting require written and not printed tickets. Party leaders quickly realized it would be necessary to have many lists written out and to provide them to voters. Thus Republicans raised money to hire scribes because they realized that many electors would leave the meeting without voting unless ballots "are previously written and in the hands of judicious men for distribution."[39] This flurry of activity was over by the early 1820s, and elections sank into apathy. Suffrage and ballot reform had not created parties, contrary to the misleading signs of a brief afterlife; rather they had helped to bury partisanship.

Indeed, it was only through the transcending of party in 1816-1817 that the old regime had been overthrown. Republicans naturally claimed the credit, and Connecticut fell in finally with the one party fluidity of national Republicanism along with many other states. But Connecticut had followed its own distinctive road to that common destination.

New Hampshire and Rhode Island, so unlike in their geography and economy, were very similar in having the least developed competitive politics in New England. Federalists and Republicans did compete in both states especially during the years 1808 to 1816 when voter turnout rose to its highest levels and ticket voting usually prevailed. In fact, turnout remained high in both states in the general elections of 1817 and 1818, though in New Hampshire the Federalists split into factions in both those years. In gubernatorial elections the politics of these small states were dominated by popular personalities who frequently ran unopposed or against a divided opposition. In Rhode Island in twenty-one gubernatorial elections from 1800 to 1820 the winner faced no opposition in a dozen years (the lieutenant governorship was sometimes contested).[40] In New Hampshire competition flourished from 1808 through 1816, but before and after Federalists suffered from lack of coherence as a party. While Republicans did organize early and manifest more of a knack for party politics, Federalists made no real effort to organize until 1808. When they did organize a system of committees reaching into towns designed to mobilize voters, New Hampshire Federalists like many of their brethren elsewhere did their best to keep their exertions secret. A recent student of New Hampshire politics concluded that the essence of early national political competition was "interaction between firm personal loyalties, salient issues, and rudimentary party apparatus."[41]

New Jersey, New York, and Pennsylvania, taken as a region ranked below the New England states and Delaware and Maryland in overall party development, though New York and New Jersey individually ranked higher perhaps than the lowest New England states. This view departs sharply from the usual one that the "big states," New York and Pennsylvania, because of their size and social complexity produced a far more sophisticated and modern politics earlier than other states. Indeed, many writers have found full-fledged parties there in the 1790s and earlier. During the Jacksonian period, of course, New York was a leader in promoting not only organized mass parties but also a party ethos which justified parties as positive ends in themselves. Recent writers have been taken with the idea that the variety of peoples and interests in eighteenth century New York early on produced the interest-group foundations on which competitive party politics easily arose.[42]

It must be admitted that a pure form of political professionalism and political entrepreneurship appeared early in New York, and that organization for the purpose of making nominations, mobilizing voters, and managing legislatures and other assemblies also advanced precociously there. Still, most organization was ad hoc, conducted as elsewhere through existing social networks; and even New York's cutthroat entrepreneurial politics did not require the existence of a two-party system which conformed to the patterns later established (see Table 2.3).

Table 2.3 Party Development in the Midatlantic States, 1800-1820

Estimated Levels of Party Activity				
	Electorate	*Office (legis.)*	*Organization*	*Overall*
New Jersey	med-Med	(low-Med)	(low-Med)	med-MED
New York	low-Med	(low-Med)	(low-Med)	low-MED
Pennsylvania	med-Low	(high-Low)	(med-Low)	high-LOW

By the late 1790s New York City and Philadelphia had advanced further than anywhere else in the country in partisan consciousness and organizational techniques. Yet even in the two cosmopolitan metropoli, party growth was uneven and a two-party system could not be said to exist, at least, not on the basis of evidence presented to date. In New York City, for example, the Democratic-Republicans moved far toward being a party even by 1800, but the Federalists did not attain the Republicans' level of organization or duration.[43]

Parties in New York state in the early national period have been characterized as "simply organizations for the nomination of candidates and for the conquest of administrative and political offices." New York's shifting parties lacked ideology and social coherence and were in effect relatively durable factions which relied on great men or notables for leadership and impetus. In this milieu, "flux, fluidity, and uncertainty were the rule."[44] A recent study of county election data in statewide races from 1792 to 1827 showed that only between the years 1809 and 1816 was there "an interlude of relative electoral stability."[45]

In Pennsylvania, the development of two parties was even weaker. Republican dominance was so strong after 1800 that the excitement and uncertainty in the state's politics for the next quarter century sprang primarily from wrangling among the Keystone State's Republican factions.[46] In 1811, while furious electoral battles were being waged in various states, Simon Snyder, a "Republican"gubernatorial candidate, won election with almost 54,000 votes over the inconsequential opposition of two "Federalist" opponents, who received 3,610 and 383 votes with 1,658 scattering. In state senate races that same year, as far as may be determined from incomplete data, Republicans frequently ran against one another or without opposition. The 1812 Presidential election consisted of a contest between two Republican factions which did not reflect accurately Republican control of the state.[47]

Though the assumption that Jeffersonian New York and Pennsylvania led the way in producing political organizations comparable to Jacksonian parties has flourished for a long time, New Jersey has recently attracted notice for its political development.[48] The state in fact outdistanced its two big neighbors in party growth and resembled the medium New England states in having sporadic outbursts of electoral competition alongside periods of quiescence. The former resulted from Federalists deciding to make a run for it, but after 1800 New Jersey was largely in Republican hands. In the twenty years after 1800 Federalist strength in the state legislature fell below 40 percent eleven times and to 30 percent or below four times. In Congressional races throughout the period, the Federalists were often simply not in the field (see Table 2.4).

Table 2.4 Federalist Percentage of the Vote in Congressional Elections, New Jersey, 1796-1822

Year	Percent	Year	Percent
1796	65	1810	–
1798	40	1813	52
1800	49	1814	48
1803	–	1816	–
1806	–	1820	–
1808	44	1822	–

SOURCE: Rudolph V. Pasler and Margaert C. Palser, *The New Jersey Federalists* (Rutherford, N.J., 1975), p. 202.

NOTE: The legislature has not been studied directly.

Enough information exists regarding New Jersey to state that two-party competition developed only partially in the early national period and, as elsewhere, waxed most intensely just before 1801 and later in response to the Embargo (1808) and War of 1812. There also existed a distinct sectional basis to parties with organizations growing in different regions. Republican majorities and organization flourished in east Jersey and after 1800 Republican leaders tried to recruit influential men in west Jersey and gradually to extend Republican organization throughout the state. But west Jersey remained mostly Federalist and Republicans frequently did not contest elections there, even after 1810. Federalist organization remained even more sectionally confined and the most recent students of New Jersey Federalism have argued that Quaker dominated Burlington County in important ways *was* New Jersey Federalism, providing its leadership core during periods when Federalists made state politics competitive and keeping it alive even into the "Era of Good Feelings." In any case, New Jersey Federalism did draw life primarily from west Jersey, though Republicans made more inroads into their redoubts than vice versa.[49]

Federalists had reigned in New Jersey in the 1790s and had turned back the onrushing—and organizing—Republicans in 1800, when party organization was emergent among both groups. After Jefferson's national victory, however, Federalists lost the state for the first time in 1801. Party battles continued to rage in the next two years, but from 1804 through 1807 a period of relative calm prevailed as Federalist efforts tailed off. In 1808 the Federalists returned to the field with greater exertions than ever, but the Republicans, responding in kind, won by a comfortable majority. The onset of war regenerated Federalist hopes and also gave them the new label of "Peace party." This allowed them to strike a nonpartisan pose and to exploit a powerful reaction against the war. After a frenzied campaign and a large turnout the "Peace party" squeaked back into control of the state for the first time in over a decade. Aside from opposition to the war, their major policy was an effort to insure that they would stay in power. They awarded themselves the disposition of New Jersey's electoral votes in the presidential election of 1812 by changing the mode of choosing electors from a popular election to one by the legislature. They kept congressional elections popular, but changed them from a general election; new gerrymandered districts were introduced with the result that four of six congressmen next elected were Federalists.

Republicans came storming back the next year, won state control, and repealed the laws relating to elections as well as some Federalist antiwar pronouncements. In 1814 the Federalists fought one more full-scale campaign, as the Friends of Peace; and both parties probably reached the height of their development as electoral machines, with the Federalists employing Washington Benevolent Societies to help mobilize votes. Hereafter, partisan competition declined rapidly, and after 1814 Federalists never again ran tickets in every county in the state. Even during the period 1801 through 1814 they had not held a state convention, or its equivalent, every year. In the late teens and early twenties Federalists still kept control of their traditional western strongholds, and a loyal though dwindling following cast votes for Federalist tickets in those areas. But party lines frequently blurred after 1815, factionalism grew, Federalists and Republicans cooperated in business and politics, and from 1817 to 1829 the Republican governor was a former Federalist who had left Federalist ranks just at the end of the War of 1812.[50]

Party blocs in the legislature appear to have followed a similar pattern. They probably held relatively firm in the years 1801-1804, and

1808-1814, and especially during 1812-1814. Walter R. Fee observed that by 1817 any party coherence in the legislature had disappeared.[51]

Patronage practices in New Jersey also evidenced partisan norms which operated at different levels of intensity at various times, and, in this case, seem never to have prevailed completely. The Republicans did reward those who worked for the Jeffersonian cause: thus, of 256 activists during the period 1800 to 1816 identified by Carl Prince nearly two-thirds held appointive office. But overall less than one-fourth of all state and federal appointees were veteran Republicans, which leaves open the possibility that many of the remaining three-fourths were not chosen according to party criteria. Opponents and neutrals often may have simply been allowed to stay in office. In fact, as Fee observed, the Federalists enjoyed "a large number of political appointments," which elicited complaints from hard-line Republicans on many occasions; Federalists were not excluded as much as they might have been, party differences and rhetoric notwithstanding.[52]

Thus there were Federalist and Republican parties in New Jersey, but party growth was incomplete and only approached being systematic. Parties developed more than in New York and Pennsylvania, but not quite so much as in two other nearby states, Maryland and Delaware. These two small border states resembled the medium to high New England states in party activity (see Table 2.5). In Delaware elections were close throughout the period and turnout extremely high. Indeed, in nearby Pennsylvania from 1792 to 1811 voter turnout in gubernatorial voting averaged 35 percent while in little Delaware it averaged 60 percent, and it ranged from 19 to 56 percent in the big state and from 48 to 81 percent in Delaware.[53]

Table 2.5 Party Development in Maryland and Delaware, 1796-1820

A. Estimated Levels of Party Activity

	Electorate	*Office (legis.)*	*Organization*	*Overall*
Maryland	low-High	(low-Med)	(high-Med)	(high-MED)
Delaware	low-High	(low-Med)	(low-Med)	(med-MED)

B. Competition in Gubernatorial Elections

Maryland	1796	1816
Delaware	1800	1820

Federalists enjoyed unusual strength in Delaware; though elections generally were close, Federalists won most of them from 1800 to 1820. Yet the close aggregate vote concealed imbalances at the county and hundred levels; those imbalances reflected the fact that development of political organization proceeded at very different rates in Delaware's three counties. In New Castle County in the late 1790s Republicans presented tickets nominated at meetings representing localities in the county. New Castle was Republican but in Kent and Sussex counties, where Federalists generally prevailed, Republican organization came much more slowly. Federalist organization in their downstate strongholds, moreover, tended to be secret and elitist until 1811.[54] When Delaware became more strongly Federalist during the War of 1812 it was mostly because Kent and Sussex were overwhelmingly so. After 1816 Federalist unity deteriorated and at the same time Federalists made small inroads in New Castle. By 1820 split ticket voting was common and many candidates were blurring party and calling themselves "Federal Republicans."[55]

Of Maryland John Adams said in 1776: ". . . it is so eccentric a colony—sometimes so hot, sometimes so cold, now so high, then so low—that I know not what to say about or expect from it. . . ." Though early national politics in Maryland also had peculiarities, it displayed patterns which, while often contradictory or ambiguous, resembled those found in other states.

At first glance politics from 1800 to 1820 displays signs of vigorous party activity: high turnout, closely contested elections, shifting party fortunes, and high partisan consciousness—though information on party activity in the legislature and on patronage is also lacking here. Eighteenth century Maryland, however, was not a democratic arena where interest groups or the masses freely disported. Post-Revolutionary Maryland was a gentry-dominated, hierarchical society whose politics were run by competing factions of aristocrats. Maryland's new constitution was the "most conservative of all the new state constitutions." When more men went to the polls to vote after the 1790s, the basic conditions of elite influence did not change. Federalist and Republican politics, though competitive, retained the basic relations between the influentials on top and deferentials in the middle and at the bottom, and thus kept much of its nonpartisan, even antipartisan character.[56]

One student of Maryland politics, Whitman H. Ridgway, has drawn a sharp distinction between the "first" and "second" party eras in Maryland. In the Federalist-Republican period, he observed a highly traditional "ruling establishment . . . both conservative and elitist." Family connections remained extremely important and social and economic status was closely connected to political leadership. Few candidates actively campaigned for office, but set traditional methods of influence in motion to gather support.[57]

Because there were no statewide elections, state party organizations did not exist. In the counties "tight-knit, hierarchical organizations developed" which nominated candidates, decided policy, directed campaigns, and mobilized voters. But county organizations did not develop in all parts of the state. "One or the other of the organizations so dominated the politics of Baltimore city and southern Maryland that the other rarely bothered to run a candidate." Thus, some nine to eleven counties of nineteen statewide had "fairly active" parties while in the rest parties were "rather inoperative."[58] In Baltimore city the Republicans possessed a "remarkably complete organization" by 1800, but Federalist campaigns, "collapsed even before they were launched" and "it appears that the Federalist party never created a party organization in the city."[59] This meant that the Baltimore Jeffersonians, though capable of standing united against an infrequent Federalist or external threat, normally existed in a state of factional confusion and only rarely appeared to be a coherent political organization.[60]

Table 2.6 summarizes the frequency of contested elections in Maryland's counties in major elections, with "contested" being liberally defined to include any time when the minority collected at least 10 percent of the total vote.[61] In contested elections turnout rose and the electorate displayed a high degree of stability, with voters who cast ballots for Federalists in 1796 overwhelmingly continuing to vote for Federalists in later elections.[62]

Table 2.6 Number of Contested Counties in Maryland Presidential and Congressional Elections, 1796-1816

Election	No. Contested Counties	Election	No. Contested Counties
1796 P	10	1808 C	16
1798 C	10	1810 C	6
1800 P	13	1812 C	12
1801 C	11	1812 P	15
1803 C	7	1814 C	12
1804 C	5	1816 C	14

In the period 1801 to 1807 parties can barely be said to have existed, much less a "party system." Moderation seemed to prevail. Federalists had controlled the state until 1800, but when Republicans won the legislature that year, they reelected the Federalist governor and sent another Federalist to the United States Senate. Though Republicans developed what one historian has called an "unsurpassable organization," it seems to have been increasingly unneccessary—in the 1804 congressional elections six of seven Republicans were unopposed.[63] Federalists had been riven with divisions since the late 1790s and Republicans had exploited their opponents' lack of unity; but with the Embargo in 1808 the Republicans divided and the Federalists recaptured a majority of the House of Delegates, won two of eleven electoral votes, and contested most congressional elections. Though they slipped back in 1809 and 1810, the Federalists extended their organizational efforts in 1811 to include a Washington Benevolent Society, and the Republicans in turn responded with more organization. In 1812 Federalists won the state legislature again but only because of Republican divisions—there were actually more Republican total votes. Further, though Madison won only six of the state's eleven electoral votes, two of the lost votes went to Republicans who ran as Republicans opposed to Madison and the war.[64]

Even in the midst of renewed competition, central Federalist organizational efforts remained secret, though Republicans were public. Moreover, the fluctuation of political competition from 1808 to 1812 and after showed its acute sensitivity to political events.[65] Even during the period 1811-1815, when political competition and electoral mobilization became most intense, about one-fifth of the counties remained noncompetitive. Twice as many went uncontested in the 1812 congressional elections. Some degree of office-specificity prevailed in voting, with majorities and turnout varying significantly in presidential, congressional, and state assembly elections.[66]

Thus, Maryland and Delaware showed remarkable levels of political activity during the early national period, unevenly distributed across their landscape. Party development, as in other areas, remained incomplete, and at different levels in different sectors of political activity.

THE SOUTH AND WEST

"While the mobile, many-sided, restless democracy of New England, New York, and Pennsylvania . . . [fought itself] the society of the Southern states was classically calm. Not a breath disturbed the quiet which brooded over the tobacco and cotton fields between the Potomac and Florida. A Presidential election was taking place [1804], but the South saw only one candidate. . . . From the St. Mary's to the Potomac and the Ohio, every electoral voice was given to Jefferson."[67] Henry Adams exaggerated, and yet the general picture of a South without two organized parties is one of considerable accuracy. Many other historians have failed to acknowledge the fact that party competition did not exist in the South: the fits and starts of the 1790s reached a high point of half development in 1800 and after that regressed or disappeared.[68] A more accurate description of early national politics than Adams's, however, would characterize the South as disturbed by "intense factional politics on the state and local level and a listless one-party system on the national level."[69]

Virginia was typical. Though in 1800 Virginia Federalists avoided association with northern Federalism by putting forth "The American Republican Ticket" and ignoring President Adams, they did mount an organized election campaign of sorts. Traditional political patterns still existed, and no sooner had the rudiments of party competition emerged than "Jefferson's victory sounded the knell for the two-party system in Virginia."[70] This occurred throughout the South, even after Federalists there awakened during 1808-1809 and 1812-1815. Southern Federalism felt the quickening energy of the Embargo and War of 1812, but it "seldom approached and almost never equalled the level of support . . . in 1800."[71]

There exists for the South Atlantic legislatures from 1800 to 1812 just the kind of study which is needed for other states, namely a systematic inquiry into roll call voting and party action by the legislatures. In general, party mattered little in the legislative proceedings of Virginia, North Carolina, South Carolina, and Georgia. Party voting appeared only on a few roll call votes on "issues directly affecting the parties themselves rather than the state as a whole."[72] In other ways party absented itself: from speakership elections; from influencing the makeup of important committees which the minority sometimes controlled; and from routine newspaper lists of assembly members. Republican majorities, in fact, not only did not regularly use caucuses but sometimes allowed an occasional Federalist to be speaker. "Party affiliation was indeed well marked; almost every member considered himself a Federalist or Republican when national issues were at stake. But this strong partisanship rarely filtered down to state questions. . . ."[73]

In North Carolina Federalism was perhaps stronger than anywhere else in the South, and thus some degree of party competition existed there. The Federalist proportion of the legislature (though the legislature seldom acted on party lines) never fell below 25 percent, and during the War of 1812 it climbed to 40 percent and was still 33 percent in 1816. In 1808 and 1812, opponents of the national administration, "chiefly Federalists," won one-third of the presidential vote and in 1808 and 1813 North Carolina sent three Federalists to Congress.[74]

Yet Republicanism was strong and confident enough, and party weak enough, for Republican legislatures to elect moderate Federalists to the governorship several times after 1799, and to elect a Federalist speaker of the house in 1816. Federalists were by no means excluded from other offices either (as they were in Virginia and to a lesser extent in South Carolina and Georgia), except for the office most tied to national politics, United States senator. And while Federalism was spread across the state, its greatest strength lay in the Upper Cape Fear or Fayetteville district, which Broussard called "probably the firmest [Federalist] party stronghold outside New England." Like Burlington County, New Jersey, Federalists dominated so much from 1800 to 1817 that frequently Republicans did not contest elections, and like Burlington County Cape Fear was the heartland of Federalism, supplying 67 percent of its legislative seats from 1800 through 1816.[75]

In the Western states of Kentucky, Tennessee, and Ohio, politics much resembled the southern pattern. Republicanism prevailed throughout the region and whenever a question arose pertaining to national politics, Federalists were hopelessly outnumbered. State politics obeyed their own scripts apart from national patterns. Available election returns show that multiple candidacies and lopsided results were common.

Kentucky and Tennessee lacked party politics in any form during the early national period—except for the one-party politics of Republicanism and its factionalism based on sectional and personal rivalries. In Tennessee for over forty years elections were contested by factions led by leaders of no acknowledged partisan loyalties. There was "never any vestige" of a Federalist party, and national politics played no role.[76] In Kentucky politics also displayed little partisanship because Federalism had no force. Political organization before 1820 was "exceptional."[77]

Ohio manifested the only glimmer of partisanship in the West. In 1802 Federalist and Republicans organized several counties, but thereafter the universal Western and Southern pattern prevailed: Republican dominance and Republican factionalism. In 1810 Republican Tammany societies appeared in Ohio, but these elicited criticism and opposition from Republicans as well as Federalists. The War of 1812 brought a Federalist "revival," including Washington Benevolent Societies. But the Federalist upsurge failed. "Restricted to a handful of counties, it was important more for alarming Republicans and enforcing their unity. . . ."[78] Thus, while Ohio politics showed more potential for competition than other Western states, at no time did a two-party system take hold.

THE SOCIAL BASES OF THE FEDERALISTS AND REPUBLICANS

Men did not become Federalists and Republicans simply because of differences in thought or because of their reactions to events or to issues decided on their merits alone. Different attitudes, beliefs, and ideologies sprang in significant measure from men's location in the social structure, their cultural heritage, and the kind of communities in which they lived. The presence or absence of various groups in communities, or, in short, the subcultural spectrum or mix, had a powerful impact on patterns of political alignment. While ethnic and religious groups usually voted heavily for one of the parties, variations from this general pattern could be induced by geographic or economic conditions or by peculiar demographic situations, not to mention the unpredictable impact of events and personalities. While no one doubts that social attributes powerfully influence men's holding to Federalist or Republican ideologies or their following certain leaders, it is at least as important to stress that the social group bases of politics were powerful and pervasive before Federalists or Republicans ever appeared and that parties did not structure or express all sociopolitical conflict in the early national period.

Before considering the social variables shaping political preferences, a warning is necessary. While patterns of social group division may be discerned, this does not justify terming the network of group relations, perceptions, and reference group behavior a party system. True, the political alignments of this period were to some extent distinctive compared to earlier and later patterns, and to some degree they continued historic cleavages in American politics; but the existence of these conditions does not prove that a party system had evolved. The many strands of social connection and group relations may be thought of as a system only by abstracting them from their historical context. These strands may appear similar to those patterns which exist within a framework of institutionalized political parties, but without such a framework mere political coalitions of diverse social groups cannot develop into a two-party system. In addition, while the Federalist and Republican coalitions were relatively stable in some places, in others they were short-lived or subject to large shifts and realignments.

Despite all that has been written in both local and general studies about Federalists and Republicans, generalizations about their social support must be tentative. It seems that too much is known and at the same time too little. Perhaps it is a matter of having much impressionistic information and not enough systematic analysis of Federalist and Republican social bases over time. A good deal is known—or thought to be known—about social group tendencies in the 1790s through 1800, but not much about the period from 1808 to 1816 or after, when most states experienced their peaks of Federalist-Republican competition.[79] David H. Fischer in his *The Revolution in American Conservatism* (1965) provided what is still one of the best overall discussions of this question, but its limits are quickly suggested by his own title: "Patterns of Partisan Allegiance, 1800,"[80] and this in a book which argued persuasively that the Federalists enjoyed a rebirth and that the most intense political competition came after 1808.

Fischer found at least five "patterns" including a contrast between growing and static regions, another based on prior political loyalties, and two others deriving from ethnicity and religion. But the "most pervasive pattern," and the one to which he gave most attention, was that "established elites in most states were Federalist: their challengers . . . Jeffersonian."[81] This emphasis has been a staple of early national political history. Countless historians have agreed that Federalists represented old wealth and prestigious occupations, and Federalists themselves have been quoted numberless times in illustration of their self-image as the wealthy, wise, virtuous, and respectable. This pattern seems to have held in New England. While Republican leaders there were neither poor nor merely average men, they were newly risen, or rising, or from less respectable backgrounds; even if descended from old families, they were often somehow mavericks or men marginal to the elite.[82]

Outside of New England, the pattern becomes far less predictable. In the Middle Atlantic and Border states, old, established families of wealth and status were frequently Republican as well as Federalist; in the South and West elites probably had a Republican tendency, certainly by 1800 or soon after. Within states or regions the power structure of various communities could differ widely, from highly centralized and stable oligarchies in which a few families stood at the top in most ways social and political to relatively open, plural polyarchies with differentiated elites. This was the case, at least, in Maryland, where, in addition, Republican leaders usually came from the upper levels of society.[83] Given the similarity of Federalist and Republican leaders' social standing outside New England, it follows that during the formative stages of the parties, as Richard Buel has observed, "the disposition of the regional leadership was often more critical than anything else in determining the political complexion of an area."[84]

The leadership's dispostion toward England and things English was a powerful shaper of political alignments, probably more influential overall than wealth and occupation. Robert Kelley has recently called attention to the operation of the cultural variable in early national politics by focusing on the ways that it tied together the questions of relations with England, how much government, and who would govern. He characterized the Federalists as a combination of the "moralistic republicans of New England" and the "nationalist republicans of the Middle states" who, with support from former Loyalists

> set out during Washington's years to build a strong and vigorous nation modeled on English lines. It was to be Anglicized in political style, Atlantic and eastward looking in its orientation, commercial and developmental in its economics, and friendly with England. Abroad, its enemy was to be England's enemy: France, and that nation's radicalism, irreligion, and egalitarianism. At home, Federalists wanted the American economy to be given general direction by financial institutions patterned after the Bank of England. As a political outlook that flourished primarily among the ethnically English, Federalism's heartland lay in New England and among the Anglicized Middle States aristocracy.[85]

Thus, to say that Federalists were elitist and pro-English is to say almost the same thing. They favored an American version of an English government and society. This helps us to understand part of what separated them from those Republican leaders who were otherwise of comparable upper class status. The English affinities of Federalist elites were evident in places as diverse as Portsmouth, New Hampshire, Boston, the Connecticut Valley, New York City, Philadelphia, eastern Pennsylvania, west Jersey, the Northern Neck and Tidewater of Virginia, Delaware's two lower counties, Maryland, and South Carolina.[86]

While New England was the heartland of the ethnically English—or of that cultural compound known as Yankee—neither an English nor a Yankee background ensured a uniform Federalist vote. While Yankee settlement in western New York and Ohio created areas of Federalist strength, within New England many Yankees defected to the Republicans.[87] Many forces contributed to New England's division, but the principal solvent of Federalist cultural-political hegemony was religion. At one pole stood the Congregational clergy of Massachusetts, Connecticut, and New Hampshire, nine out of ten or more staunchly Federalist and many of them energetic politicians in the late 1790s and early years of the century. They were followed by their parishioners who were supporters of the church-state relationship in those states and who lived in towns tending toward homogeneity in religious sentiment and in traditional respect for ministers.[88] At the other pole stood dissenting religious groups—particularly the Baptists, Methodists, and Universalists, as well as some Episcopalians who endured the cost and stigma of religious establishments in which they did not believe. In the middle were moderate Congregationalists and Unitarians, some of whom were Federalists and some of whom were Republicans. Only a minority of non-Congregational groups were Federalist, and the Congregationalists while mostly Federalist nevertheless divided between the parties. The orthodox and those most involved in religious life probably had a strong Federalist bent, but it is important to note that Congregationalists made up an important part of the Republican camp—without them the Republicans could have won no elections in New England.

Episcopalians both in and out of New England were usually Federalists, reflecing their generally high status, Anglican tastes, and elitism. Yet some tended to be Republican from the start, and Republicans gave them a prominence out of proportion to their numbers. In Connecticut Episcopalians began as Federalists, but the opposition to the Standing Order tried for years to lure them away, hoping to exploit their lack of rapport with the aggressively puritan Federalists and their clerical allies. Between 1811 and 1818 the Episcopalians do seem to have shifted away from the Federalists to the Toleration party, Unionists, and Republicans.[89]

Quakers probably were less divided and acquired a strong reputation for Federalism. In their traditional homeland of west Jersey and southeastern Pennsylvania, Quakers indeed constituted an important part of the Federalist interest. New Jersey's chief Federal stronghold was Quaker-dominated Burlington County, where influential Quaker manufacturers supported moral reform and directed the votes of deferential workers and dependents. In Ohio Quaker areas supported the Federalist "revival" of 1812-1816. In Massachusetts, however, some Quakers were Republican, which probably owed much to the historic persecutions of Quakers by the religious establishment—now identified with Federalism.[90]

Presbyterians in New England and Scots-Irish Presbyterians in New York probably had a strong Republican tendency, but the Scottish Presbyterians of the Upper Cape Fear region in North Carolina helped to make that district one of the distinctive Federalist areas of the South.[91] Similarly, while Methodists in New England may have usually voted Republican, rural Methodists in Delaware's two lower counties supported Federalism. But the Delaware Methodists were not only of English stock but also had been Anglican before the Revolution.[92] Thus, if religion could divide the "ethnically English" and Yankees in their politics, ethnicity too could operate as a powerful force, in some cases accounting for the deviation of certain religious or other groups from expected patterns.

Outside of New England there existed much less ethnic homogeneity and the largest non-English groups tended to be Republican, notably the Scots-Irish and the Germans. The Scots-Irish tended to be Republican apparently in the district of Maine (part of Massachusetts to 1820), in New York and especially in Pennsylvania, and in northern Delaware. In Virginia's Shenandoah Valley, however, they probably were Federalist.[93]

The Germans traditionally have joined the Scots-Irish in historians' accounts as the second major ethnic group most reliably Republican. It has long been accepted that the Pennsylvania Germans initially supported the Federalists in the mid-1790s, but in the late 1790s switched permanently to the Republicans because of revulsion for the Federalists' Alien Law and direct tax. While it seems reasonable that Germans did become Republicans, little systematic evidence has been presented, practically none about their activities after 1800, and no effort has been made to differentiate the Germans into subgroups, though they are occasionally referred to as German Lutherans.

The Federalists' English mentality and nativism probably repelled many Germans and other ethnic and religious groups. The numbers of incoming French and Irish Catholics were not great, nor was the number of Jews large, but these groups were probably strongly Republican. Under the circumstances the few Irish Protestants predictably became vocal Federalists.

The two most ethnically diverse states were of course New York and Pennsylvania, and it was no accident that they were so lopsidedly Republican that competitive party politics never developed to maturity. In Pennsylvania the Germans and Scots-Irish formed part of the Republican coalition while in New York, Germans, Scots-Irish Presbyterians, and the old Dutch tended to be Jeffersonians along with an even more heterogeneous array of ethnocultural groups in New York City.

The claim that demographic changes and voting were related should for now be treated with skepticism. As Fischer put it, Federalist regions "were mature, static, homogeneous, and ingrown. Jeffersonian areas . . . tended to be immature, fluid, and dynamic." He found too that the rate of population growth was the single variable correlating more closely with voting than any other. "Dynamism, expansion, and mobility appear, generally, to have distinguished Republican regions from those in which Federalism flourished." Most historians have found this idea attractive, and recently Robert Kelley linked this notion to his cultural interpretation, asserting that "Jeffersonian ideology was that of the most flourishing and rapidly growing culture groups in national life." Paul Goodman, on the other hand, associated cultural diversity and social development both with Republican voting and even more with the development of competitive party politics.[94]

There are several problems wih this thesis, the most obvious being the difficulty of knowing whether community-type as such was the important variable or whether this is just another way of measuring the presence or absence of various religious and ethnic groups. Were not many "dynamic" and Republican-voting communities in New England, for example, those with large numbers of dissenters? Were not many dynamic places in the Middle Atlantic and Border states also areas of ethnic diversity? Given the overlap between these patterns or variables it is difficult to know how much weight to assign independently to the growth-stasis thesis. Further, when tested at the township level in New Hampshire and Massachusetts, no strong correlation emerges between rate of population change and party vote.[95]

Finally, while the social bases of Federalism and Republicanism probably exhibited a good deal of stability in several states, it may be that further inquiry will reveal that change and fluidity registered high levels as well when compared to later party eras and particularly to the mature Democratic-Whig party system. Indeed, in viewing the actions of social groups and of party fortunes in the states between 1796 and 1824, evidence of shifts and changes characteristic of realignment periods pop up continuously. That is, the early national period seems to display many instances of sudden shifts of loyalty, defections, revamped coalitions, and party emergence and submergence. These symptoms were characteristic of such decades in the nineteenth century as the 1850s and 1890s when realignments took place. This makes sense when it is kept in mind that during the Federalist-Republican era parties were still being created.

CONCLUSION

A variety of political patterns existed throughout the regions, states, and commmunities of the new nation. Federalist-Republican competition—as well as some between political groups less sharply defined —produced some extraordinary levels of cadre activism and voter turnout at various times and places.[96] Massachusetts, Maryland, Delaware, New Jersey, and Vermont perhaps displayed the highest levels of competition and party development, but within any region or, indeed, within any state, party growth remained incomplete with respect to the three major elements of parties as institutionalized entities: parties in the electorate, as organizations, and in the legislature. Of course, parties always have remained incomplete in their geographic extension because of the noncompetitive character of many constituencies during any party era. But a special problem is posed by this condition during the creative phase because full levels of institutional growth were not yet achieved either. Thus, the burden of proof is on those who assert that something "national" and "systematic" did develop.

Compared to the later Whigs and Democrats, the Federalists and Republicans remained half-developed and not explicitly institutionalized. Federalists and Republicans mounted impressive efforts to get out the vote and made use of caucuses, meetings, "conventions," and whatnot to nominate candidates. But Federalist and Republican organizations did not take on a life of their own. Some of their methods startle in their resemblance to post-Jacksonian "usages," but Federal-Republican organizations did not emerge as explicit ends in themselves. That would come in the Jackson-Van Buren period.

Federalist and Republican parties came into being under the stimulus of events, usually national and sometimes local. When the pressure of issues retreated, Federalist and Republican organizations collapsed. The early national correlation between organizational effort and events and issues was almost perfect: no coefficient can be calculated to express it, but no historian can avoid it. By contrast, Democratic and Whig organizations sought routinely to avoid or absorb issues and men. Jackson was the "Old Hero," but after him, with a Van Buren or Polk, personality, reputation, deeds, charisma, all counted for less. Issues and events created Federalist-Republican competition and led it through a rollercoaster career. Whig and Democratic organizations sought success by transcending (some would say avoiding) issues; of course they could not be completely successful, but the contrast in intent is striking and revealing.

Under Democrats and Whigs, the convention system operated openly and according to a well-defined series of steps. In recent years historians have dissected the apparently open and representative structure of this convention system to point out that, although a great number of persons participated along the way, the major decisions still were made by oligarchies of professional politicians managing things behind the scenes. Yet if Democrats and Whigs excelled in public appearances while continuing a large measure of the elite control that existed previously, the Federalists and Republicans hardly had bothered with "cosmetics." The Federalists kept their organization as well hidden from public view for as long as they could (when they had it). Republicans in various places showed their hand earlier than the Federalists, but they too hid party committees from public view and in some places kept them hidden well into the 1800s.

The secrecy and ad hoc nature of much political organization in the first era and the regular, public operations of party in the next shows clearly the different place of party in each. So too did the contrasting directions in which the convention process flowed in each case. In the Democratic-Whig period, for example, gubernatorial candidates would be nominated after a succession of conventions beginning at the local level and moving on up through successively higher levels. In the Federal-Republican era gubernatorial candidates would be nominated at "respectable meetings of Federalists (or Republicans) from throughout the state" or at mixed caucuses (i.e., of the party's state legislators joined by other leaders); then county meetings or committees would be set in motion by a state committee (or a committee of the meeting or caucus); and finally town and local committees or meetings would make plans to mobilize the party's vote on election day. In the early national period, candidates would be chosen, addresses issued, and then the faithful would be mobilized from the top down. Of course such organization occurred far less frequently from 1796 to 1824, whatever its procedure, than it did after the mid-1830s. But the main point here is that the flow of action went in completely opposite directions in these two eras. Despite the fact that in both eras central party oligarchies exercised considerable control, the differences between them go to the heart of political culture.

The techniques of mobilization which sprouted in the early republic and which seem so "modern" differed substantially from later campaigns. Federalists and Republicans, though they spoke of "electioneering" and "exertions" and "influence," did not think of campaigns as sustained, all-absorbing ways of life, because they were not yet professional politicians. As often as we might pay tribute to the innovations and mass orientation of Federalist and Republican voter mobilization, it must also be added that their efforts, however intense, were usually of short and temporary duration, coming mostly just before elections.

Finally, Whigs and Democrats accepted party competition as legitimate, even natural, and good. Though there was some lingering antipartyism in the 1830s, mostly among Whigs, basic attitudes to party and organization had changed and the popular climate was completely different. At least political leaders had changed and their defending, justifying, and even celebrating the operation of party politics did most to create a favorable atmosphere. No doubt their positive orientation to parties went in advance of the rest of the population. Disappointed politicians, moralists in politics, and especially leaders of challenging movements or third parties, frequently expressed antiparty sentiments during the antebellum period and beyond, testifying to the continuation of substrata of hostility and ambivalence toward parties among the electorate. But Federalists and Republicans had simply never accepted the idea of competitive party politics. Both groups, as several recent writers have emphasized, saw victory in terms of conversion or elimination of opposition.[97] Ideally, parties or factions would collapse into a unitary state. Political organization was thus a means to an end, not an end in itself.

Federalists and Republicans each saw themselves as saviors of the republic and their enemies as its ruin. When the smoke cleared after the War of 1812 and when the fires of partisanship had damped down, political leaders in the 1820s looked back and began to believe that political competition had been a good thing in itself. Republicans, of course, had special reasons to celebrate the process since deliverance had been gained on their terms, or at least under their auspices. And so the means as well as the result came to be honored. In that way, despite themselves, Federalists and Republicans, first through their actions and secondly through the unintended consequences of their contest for power, helped prepare the way for party organizations which would have an institutional life of their own.

NOTES

1. Joseph Charles, *The Origins of the American Party System: Three Essays* (Williamsburg, Va., 1956). William Nisbet Chambers, *Political Parties in a New Nation: The American Experience, 1776-1809* (New York, 1963).

2. Examples of a national or top-down approach include: Chambers, *Political Parties in a New Nation*; Noble E. Cunningham, Jr., *The Jeffersonian Republicans: The Formation of Party Organization, 1789-1801* (Chapel Hill, 1957). For an emphasis on local origins, studies include: Paul Goodman, *The Democratic-Republicans of Massachusetts: Politics in a Young Republic* (Cambridge, Mass., 1964); Alfred F. Young, *The Democratic Republicans of New York: The Origins, 1763-1797* (Chapel Hill, 1967); and Richard G. Miller, *Philadelphia—The Federalist City: A Study of Urban Politics*, 1789-1801 (Port Washington, N.Y., 1976).

3. For elaboration of this argument, Ronald P. Formisano, "Deferential-Participant Politics: The Early Republic's Political Culture, 1789-1840," *American Political Science Review* 58 (June 1974): 473-87; also see Paul Goodman, "The First American Party System," in *The American Party Systems: Stages of Political Development*, ed. William Nisbet Chambers and Walter Dean Burnham (New York, 1967), p. 86.

4. For an analogous critique of modern voting studies, see Gerald M. Pomper, "From Confusion to Clarity: Issues and American Voters 1956-1968," *American Political Science Review* 68 (June 1972): 427.

5. Compare the levels of cohesiveness in congressional voting for New England representatives with those for Middle Atlantic and Southern representatives; see Rudolph M. Bell, *Party and Faction in American Politics: The House of Representatives, 1789-1801* (Westport, Conn., 1973), pp. 19, 24-30.

6. Linda K. Kerber, "The Federalist Party," in *History of U.S. Political Parties: 1789-1860 From Factions to Parties*, ed. Arthur M. Schlesinger, Jr. (New York, 1973), 1:10.

7. Standard works include: Manning J. Dauer, *The Adams Federalists* (Baltimore, 1953); Stephen G. Kurtz, *The Presidency of John Adams: The Collapse of Federalism, 1795-1800* (Philadelphia, 1957). See also Kerber, "The Federalist Party," pp. 14-15 and Richard H. Kohn, *Eagle and Sword: The Federalists and the Creation of the Military Establishment in America, 1783-1802* (New York, 1975), pp. 256-73. Federalists even contemplated trying to stop Southern and Western congressmen from sending circular letters to their constituents because they broadcast partisan opposition; Noble E. Cunningham, Jr., ed., *Circular Letters of Congressmen to Their Constituents 1789-1829: 1st Congress to 9th Congress 1789-1807* (Chapel Hill, 1978), 1:xxxvii-xl.

8. Kerber, "Federalist Party," p. 19.

9. At the same time it is possible to agree with Cunningham's observation that the election of 1800 was "more than any Presidential election that had preceded or would follow for at least a generation . . . a *party* contest." Noble E. Cunningham, Jr., "Election of 1800," in *History of American Presidential Elections, 1789-1968*, ed. Arthur Schlesinger, Jr., and Fred L. Israel, 3 vols. (New York, 1971), 1:100.

10. Cunningham, "1800," pp. 129-30.

11. Manning J. Dauer, "Election of 1804," in *American Presidential Elections*, ed. by Schlesinger and Israel, 1:160, 165; Henry Adams, *History of the United States of America During the Second Administration of Thomas Jefferson*, 9 vols. (New York, 1890), 2:148-49.

12. Irving Brant, "Election of 1808," in *American Presidential Elections*, ed. by Schlesinger and Israel, 1:190.

13. Brant, "Election of 1808," 1:214; Adams, *History of Jefferson's Second Administration*, 2:283-87.

14. Norman Risjord, "Election of 1812," in *American Presidential Elections*, ed. Schlesinger and Israel, 1:249, 252-53, 255-57, 259.

15. Risjord, "Election of 1812," 1:254-55. The fullest discussion of this subject is in David Hackett Fischer, *The Revolution in American Conservatism: The Federalist Party in the Era of Jeffersonian Democracy* (New York, 1965), pp. 83-90.

16. Lynn W. Turner, "Elections of 1816 and 1820," in *American Presidential Elections*, ed. by Schlesinger and Israel, 1:307-8. Cunningham, "Election of 1800," 1:105. On the lack of national organization throughout the period, see James S. Chase, *Emergence of the Presidential Nominating Convention, 1789-1832* (Urbana, Ill., 1973), pp. 12-18.

17. Turner, "Elections of 1816 and 1820," 1:301, 315. The number of states using legislatures, nine, remained constant from 1816 to 1820.

18. Compare James Sterling Young, *The Washington Community, 1800-1828* (New York, 1966) and Harry William Fritz, "The Collapse of Party: President, Congress, and the Decline of Party Action, 1807-1817" (Ph.D. dissertation, Washington University, 1971). In House speaker elections two-party contests appeared only in 1799 and 1813, and Republicans competed among themselves otherwise; Gerald R. Lientz, "House Speaker Elections and Congressional Parties, 1789-1860," *Capitol Studies* 6 (Spring 1978): 66-69. The zenith of the Republican party's congressional effectiveness came in its uniting in 1812 on the issues of preparedness and war, but even the party did not function as coherently on other issues; Harry W. Fritz, "The War Hawks of 1812," *Capitol Studies* 5 (Spring 1977): 40-41.

19. Carl E. Prince, *The Federalists and the Origins of the U.S. Civil Service* (New York, 1977).

20. J. H. Plumb, "The Growth of the Electorate in England From 1600 to 1715," *Past and Present* 45 (November 1969): 90-116.

21. These generalizations are based in part on my own work in progress, "The Transformation of Political Culture: Massachusetts Parties and Voters, 1790's-1840's"; in part on Paul Goodman, *Democratic-Republicans of Massachusetts*, and James M. Banner, Jr., *To the Hartford Convention: The Federalists and the Origins of Party Politics in Massachusetts, 1789-1815* (New York, 1970).

22. Walter H. Crockett, *Vermont: The Green Mountain State*, 5 vols. (New York, 1921), 3:67-73; Roger H. Brown, "A Vermont Republican Urges War: Royall Tyler, 1812, and the Safety of Republican Government," *Vermont History* 36 (Winter 1968): 13-18; Zadock Thompson, *History of Vermont, Natural, Civil and Statistical* (Burlington, Vt., 1833), p. 210.

23. Crockett, *Vermont*, 2:588-612; 3:3-126; Thompson, *History of Vermont*, pp. 201ff.

24. LaFayette Wilbur, *Early History of Vermont*, 4 vols. (Jericho, Vt., 1902), 3:163-65.

25. Thompson, *History of Vermont*, pp. 201-8, 214, 220, 223.

26. Edward Brynn, "Patterns of Dissent: Vermont's Opposition to the War of 1812," *Vermont History* 40 (Winter 1972): 21-24.

27. Edward Augustus Kendall, *Travels Through the Northern Parts of the United States in the Year 1807 and 1808*, 3 vols. (New York, 1809), 1:173.

28. Quotation from Brant, "Election of 1808," 1:189. Parties did not exist in the 1790s though some dissent with the Standing Order surfaced and presaged later Republican opposition. James R. Beasley, "Emerging Republicanism and the Standing Order: The Appropriation Act Controversy in Connecticut, 1793 to 1795," *William and Mary Quarterly* 29 (October 1972): 586-610.

29. This account of Connecticut politics relies heavily on Richard J. Purcell, *Connecticut in Transition: 1775-1818* (Middletown, Conn., 1963; original edition, 1918), pp. 119, 122-26, 134-35, 139-40.

30. Norman L. Stamps, "Party Government in Connecticut, 1800-1816," *Historian* 17 (Spring 1955): 174-75, 179; Purcell, *Connecticut in Transition*, pp. 125-26.

31. Alan William Brownsword, "Connecticut Political Patterns 1817-1828" (Ph.D. dissertation, University of Wisconsin, 1962), p. 74.

32. Regarding the caucus, Stamps, "Party Government," pp. 179-80. Jarvis Means Morse, *A Neglected Period of Connecticut's History, 1818-1850* (New Haven, 1933), p. 30, said that in 1818 Republican legislators numbered 120, Federalists 70, and Independents about 20.

33. In 1806 the Republican general committee exhorted town managers: "No church ever remained pure, if it feared to excommunicate bad members: No army could ever succeed, if it always kept out of sight of the enemy, for fear of losing men: No party can be respectable, if it fails to act on principle and system. . . . If any expect that each one shall lead himself, he believes in a more perfect democracy than we do. The most perfect democracy of which society is susceptible, is that in which each part performs its disinct functions *in connection with the whole*." Quoted in Stamps, "Party Government," pp. 188-89.

34. Purcell, *Connecticut in Transition*, p. 190; also pp. 191, 205; regarding justices, pp. 132-33.

35. Stamps, "Party Government," p. 175.

36. Purcell, *Connecticut in Transition*, pp. 153-76.

37. Ibid., pp. 177-86. In the legislature party coherence seems to have followed an even more erratic pattern, rising from 1801 through 1804, fading during 1805-1807, reviving in 1808, and breaking down again during the Republican decline (1809-1814). Republican representation in the assembly fell

to 36 in the fall of 1814, ibid., pp. 166-68, 185-86; Stamps, "Party Government," 181-86, 187-88.

38. Purcell, *Connecticut in Transition*, pp. 188, 212-16, 220-32, 259-60. Morse, *A Neglected Period*, pp. 36-65. For election returns I relied on Phillip J. Lampi, compiler, "American Election Returns, 1789-1824," American Antiquarian Society, forthcoming.

39. Brownsword, "Connecticut Political Patterns," pp. 88, 89.

40. In Rhode Island in 1811 ticket voting for governor, lieutenant governor, treasurer, and ten senators prevailed; but in 1812, while the Federalist vote in towns and counties for governor, congress, and president showed slight variance, the Republican vote varied greatly, party because of the unpopularity of Madison and his congressional supporters in New England. In 1816 the Republicans did not contest the congressional election, but the state election of 1817 was a very competitive contest in which Republicans won after a decade of Federalist success. Lampi, comp., "American Election Returns." Patrick T. Conley, *Democracy in Decline: Constitutional Development in Rhode Island, 1776-1841* (Providence, 1977), suggests the weakness of parties.

41. Sue Taishoff, "New Hampshire State Politics and the Concept of a Party System," *Historical New Hampshire*, 31 (Spring-Summer 1976): 38. For a different view of New Hampshire politics, see Donald B. Cole, *Jacksonian Democracy in New Hampshire, 1800-1851* (Cambridge, Mass., 1970), pp. 16-46; and especially Mark D. Kaplanoff, "From Colony to State: New Hampshire, 1800-1815" (unpublished manuscript, Cambridge University, England, 1974.) Ticket voting appears to have been strong in 1812 and fell off by 1816; see Lampi, comp., "American Election Returns." The weakness of the Republican party in the legislature is implied in William G. McLoughlin, "The Bench, The Church, and The Republican Party in New Hampshire, 1790 to 1820," *Historical New Hampshire* 20 (Summer 1965): 26-28.

42. For example, Patricia U. Bonomi, *A Factious People: Politics and Society in Colonial New York* (New York, 1971).

43. Arthur Irving Bernstein, "The Rise of the Democratic-Republican Party in New York City, 1789-1800" (Ph.D. dissertation, Columbia University, 1964), pp. 55, 255, 358, 393, 400-402, 406, 414, 421, 425-29.

44. Alvin Kass, *Politics in New York State, 1800-1830* (Syracuse, N.Y., 1965), pp. 9, 16-17, 19.

45. Lee Benson, Joel H. Silbey, and Phyllis F. Field, "Toward a Theory of Stability and Change in American Voting Patterns: New York State, 1792-1970," in *The History of American Electoral Behavior*, ed. Joel H. Silbey, Allan G. Bogue, and William H. Flanigan (Princeton, 1978), p. 85. Interyear correlations in this period were high: "In three gubernatorial, one lieutenant gubernatorial, and four state senate races, the mean Democratic correlation was .80, the median .83." Yet even this period was not completely stable.

46. For a more detailed analysis of the literature on Pennsylvania's parties, Formisano, "Deferential-Participant Politics," *American Political Science Review* 58: 476-77; Also, Sue Taishoff, "Parties, Political Culture, and Latent Values: The Fries Rebellion and Partisan Behavior in Southeastern Pennsylvania, 1790-1808" (unpublished seminar paper, University of Virginia, 1973). No

regular two-party conflict existed in a small town in northeast Pennsylvania from 1812 to 1820. Joseph John Hogan, Jr., "The Social Economy of a Country Town, Montrose, Pennsylvania, 1800-1812" (Ph.D. dissertation, State University of New York, Binghamton, 1975), pp. 23-49. Lampi, comp., "American Election Returns."

47. Risjord found Federalist organization in Pennsylvania "quite weak"; "Election of 1812," 1:266-67.

48. Risjord said that "New Jersey possessed what may have been the most sophisticated electoral machinery in the nation"; "Election of 1812," 1:251.

49. Rudolph V. Pasler and Margaret C. Pasler, "Federalist Tenacity in Burlington County, 1810-1824," *New Jersey History* 77 (Winter 1969): 197-210; Walter R. Fee, *The Transition From Aristocracy to Democracy in New Jersey, 1789-1829* (Somerville, N.J., 1933), p. 188. In 1810 and 1811 Republicans ran no ticket in Burlington County.

50. Fee, *Transition From Aristocracy to Democracy*, pp. 88-89, and passim. Fischer, *Revolution in American Conservatism*, observed that Federalists only occasionally used committees from 1801 to 1808 (p. 62n) and presented descriptions of Federalist organizations in 1808 and 1812 (pp. 67, 118). His partial election data showed "No clear party cleavage" for 1803, 1806, 1820, 1824, and 1826, and competition and high turnout for 1808 and 1814 (p. 188). The 1814 votes for State Council and Assembly showed a high congruence with congressional returns; Lampi, comp., "American Election Returns."

51. Fee, *Transition*, pp. 130-31, 182-83, 195-97, 214-15, 227-32, 235-36.

52. Carl E. Prince, *New Jersey's Jeffersonian Republicans: The Genesis of an Early Political Machine, 1789-1817* (Chapel Hill, 1967), pp. 223, 245; Fee, *Transition*, pp. 139, 143; after 1815 patronage criteria loosened even more, ibid., pp. 212, 224.

53. David P. Peltier, "Party Development and Voter Participation in Delaware, 1792-1811," *Delaware History* 14 (October 1970): 95-96.

54. Peltier, "Party Development in Delaware," 78, 82-84, 85-86; John A. Munroe, *Federalist Delaware, 1775-1815* (New Brunswick, N.J., 1954), pp. 200-59.

55. Peltier, "Nineteenth Century Voting Patterns in Delaware," *Delaware History* 13 (April 1969): 220-221; Peltier, "Party Development in Delaware," 171; Lampi, comp., "American Election Returns,".

56. The quotation on constitutions is from Ronald Hoffman, *A Spirit of Dissension: Economics, Politics, and the Revolution in Maryland* (Baltimore, 1973), p. 271; Philip A. Crowl, *Maryland During and After the Revolution: A Political and Economic Study* (Baltimore, 1943), pp. 11-15; David Curtis Skaggs, *Roots of Maryland Democracy: 1753-1776* (Westport, Conn., 1973), pp. 18-23, 41-42, 45-53; Aubrey C. Land, *The Dulanys of Maryland: A Biographical Study of Daniel Dulany, The Elder (1685-1753) and Daniel Dulany, The Younger (1772-1797)* (Baltimore, 1955), pp. 320-31; L. Marx Renzulli, Jr., *Maryland: The Federalist Years* (Rutherford, N.J., 1973), pp. 22-23, 29-33.

57. Whitman H. Ridgway, *Community Leadership in Maryland, 1790-1840: A Comparative Analysis of Power in Society* (Chapel Hill, 1979).

58. David A. Bohmer, "The Maryland Electorate and the Concept of a Party

System in the Early National Period," in *The History of American Electoral Behavior* ed. Joel Silbey, Allan G. Bogue, and William H. Flanigan (Princeton, 1978), pp. 151, 156.

59. William Bruce Wheeler, "Urban Politics in Nature's Republic: The Development of Political Parties in the Seaport Cities in the Federalist Era" (Ph.D. dissertation, University of Virginia, 1967), pp. 199, 201, 208.

60. Idem., "The Baltimore Jeffersonians, 1788-1800: A Profile of Inter-Factional Conflict," *Maryland Historical Magazine* 66 (Summer 1971): 160-64.

61. Table 2.6 is adapted from Bohmer, "Maryland Electorate," p. 153. The original showed convincingly that turnout in contested counties ran higher than turnout in uncontested. In 1818 in six of eight congressional districts there were no party contests.

62. Bohmer presented both aggregate and individual voting data for two counties (1796-1802) in support of this point; "Maryland Electorate," pp. 154-69.

63. Renzulli, *Maryland*, pp. 217, 232-33.

64. Victor Sapio, "Maryland's Federalist Revival, 1808-1812," *Maryland Historical Magazine* 64 (Spring 1969): 8, 17; Renzulli, *Maryland*, pp. 249, 252-53; in 1809 when Congress repealed the Embargo the entire Maryland delegation voted for repeal including Republican Senator Samuel Smith, a former backer of the measure; John S. Pancake, "Baltimore and the Embargo 1807-1809," *Maryland Historical Magazine* 47 (September 1952): 183-84.

65. Renzulli, *Maryland*, pp. 311ff.; Sapio, "Maryland's Federalist Revival." Fischer presented tables depicting Federalist organization in 1811 and 1815 and said that Maryland Federalists had conventions in embryonic form as early as 1811: "They were secret but conventions nonetheless—meetings of delegates from the counties chosen not by the people but by local elites for the purpose of making nominations and deciding party policy"; *Revolution in American Conservatism*, p. 75, also p. 82.

66. Lampi, comp., "American Election Returns," is incomplete but nevertheless suggestive: see returns for 1811 state senate, and 1812, 1813, and 1815 assembly, and 1812 president and Congress.

67. Adams, *History of the United States*, 2:200-01.

68. Lisle A. Rose, *Prologue to Democracy: The Federalists in the South 1789-1800* (Lexington, Ky., 1968); Risjord, "Election of 1812," 1:252. Electioneering, conversely, was more open in South than in New England and other regions; Noble E. Cunningham, Jr., ed., *Circular Letters of Congressmen*.

69. Burton W. Folsom, II, "Party Formation and Development in Jacksonian America: The Old South," *Journal of American Studies* 7 (December 1973): 217.

70. Richard R. Beeman, *The Old Dominion and the New Nation, 1788-1801* (Lexington, Ken., 1972), pp. 224, 237-38. In the Virginia Tidewater, "isolated pockets" of Federalism existed after 1800 "due largely to the continuing influence of prestigious families"; Norman K. Risjord, "The Virginian Federalists," *Journal of Southern History* 38 (November 1967): 507.

71. James H. Broussard, "Regional Pride and Republican Politics: The Fatal Weakness of Southern Federalism, 1800-1815," *South Atlantic Quarterly* 73 (Winter 1974): 23.

72. Idem, "Party and Partisanship in American Legislatures: The South Atlantic States," *Journal of Southern History* 43 (February 1977): 48.

73. Ibid., p. 52.

74. Idem, "The North Carolina Federalists, 1800-1816," *North Carolina Historical Review* 55 (January 1978): 19.

75. Ibid., pp. 19, 20, 21, 22-23, 25.

76. Richard P. McCormick, *The Second American Party System: Party Formation in the Jacksonian Era* (Chapel Hill, 1966), pp. 222-24. Thomas Perkins Abernathy, *From Frontier to Plantation in Tennessee: A Study in Frontier Democracy* (Chapel Hill, 1932), pp. 164-81, 221ff. Abernathy characterized the period 1796-1819, compared to those before and after, as one of political quiet in Tennessee, because the old elite created by the Revolution simply jockeyed for office and frequently faced no opposition, pp. 351-52.

77. McCormick, *Second Party System*, p. 212. The Madisonian Republicans did some organizing in 1812 and easily swamped a Clintonian boomlet. Though not concerned primarily with politics, Niels Henry Sonne throws considerable light on Kentucky's political culture in his book, *Liberal Kentucky, 1780-1828* (New York, 1939).

78. Donald J. Ratcliffe, "The Experience of Revolution and the Beginnings of Party Politics in Ohio, 1776-1816," *Ohio History* 85 (Summer 1976): 208-17; McCormick, *Second Party System*, pp. 258-61; Homer C. Hockett, *Western Influences on Political Parties to 1825: An Essay in Historical Interpretation* (Columbus, Ohio, 1917), pp. 55-80; Lampi, comp., "American Election Returns," elections of 1807, 1808, 1812. From 1802 to 1812 Ohio Federalists could affect the outcome of intra-Republican struggles for power, Stephen Carey Fox, "The Group Bases of Ohio Political Behavior, 1803-1848" (Ph.D. dissertation, University of Cinncinnati, 1973), pp. 103-11. In 1819 "rudimentary political machines" surfaced as part of an anti-Bank of the U.S. movement; ibid., p. 127.

79. Taking Massachusetts as an example, Goodman's *Democratic-Republicans* and Banner's *To the Hartford Convention* are superior to most studies in this respect, yet both end about 1815, while Federalists and Republicans still battled on in the 1820s, with the Republicans displacing the Federalists as the state's majority party in 1823 and 1824 even after the Republican district of Maine separated from Massachusetts to become a state itself in 1820.

80. Fischer, *Revolution in American Conservatism*, pp. 201-26.

81. Ibid., pp. 203-11.

82. Goodman, *Democratic-Republicans;* Kaplanoff, "From Colony to State"; and Purcell, *Connecticut in Transition*. Very suggestive on this point is Dorothy Ann Lipson, *Freemasonry in Federalist Connecticut, 1789-1835* (Princeton, 1977).

83. Ridgway, *Leadership in Maryland*. Paul Goodman, "Social Status of Party Leadership: The House of Representatives, 1797-1804," *William and Mary Quarterly* 25 (July 1968): 465-74, found that New England and Middle State Federalist representatives came from more socially prominent backgrounds than Republican congressmen, while southern Republican representatives resembled northern Federalists in their elite status.

84. Richard Buel, Jr., *Securing the Revolution: Ideology in American Politics, 1789-1815* (Ithaca, N.Y., 1972), p. 75.

85. Robert Kelley, *The Cultural Pattern in American Politics: The First Century* (New York, 1979), pp. 115-16.

86. Ibid., pp. 125-26; Goodman, "First Party System," p. 79; Fischer, *Revolution in American Conservatism*, pp. 207, 214, 221; Buel, *Securing the Revolution*, pp. 72-90.

87. Dixon Ryan Fox, *Yankees and Yorkers* (New York, 1940); Ratcliffe, "Beginnings of Party Politics in Ohio," p. 213; Stephen Fox, "Ohio Political Behavior," p. 105.

88. Goodman, *Democratic-Republicans*; Banner, *To the Hartford Convention*; Purcell, *Connecticut in Transition*; Cole, *Jacksonian Democracy in New Hampshire*; Kaplanoff found a closer association between religion and voting than between economic development and voting; "From Colony to State," pp. 139-50.

89. Kelley, *The Cultural Pattern*, p. 125; Purcell, *Connecticut in Transition*, passim.

90. Pasler and Pasler, "Federalist Tenacity in Burlington County," pp. 197-200; Ratcliffe, "Beginnings of Party Politics in Ohio," p. 213; the statement about Massachusetts is based on my examination of electoral data and local histories.

91. Kelley, *The Cultural Pattern*, pp. 120, 127; Broussard, "North Carolina Federalists," p. 20.

92. Goodman, "First Party System," p. 79. Jefferson described Delaware as virtually "a county of England" in its politics; quoted in ibid., p. 79.

93. Kelley, *The Cultural Pattern*, p. 125, said they were Republican in Virginia, but Goodman seems more in line with other descriptions of Federalist strength in Virginia, "First Party System," pp. 82-83.

94. Fischer, *Revolution in American Conservatism*, pp. 213, 215; Kelley, *The Cultural Pattern*, p. 126; Goodman, "First Party System," pp. 65, 84-85.

95. Kaplanoff, "From Colony to State," pp. 88-89, 369-70. I have calculated correlations for all counties in Massachusetts using township level data 1800-1810: in eastern Massachusetts there tended to be a slightly positive relation between Federalist vote and population change (the reverse of what the usual thesis holds), and in Worcester and the western counties a slightly negative relationship.

96. For example, the Connecticut "Toleration ticket" vs. the Federalists who always refrained from admitting they were a party; various "Peace" tickets and coalitions of 1812-1815; Madisonians vs. Clintonians, and others.

97. Buel, *Securing the Revolution*; Michael Wallace, "Changing Concepts of Party in the United States: New York, 1815-1828," *American Historical Review* 74 (December 1968): 453-91; Richard Hofstadter, *The Idea of a Party System: The Rise of Legitimate Opposition in the United States, 1780-1840* (Berkeley, 1969); Daniel Sisson, *The American Revolution of 1800* (New York, 1974); Young, *The Washington Community*.

*William G. Shade**

POLITICAL PLURALISM AND PARTY DEVELOPMENT: THE CREATION OF A MODERN PARTY SYSTEM: 1815-1852

3

The most striking characteristic of the United States in the four decades after the War of 1812 was the dizzying pace of social and economic change. It was during these years, according to Frederick Jackson Turner, "that the new republic gave clear evidence that it was throwing off the last remnants of colonial dependence."[1] A rapidly expanding society on the move, the United States was neither "traditional" nor "modern," but enmeshed in the process of creating an individualistic and politically democratic society for white men. Beginning in the 1820s economic growth and geographic mobility reached unprecedented levels. Increasing religious fragmentation and ethnic heterogeneity forced a widespread acceptance of cultural pluralism and a debate over its meaning for American society. These decades also witnessed a radical transformation of the nation's political system. By the 1840s the creation of two relatively modern parties signaled the advent of the "second American party system."[2]

Political parties are far less common and more variable organizations than most historians have assumed. Recent historical studies have traced the different meanings given to the term "party" since the seventeenth century and examinations of the politics of "emerging nations" have heightened our awareness of the unique nature of competitive two-party systems and the variety of political structures that are called "parties." These works have induced a proper skepticism about the nature of past "parties" and have led historians to question how well developed parties were at the specific times in the past when

*I would like to thank Ellen Weiss, Ronald P. Formisano, and Sue Taishoff for their help with various aspects of this essay.

they supposedly carried out the textbook functions assigned to modern parties.[3] The main purpose of this essay is to date more precisely the phases in the development of the second party system and to compare and contrast the characteristics of these phases.

The period discussed here was a transitional one in which the expansion of political democracy altered the electoral environment in numerous ways that affected the emergence of modern parties. The most important change involved extending the suffrage.[4] Throughout the first half of the nineteenth century property qualifications were gradually lowered and then replaced with taxpayer qualifications and residency requirements or abolished entirely. The confusing array of suffrage requirements for different offices gave way to a more egalitarian standard. As a result, the electorate came to include almost all adult white males. Economic and religious qualifications for officeholding were removed, and an increasing number of state and local offices became elective. By making electoral units smaller and polling places more accessible, voting was made easier. Provisions governing the electoral process became more uniform throughout the country as viva voce voting gave way to the secret ballot and later, in the mid-1830s, to printed ballots.

The recent insistence by historians that Andrew Jackson personally had little to do with the advance of political democracy is well documented, but their assumption that this process was completed before Jackson's elevation to the presidency is erroneous.[5] In 1828 fourteen states still had some sort of property or taxpayer qualification for voting.

The decade of the 1830s brought most of these democratic changes to the antebellum South. But not until the 1840s did Connecticut, New Jersey, and Louisiana drop their taxpayer qualification. Following the Dorr War in 1842 Rhode Island revised its ancient constitution, elimnated a property requirement, and allowed native-born citizens who paid one dollar in taxes to vote. Virginia finally abolished the state's property requirement in 1851, but South Carolina continued to hold out until Reconstruction.

Furthermore, expansion of the suffrage was not always accompanied by other democratic reforms. New Jersey had long had nearly universal white manhood suffrage, but the state did not make the office of governor elective until 1844. Illinois which also had broad suffrage had an elected governor from the time it entered the Union in 1818 but retained viva voce voting until 1848. Pennsylvania made judges elective in 1838, but refused to remove the taxpaying requirement for voting. Although Kentucky had early adopted most democratic reforms, its county governments remained as oligarchic as those of

Virginia. "Free Suffrage" continued to be an issue in North Carolina until 1857, because that state retained a property qualification to vote in elections for the state senate. Finally, throughout the South, progress toward representation based upon population and the acceptance of political individualism was hindered by the existence of slavery.[6] During these years, some combination of "people and property" survived as the basis of representation in most states.

Changes in the political environment, however, indicated a reorientation of American political culture that reflected the increasingly pluralistic nature of the society. During these years, the traditional view of political parties as illegitimate expressions of corrupt self-interest declined as the conception of a politics of conflict implicit in political individualism gained wider popularity.[7] An increasing number of Americans accepted the view that in a pluralistic society parties were necessary instruments of interest aggregation and conflict resolution. As with the movement toward political democracy, this change proceeded slowly at different rates in different areas. While the majority of New York politicians seem to have accepted a favorable conception of parties and partisanship by the end of the 1820s, this view spread only slowly to the other states. Antipartyism remained and was expressed sporadically by diverse groups. In general, Whigs never fully embraced party politics and Zachary Taylor ran a "no party" campaign in 1848.[8]

As the constitutional environment changed and a majority of Americans came to acknowledge the legitimacy of political parties, the basic outlines of modern party machinery appeared. Traditionally, nomination procedures for federal as well as state offices were quite informal and candidates' names were placed before the voters in a number of different ways. To the degree that there can be said to have been party control, it was exercised in a semi-secret fashion through some form of legislative caucus or state convention and was short-lived, appearing only at election times. The convention system which replaced these traditional procedures was, as Richard McCormick has noted, "the most conspicuous feature of the highly elaborated organization developed by parties in this era."[9] Although the stated purpose of conventions was nomination, they also provided rudimentary campaign organizations for the parties. The overthrow of "King Caucus" in the 1820s, however, represented the beginning rather than the culmination of a process that was not yet completed at the time of the dissolution of the second party system.

The nomination of presidential candidates by national conventions was accepted only haltingly during the 1830s. In preparation for the election of 1832, three conventions were called to select presidential and vice-presidential tickets. Previously, a variety of modes of nomination had been used for these offices. The best known was the congressional caucus, but in the 1820s the opponents of caucus domination exaggerated its role. In 1824 a rump caucus of sixty-six Republican congressmen nominated William Crawford, who ran a poor fourth in the popular balloting to candidates put forward by resolutions of state legislatures. A national convention was first used to nominate candidates in 1831 when the Anti-Masons chose William Wirt and Amos Ellmaker. Later that year a "National Republican Convention" supported Henry Clay and Pennsylvanian John Sargent. Finally, early in 1832 a convention of "Republican" delegates, meeting in Baltimore "for the Purpose of Nominating a Candidate for the Office of Vice President," endorsed Jackson's choice of Martin Van Buren as his running mate. Although the Democrats returned to Baltimore three years later to tap Van Buren and Richard M. Johnson for the election of 1836, these initial conventions did not signal the advent of well-developed modern parties. "Despite the conventions and the committees," as Roy Nichols argued, "it was still *caudillo* politics."[10]

This is clearly reflected in a closer look at the elections of 1832 and 1836. Faced with a multiplicity of party labels, historians have too often forced a complex and unstructured situation into the familiar two-party mold. Yet, the nature of party labels offers a crucial clue to the level of party development. Most of the labels used by historians to describe the parties of the late 1820s and early 1830s can be found in the sources, but the personal nature of these affiliations stands out—the "Jackson party," the "Adams party," the "Calhoun party," and the "Friends of Clay" are typical. Others termed themselves members of the "Administration party" or the "Opposition." Nearly everyone claimed to be a "Republican;" and when the term "National Republican" gained vogue in several northern states in 1832, the usage proved to be short-lived and had little specific reference to an institutionalized party. Indeed, it was the diversity rather than the uniformity of party labels that characterized the election of 1832.[11]

Historical analyses of the 1832 election have oversimplified this rather complex situation. Despite the fact that in eight states three separate tickets were in the field, historians have treated 1832 as a two-party contest.[12] They have ignored the "Democratic Anti-Masons' " label and counted the party's votes for Henry Clay. It is difficult to judge Anti-Masonic strength precisely, but it was clearly an important element in the election. In the states of New York and Ohio political deals swung Anti-Masonic voters to Clay. In Pennsylvania, Wirt received 67,000 votes as the only alternative to Jackson. Elsewhere, the

Anti-Masons won in Vermont, and did well in three-party contests in Massachusetts, Rhode Island, and Connecticut. The variety of Jackson tickets casts doubt upon the capacity of the party managers who had met in the Baltimore convention to control the election. A Jackson-Barbour ticket appeared in seven Southern states, and in Pennsylvania Jackson's running mate was native son William Wilkins. Even ignoring South Carolina's vote for John Floyd and Henry Lee, the election hardly fits the pattern of a well organized two-party contest.

The waters of presidential politics remained clouded four years later. Again the election was not a two-party contest; five presidential candidates and eight tickets received electoral votes. Although the "Democratic Republicans" did hold a convention and presented a semblance of party organization, Van Buren's Virginia electors refused to support Johnson and cast their twenty-three votes for William Smith of South Carolina. For the only time in American history, the Senate was forced to select the vice-president. The multiplicity of candidates grew because of the disorganization of Van Buren's opponents who struggled to make a virtue of disunity by emphasizing traditional antiparty arguments. Contemporary Democrats countered with the charge that the use of regional candidates was designed to appeal to sectional interests and throw the election into the House. However, little evidence exists that any group was sufficiently in control of Whig strategy to execute such a Machiavellian design.[13] Nominations of the so-called Whig candidates emerged in a traditional fashion from the states, and the label "Whig" was not universally used to designate the various opposition tickets.

The Whig convention of 1839, which nominated William Henry Harrison and John Tyler, ushered in a new period in the organization of presidential politics.[14] After that date, presidential and vice-presidential nominations were increasingly contested within party conventions and generally uniform national support was given to the chosen candidates. Conventions also adopted the practice of drawing up platforms formally expressing the party's basic principles. Just as they had taken the lead in developing campaign organization, the Democrats, or "the American Democracy" as they officially termed themselves, presented the first modern platform in 1840. At the time, Calhoun and his followers wanted to bind their northern allies to their own conception of a government of limited powers. Subsequently, similar documents were issued in 1844, 1848, and 1852. The Whig conventions of 1839 and 1848 avoided formal platforms, but those of 1844 and 1852 issued documents similar in structure and intent to those of the Democrats.

While the decade of the 1840s witnessed the emergence of modern party structures, even then their development remained incomplete. Organizations analogous to national committees appeared in 1844; but only the Democrats officially elected a national party chairman and his duties were limited to the campaign of that year. Four years later the Democrats chose a national committee that was to carry over until the next election, but the Whigs failed to follow their example. Although all the aspects of modern party machinery were not yet in place, institutional structures quite unlike anything that preceded them had emerged to organize political conflict in America.

American political culture and political structure obviously changed greatly during these years. Political individualism advanced; partisan conflict attained a new degree of legitimacy; and the outlines of modern party structures emerged. These changes, however, took place more slowly and were less elaborate than most recent historians have believed. Democratic reform was limited; southern radicals and northern evangelicals retained a traditional hostility to party politics; and party organization remained in an incomplete state of development. By turning to electoral behavior one can date more precisely two phases in the evolution of the "second party system" and the emergence of modern parties in America.

Looking at the nation as a whole the presidential elections from 1824 to 1852 fall into two groups, each of which represents a distinctly different phase of party development.[15] The correlation of the vote for Jackson in the first three of these elections—Phase I (1824-1832) was relatively high, but it bore little relation to the 1836 vote for Van Buren. That election began a new and relatively stable era—Phase II (1840-1852) in which the distributions of Democratic strength from one election to the next were highly intercorrelated.

The election of 1836 was a transitional one that reflected some of the characteristics of both phases. Turnout in the last two presidential elections of the first phase and in 1836 was moderately high, but it lagged below that for state elections.[16] The second phase initiated a fifty-year period of high and consistant popular interest in American presidential elections. Along with the jump in turnout, there was a shift in the sectional patterns of party support. The elections of the first phase were distinctly sectional; the candidates obviously appealed to different parts of the country. New England went radically one way in each of these elections while the slave South leaned in the opposite direction. Richard McCormick has argued that the second party system evolved with each successive presidential election, spreading from the Middle States where it appeared in 1828 to New England in 1832 and penetrating the South finally in 1836.

Figure 3.1 Correlations Between Adjacent Presidential Elections

The United States: Jackson-Democratic Vote

Table 3.1 Sectionalism and Presidential Elections: Jackson-Democratic Vote (in percentages)

	1824	1828	1832	1836	1840	1844	1848	1852
United States	43	56	55	51	47	50	42	51
New England	0	32	40	51	45	46	37	44
Middle Atlantic	69	56	54	53	49	50	36	51
Old Northwest	39	54	56	48	46	50	47	51
Border	37	55	50	46	45	49	47	52
South Atlantic	46	77	83	53	46	51	48	57
Southwest	83	88	63	49	48	54	50	57
CRV*	57	30	23	5	3	5	13	8

*Coefficient of Relative Variation is based on the mean and standard deviation of the six sections.

But historians have generally overemphasized the political importance of "Sections" in the 1820s and 1830s. States were the most important entities and most evidence of sectionalism—with the exception of that relating to slavery—represented only short-term shared interests of sets of continguous states. In the first phase most states gave their vote heavily to one candidate and there was little intrastate competition. Where compeition did exist, it did *not* reflect the development of two national parties. In 1832 the voters of four states split their votes among three candidates. Only six states in that election had viable two-ticket contests; but the same tickets did not battle in each of these states! Four years later the number of two-ticket contests doubled, but the confusion of tickets increased.

A new phase characterized by high turnout and two-party competition in all of the states (except South Carolina) appeared in 1840. With this the nature of the presidential contest changed from one rooted in cohesive state interests to one structured by national parties that penetrated into the states. This change came in two distinct steps. Competition appeared in most states between 1834 and 1836; participation increased between 1836 and 1840. While the latter was undoubtedly influenced by the Panic of 1837, shifts in the partisan allegiances of social classes had little to do with these changes.[17]

Between 1824 and 1832 the vote for Jackson fluctuated widely from state to state—in fact, he received no votes in New Hampshire in 1824 and 100 percent of Mississippi's vote in 1832. There was still a wide range in the Democratic vote in 1836; after 1840 the difference between the states giving the highest and lowest Democratic vote seldom exceeded 10 percent, and generally it was within a 5 percent range. Similarly, the Adams vote in 1828 correlated only moderately with both the Adams vote of 1824 and the Clay vote of 1832, and the latter was not correlated with the vote for any of the candidates in 1836. In contrast, relatively high correlations existed between elections for both parties from 1840 to 1852.

Closer examination at the state level clarifies the vast differences between the two phases. While a variety of patterns existed in both phases, what stands out is the diversity of these patterns in the first phase and their similarity in the second phase. It was only after the late 1830s that American parties exhibited the characteristics that historians invariably have associated with them. The seeming stability in Figure 3.1 was not reflected in the voting at the state level. Nor did contiguous states have similar patterns. The contrasting levels of party development in each phase can be seen in the autocorrelations within each state. To illustrate this, the following discussion will focus on six states that reflect three different patterns. The pairing of these states indicates that the patterns were not sectional.

Pennsylvania and Mississippi had similar patterns in presidential elections from 1824 to 1852. If one looks only at the percentage of the vote given to Jackson, these two states seem to move in opposite directions. In each successive election his proportion of the vote increased in Mississippi and declined in Pennsylvania. However, the correlation of the county returns in each of these elections shows that in both states the close relationship between the 1824 and 1828 votes was significantly eroded by 1832. In Pennsylvania the correlation between 1832, when Jackson was challenged by the Anti-Masonic candidate Wirt, and 1828 fell to .74. In Mississippi, where the regular Jackson-Van Buren ticket faced a Jackson-Barbour ticket, it was even lower, a mere .20. Four years later a relatively new pattern appeared and both of these states established consistent partisan distributions in presidential elections that remained stable through 1852.

Figure 3.2 Correlations between Adjacent Presidential Elections, Mississippi and Pennsylvania: Jackson-Democratic Vote

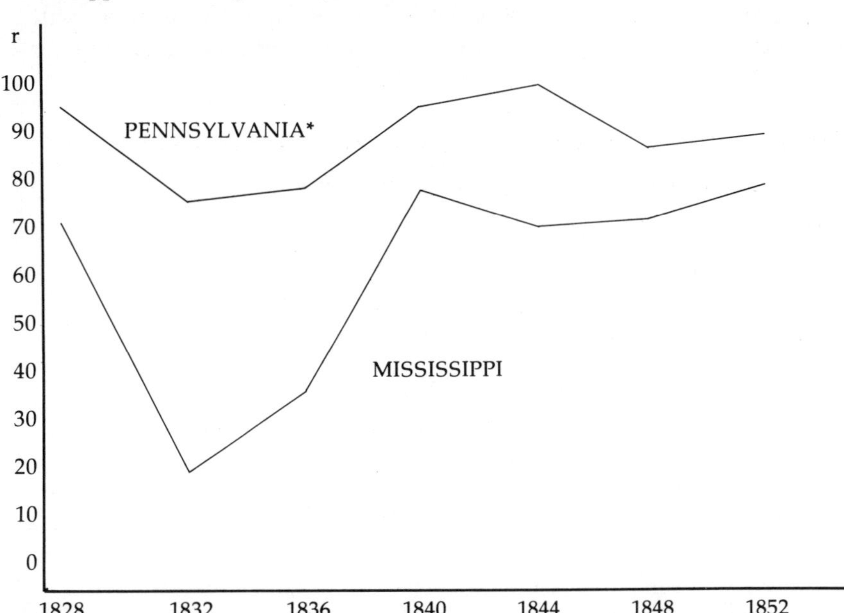

*The 1828 Jackson vote is correlated with the vote for Crawford and Jackson in 1824.

New Jersey and New Hampshire followed a different course in the first phase before settling into a similarly stable pattern in the second phase. The Jackson-Democratic proportion of the vote in the former state was close to 50 percent throughout the entire period from 1824 to 1852. The early appearance and clear evolution of party labels beginning in the 1820s make the state unique in its early stability. Yet, the pattern of electoral response showed some fluctuation in the 1830s. Jackson's vote in 1828 was only moderately correlated with the previous election, but it was closely related to that of 1832. Although turnout remained high, the patterns of the vote changed and the correlations between each election from 1832 to 1840 declined before electoral stability and even higher turnout appeared in the next decade. New Hampshire shifted from one of the states in which neither Jackson nor Crawford received a significant vote in 1824 to the most Democratic state in the nation in 1836. It then settled down as a consistently Democratic state giving approximately 55 percent of its vote to the party throughout the 1840s. Turnout also fluctuated a great deal more than it did in New Jersey. In 1836 only 37 percent of the white adult males voted, but an unprecedented 83 percent went to the polls four years later. The election of 1832 was highly correlated with 1828; then, as in New Jersey, the two succeeding elections registered declining correlations with their predecessors until the election of 1840 reversed that erosion and introduced a higher level of stability.

Virginia and Illinois exhibit a third pattern. In the former, which retained a property qualification for voting until 1851, turnout rose

Figure 3.3 Correlations Between Adjacent Presidential Elections,

New Jersey and New Hampshire: Jackson-Democratic Vote

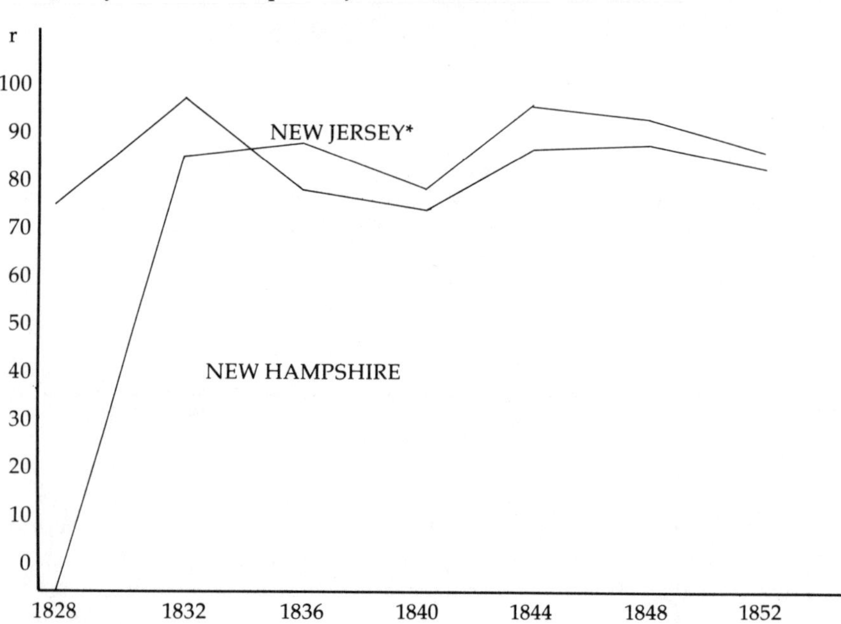

from 12 percent to 35 percent by 1836. In 1840 it jumped 20 points and remained stable until 1852 when, under the new state constitution, it reached 64 percent of the white adult males. Although Jackson won easily in 1828 there was little correlation between that vote and the 1824 distribution. However, the 1828 pattern was repeated four years later when an obvious reshuffling of the electorate took place. The election of 1836 in Virginia correlated poorly with either 1832 or 1840. The election of 1840 ushered in a decade of relative party coherence. In Illinois it is difficult to determine just whom the voters wished to support when they chose certain electors in 1824, and turnout declined in each election between 1828 and 1836. As in Virginia there is a relationship between the vote in 1828 and 1832 but little between that in 1832 and 1836. In 1840 turnout doubled, the correlation between elections went up, and a stable partisan pattern emerged and persisted throughout Phase II.

Obviously there were many differences between voter behavior in these six states, but the patterns described illustrate two points. In

Figure 3.4 Correlations Between Adjacent Presidential Elections,

Illinois and Virginia: Jackson-Democratic Vote

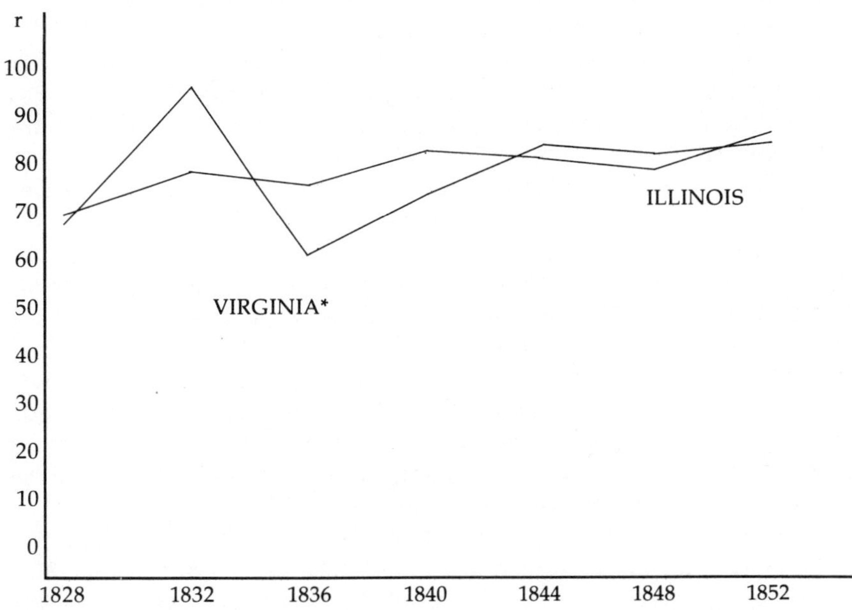

*The 1828 Jackson vote is correlated with the vote for Crawford and Jackson in 1824.

terms of the development of the second party system, Phase I was characterized by a diversity of responses in turnout and distribution of the vote within the states, while Phase II witnessed a uniformity of voter behavior throughout the country. It was not a matter of sectional responses, but of the outgrowth of behavior within the states. Not only did New Jersey differ from Pennsylvania in Phase I, but both states differed from New York. Missouri and Alabama followed fairly similar patterns, but each differed from the neighboring states of Illinois and Mississippi.[18]

Although state elections did not occur at the same time as presidential elections, they also reflected two phases of development that coincide with those uncovered in presidential elections. The patterns of development varied from state to state, but by 1840 most states exhibited markedly similar characteristics. In Phase I state politics was dominated by cliques like the Albany Regency and the Richmond Junto and displayed a great deal of intrastate regionalism. Eventually this situation gave way to one in which parties controlled the nomination and election of state officials. By the mid-1820s the convention system provided the formal organization of state parties in the Middle States where the idea had first taken root. In New England, conventions coexisted with other forms beginning in the early 1830s but it was not until the end of that decade that the system penetrated most Southern and Western states.

Statewide parties seemed to appear in Pennsylvania in the 1820s, although their labels—the "Family party" and the "Amalgamation party"—indicate a rudimentary state of development; for example, the gubernatorial elections of 1817 and 1823 show quite similar patterns of response.[19] However, this structure was short-lived and disappeared in 1829 when George Wolf, a member of the "Family party," faced the Anti-Masonic candidate, Joseph Ritner. Wolf and Ritner ran against each other again in 1832, but the returns reveal only a moderate correlation between these elections. Three years later a split in the Democratic party finally allowed Ritner to win. Although the Democrats were split into "Wolves" and "Mules" and Ritner ran as a "Coalition" (Whig and Anti-Mason) candidate, the outlines of two-party politics had emerged. Throughout the 1840s gubernatorial elections correlated highly with each other and turnout lagged below the presidential elections even when both were held in the same year.

New Hampshire also had a brief period of stability in Phase I, but the pattern was different than that of Pennsylvania.[20] During the 1820s most elections were regional-factional affairs between candidates who termed themselves Republicans. Both Levi Woodbury and Benjamin Pierce won convincingly in one year and then were beaten in the following election. From year to year political leaders shifted their loyalties. A certain stability appeared in the four years following 1828, but this gave way quickly to a series of elections in which the voters showed little interest. In 1838 two-party competiton appeared and persisted for four years; beginning in 1842 after some reshuffling, New Hampshire witnessed nearly a decade of fairly stable and competitive three-party politics.

Another pattern appeared in the Western states of Illinois and Mississippi. In each state the gubernatorial elections of the 1820s and early 1830s featured three or four candidates who did not clearly adhere to any party affiliation. Illinois politics during these years is generally discussed in relation to the personality of Ninian Edwards who had been described as campaigning "like a feudal lord asking the suffrage of his vassels."[21] Stability did not begin to emerge until 1838, and there were fluctuations until the mid-1840s.

Mississippi showed a similar pattern, but party stability was achieved earlier.[22] The elections before 1835 generally featured three or more candidates, and those that were two-candidate contests—1829 and 1833—showed little relationship to each other. A stable pattern began to emerge in the late 1830s; after 1839 consistently high interelection correlations characterized the partisan distributions. As in the other states discussed above, well-organized parties dominated the state's elections in the 1840s.

Other states exhibited patterns of development that were at variance with those from these four states. In New York one can divide these years into three "suberas" of electoral behavior: 1817-1827, 1828-1838, and 1839-1853. The pattern in Missouri was similar to that in Pennsylvania, although there was a consistently lower relationship between the elections after 1836. In Alabama the gubernatorial elections continued to feature three to five candidates through the 1840s and correlations between regular Democrats were modest. The situation in Virginia should warn against an easy belief in the degree to which parties had developed by Phase II. The state did not have popular elections for governor. The fragmentary election results for the legislature confirm the conception of two phases of development during these years, but there seem to have been two suberas in Phase II. Between 1834 and 1842 relatively stable two-party politics existed, but that gave way to an unstable situation in which the Democratic party was riven by factional disputes. That these fights did take place within the party structure is important, but it does show the limited development of parties during the second party system and its fragility in the South.

Historians have traditionally assumed that those people who voted

Table 3.2 Correlations between Adjacent Gubernatorial Elections: Jackson-Democratic Vote

Illinois (r)		Pennsylvania (r)		Mississippi (r)		New Hampshire (r_s)			
1822/1826	−.12	1817/1823	.76	1817/1829	**	1823/1824	.66	1841/1842	.84
1826/1830	.35	1823/1826	**	1829/1831	.33	1824/1828	**	1842/1843	.87
1830/1834	.22	1823/1829	.08	1831/1833	.61	1828/1829	.92	1843/1844	.82
1834/1838	.53	1829/1832	.62	1833/1835	.41	1829/1830	.91	1844/1845	.83
1838/1842	.65	1832/1835	.89	1835/1837	.48	1831/1831	.99	1845/1847	.71
1842/1846	.64	1835/1838	.87	1837/1839	.40	1831/1832	.48	1847/1848	.98
1846/1848	.81	1838/1841	.94	1839/1841	.99	1833/1838	**	1848/1849	.96
1848/1852	.90	1841/1844	.97	1841/1843	.77	1838/1839	.99	1849/1850	1.00
		1844/1847	.96	1843/1845	.91	1839/1840	.88	1850/1851	.88
		1847/1848	.97	1845/1847	.65	1840/1841	.79	1851/1852	.91
		1848/1851	.93	1847/1849	.50				
				1849/1851	.74				

for one party in presidential elections voted for the candidate of the same party in state elections. Yet, the situation during these years was more complex, and especially so before the mid-1830s. McCormick and others have acknowledged the "dual" politics in the Midwestern states in the 1820s and early 1830s when separate organizations contested state and federal elections. An examination of the vote for the candidates supposedly associated with the same parties again reveals a difference between Phase I and Phase II.

As one might expect from the existence of multiple candidacies, it is impossible to find any relation between patterns of the vote in gubernatorial and presidential elections in Mississippi and Illinois before the mid-1830s. In the former state, the gubernatorial election of 1835 showed virtually no relation to the presidential election of 1836. After a period of transition, fifteen years of electoral stability began with the election of 1839. Illinois lagged a bit behind Mississippi. The gubernatorial vote of 1838 correlated with the presidential vote of 1836, and, to a lesser degree, with that of 1840, but the election of 1842 showed little relation to the presidential and the gubernatorial elections on either side of it. A consistent correlation between elections at the state and local level did not appear until 1844.

This shift from relative chaos to relative stability in elections was not entirely a Western phenomenon, although the Western states never reached the same level of stability as the demographically less volatile Eastern states. A transition could also be found in the East where some development of state parties occurred earlier. Because its elections involved contests between two separate tickets, most historians have accepted the existence of two parties in Pennsylvania from 1817 to 1835. In actuality, the relationship between gubernatorial and presidential elections fluctuated wildly until the mid-1830s. After the gubernatorial election of 1838, there was a high and consistent relationship through 1852. Returns from New Hampshire show an inconsistent relation between sets of elections until the late-1830s when stability emerged. Those for Virginia urge caution. While no correlation between legislative and presidential elections could be found in Phase I, the correlations in Phase II are not consistently high. The legislative and presidential returns correlate highly with each other in both 1836 and 1844. The elections of 1840, the first gubernatorial vote in 1851, and the presidential election of the following year, however, show more moderate correlations.

The electorial behavior of American voters between 1815 and 1853 can best be viewed in terms of two phases which help clarify the situation only hinted at in the examination of legal change and the evolution of party structures. The mid-1830s were a crucial period

Table 3.3 Correlations between Adjacent Presidential and State Elections: Jackson-Democratic Vote

Illinois (r)		Pennsylvania (r)		Mississippi (r)		New Hampshire (r_s)		Virginia (r_{tet})	
P24/G26	−.01	P24/G26	.31	P24/G25	**	P24/G24	**	P36/HD36	.98
P28/G30	.56	P28/G29	−.03	P28/G29	.67	P28/G28	.98	P40/HD40	.87
P32/G34	.42	P32/G32	.66	P32/G33	.32	P32/G32	.40	P44/HD44	.96
P36/G38	.86	P36/G35	.90	P36/G35	.46	P36/G36	**	P52/G51	.87
P40/G42	.65	P40/G41	.98	P40/G41	.91	P40/G40	.93		
P44/G46	.88	P44/G44	.99	P44/G45	.68	P44/G44	.82		
P48/G48	.90	P48/G48	.89	P48/G49	.78	P48/G48	.87		
P52/G52	.99	P52/G51	.98	P52/G53	.73	P52/G52	.87		

although the modern typology of critical realignments seems inapplicable. In the years before 1836 regional interests and elite politics dominated both presidential and state elections. Patterns of development within the states varied greatly. It was an age of what V. O. Key, Jr.—speaking of a different time—termed "friends and neighbors" politics.[23] Only after the mid-1830s did voters begin to respond to candidates in a partisan fashion. A sense of party identification emerged and the voters went to the polls in the 1840s with a conviction that they were either Democrats or Whigs.

The function of a political party involves not only electoral politics but also the organization and control of legislative bodies. Most historians have insisted that parties during these years were effective in the legislative realm, but this sector of party activity has not received so much attention as electoral politics. The problem of assigning party labels to congressional candidates before 1835 is more difficult than it might appear from traditional discussions. The most detailed examination of the House of Representatives during these years concluded: "By the end of Jackon's second term most congressmen can be classified by party, but for much of the period between 1825 and 1837 such classifications are much more difficult to make and in many cases impossible."[24] Throughout the 1820s and well into the 1830s the influence of party affiliation on the election of congressmen was minimal. In the late 1820s New Jersey, Delaware, and Ohio initiated the nomination of congressional candidates by party conventions and the procedure gradually spread during the next decade. Until 1828 there was no relationship between congressional and presidential elections and even after that date a fluid situation existed in off-year elections until the late 1830s.

A careful examination of the typical "test votes" upon which historians have generally relied leaves the clear impression that from the beginning of Monroe's administration until the final two years of Jackson's, patterns of voting behavior in the Congress basically reflected high cohesion within state delegations.[25] The sectionalism that Turner and his followers uncovered was an artifact of the aggregation of these state-centered responses. Given the types of issues under consideration—internal improvements, public lands, tariffs, and Indian policy—one can readily understand the reasons for high cohesion. It is actually far less difficult to comprehend the existence of this pattern than to explain why it gave way to one structured by partisan conflict.

This period witnessed few changes in the rules or structure of either house of Congress although the importance of standing committees continued to grow. A most important procedural change signaled the advent of partisanship. In 1846—well into Phase II—the Senate made party organizations responsible for committee assignments. The effectiveness of parties in Congress, however, can be charted more clearly by focusing on the contests for speakership of the House.[26] By using the number of candidates polling at least twelve votes and the percentage of the vote gained by the two leading candidates, one can show an organizational revolution (preceded immediately by a chaotic election and followed by a decade of uniformity) which appeared with the onset of the Twenty-fourth Congress in December 1835. After that date only the elections of 1839 and 1849 disrupt the pattern of well-managed party control. While the organization of Congress at this time offers a fertile field for future research, it seems clear from the effect of party influence on the speakership contests that one can also divide congressional organization during these years into two distinct eras separated by a transitional period in the mid-1830s.

This impression is further enhanced by an examination of roll call voting. The works of Thomas Alexander and Joel Silbey have demonstrated the importance of congressional parties in the years after 1835 throughout the entire life of the second party system.[27] In the House, Democratic cohesion from the Twenty-fourth through the Twenty-seventh Congress (1835-1843) was high: nearly two-thirds of all votes united 90 percent of the party. Whig cohesion lagged and 90 percent of the party did not vote together in 60 percent of the roll calls until the Twenty-sixth Congress. This level declined in the Twenty-seventh Congress, but returned in the next three Congresses (1843-1849). Democratic cohesion was at its highest in the Twenty-seventh Congress, while the Whigs reached their peak in the Twenty-ninth Congress. Clearly, parties were strongest in the 1840s, but even after 1849, when sectionalism increasingly intruded into Congress and cohesion declined, party affiliation remained important.

This picture of Phase II contrasts sharply with that presented in studies of congressional voting behavior in Phase I. After more than a decade during which congressional parties had little effect—if they can be said to have existed at all—the Nineteenth Congress (1825-1827) revealed the outlines of "Adams" and "Jackson" parties.[28] Actually only about one-half the members expressed a clear presidential choice; this hardly constituted "a party system." The importance of living arrangements—the messes—continues to be a matter of argument; however, there is little doubt that during Phase I state delegations presented a united front. In the late 1820s fifteen of the twenty-six delegations were unanimous in their votes and the mean index of cohesion was 77.9 for those roll calls used to prove the existence of the "Adams" and "Jackson" parties. In this limited sense congressional parties existed in the Twentieth Congress, but they shaped voting responses on only a few issues and, like the presidential politics of the day, were basically rooted in geography.

This situation has misled historians. Most have accepted the primacy of congressional parties after the mid-1820s. But the usual "test votes" upon which historians rely hardly show this pattern, and it would seem that state and regional influences continued to be dominant well into Jackson's second term. It is diffcult to find any clear organization of Congress before 1834. Leading issues such as tariffs and internal improvements continued to be determined by local interests. Questions concerning public lands, particularly Clay's distribution proposal, united the antiadministration forces, but split Jackson's northern supporters, as did the original bill to recharter the Bank of the United States. Even the highly emotional question of Indian removal —the key measure of Jackson's presidency—split the Jackson forces and it is best understood in terms of local responses.

It is quite possible that these "test votes" to which historians have consistently turned represent exceptions rather than examples of partisan control of the legislative process. To weigh this possibility we can examine all of the roll calls from the two sessions of the Twenty-second Senate which met between December 1831 and March 1833. This Senate dealt with what are generally considered the major issues of these years: tariff and nullification, the Bank of the United States, Clay's distribution bill, Indian policy, and crucial divisive appointments—such as Van Buren's to the Court of St. James and Samuel Gwin's as Register of the Land Office in Mississippi.

The importance of party in the Twenty-second Senate was distinctly less than can be seen in a similar analysis of the Twenty-ninth Senate, which typified Phase II.[29] In the later Senate, 15.5 percent of all the roll calls in the first session and 16.6 percent in the second session pitted 90 percent of one party against 90 percent of the other party. This was not the case for a single vote in either session of the Twenty-second Senate. On an additional 42 percent of the roll calls in the first session of the Twenty-ninth Senate and 51 percent in the second session, 90 percent of at least one party voted against a majority of the other, but only nine roll calls during the entire Twenty-second Senate (2 percent) met this criterion. Mean indices of party cohesion and of party likeness both reveal an extremely low level of party development in the midst of Jackson's presidency. These patterns coincide with those of the "test votes" and reinforce the impression that during Phase I roll call responses in Congress reflected the influence of state interests rather than parties.

Given the federal nature of the Union and the extreme importance of the states at the time, we must also examine legislative parties at the state level if we wish to assay the importance of parties in the processes by which the American people were governed. Historians have realized the importance of state legislative behavior, but few have examined any more than a handful of test votes on a single issue, such as banking. Two questions are crucial: When did parties begin to exert an important role in legislative behavior (particularly relative to intrastate sectional differences)? When did the issue orientation of state legislative parties tend to take on patterns that were similar in most of the states?

Studies of three states do offer hints that the development of legislative parties mirrored electoral changes. The most detailed study of any state legislature is that of New Jersey by Peter Levine. That study examines every roll call in both houses between 1829 and 1844.[30] Because of the early appearance of labels and the consistent Democratic percentage in presidential elections, he argues that parties were "highly structured" by 1829 and "after a period of coalitional reshuffling stabilization emerged in 1834." Yet when considered in relation to the institutionalization of party-in-the-legislature, three stages of development are evident from his data. Even on appointments, the percentage of partisan roll calls was lower before 1834 than after. Most substantive roll calls at the time generated no party conflict at all and appear to have been dictated by local interests. Between 1833 and 1837, in a rather irregular fashion, one-half of the roll calls began to involve a reasonable majority of one party against a reasonable majority of the other. In the final stage between 1838 and 1844 clear partisan conflict dominated a number of issues and could be found in lesser degrees on most others.

Studies of Illinois and Virginia have yielded similar results. Between 1834 and 1841 Illinois legislative behavior went through two stages.[31] The Ninth and Tenth General Assemblies (1834–1837) were characterized by low party cohesion and little difference between the parties. After 1837 the situation changed and partisanship became increasingly important in the roll calls of the Eleventh and Twelfth Assemblies. Party affiliation in Virginia had little to do with elections in the early 1830s and there was no relation between the presidential choice of a county and the way its delegates voted in the Assembly.[32] A radical change had taken place by 1835. Party labels were more apparent and high levels of cohesion could be found for both parties. The mean index of party likeness was 51.8, and 27 percent of all roll calls united 90 percent of one party against 90 percent of the other. Almost exactly the same pattern was presented five years later. In the mid-1840s, however, mean party cohesion fell and party likeness skyrocketed. This was the product of factional infighting among the Democrats in a somewhat unusual session, but legislative parties in Virginia were probably less stable than elsewhere.

In each of these three states, the timing of legislative party development resembled that of electoral parties. Still it is quite clear that on the national level the simple assumption that the two were always correlated is unwarranted. The later years of the 1840s are still poorly understood although it seems reasonable that in most states parties maintained their strength. The conception of at least two phases of development in party influence in state legislatures is also consistent with the findings of an analysis of 250 roll calls from six legislatures between 1833 and 1843.[33] Although intended to show something else and based on very traditional test votes, the analysis clearly revealed low levels of party development before 1837 and relatively high levels after that date. More important, this is the only study that compares the growth of party cohesion in several states simultaneously, and it supports the view that by the 1840s local interests were giving way to national party affiliation in determining some crucial aspects of legislative behavior.

While obviously a good deal more work needs to be done, the development of legislative parties at both the federal and state levels reflected the two phases uncovered in electoral behavior. In Phase I fairly consistent groupings emerged in the Congress which were related to the impending presidential election. These "parties," however, were rooted in state interests, short-lived, affected only selected issues, and exerted little organizational control. At the end of Jackson's second term, this changed; two parties increasingly dominated congressional behavior and reached their height of influence in the mid-1840s. In a somewhat similar fashion legislative parties emerged within the states. As with electoral behavior, this process varied and was not a carbon copy of that at the national level. In most states—New Jersey was an exception—party labels did not appear until the mid-1830s. The economically troubled year of 1837, which forced state legislators to consider economic policies, represented a watershed between Phase I and Phase II. After that date, the importance of parties spread. By the 1840s Whigs and Democrats began to take distinguishable positions that transcended state boundaries.

Thus, after a brief transitional period in the mid-1830s, parties emerged in a relatively modern form to structure American politics at both the state and federal levels to a greater degree than ever before. As the example of Virginia suggests, historians must be careful to view this matter in relative terms and not overrate either the level of development of the second party system or the extent of its penetration into the American political system. It is obvious, however, that a new level of party development characterized electoral and legislative politics in both the federal and state governments.

A two-phase conception of development during the second party system helps clarify certain problems concerning the changing nature of American political elites during these years. Systematic studies of political leadership in early America are incredibly sparse even at the national level. Those which exist tend to reflect traditional conceptions of American political history and focus on such questions as "Were the Whigs a Class Party in Alabama?"[34] In their desire to characterize the differences between the major parties, historians have ignored the relation between the changing nature of elites and political development. The position and role of elites are a function of political culture, and differences between elites at different stages of development are undoubtedly more significant than socioeconomic differences between contemporary party leaders which have been shown to be modest.

The traditional view was that "rotation in office" or the "spoils system" instituted by Jackson democratized the federal government. However, it is not clear when or why these changes took place and several recent scholars have insisted that this process represented the "modernization" of the civil service.[35] It is doubtful that this was Jackson's intention, and his policy did not lead to an efficient government. At some point during this period the civil service became the instrument of party and its quality—or at least ability to cope—declined. The "Old Hero" took a very personal and traditional approach to appointments; some of his subordinates in the course of administrating their departments did attempt to find ways to institutionalize honesty. The classical republican demand for "rotation in office," however, was never realized. Instead the "rotation" that characterized the 1840s and early 1850s resulted from what eighteenth century republicans would have disdainfully called the "baneful influence of party."

Jacksonian "reform" was not so sweeping as opponents charged; not did it precipitate the rise of a "new class." Jackson's appointments to high level positions in the civil service differed little in socioeconomic status from those of Jefferson. A close analysis of Maryland also shows that during the 1830s traditional leaders still called the tune, while the dancers came only in a glacial fashion from more moderate backgrounds. The greatest differences between Jackson's appointees and Jefferson's was their regional origins. By the 1840s ethnicity also began to affect appointments and the number of foreign-born, particularly Irish, increased in the Customhouse Service.[36]

During the 1830s and 1840s there were also few socioeconomic differences between those who held elective office as either Whigs or

Democrats.[37] Occupational differences existed in some Northern states, but these were less pronounced in both the West and the South. Differences in wealth were minimal; those having a formal education favored the Whigs in New England and the Democrats in the South. The available fragments of evidence which do exist indicate that leaders of both parties in Phase II came from slightly lower social origins than those who dominated both state and national politics from the establishment of the federal government through Jackson's presidency. Traditional modes of nomination emphasizing the importance of militia companies and socially prestigious organizations like the Masons remained dominant into the 1830s, but the introduction of the convention system offered a new source of mobility to those willing to accept party discipline. The much touted "decline of deference" shifted the relationship between the political elite and the voters, and the "emergence of the politician" signaled the creation of new political structures by elements with slightly lower social origins than those of political activists earlier in the century. But it must be emphasized that this process was a slow one that was, in socioeconomic terms, more cosmetic than real.

More important, the politicians of the 1840s saw their role within the system differently. Their understanding of "representation" changed and they increasingly tended to share ethnocultural or ideological perspectives with their followers instead of insisting on their own natural superiority engendered by economic and social prominence. Yet, this commonly accepted set of conclusions needs precise documentation if this shift is to be explained. It is at present unclear when this "democratization" of elected officials and bureaucrats occurred, but a reasonable hypothesis is that it accompanied the shift from Phase I to Phase II.

Although there were those politicians who continued to insist on the role of "moral courage" and independence, a new legislative style appeared in Congress in Phase II. Throughout Phase I congressional leaders spoke of a "Senate of equals of men of individual honor and personal character and of absolute independence" and a House in which "every member is a peer and no man led."[38] By the 1840s this had become a minority position. Independence gave way to party discipline. In dealing with each other these politicians demonstrated a flexibility in compromising on issues and a keen respect for the manipulation of parliamentary procedures.

At the same time the behavior of the voters also changed greatly. Previously, far too little attention has been given to shifts within these years. Thus, one historian characterized the voting behavior of this "system" according to the election of 1832 and another according to the election of 1844. The most widely read study of the "Jacksonian period" assumed a monolithic and consistent two-party structure for the entire period. Attempts to characterize the political struggles at this time have not been closely attuned to the delineation of phases of electoral and party behavior. In Phase I, presidential elections may have played a primary role in structuring certain aspects of the party system. But to argue that the developed parties of the 1840s were characterized only by presidential elections is incorrect. Similarly, the Panic of 1819 did affect state parties in the early years of the troubled 1820s, but the political alignments of that decade were incomplete at best and did not endure.[39]

The assumptions of traditional historians have impeded our understanding of a complex situation. Some of the questions posed by contemporary students of political systems cannot be answered with any precision by historians, because, in part, they are not relevant to the political system that is being examined. The focus upon the influence of class within a fairly homogeneous national political arena led Arthur Schlesinger, Jr., to emphasize that "classes rather than sections" were the dynamic elements in American politics.[40] Most of the revisionist literature of the past three decades has focused upon his simplistic claims of class allegiance and has shown that such economic distinctions among the mass voters were difficult to find. Where they did exist first order differences tended to disappear when other variables were introduced. Thus, little empirical support for the traditional view can be found.

Less examined has been the basic conceptual flaw in the traditional view—the assumptions of a nationwide consciousness of economic place (some clear sense of whether one resided in "the house of Have" or "the house of Want") and of the existence of a politically integrated national electorate. The idea of a national electorate at that time is an abstraction covering a complex mosaic of state and local electorates and any sense of economic place was relative to local situations which varied from community to community. Studies of voting behavior must begin by identifying the politically relevant conflict groups within the states and localities and then examine the process by which political entrepreneurs were able to draw together and relate them in a coherent fashion to groups in other states. The low level of social and economic integration within what was then referred to, not inaccurately, as "a confederation of independent republics" makes generalization from even the most brilliantly executed "case studies" dangerous.

Presidential elections in Phase I featured a unified response from voters in most states that gave a sectional pattern to the overall picture. Where competition did exist, it tended to reflect intrastate regionalism. Although there was little correlation between gubernatorial and presidential elections, state politics everywhere mirrored the various economic interests, ethnic differences, and spheres of elite kin-group hegemony that contributed to such regional differences. Cliques rather than modern parties structured the politics of Phase I.

The term "party" was used to describe various different groups within the states. In the wake of the depression beginning in 1819 a number of "Relief" parties appeared, and in Kentucky this led to the polarization of state politics into "New Court" and "Old Court" parties. At about the same time a "People's party" appeared in New York to oppose the Albany Regency and to support the popular election of presidential electors. Yet these, like Pennsylvania's "Family party" or the "Georgia Machine" in Alabama, were short-lived, unstructured organizations with social bases indistinguishable from their opponents.[41]

Two other "parties" which appeared in the late 1820s might be treated better as social movements. Both the Anti-Masons and the Workingmen presented some semblance of organization and continued to run candidates in some states for nearly a decade before being assimilated into the two major parties that emerged in the late 1830s.[42] It is of interest in relation to traditional views that the religiously oriented Anti-Masonic party attracted far more voters and developed a more elaborate national structure than the Workingmen. While they did effectively organize in a number of Eastern cities, the Workingmen had no national organization or national unity. Within New York City successive Workingmen's organizations were different in their composition despite their identical labels. One can define the social bases of these groups in different areas, but even under a single label—whether Anti-Mason or Workingmen—many separate factions functioned and followed different paths into the orbits of the major parties.

Although parties developed earlier in some states than in others a fragmented situation continued to exist throughout most of the 1830s. No single event precipitated the birth of modern party organization, but the Panic of 1837 created an environment of anxiety and distress which enabled political entrepreneurs to knit together the coalitional structure of the second party system. Not only have traditional historians failed to date this process but also they have overrated the results. Even at the height of its development, the second party system failed to produce a high degree of political integration. Its cohesiveness depended upon the willingness of northerners to allow the South to control its "peculiar institution" and the flexibility of politics in a federal system with a modest communications network.

During Phase II voting patterns stabilized and a new degree of integration of state and national politics appeared. In each state the Democrats and the Whigs assumed positions shared by their fellow partisans throughout the country. The behavior of the voters, however, reflected the unique social and economic situations within each of the states. The social basis of party politics in the South seems to have differed from that in the North. Yet, quite in contrast to traditional views, recent voting studies from all parts of the country "suggest that the relative wealth of citizens had little to do with their party preference."[43]

In the North one can find some occupational and status differences between Whigs and Democrats, and a strong Whiggish bias existed among the super-rich in northern cities. But the major distinctions between the rank and file of Whig and Democratic voters grew from their relation to certain ethnoreligious communities.[44] For the most part recent studies counsel caution with regard to traditional conceptions concerning an "immigrant vote" and a reductionist stance viewing denominational affiliation as an indicator of economic class only. Immigrants divided their vote in New York and Pennsylvania. In these states the "invisible immigrants"—the English, Scots, and Welsh—were Whigs. While the Irish and the German newcomers better fit the traditional picture of strong Democratic support, both groups were split by religious differences. The political behavior of Irish Catholics who were Democrats, virtually to the man, stood in sharp contrast to that of the Irish Protestants who were predominantly Whigs. Among the Germans the minority sects, such as the Brethern and the Moravians, bitterly opposed the majority who were Catholic, Lutheran, or German Reformed. Such denominational differences affected the members of these ethnic groups who had lived in the United States for several generations, but political behavior was also related to doctrinal disputes within denominations which reflected differences in religious style. Most northern Presbyterians tended to be Whigs, but in the Middle states the Old School "party" leaned toward the Democrats. In Illinois Baptists favoring home missions tended to be Whigs, while those who opposed home missions supported Jackson and his followers. Often these differences in religious style were only aspects of other forms of group hostility. In the lower Midwest, settlers from the upland South almost invariably clashed with the Yankees who moved into the area in the 1820s and 1830s. Generally these group conflicts had economic overtones as well, but multivariate analyses have emphasized the primacy of ethnoreligious factors in defining political cleavage during these years. The shared values and group perspectives of these ethnocultural communities enabled their members to comprehend the meaning of political action in personally relevant terms. Even partisan response to economic issues must be understood in relation to the economic orientation consonant with the group's values.[45]

Historians still know very little about voting behavior in the South. Wealth and occupation had only minor relation to political preference although both were probably more important than in the North. The Democratic allegiance of the Germans in Virginia, the Catholics and foreign-born in Louisiana, the handful of Episcopalians and Presbyterians in Georgia and Arkansas, as well as the contrasting roles of Germans and native-born Presbyterians in Missouri all indicate a certain relevance of ethnic and religious differences in these states. But the dominance of Anglo-Protestants, particularly Methodists and Baptists, in most of the South, and the compartmentalized nature of religious outlooks in that section have stymied attempts at an ethnoreligious synthesis. Studies of Mississippi, Alabama, Georgia, and Virginia have connected Whig sentiments with flourishing economic areas that had "commercial contacts with the outside world."[46] Yet, even in those states economics fails to account for most Whig voters. Political leaders drawn from the social and economic elite retained a personal following. County studies which have emphasized the importance of kin relationships—"friends and neighbors" politics—and the continuing impact throughout the South of intrastate regionalism suggest that certain aspects of Phase I were simply extended and redefined during Phase II to relate to national issues and a few relevant perspectives shared with their northern counterparts.[47]

This examination of the phases in the development of the second party system suggests that historians have only begun to solve the problems related to stability and change in the American political system. The conception of five successive party systems each lasting a generation separated by brief intensive periods of "critical realignment" has reoriented historical understanding of American party development.[48] Yet, further refinements such as those suggested here need to be examined before historians will be able to explain adequately the causes of "realignment" and the level of development exhibited by each system.

Within the years traditionally encompassed by the second party system there were two phases with quite different characteristics. Phase I was distinguished by a lack of party development and by the very sporadic and unsystematic nature of its parties. Thus, the parties of Phase I resembled those of the two decades following the adoption of the Constitution. Congressional parties in the late 1820s and early 1830s seem to have been even less cohesive than those of the 1790s or the period of crisis relating to the War of 1812. The organization of the presidential elections of 1828 and 1832 was, however, definitely superior to that created in either 1800 or 1812, but state politics continued to display intrastate regionalism and oligarchic control. The appearance of grass roots parties in Phase I did mark the beginnings of a less deferential response on the part of voters, but generally these parties remained unrelated to those involved in the contest for the presidency.

In contrast the party system that clearly emerged during Phase II resembled the so-called third party system which stabilized following the Civil War. In one aspect Phase II seems to have been unique; for a decade and a half of its existence, party competition penetrated all but one of the states.[49] Yet, in every other way it exhibited a lower level of party development. Partisan identification and the integration of state and federal politics measured by the correlation between elections at both levels were less pronounced in Phase II than in the later period. Congressional partics reached new organizational heights in the 1870s and for two decades partisanship dominated roll call voting to a greater degree than at any other time in American history.

At present, it is nearly impossible for the historian to explain with any precision why Phase II—the "normal" or stable phase of the second party system—appeared when it did, or why it failed to reach the level of development that characterized the "normal" phase of the third party system. The increased intensity of voter participation, the modification of the "rules of the game," fresh patterns of partisan allegiance, and clear party identification would indicate that something resembling a "critical realignment" had taken place. However, the application of this concept is fraught with difficulties. The period of stability did not begin in the 1820s as Walter Dean Burnham assumed, and it did not last a generation—thirty to thirty-eight years—as his general theory implied. The most crucial problem is that in Phase I a stable pattern of party alignment did not exist. Party allegiance, as Burnham used the term, appeared for the first time in American history in Phase II.

The newly developed political structures which held the voters' loyalty throughout the 1840s were the first "constituent" parties in American history. Their concern with the integration and aggregation of diverse groups of supporters was dictated by the fragmented and pluralistic nature of American society. The coincidence of the Panic of 1837 and the onset of Phase II suggests the primacy of economic factors in producing "stress in the socioeconomic system." Yet, it is impossible to weigh the relative amount of stress generated by economic growth, immigration, geographic and social mobility, or religious revivalism. The rate of change and the number of sectors of life being transformed simultaneously indicate that a multidimensional concept such as "social mobilization" is more appropriate to understanding the nature of the social stress which preceded Phase II.[50]

Historians have not systematically studied the relationship between socioeconomic change and political development at different periods in the American past and, thus, lack the rudimentary theoretical tools to explain the genesis of relatively modern political parties during these years. They have recognized, however, the destabilizing nature of social change at this time and associated this with the "birth" of modern parties. The end of the Napoleonic Wars removed the threat of foreign intervention; the republic seemed secure for the first time since the Revolution. Yet, the 1820s began a period of unprecedented economic growth and development. The "Transportation Revolution" scattered Americans into the interior in greater numbers than ever before and encouraged the urbanization of the Northeastern states. The native population continued to grow at an extraordinary rate while an increasing number of immigrants poured into the country. All of Karl Deutsch's indicators of "social mobilization" reached critical levels.[51]

The expansion of the transportation system began to tenuously join together numerous dispersed island communities, but the United States was also becoming an increasingly pluralistic society in which social and economic change tended to create new areas of conflict. Church membership rose dramatically during the first thirty years of the nineteenth century, but the Second Great Awakening was also the source of Protestant sectarianism and virulent anti-Catholicism. The social diversity caused by immigration spawned ethnic conflict; economic growth heightened differences in wealth and generated new class antagonisms. The elevation of "marginal men," hosts of new organizations, riots, expansion of the media and political activity, and increased demands on government characterized these years. Modern political parties were one of the many institutional structures created by Americans to bring order out of an increasingly chaotic world.

But the rate of social and economic change fails to explain the appearance of modern parties in the 1830s. It provided the environment for human action. Parties were "invented" by politicians seeking power for their own diverse reasons by providing new means of interest aggregation, of political recruitment, and of rationalizing government at both levels of the federal system. For years individuals and groups had sought to structure the political process. Their successes were limited to short-term control of legislative bodies or the mobilization of the electorate in the smaller states. The key to their success in the 1830s was the development of communications technology which made possible not only statewide but nationwide networks.

NOTES

1. Frederick Jackson Turner, *The Rise of the New West, 1819-1828* (1906, reprint ed., New York, 1962), p. 25.

2. Richard P. McCormick, *The Second American Party System: Party Formation in the Jacksonian Era* (Chapel Hill, 1966).

3. Giovanni Sartori, *Parties and Party Systems: A Framework for Analysis*, vol. I (Cambridge, England, 1976), discusses many of these problems.

4. Chilton Williamson, *American Suffrage from Property to Democracy, 1760-1860* (Princeton, 1960) is the standard study.

5. Cf. Marvin Meyers, *The Jacksonian Persuasion: Politics and Belief* (1957, reprint ed., Stanford, 1960), p. 238. This is less true of older studies.

6. Fletcher M. Green, *Constitutional Development in the South Atlantic States, 1776-1860: A Study in the Evolution of Democracy* (Chapel Hill, 1930), pp. 144-304; and Charles S. Sydnor, *The Development of Southern Sectionalism, 1819-1848* (Baton Rouge, 1948), pp. 275-93, deal with all of these questions and support the view taken here.

7. On the growing acceptance of parties, see Richard Hofstadter, *The Idea of a Party System: The Rise of Legitimate Opposition in the United States, 1780-1840* (Berkeley, 1966); and Michael Wallace, "Changing Concepts of Party in the United States: New York, 1815-1828," *American Historical Review* 74 (December 1968): 445-68. The rise of political individualism is the subject of J.R. Pole, *Political Representation in England and the Origins of the American Republic* (Berkeley, 1966).

8. An excellent contemporary discussion is Thomas Ford, *History of Illinois From its Commencement as a State in 1818 to 1847* (New York, 1854). As late as July 21, 1835, *The Globe* praised Edmund Burke and used "party" in a strictly Burkean sense. Hofstadter and Wallace exaggerate the degree of this transition and place the acceptance of parties in the country as a whole at least a decade too early. See Ronald P. Formisano, "Political Character, Anti-partyism, and the Second Party System," *American Quarterly* 21 (Winter 1969): 683-709; Sidney Nathans, *Daniel Webster and Jacksonian Democracy* (Baltimore, 1973); Jean E. Friedman, *The Revolt of the Conservative Democrats: An Essay on American Political Culture and Political Development, 1837-1844* (Ann Arbor, 1978); and Stephen C. Fox, "The Group Bases of Ohio Political Behavior, 1803-1848" (Ph.D. dissertation, University of Cincinnati, 1973).

9. McCormick, *The Second American Party System*, p. 349. See also James S. Chase, *Emergence of the Presidential Nominating Convention, 1789-1832* (Urbana, Ill., 1973).

10. Roy F. Nichols, *The Invention of the American Political Parties: A Study of Political Improvisation* (New York, 1967), p. 313.

11. One of the few historians who commented at any length on this was Samuel Gammon, *The Presidential Campaign of 1832*, Johns Hopkins University, Studies in Historical and Political Science, vol. 40 (Baltimore, 1932), pp. 155-62.

12. A typical example is Robert Remini, "Election of 1832," in *History of*

American Presidential Elections, 1789-1968, ed. Arthur M. Schlesinger, Jr. and Fred L. Israel, 3 vols. (New York, 1971), 1: 495-574.

13. The traditional view is repeated in two recent studies of the election: Sister Mary R. Bartus, "The Presidential Election of 1836" (Ph.D. dissertation, Fordham University, 1967); and Joel Silbey, "Election of 1836," in *History*, ed. Schlesinger and Israel, 1: 577-640. For a more detailed analysis of the change, see William G. Shade, "Martin Van Buren, Slavery and the Election of 1836," in *Martin Van Buren: Politics, Policy and the Presidency*, ed. Gerald Sorin and Donald M. Roper (forthcoming).

14. This interpretation follows Nichols, *The Invention of American Political Parties*, pp. 333-81.

15. Gerald Pomper, "Classification of Presidential Elections," *The Journal of Politics* 29 (August 1967): 535-66.

16. On turnout see Richard P. McCormick, "New Perspectives on Jacksonian Politics," *American Historical Review* 65 (January 1960): 288-301; and Pole, *Political Representation*, in which results published in several earlier articles are reprinted in an appendix.

17. This point is emphasized by Silbey, "Election of 1836," 1: 596-99, and is one of McCormick's major conclusions. Charles G. Sellers, Jr., "Who Were the Southern Whigs?" *American Historical Review* 59 (January 1954): 335-46, and Frank Otto Gatell, "Money and Party in Jacksonian America," *Political Science Quarterly* 82 (June 1967): 235-52, present the traditional view.

18. Lee Benson, Joel H. Silbey and Phyllis F. Field, "Toward A Theory of Stability and Change in American Voting Patterns: New York State, 1792-1970," in *The History of American Electoral Behavior: Quantitative Studies*, ed. by Joel H. Silbey, Allan G. Bogue, and William Flanigan (Princeton, 1978), pp. 78-105. The Alabama and Missouri data are from the Inter-University Consortium for Political and Social Research.

19. On Pennsylvania see Philip Klein, *Pennsylvania Politics 1817-1832: A Game without Rules* (Philadelphia, 1940); Charles McCool Snyder, *The Jacksonian Heritage, 1833-1848* (Harrisburg, 1958); and Roger Dewey Petersen, "The Reaction to a Heterogeneous Society: A Behavioral and Quantitative Analysis of Northern Voting Behavior, 1845-1970, Pennsylvania a Test Case" (Ph.D. dissertation, University of Pittsburgh, 1970).

20. On New Hampshire see Donald Cole, *Jacksonian Democracy in New Hampshire* (Cambridge, 1970); Vincent J. Capowski, "The Era of Good Feelings in New Hampshire: The Gubernatorial Campaigns of Levi Woodbury, 1823-1824," *Historical New Hampshire* 21 (Winter 1966): 3-33; and Sue Taishoff, "New Hampshire State Politics and the Concept of a Party System, 1800-1840," *Historical New Hampshire* 31 (Spring-Summer 1976): 17-43.

21. Theodore C. Pease, *Illinois Election Returns, 1818-1848* (Springfield, Ill, 1923), p. xxiii. On Illinois see idem, *The Frontier State, 1818-1848* (Springfield, 1918); and Charles Manfred Thompson, *The Illinois Whigs before 1846*, University of Illinois Studies in the Social Sciences, vol. 4 (March 1915): 9-165.

22. On Mississippi see Edwin Arthur Miles, *Jacksonian Democracy in Mississippi* (Chapel Hill, 1960); and David N. Young, "The Mississippi Whigs"

(Ph.D. dissertation, University of Alabama, 1968). Professor Miles provided me with the 1829-1835 gubernatorial results.

23. V. O. Key, Jr., *Southern Politics in State and Nation* (New York, 1949), pp. 37-41.

24. Alvin Willard Lynn, "Party Formation and Operations in the House of Representatives, 1824-1837" (Ph.D. dissertation, Rutgers University, 1973), p. 137.

25. The test votes discussed here and the mean cohesion of state delegations in the House on each are as follows: the Bonus Bill, February 8, 1817 (64.53); the General Survey Bill, February 10, 1824 (83.67); the Tariff of 1824, April 16, 1824 (88.00); the Tariff of 1828, April 22, 1828 (84.75); the Distribution Bill, January 18, 1830 (83.75); the Maysville Road Bill, April 29, 1830 (75.79); Indian Removal, May 24, 1830 (69.35); the recharter of the Bank of the United States, July 3, 1832 (73.30); and the resolution of the Bank of the United States, April 4, 1834 (62.33).

26. James S. Young, *The Washington Community, 1800-1828* (New York, 1966), pp. 117-21. See also Gerald R. Lientz, "House Speaker Elections and Congressional Parties, 1789-1860," *Capitol Studies* 6 (Spring 1978): 62-88.

27. Joel H. Silbey, *The Shrine of Party: Congressional Voting Behavior, 1841-1852* (Pittsburgh, 1967); and Thomas B. Alexander, *Sectional Stress and Party Strength: A Study of Roll-Call Voting Patterns in the United States House of Representatives* (Nashville, 1967). Also see David J. Russo, "The Major Political Issues of the Jacksonian Period and the Development of Party Loyalty in Congress, 1830-1840," *Transactions of the American Philosophical Society* 62 (May 1972): pp. 3-49.

28. Along with Young, *The Washington Community*, see George R. Neilson, "The Indispensable Institution: The Congressional Party During the Era of Good Feelings" (Ph.D. dissertation, University of Iowa, 1968). Young is criticized in Allan G. Bogue and Mark Paul Malaire, "Of Mess and Men: The Boardinghouse and Congressional Voting, 1821-1842," *American Journal of Political Science* 19 (May 1975): 207-30. Their findings fit generally with what is said here since, as they admit, their party designations for 1821-1822 are "less than precise."

29. The Twenty-ninth Senate was analyzed in A. Lawrence Lowell's classic study, "The Influence of Party Upon Legislation in England and America," *Annual Report of the American Historical Association for the Year 1901* (Washington, D.C., 1901) 2: 319-545. The data on the Twenty-second Senate is from the ICPSR and has been analyzed with the ACCUM program written for Lee Anderson, et al., *Legislative Roll-Call Analysis* (Evanston, 1966). Sellers' discussion of six crucial votes in the Twenty-second and Twenty-third Congresses in "Who Were the Southern Whigs," pp. 338-39, also shows little party unity.

30. Peter Levine has written a number of essays which are included in his book *Behavior of State Legislative Parties in the Jacksonian Era: New Jersey, 1829-1844* (Rutherford, N.J., 1977).

31. Rodney O. Davis, "Illinois Legislators and Jacksonian Democracy, 1834-1841" (Ph.D. dissertation, University of Iowa, 1966).

32. The following is from a study in progress of Virginia, which includes an analysis of the roll calls in the Assembly during the sessions 1831-1832, 1835-1836, 1840-1841 and 1845-1846. Party labels did not appear until 1834 and thus the 1831-1832 data are quite speculative. It is based upon the reasonable assumption that the counties which voted for Adams or Jackson sent "Adams" or "Jackson" men to the Assembly.

33. Herbert Ershkowitz and William G. Shade, "Consensus or Conflict? Political Behavior in the State Legislatures during the Jacksonian Era," *Journal of American History* 58 (December 1971): 591-621. Since this essay was written, Michael F. Holt has published further corroborating evidence in *The Political Crisis of the 1850s* (New York, 1978), pp. 26-27, 115-16.

34. Grady McWhiney, "Were the Whigs a Class Party in Alabama?" *Journal of Southern History* 23 (November 1957): 510-22.

35. Lynn Marshall, "The Strange Still-birth of the Whig Party," *American Historical Review* 72 (January 1967): 445-68; Mathew A. Crenson, *The Federal Machine: Beginnings of Bureaucracy in Jacksonian America* (Baltimore, 1975). Leonard D. White, *The Jacksonians, 1829-1861* (New York, 1954), remains the classic study.

36. Erik M. Erikson, "The Federal Civil Service under President Jackson," *Mississippi Valley Historical Review* 30 (March 1927):517-40; Sidney H. Aronson, *Status and Kinship in the Higher Civil Service: Standards of Selection in the Administrations of John Adams, Thomas Jefferson and Andrew Jackson* (Cambridge, 1964); Whitman Ridgway, "McCulloch vs. the Jacksonians: Patronage and Politics in Maryland," *Maryland Historical Magazine* 70 (Winter 1975):350-62; and Leonard Tabachnik, "Political Patronage and Ethnic Groups: Foreign-born in the United States Customhouse Service, 1821-1861," *Civil War History* 17 (September 1971):222-31.

37. Lee Benson, *The Concept of Jacksonian Democracy: New York as a Test Case* (Princeton, 1961), pp. 64-85; Michael Fitzgibbon Holt, *Forging a Majority: The Formation of the Republican Party in Pittsburgh, 1848-1860* (New Haven, 1969), pp. 42-48; William A. Gudelunas, Jr., and William G. Shade, *Before the Molly Maguires: The Emergence of the Ethno-Religious Factor in the Politics of the Lower Anthracite Region, 1844-1872* (New York, 1976), pp. 43-44; Rodney O. Davis, "The Influence of Party on Political Leadership in Illinois in the Jacksonian Era," paper presented at the annual meeting of the Organization of American Historians, Chicago, 1973; Young, "The Mississippi Whigs," pp. 82-88; Thomas Alexander et. al., "Who Were the Alabama Whigs?" *Alabama Review* 16 (January 1963):5-19; Thomas Alexander et al., "The Basis of Alabama's Ante-Bellum Two-Party System," *Alabama Review* 19 (October 1966):243-76; and W. Wayne Smith, "Jacksonian Democracy on the Chesapeake: Class, Kinship and Politics," *Maryland Historical Magazine* 63 (March 1968):55-67.

38. Johanna Nicol Shields, "Variations in Legislative Style Among Leaders in the United States House and Senate in the 1840s," unpublished paper presented at the annual meeting of the Social Science History Association, Ann Arbor, Michigan, November, 1977.

39. Cf. Charles G. Sellers, Jr., "Banking and Politics in Jackson's Tennessee,

1817-1827," *Mississippi Valley Historical Review* 61 (June 1954): 61-84; Lynn Marshall, "The Genesis of Grass-Roots Democracy in Kentucky," *Mid-America* 47 (October 1965): 269-87; and Kim T. Phillips, "Pennsylvania Origins of the Jackson Movement," *Political Science Quarterly* 91 (Fall 1976): 489-508.

40. Arthur M. Schlesinger, Jr., *The Age of Jackson* (Boston, 1945). Two good historiographical essays are Charles G. Sellers, Jr., "Andrew Jackson versus the Historians," *Mississippi Valley Historical Review* 44 (March 1958): 615-34, and Ronald P. Formisano, "Toward a Reorientation of Jacksonian Politics: A Review of the Literature, 1959-1975," *Journal of American History* 64 (June 1976): 42-65.

41. A. M. Stickles, *The Critical Court Struggle in Kentucky* (Bloomington, Ind., 1929); Alvin Kass, *Politics in New York State, 1800-1830* (Syracuse, 1965); Klein, *Pennsylvania Politics;* and Ruth K. Nuemberger, "The 'Royal Party' in Early Alabama Politics," *Alabama Review* 6 (April and July 1953): 81-99 and 198-212.

42. See Edward Pessen, *Most Uncommon Jacksonians* (Albany, 1967); Walter Hugins, *Jacksonian Democracy and the Working Class* (Stanford, 1960); and Michael F. Holt, "The Antimasonic and Know-Nothing Parties," in *History of U. S. Political Parties*, ed. Arthur M. Schlesinger, Jr., 4 vols. (New York, 1973), 1: 575-737. The literature on these movements is summarized in *Jacksonian America: Society, Personality and Politics*, Edward Pessen (rev. ed., Homewood, 1978), pp. 261-79.

43. Ibid., pp. 244-45.

44. Benson, *Concept of Jacksonian Democracy*, pp. 288-328; Robert Kelley, "Presbyterianism, Jacksonian Democracy and Grover Cleveland," *American Quarterly* 18 (Winter 1966): 615-36; Holt, *Forging A Majority*, pp. 40-83; William G. Shade, "Pennsylvania Politics in the Jacksonian Period: A Case Study, Northampton County, 1824-1844," *Pennsylvania History* 39 (July 1972): 313-33; Gudelunas and Shade, *Before the Molly Maguires*, pp. 32-61; Petersen, "Reaction to a Heterogeneous Society"; Ronald P. Formisano, *The Birth of Mass Political Parties: Michigan, 1827-1861* (Princeton, 1971); Fox, "Ohio Political Behavior"; and John Rozette, "The Social Basis of Party Conflict in the Age of Jackson: Individual Voting Behavior in Greene County Illinois, 1838-1848" (Ph.D. dissertation, University of Michigan, 1974).

45. William G. Shade, *Banks or No Banks: The Money Issue in Western Politics, 1832-1865* (Detroit, 1972).

46. Alexander et al., "Basis of Alabama's Two Party System"; Young, "Mississippi Whigs," pp. 48-87; Lynwood Dent, Jr., "The Virginia Democratic Party, 1824-1847" (Ph.D. dissertation, Louisiana State University, 1976), pp. 357-98.

47. J. Mills Thornton, *Politics and Power in a Slave Society: Alabama, 1800-1860* (Baton Rouge, 1978); Donald DeBats, "Elites and Masses: Political Structure, Communication and Behavior in Ante-Bellum Georgia" (Ph.D. dissertation, University of Wisconsin, 1973); and Harry Legare Watson II, " 'Bitter Combinations of the Neighborhood': The Second Party System in Cumberland County North Carolina" (Ph.D. dissertation, Northwestern University, 1976).

48. Walter Dean Burnham, *Critical Elections and the Mainsprings of American*

Politics (New York, 1970), is the fullest statement of the theory of critical realignments. Burnham's data did not go back beyond the election of 1828 and he does not concentrate on this period to any great extent.

49. The Whig party was never strong in the new states of Arkansas and Texas. See Brian G. Walton, "The Second Party System in Arkansas, 1836-1848," *Arkansas Historical Quarterly* 28 (Summer 1969):120-55.

50. Karl W. Deutsch, "Social Mobilization and Political Development," *American Political Science Review* 55 (September 1961):493-514.

51. Deutsch's relevant indicators and critical annual percentage rates of change are growth of mass media (2.75); increase in voting participation (2.2); increase in literacy (1.2); change of residence (1.25); population growth (2.6); shift out of agriculture (.7); shift from rural to urban residence (.5); linguistic assimilation (.25); income growth (5.0); and income growth per capita (2.3).

*Paul Kleppner**

PARTISANSHIP AND ETHNORELIGIOUS CONFLICT: THE THIRD ELECTORAL SYSTEM, 1853-1892

4

The vast majority of voters on both sides are party men, who vote the same way year after year.

Josiah Strong (1891)

For Strong and other issue-conscious elites, that was a frustrating reality. Among that self-conscious, self-proclaimed group of "notables," orientations toward electoral politics were dominated by a norm of "absolute independence of party dictation."[1] Unhappily for their individual and collective psyches, relatively few Americans shared their antipartisan animus. Powerful and *positive* orientations toward political parties were broadly diffused among the late-nineteenth century electorate. Mass political culture provided little support for the gospel of "independence of party." Instead, most men believed that to have been "born, raised, and educated as Democrats [or Republicans], and to vote anything else was treason, more rank than to fight against their country."[2] And most men, in most elections, voted as they believed.

A high incidence of positive evaluations of parties is surely as alien to the electoral politics of our own day, as are the behavioral indicators

*Most of the research for this chapter comes from my larger study of the third electoral system. That research was supported by funding from the American Philosophical Society, the National Endowment for the Humanities, the Smithsonian Institution, and the Council of Academic Deans, Northern Illinois University. Since completing that book I have done additional work on the period as part of a research project supported by grants from the National Endowment for the Humanities and the National Science Foundation. These grants are being administered by NSF as grant SOC77-14155. I am grateful to all of these agencies for their assistance.

associated with such evaluations. The wide (almost wild) partisan swings that mark current elections were unknown in the nineteenth century. Partisan percentages then fluctuated within quite narrow ranges. Those electoral battles mobilized historically high proportions of the potential electorate; most men regularly participated, and their voting decisions were cued primarily by their psychological attachments to parties. In short, to most citizens the partisan outcome of elections mattered, and they behaved accordingly.

The partisan linkages that characterized the third electoral system were stronger than those prevailing in any corresponding era. Party, in both its organizational and symbolic senses, structured outcomes in legislatures and among voters. And durable party oppositions reflected powerful ethnoreligious and sectional animosities. That cleavage structure was forged in the 1850s, seared into consciousness by the experiences of the Civil War, and sustained thereafter by the combined effects of standing party attachments and current events that reinforced the salience of these types of intergroup conflict.

CHRONOLOGICAL BOUNDARIES

It took a series of electoral blows to displace the second party system. Their cumulative impact, apparent by the mid-1850s, permanently shattered the Whig party's mass base and significantly reduced the size of the Democratic coalition, while leaving its geographic base essentially intact (see Table 4.1).[3]

Severe fluctuation of the magnitude associated with critical realignments began with the 1854-1856 sequence, and at the national level party distributions stabilized by about 1868. While the 1856-1868 (or 1856-1872) election sequence showed high levels of partisan instability, these fluctuations did not substantially alter the general shape of the distributions that were already in place by 1856. By that year, in fact, the broad contours of the realigned social coalitions were reasonably clear. In most of the country, the voter movement associated with the war and its aftermath completed the process of reshuffling party coalitions by deepening and solidifying these social outlines.[4]

Wartime conditions in the Border states, and the war and Reconstruction in the South interrupted the normal operation of the electoral process. Realignment in these states was completed only after the termination of such conditions and the enfranchisement of blacks. That coincided with a resurgence of Democratic strength in other parts of the country that was associated with both a revitalized prohibition crusade and an industrial depression. With these developments, across the 1874-1876 election sequence, the third electoral system

Table 4.1 Partisan Autocorrelations by States and by Counties

	Democrat				Whig/Republican			
	United States		*Nonsouth*		*United States*		*Nonsouth*	
ELECTION PAIR	STATES	COUNTIES	STATES	COUNTIES	STATES	COUNTIES	STATES	COUNTIES
1840/1844	.836	.896	.899	.894	.836	.897	.835	.888
1844/1848	.791	.867	.794	.810	.740	.874	.882	.851
1848/1852	.800	.823	.748	.814	.601	.730	.843	.875
1852/1856	.820	.718	.758	.687	.025	.195	−.425	−.049
1856/1860*	.671	.629	.848	.852	.967	.808	.948	.900
1860*/1864	.558	.324	.558	.339	.436	.256	.436	.336
1864/1868	.830	.801	.830	.802	.837	.800	.837	.801
1868/1872	.681	.653	.773	.726	.691	.652	.777	.727
1872/1876	.749	.824	.899	.902	.762	.849	.924	.904
1876/1880	.895	.840	.939	.934	.903	.875	.945	.915
1880/1884	.902	.894	.831	.879	.879	.880	.804	.860
1884/1888	.932	.877	.914	.903	.940	.881	.900	.886
1888/1892	.770	.709	.663	.745	.793	.793	.447	.752
1892/1896	.082	.456	−.528	.159	.771	.780	.734	.719
1896/1900	.781	.674	.695	.502	.831	.823	.831	.746

*Douglas and Breckinridge Democrat 1860

reached its equilibrium, or stable, phase. That persisted until a new type of sectional polarity combined with another depression to overturn the "standing decision" that had structured party oppositions for over a third of a century.

The symptoms of the system tension that escalated to the "flash point" of realignment were apparent before the mid-1850s. In the South the decline in Whig strength between 1848 and 1852 was accompanied by a tendency toward partisan and pro-Democratic homogeneity. That indicated a sectional response, a narrowing of the voting distance among social groups, propelled by the development of a regional self-consciousness whose chief referent was a powerful strain of anti-Northernism. The high levels of factional voting and low turnout that marked the 1850 election indicated that increasing numbers of voters perceived that their demands could not be accommodated within the party system as then structured.

To the north of the Mason-Dixon line the symptoms of system strain were even more virulent. The Liberty party in the early 1840s and the Free Soilers thereafter spread the antislavery and antisouthern gospel. As they drew support from the major parties and mobilized nonvoters, their vote totals evidenced the incapacity of "politics as usual" to integrate and aggregate the demands of a growing number of northerners. The sudden emergence and widespread success of the Native American, or Know-Nothing, party in 1854 provided an even more dramatic indicator of that. While some voters displayed their "impatience" with the existing parties by balloting for minor ones, others signaled their frustration simply by not voting.[5] Turnout in the nonsouthern states over the four biennial elections between 1846 and 1852 showed a mean of 58.5 percent, compared to 68.2 percent over the 1838-1844 sequence. This severe turnout decline and increased levels of minor-party voting were unmistakable signs of system disarray.

The tensions that percolated through the society in the 1840s and 1850s cut orthogonally across the existing party cleavage. The data in Table 4.2 reveal why the existing parties were unable to deal with one critical dimension of that crosscutting tension.

Neither Democrats nor Whigs could accommodate the developing regional antagonisms. Each was literally a national party in the sense that each drew considerable voting support from every region. Parties that were regionally inclusive looked to both sides of the Mason-Dixon line for popular support and could not aggregate demands that involved powerful regional polarities. They could not, that is, without undergoing fundamental changes in characters and social coalitions, without becoming regionally exclusive parties.

The electoral transformation of the 1850s produced that effect. The

Table 4.2 Distribution of Partisan Presidential Vote by States

	Democrat				Whig/Republican			
	United States		*Nonsouth*		*United States*		*Nonsouth*	
ELECTION	$\bar{M}$	σ^2	$\bar{M}$	σ^2	$\bar{M}$	σ^2	$\bar{M}$	σ^2
1836	51.1	62.56	50.2	74.47	48.7	59.59	49.5	70.22
1840	46.4	33.98	45.9	35.40	53.2	32.83	53.6	33.98
1844	50.1	35.04	48.3	29.48	47.6	32.49	48.5	34.45
1848	45.5	89.30	42.9	91.77	47.2	56.70	46.0	56.70
1852	52.4	58.06	49.6	40.06	42.4	43.82	43.8	24.80
1856	48.0	127.23	42.6	87.42	26.2	724.68	39.3	563.58
1860*	48.2	146.41	44.5	104.65	32.1	763.41	46.6	417.79
1864	42.1	109.83	42.1	109.83	57.7	104.04	57.7	104.04
1868	45.9	133.17	44.8	122.10	54.0	133.17	55.1	122.10
1872	42.4	81.00	40.8	71.06	56.8	80.10	58.3	70.39
1876	50.6	94.09	46.9	61.46	48.4	83.72	51.8	55.05
1880	49.0	100.80	44.5	59.90	47.8	98.01	52.1	51.98
1884	49.2	94.47	44.9	42.64	47.9	69.55	51.4	28.30
1888	50.2	133.40	44.7	37.94	46.5	114.27	51.6	28.30
1892	41.9	472.19	34.5	362.52	40.2	201.35	46.6	39.18
1896	52.4	333.79	47.4	285.94	45.3	308.35	50.3	249.01
1900	48.5	224.10	42.2	76.91	48.1	200.78	54.3	50.55
1904	41.7	394.41	32.2	80.10	52.2	356.45	61.4	58.36

*Douglas and Breckinridge Democrat 1860

enormous increases in the size of the variance (σ^2) of the vote distributions in 1856 give evidence of that. On the anti-Democratic side, the Whigs were displaced by a sectional coalition whose appeal was exclusively northern and whose strongholds were in New England and in the areas of Yankee settlement to the west of that region. The Democrats became a party whose regional bastions were the South and Border areas. The relatively tight party balances in every region that had marked the second electoral era yielded to a competitive structure based upon enormous regional polarities that were expressed through partisan oppositions. The resulting party system was structured to produce policy outputs reflective of these North-South polarities.

The events of the 1850s were the proximate causes of the breakup of the second party system. But those events occurred within a context that had been shaped by earlier developments and conditioned by long-smoldering resentments. That the sectional controversies of the 1850s culminated in secession and war, while similar debates in earlier decades had been confined to hostile exchanges among elites, indicates an intervening change in mass opinion. The roots of that change lay in the religious revivals of the 1820s and 1830s. For Charles Grandison Finney preached a new understanding of the nature of man and thus transformed the outlook of those who experienced the revivals and internalized their ethos.[6]

Free will and the agency of man in conversion were the essentials of that ethos. These two tenets, in turn, shaped the abolitionist movement. For if every man was a free moral agent, then enslavement denied him his own moral responsibility. Slavery's lack of liberty was thus inconsistent with the revivalist emphasis on free will. Moreover, it was not merely that slavery was wrong, it was sinful. And true believers could not passively tolerate the continued existence of this or any other sin. God commanded the saved to work for the good of others, to save others from sin even when those others saw no sin.

The revivalist ethos made another contribution to political culture. It brought to politics the spirit of the religious enthusiast, the true believer convinced of his righteousness. That disposition endowed politics with a right vs. wrong, a with-us-or-against-us attitude. The disposition of the coalition-building politician inclined toward political responsibility, which included compromise among contending views and the development of joint preference orderings of objectives; but that of the religious enthusiast valued ultimate responsibility and spoke of "higher laws" that admitted of no compromise.[7]

The revivals and the disposition which they inculcated underlay the attitudinal transformation that made the realignment of the 1850s possible. The diffusion of that disposition led increasingly large numbers of people to involvement in the benevolent enterprises that revivalists saw as an integral part of the salvation experience. That cluster of interlocking mission, tract, Sunday school, education, and temperance societies provided an organizational base for the elimination of sin. Commitment to these organizations led to involvement in pressure-group politics and, slowly, reluctantly, but inexorably, to involvement in electoral politics.

The revivalist disposition impacted electoral politics by unleashing several distinctive streams of emotions that ultimately converged to shatter the existing party system.[8] It shaped the abolitionist crusade and directed the energies of some abolitionists into political antislavery. That served to heighten regional self-consciousness and, by imbuing the drive with an all-or-nothing moralism, to escalate the levels of North-South tension. When such uncompromising moralism was brought to bear on other public questions, old partisan attachments were shaken, new support clienteles emerged, and an exclusively sectional coalition was able to gain control over the region's, and the nation's, policy-making institutions.

The emergence of single-issue antislavery parties, Liberty and Free Soil, probably made few new converts to the holy crusade against the sin of slavery. However, by channeling abolitionism into electoral politics, by making slavery an object of mass cognitions and providing a partisan alternative for the expression of attitudes, they had other behavioral consequences.

First, they weakened the commitments of some voters to the major parties. The Liberty party in 1840 and 1844 drew support among Yankee-stock and Whig voters. The Free Soil party was less narrowly and overtly a religious crusade than the Liberty party had been, and between 1848 and 1852 it was able to broaden the mass base of political antislavery. Its appeal was still strongest among Yankee-stock voters, but it was not as exclusively confined to Yankees with Whig voting habits as the Liberty party had been. In New England as well as in areas settled by Yankees in New York, Pennsylvania, and the Midwest, the Free Soil party cut into the voting support of both major parties. The effect, at the aggregate level, was to reduce the major parties' proportionate share of the total vote cast. In no presidential or congressional election between 1842 and 1850 were either the Democrats or Whigs able to poll as much as 50 percent of the total nonsouthern vote.[9] At the individual level, such movement weakened the psychological attachments of these voters to their old parties.

Second, both Liberty and Free Soil helped to condition northern mass opinion in another way. By alerting northerners to the aggressions of the slave power, they injected anti-Southernism into mass politics. Perhaps, only their die-hard supporters read their tracts or listened to their speeches. However, by raising such themes, Liberty and Free Soil forced responses from the major parties to stop the erosion of their own mass coalitions. The Whig response was an anti-Southernism as forceful in tone as that of the Liberty or Free Soil parties. The Democrats' response emerged hesitantly, gave more evidence of tactics than of conviction, and never reached the white-hot levels that characterized the Whig, Liberty, and Free Soil charges. Through such responses, however, antisouthern themes reached an audience much larger than the voting supporters of the antislavery parties. Anti-Southernism and its concrete referents became a part of the political vocabulary and the political outlook of increasingly large numbers of northern citizens.[10]

Political antislavery, imbued with attitudes of uncompromising morality, stoked the fires of sectional controversy, but it was only one way in which religious enthusiasm contributed to the emerging tensions that destroyed the prevailing party system. Other groups whose political cultures had come to involve revivalist dispositions became dissatisfied with "politics as usual" for different reasons. Some were fired by temperance and sabbatarian zeal and sought to translate their versions of God's will into public policy. They quickly became disillusioned with political parties that pandered to the "saloon vote" and evaded what they saw as righteous and uncompromisable demands. Others were driven by what they perceived as the growing menace of popery. To them Catholics were aggressively subversive of American values and the major parties were not equally aggressive in resisting that peril. The increasingly widespread diffusion of such sentiments and evaluations of parties further expanded the size of the potential support clientele that was manifestly dissatisfied with the prevailing party system.[11]

To growing numbers of citizens, and for descriptively distinctive reasons, "politics as usual" proved inadequate. By the mid-1850s the attitudes and emotions created by a political antislavery that weakened party loyalties while teaching the lessons of anti-Southernism, by an unleashed temperance and sabbatarian enthusiasm, and by a renascent and driving antipopery converged to shatter existing coalitional arrangements. While these factors can be separated descriptively, it is important to bear in mind that they coexisted in life and thought and "permeated one another with emotional resonance."[12] The tensions that they created and the "derangement of parties" that they set in motion were visible before Bleeding Kansas become an object of public concern.[13] The resulting streams of disaffected voters were neither easily nor rapidly fused into a cohesive partisan alternative.

Neither Democrats nor Whigs escaped the convulsive effects of a religious enthusiasm turned loose on electoral politics. The Free Soil party cut into the Democrats' Yankee voting support. And as temperance, sabbatarian, and anti-Catholic attitudes became increasingly salient, the loyalties of even more Yankee and other native-stock Protestant Democrats were shaken. Antipopery had appeal even among some of the foreign-stock groups in the party's coalition—especially the Dutch and Norwegians in the Midwest and the German Sectarians both there and in the Midatlantic area. The consequence was a sharp reduction in the size of the Democratic voting coalition. For the Whigs the effect was more drastic; that party's coalition was literally shattered. Liberty party moralism had its greatest appeal among Yankee Whigs, and the Free Soil party enlisted the support of even slightly larger numbers of that group. In the face of this steady hemorrhaging of Northern strength, the Whigs' sudden decline in the South in 1852 demoralized the party's leaders everywhere and accelerated its dissolution in the North. By 1854 northern Whiggery was in nearly total disarray. Know-Nothings in some locales and Independent, Fusion, or People's candidates in others drew heavily from Whig ranks. While the party organization persisted beyond the 1854-1856 sequence, as a party in the electorate Whiggery had ceased to be the major opposition to the Democrats.

The destruction of the sectionally inclusive Whig party was one development; its replacement by a sectionally exclusive Republican party was quite another. Creating an anti-Democratic *party opposition* was more protracted and agonizing an enterprise than has generally been recognized. The Republican party did not emerge spontaneously in 1854. In fact, what emerged then was not a *party* at all; it was a loosely structured, popular front coalition of anti-Democratic voter groups. To unite these separately designated groupings into a single party required purposive efforts by party-building elites. Those efforts had to be directed at sublimating potential conflict among the groups comprising the popular front to produce a "joint preference ordering" that emphasized opposition to "Democracy" and all that that party symbolized.[14]

The mechanics and speed with which this party building occurred varied from place to place. In some states the Native Americans, instead of nominating their own tickets in 1854, cooperated with Whigs, Free Soilers, and anti-Nebraska Democrats. In other locales, however, the Know-Nothings were not amalgamated into the popular front until after the 1854 election. And in still other places, the fusion arrangements were tenuous and incomplete even on the eve of the 1860 election.[15]

What was less variable were the themes that anti-Democratic party builders wove together symbolically to tap preexisting emotions, to imbue them with partisan salience, and to fashion their mass coalition. Two such themes predominated: antipartyism and anti-Southernism.

Antiparty themes resonated positively with the dispositions of groups that had been trying for a decade or more to translate their conceptions of righteousness into public policy. Whether that involved the extirpation of slavery, the elimination of demon rum, a political response to the growing Catholic menace, or some combination of these ingredients, such groups shared the conviction that only an "all absorbing party spirit" had frustrated their efforts. Attacks on that "party spirit" could "represent" their political characters and could mobilize their voting support.[16]

Political symbolism that employed antisouthern themes and code words was designed for the same purpose. Denunciations of slavery and of the aggressive spirit of the slave power conveyed a sense of psychological linkage between the political characters of the groups holding such attitudes and that of the political leaders articulating them. And to such groups the code words referred to more than the South's labor system. Consistent with their evangelical values, they regarded whatever limited the operation of man's free will, his right to do right, as a peril to the individual's and society's salvation. Such restraints were violations of God's law, sins to be eliminated. Whether the bondage of the black to his white owner, or the immigrant to the dictates of the pope, or any man to the influence of King Alcohol or to the Spirit of Party, these were all sinful forms of "slavery" that restrained free will.[17]

The fact that anti-Democratic party builders wove such themes together symbolically did not mean that they believed that temperance and sabbatarian support, anti-Catholicism, and opposition to slavery were predispositions equally and strongly held by all of the groups to which they aimed their appeals. It implied, however, their perception of a broad and politically salient attitudinal consonance. And antiparty and antisouthern themes became the least common denominators expressive of that shared psychological rapport.

Over the years between 1854 and 1860, the use of such themes helped to begin the process of developing the anti-Democratic popular front into a political party. They also helped marginally to expand its mass voting base. Developments after 1860 accelerated the rate of movement by some groups away from the Democrats, solidified the anti-Democratic coalition, and transformed it into a *party* opposition.

Secession and Civil War changed the context within which election battles were fought. The with-us-or-against-us moralism that earlier had penetrated the political culture now created a context that was not supportive of oppositional politics. In a morally overheated atmosphere in which proximate events were endowed with ultimate meaning, dissent was transmuted into "treason" and political opponents into "Copperheads."[18] The events of the war, Democratic behaviors, and the aura that the anti-Democrats bestowed upon themselves all reverberated with emotional resonance to give new legitimacy to anti-Democratic voting. They combined as well to solidify the Republicans as a party in the electorate.

A party exists when its officials, activists, and voters consciously identify with a common name and symbols. A party may be said to have developed voting clienteles when as an institution it has become a positive reference group inducing habituated loyalty, and when its symbols have become positive reference symbols providing cues to the political cosmos.[19] "Republican" as a party in the electorate developed more slowly than it did as a band of officeholders or political activists. That development involved three distinct stages that can only be tersely demarcated here.[20] First, in the mid-1850s a broad series of social groups cohered as an anti-Democratic popular front, held together largely by shared negative evaluations of all that the Democratic party represented and symbolized. Second, the wartime efforts by Republican party builders expanded the front's mass base and habituated the groups that comprised it into anti-Democratic voting practices by the use of "Union" and "patriotic" symbols. That entailed as well a conscious avoidance of the Republican label and of references to those socially divisive questions that had structured party oppositions prior to 1854. Third, by 1868 and 1870 Republican party builders began to behave as we typically expect party leaders to behave. They used "Democrat" as a negative reference symbol and "Republican" as its positive counterpart. Such usage implied a perception that a large number of voters had come to identify positively with that symbol and to use it to guide their voting choices.

Whether as a loosely structured popular front or as a fully developed party in the electorate, the Republicans differed from the Whigs in important respects. First, because the Republican party combined the Whig party's mass base with the support that it attracted from large numbers of Yankees who had earlier been Democrats, it was more clearly a Yankee party than Whiggery ever had been. Second, despite its dominant Yankee character and tone, it was also the party of the "Union" and "loyalty," and attracted support among foreign-stock voter groups that had long been anti-Whig. Among some of the Dutch and Norwegian pietists that attraction was reinforced by the fact that the Republicans, as the Whigs did earlier, projected an anti-Catholic aura. Thus, unlike the Whigs, the Republicans were able to unite native and immigrant pietists into a single though often uneasy coalition; and unlike the Whigs, the Republicans were unmistakably a sectional party. That sectional character had the most immediate implications for the subsequent shape of national policy. What underpinned that sectional dominance and made it possible was the coalitional reshuffling set in motion by a religious enthusiasm unleashed on electoral politics.

SYSTEM CHARACTERISTICS

The partisan cleavage of the third electoral era pivoted on twin fault lines of cultural conflict. The first involved a value-and-interest clash between Yankee moralist subculture and white-southern subculture. The second, in the Northern states, entailed a religious value conflict between pietist and antipietist subcultures. That party system, rooted in basic value differences, forged in the morally charged atmosphere of the 1850s, and broadened and reinforced during the war, endured through 1892. Party identifications formed under conditions of emotional and moral intensity were not facilely abandoned.

However, the system's stable phase—from 1876 to 1892—was just that, a stable, and not a static, phase. There were fluctuations and electoral changes, but neither these nor subrealignments in particular states transformed the shape of the electoral universe.

In its equilibrium phase, the third electoral era was marked by a tight partisan balance, relatively low levels of election-to-election fluctuation, and historically high rates of voter mobilization. Table 4.3 provides an overview of these characteristics for the nation and for each of its regions.

The relatively narrow Democratic lead at the national level was built from the party's virtual dominance in the South and its smaller but still secure lead in the Border states. Democratic strength in these areas, which together held 28.4 percent of the nation's 1880 electorate, more than offset the secure Republican leads in New England and the West North Central states, regions whose combined voting population was 21.5 percent of the nation's total. The electorally more important areas of the country, the Midatlantic and East North Central with 45.9 percent of the total electorate, were also the most closely competitive. In these areas the Republican margins were tenuous at best. Moreover, in both of these regions and in New England, the size of the Republican lead declined from the beginning of the stable phase to its end.

As the longitudinal standard deviations indicate, party percentages did not fluctuate widely from one election to the next. The amounts of

Table 4.3 Empirical Characteristics of the 1876-1892 Stable Phase

	$\bar{M}$	Longitudinal σ		Minor Parties	Turnout	
	Lead	Dem.	Repub.	$\bar{M}$ %	$\bar{M}$	σ
United States	3.52D	3.20	4.89	8.4	71.3	7.51
Nonsouth	2.57R	3.83	4.27	8.1	75.5	7.49
New England	10.57R	4.21	2.23	4.9	66.3	6.24
Middle Atlantic	1.81R	6.50	2.62	6.3	77.9	8.78
East North Central	2.42R	2.93	2.04	5.7	79.4	7.39
West North Central	21.00R	6.56	5.55	14.1	73.9	8.40
Confederate	31.36D	3.41	9.42	9.8	56.5	9.10
Border	13.82D	2.47	5.83	6.7	75.1	9.72
West*	6.51R	8.47	3.04	7.8	60.9	6.23

*Mountain and Pacific States

longitudinal volatility were not uniform across regions, or even across parties within the same region. The relatively high standard deviations for the Republicans in the South and for the Democrats in the West reflected their incapacities to develop stable parties in the electorate in those areas. The post-Reconstruction problems of the Republicans in the South have been adequately chronicled. It is sufficient to notice that their frequently employed tactic of abandoning their own party label and fusing with minor parties had the effect of inhibiting the development of the strong psychological bonds between voters and party symbols that typify a stable party in the electorate. Though their position was less dire than that of the Republicans in the South, western Democrats experienced analogous difficulties. And these were complicated somewhat by the fact that, due to continued streams of westward migration, the size and composition of the electorate there were more susceptible to short-term volatility than elsewhere. Yet even in the face of these ostensible anomalies, what stands out is the long-term stability of partisan percentages.

Underlying that stability, however, was a secular trend of some importance. A longitudinal indictaor of that trend is presented in Table 4.3, the mean percentage of the total vote polled by minor parties. The trend was most evident in the West North Central area, the South, and the West. Two of these were regions characterized by virtual one-party dominance. The West was not, of course, but the Republican lead there was only sporadically challenged by the Democrats and actually widened over the course of the stable phase. In other areas where electoral competition was higher, the smaller amounts of minor party voting had greater impact upon the partisan balance than in these three regions.

Minor party voting may generally be viewed as a sign that some voters are dissatisfied with the alternatives offered by the major parties. Demands important to some groups of citizens were not being integrated and aggregated by either of the major parties as then constituted. What those demands were and which citizen groups were concerned with them can be determined only by close analysis of the particular minor parties and of the social composition of their voting clienteles. While that is not feasible here, it is possible to make at least some broad distinctions.[21]

In the South and West North Central areas much of the minor party vote resulted from the failure of "politics as usual" to provide a partisan alternative that could compete viably with the dominant party. Minor party support emerged from long-standing political-structural conditions more so than from social-structural change that induced new tensions. The minor parties that developed under these conditions typically drew their voters from social groups that normally supported the minority major party. They did not cut appreciably into the vote of the dominant party.[22]

Of course, not all minor parties that arose under conditions of one-party dominance were simply surrogates for the weaker of the major parties. When new social tensions were both intensely felt and broadly diffused, minor parties of a wholly different type developed. These were able to cut into the voting coalitions of both major parties. Their crosscutting capacity indicated disaffection even with the majority coalition. Under conditions of single-party dominance, mobilizing the discontented within the hegemonic party was a necessary prerequisite to the dissolution of the prevailing party system. Such characteristics typified the minor parties that emerged in the West and West North Central areas, and to a lesser extent the South, in 1890 and 1892.[23] They were harbingers of an impending critical realignment.

In contexts where competition between the two major parties was strong, minor party voting was an unambiguous sign of the incapacity of either major party to integrate some set of citizen demands. Much of the nonsouthern Greenback vote in 1878 and the support for the variously named Labor parties in 1886 emerged from this incapacity. Socioeconomic tensions, intensified by crisis (i.e. strike) conditions, produced flashes of support for left-oriented minor parties. The citizen demands that underlay that voting support were not (and could not be) integrated and aggregated by the party system as then structured. These demands were essentially class-oriented, and the coalitions of each of the major parties cut across class boundaries. Their coalitions were structured along lines of ethnoreligious polarities and the resulting trans-class coalitions made them inadequate vehicles for the articulation of class exclusive interests.

While sporadically high levels of voting for minor parties of left *tendence* revealed one type of social tension that could not be accommodated by the existing party system, the Prohibition party pointed to another. In most contexts the natural home of supporters of the cold water cause had long been the Republican party. But the Republican party grew pragmatic, and especially so as demographic trends increased the electoral size of those groups to whom prohibition was anathema. To win elections Republican elites gradually turned the party away from its earlier strident moralism and support for the prohibition crusade. At least that was the perception—and it was essentially an accurate one—of the single-minded zealots who fashioned the Prohibition party. It is not necessary here to dwell on the difficulties faced by antiparty moralists when they try to create a political party. Neither is it necessary to recount either the frequency with which their candidates lost elections or the wide margins of their defeats. It is only necessary to draw attention to the fact that Prohibition voting reflected the same types of conditions that prompted support for other minor parties. Their voters perceived that neither major party addressed the concern that they viewed as the most important question of the day, the elimination of the sinful liquor traffic.

But there was a difference. Over the course of the 1870s and 1880s, Prohibitionists behaved ambivalently; they seemed to see their organization as a pressure group as much as a political party.[24] True, it did not operate as we expect a pressure group to function; it did not petition and lobby legislators. Instead it entered electoral politics; it nominated candidates and campaigned for them, though without any realistic expectation of electing them. Yet other actions provide revealing insights. Prohibitionists were often reluctant to nominate candidates in districts if that imperiled the election chances of friendly Republicans. They frequently used the threat of a separate nomination to elicit a public commitment of prohibition support. At other times Prohibitionists were willing to abandon partisan electioneering to concentrate on prohibition referenda. In these and other ways they revealed their commitment to the cause at the expense of the party. Their realistic objective was to pressure one of the major parties—and there was never any doubt that they had the Republicans in mind—to champion the cause of prohibition.

Votes for Prohibitionists, as for Greenbackers, Labor candidates, and Populists, gave evidence that not all citizens were satisfied with the prevailing structure of party oppositions. Social and demographic changes created new tensions, imparted political salience to new issues, and led some groups to perceive that the old party system could not address these new matters that had become of great concern to them. But the size of this disaffected group should not be exaggerated; everywhere, as the levels of minor party voting indicated, it was relatively small, especially when compared with the high levels of mass mobilization that characterized the electoral system. There was no "closet" majority waiting only to be drawn to the polls by a party or candidate who offered the nineteenth century version of "a choice not an echo."

High levels of voter turnout were a hallmark of the third party system (see Table 4.3). These characterized more regions, more states, and higher proportions of the voting population than ever before or since. And not only were turnout rates high, they were increasing, except in the South.[25] Of course, some elections drew higher proportions of the electorate to the polls than others. The regular pattern showed higher turnout in presidential years than in off years. But the magnitude of the turnout drop from presidential to off-year elections was considerably lower than it regularly has been for similar election pairs since 1900.

Strong partisan competition nationally and in the most populous regions of the country, considerable longitudinal stability in partisan percentages, and high rates of electoral mobilization were indicators of an electoral universe in which party identifications mattered to most citizens. It was those partisan attachments, not the candidates' attractiveness or a shifting mix of current events and associated issues, that primarily guided voting behavior and structured election outcomes. As its elite critics lamented, it was an era of intense partisanship, one in which party managers expended their energies to mobilize the faithful. The parades, rallies, and processions, that in the eyes of some observers gave American campaigns the appearance of a "traveling circus," were designed to reactivate and reinforce those standing loyalties and to translate them into voting decisions.[26]

If party loyalties were strong and served as cues to voting behavior, then we should expect to find relatively low rates of defection or cross-party voter movement. We should expect, for example, that the overwhelming majority of those who cast Democratic ballots at one election did so again and again. We should expect to discover, too, that such behavior characterized the supporters of each of the major parties, though not necessarily to the same degree. Conversely, of course, there should have been quite low rates of voter movement between the two major parties.

We can apply regression estimation procedures to county-level voting data to determine to what extent the behavior of voters over the 1876-1892 sequence squared with these expectations. In this instance, the application of regression techniques to ecological data enables us to derive estimates of the transitional probabilities of partisan selection from one election to the next. For example, if we regress Democratic party turnout across some set of counties at one election on the same measure at the previous election, the sum of the resulting intercept and regression coefficient provides a relatively unbiased estimate of the proportion of Democratic voters at the first election who repeated their Democratic choice at the second.[27] And the intercept by itself provides a similar estimate of non-Democrats at the first election who made a Democratic voting choice at the second. The data presented here derive from calculating such estimates across the counties within three regions for each of the pairs of presidential elections over the 1876-1892 period. The separate estimates for each of these pairs have then been summed and divided by the number of election pairs (N=4) to obtain a mean (or average) across the entire time period. To obtain the estimate of cross-party movement, the proportions of Republican-to-Democrat and Democrat-to-Republican party switchers have been added for each election pair; those totals have then been summed across the four election pairs and the means calculated.

The pattern evident from the data in Table 4.4 is what one would expect of a highly partisan electorate.

Table 4.4 Estimates of Partisan Stability, 1876-1892 (in percentages)

	Democratic Repeaters	Party Switchers	Republican Repeaters
NORTH	94.0	5.1	90.9
MIDWEST	93.2	5.4	84.8
SOUTH*	82.8	8.8	85.2

*Border and Confederate States

In both the North and Midwest Democratic voters were more stable partisans over successive election pairs than Republican voters were. And the difference in the Midwest (8.4 percentage points) was of considerable substantive importance given the tight competitive pattern that marked much of that area. The differences in both areas, though not strikingly large, probably reflected the fact that more normal Republicans than Democrats had internalized antiparty norms. Values of that type were especially important to Yankee evangelical pietists who were an important Republican support group. But these differences should not deflect attention from the significant similarity—an overwhelming proportion of voters who cast Democratic or Republican ballots in one election repeated that same partisan selection in the next one. In fact, the proportions of party switchers were typically lower than the proportions of partisans who abstained from voting in a subsequent election.

The South presents only a slightly different picture. The level of Democratic stability was lower and the rate of party switching was slightly higher than elsewhere. And the final two election pairs exhibited signs of the growing pool of nonvoters that soon thereafter would become a distinguishing feature of the electoral universe in that region. Yet even with these caveats in mind, the rates of partisan stability remain impressive.

The equilibrium phase of the third electoral system was a period of intense and stable partisanship. Voters not only turned out for elections at historically high rates, but they regularly were guided in their voting choices by their standing attachments to parties. To the majority of voters, the labels of the major parties were positive reference symbols that guided their voting decisions.

PARTISANSHIP AND SOCIAL STRUCTURE

To say that most voters made their decisions on the basis of their partisan identifications is also to say that election outcomes were structured primarily by those "standing decisions." In other words, partisan identification was the single most important variable underlying the observed distribution of the vote.[28] But that observation does not end the analysis, nor does mere invocation of the term partisan identification constitute a self-evident explanation. Instead, it is necessary to inquire into the social roots of those standing party attachments to understand the causes of party identification.

Who socially were the normal Democrats and the normal Republicans during the stable phase of the third electoral system? What were the systemic implications of that prevailing structure of social-group partisanship? We can begin to respond to these questions by summarizing briefly the pertinent findings of a number of studies of the social bases of mass voting behavior during that period.[29]

The cleavage underlying mass politics in the South and Border areas was quite distinct from that shaping northern party oppositions. The sociopolitical contexts within which party identifications were formed differed materially. The experiences of the war, black enfranchisement, and Reconstruction in some of these states combined to shape citizen orientations to electoral politics, to redevelop both major parties, and to redefine the meanings of partisan attachments. The strong antinorthern and anti-Republican dispositions that underpinned the secession of eleven states and the wartime internal discord within the loyal slave states were given specific referents and were intensified after 1861. While the details varied from place to place, a common consequence resulted. The reconstituted Democratic party came to represent "white man's government"; it was a "white man's party" dedicated by its acts as well as its rhetoric to the preservation of white political dominance. And "Republican" came to be perceived, by most white and blacks, as representative of "black rule." These perceptions largely structured partisan identifications and thus mass voting behavior.

In the states of the former Confederacy mass politics reflected racial polarities of a magnitude that were unknown in the North until the 1960s. More than two-thirds of the blacks who cast Republican ballots, and better than four-fifths of the whites voted for the Democratic party. Republican voting support was confined to black voters and to mountain-county whites.[30] The latter continued to vote as they had in antebellum days, in opposition to their natural enemies, the tidewater aristocrats. Their commitment to Republicanism was not impacted by their antiblack attitudes because the relatively small numbers of blacks in the mountain counties posed no realistic threat of black dominance over local governments.

The more heterogeneous population compositions of the Border states and the smaller relative sizes of their black populations produced partisan coalitions whose specific contents differed from those in the South. But the same types of behavioral influences were at work. The Democrats defended "white government" and mobilized the support of most white voters, while the Republicans depended upon black voters and whichever white voter groups did not perceive blacks as threats to local political control. The absence of that perception, even where the statewide proportion of blacks was comparatively low, was a vital predisposing condition. For example, in Maryland's western counties, where there were few blacks, voter groups behaved much like their social counterparts in New York or Ohio. But in the eastern shore counties, where the black population was heavy, these same voter groups responded with cohesive antiblack and pro-Democratic voting behavior.

The voting patterns exhibited by the northern electorate were more complex. The heterogeneity of its population composition, the geographically asymmetrical distribution of its social groups, and long-term demographic change produced what appeared to be a jumbled mix of patterns, but there was order under that seeming chaos and structure in the central tendencies of social group partisanship.

In the Northern states ethnic and religious conflict structured party oppositions. Partisan cleavage reflected value conflicts rooted in "primordial attachments" derived from a shared social existence, "immediate contiguity and kin connection mainly, but beyond them, the givenness that stems from being born into a particular religious community, speaking a particular language, . . . and following particular social patterns."[31] While there were exceptions and variations, the general shapes of party coalitions followed ethnoreligious lines. Specifically, the Republicans drew majority voting support among these native-stock groups: Baptists, Congregationalists, Episcopalians, Free Will Baptists, Methodists, Presbyterians, and Quakers. And they also attracted the bulk of the ballots cast by black voters irrespective of their religious connections. The immigrant groups comprising the Republican coalition included majorities of British-stock voters, English Canadians, and the less confessional groups of German Lutherans, German Sectarians, Norwegian and Swedish Lutherans. The Democratic party in the electorate enlisted majority support from the highly confessional German Lutheran groups, German Reformed groups, and among all subgroups of Catholic voters except the French Canadians. Southern-stock Baptists, Methodists, and Presbyterians were also heavily Democratic. Two quite different groups, the Disciples of Christ and French Canadians, split their vote about evenly between the two major parties.

Descriptive statements of central tendencies are not designed to account for the behavior of every group member, nor even for the collective voting choice of the group in all contexts and under all conditions. For example, while Missouri Synod German Lutherans generally were strong Democrats, where they perceived that party as the "Catholic party" they displayed a clear pro-Republican voting pattern. While Norwegian Lutherans generally were strongly Republican, their communities settled prior to the mid-1850s showed lingering traces of their former Democratic bias. So it was, too, but in the opposite partisan direction, with the more pietistic German Lutheran groups in New Jersey, New York, and Pennsylvania. In both of these types of cases and some others, older partisan attachments had been crosscut by new political realities in the 1850s and thereafter. Originally, these groups had seen Democratic voting as a means of defending their values against the anti-immigrant impulses of the Whigs. But as the political context changed, and as they increasingly associated the Democratic party with "treason," Catholicism, and demon rum, some group members—perhaps only those newly entering the electorate—swung to the Republicans, the self-styled and widely perceived "party of great moral ideas." Such movement produced an aggregate vote division that was much less Democratic than it had been earlier.

Religious dispositions did not operate in isolation. Ethnic and economic identifications also played roles. Thus, throughout the Midatlantic and Midwestern states Yankee pietists were more cohesively Republican than any other group of that religious temperament. Ethnic and religious identifications in that group overlapped and reinforced each other. In other groups ethnic and religious identifications came into conflict. Native-stock Catholics, for example, were often cross-pressured between their religious outlooks and their anti-immigrant attitudes. They consistently exhibited the lowest rates of Democratic partisanship of any of the Catholic subgroups except the French Canadians. In the Midwest the French Canadians were rather strongly Democratic, but in the East they were electorally divided and even gave the Republicans marginal majorities in some contexts. In places like Massachusetts, French-Canadian group consciousness collided with Irish Catholic aggressiveness. That conflict often led the French Canadians to vote against the Irish party, the Democrats.

For some groups in some locales, partisan proclivities may also have been reinforced by economic identifications. Among some of Boston's Irish, for example, a shared sense of economic deprivation served to reinforce their religiously rooted partisanship. Suffrage laws in Rhode Island that discriminated against the foreign born imbued that state's partisan cleavage with clearer signs of economic polarity than those in any other Eastern state. Within groups economic identifications crosscut ethnic and religious ones and tended at times to produce distinctive rates of subgroup partisanship. In one Illinois sample, for instance, religious ritualists who were businessmen or white-collar workers were more Republican than others who shared that religious disposition but were unskilled laborers or skilled blue-collar workers. The partisan differences between the religious groups remained wider than the differences within the groups, however.[32] Some particular conditions—strike situations and general economic downturns were the most significant—increased the salience of economic identifications. Under such conditions older attachments tended to break down and the aggregate rates of the group's partisanship shifted, at least temporarily.

Explanations of mass politics must take into account the specific contexts, the particular conditions, and the historical experiences of the group. All of these converge to shape group voting behavior. And just as contexts, conditions, and group experiences have varied widely in this society, there is no monolithic uniformity in the ways in which social determinants combined to influence voting decisions. By their nature descriptions of central tendencies must cut across such variations. They derive from examination of group behavior across a variety of contexts and conditions and aim at summarizing the regular patterns of that behavior. In that sense they suffer the weakness of any generalization: there are always exceptions. But the latter acquire analytical meaning in relation to the generalization for which they are the exceptions. Thus, while admitting the great variety of the human experience and the fact that citizen orientations toward politics and parties have always been shaped by multiple reference groups, it is still useful to describe the observed central tendencies of group voting behavior. It is equally useful to analyze the structure of partisanship that emerges from describing those patterns for a large number of discrete social groups.

The structure of social group partisanship that prevailed across the stable phase of the third electoral system was one that arrayed groups of predominantly pietistic religious disposition against those of ritualist or salvationist outlooks. The pietist disposition was active and fervent; it was shaped by the experience of individual regeneration. To the pietist salvation required that change of heart that resulted from being "born again." That transforming experience induced in the saved a "habitual disposition" to behave rightly.[33] And for the pietist right behavior entailed a divinely imposed responsibility to "make holy" his society. This dimension of the pietist disposition had direct behavioral and eventual partisan salience. For those who believed that they had a God-given responsibility for the moral integration of the community would not be reluctant to mind the moral business of others. And as they turned to that task and brought to their activity all of the ardor of the religious enthusiast, they came into conflict with other groups whose dispositions were incompatible with their own.

We can distinguish two categories of antipietist temperament. The ritualist disposition was a nonemotional one; it did not value that "born again" experience that was central to the pietist outlook. To the ritualist salvation resulted from the bestowal of God's grace through the mediation of the church and the sacraments it administered. Visible membership in the church and adherence to its creeds and practices were the route to that grace. Surely, ritualists believed in "good works," but never with the same imperative linkage to salvation that was essential to the pietist outlook.

In some ways the second antipietist disposition resembles the pietist one. Salvationists—e.g., southern Baptists, Methodists, and Presbyterians—certainly practiced emotional faiths; and they gave to the conversion experience the same centrality as pietists.[34] But there was a difference and one that had immense behavioral significance. To the salvationist the assurance of salvation lay in the conversion experience itself, and not (as with pietists) in the "good works" that necessarily ensued. At the moment of conversion man "passed from death unto life." Thus the conversion experience, achieved through God's mercy and not by any act of free will on man's part, was separable from the life that followed. "Born again" salvationists were expected to practice Christian morality and to work and pray for the conversion of others. But there was no connection between these expectations and any divine imperative to transform their culture in the name of Christ.

The ritualist and salvationist dispositions shared several common elements that set them apart from the temperament of pietists. The focus of both was on the salvation of the individual and not the moral integration of the community. Both believed that sin and salvation were personal matters, and not ones inherently of public concern. Each prescribed codes of good moral conduct for their believers but neither sought to enshrine these in public law. Both distinguished religious activities from secular ones and rejected holistic conceptions of the oneness of all human activity.

These contrasting outlooks, or dispositions, produced different orientations toward politics. The twin pietist commitment to the unity of all activity and to the moral integration of the community produced an orientation that saw political action as simply another way of doing the work of the Lord. The command was to sanctify society, and that required that they channel all activity to that objective. These purposive desires and cognitions shaped pietist political culture, that set of "internalized expectations" that defined the political roles of group members and that regularized their patterns of political behavior.[35] When pietists set out to use the political process to create their version of the "holy" society, they helped give shape and partisan bearings to ritualist and salvationist political cultures.

Parties and party activities did not create these antagonistic political cultures. The causal flow was in the opposite direction. Antagonistic relations between (or among) group political cultures generated party oppositions. As pietists turned to political action to sanctify their society, they evoked powerful responses from antipietist groups. Originally, of course, these group conflicts focused on specific matters: a prohibition law, a Sunday-closing ordinance, an antislavery measure, or some attempt to outlaw parochial schools. Since such conflicts involved the shape of public policy, they inevitably spilled into electoral politics. As they did and as the combatants sought to elect to public policymaking positions men who "represented" their dispositions, party coalitions began to take shape. The reasons for the initial party selection were specific to a given situation. As memories faded, and a group membership turned over, the specific reasons became stereotypes, "pictures" in the mind through which group members interpreted their political worlds. In time, through habituated and group anchored partisan response, the party as an institution became a positive reference symbol. This resulting sense of party identification then served as a kind of "self-steering mechanism" that guided and shaped responses to new political stimuli. Through such complex psychological processes group political cultures came to acquire partisan bearings.[36]

The religious revivals of the 1820s and 1830s had begun the process of transforming northern mass opinion. That transformation underlay the realignment of the 1850s. The breakup of the Whig coalition, the contraction of the Democratic mass base, and the rise of a new coalition produced a redefinition of the meaning of partisanship. Among large numbers of native Baptists and Methodists in New England, for example, "Democracy" had long represented their side in the struggle against Congregationalist-Presbyterian dominance. Among Dutch Calvinists and Norwegian Lutherans in the Midwest, voting for Democrats had expressed opposition to the anti-immigrant outlooks of Yankee Whigs; but as large-scale immigration altered social contexts, as group perceptions changed, and as both combined to project new questions into the political arena, increasing numbers of these (and other) groups came to perceive discordance between their "standing decisions" and their group values. That led some to minor party voting and others to withdraw from the participating electorate. The emergence of a new coalition, fashioned at the grass roots by pietist enthusiasts, mobilized these disaffected Democrats, who became allied with the bulk of the old Whig coalition.

Secession, war, and the Democratic party's aura of "treason" diffused negative evaluations of the party even more broadly. That produced increased rates of nonvoting among normal Democrats and swelled the pluralities and proportions polled by their opponents. Support for the "Union" and "loyalty" legitimized and habituated anti-Democratic voting and developed a "Republican" party in the electorate. The depression of 1873-1874 combined with another outburst of temperance zeal to reactivate latent Democratic loyalties, mobilize larger numbers of normal Democrats, increase the size of the Democratic vote, and inaugurate the stable phase of the third electoral era.

The party loyalties forged in the 1850s and 1860s remained largely intact for more than one-third of a century. That they were able to withstand a variety of types of economic and social change over that period testified to the intensity with which they were held. It testified also to the fact that the dispositions that shaped them remained salient to postwar electoral battles.

Pietist-antipietist conflict did not end when Lee surrendered his sword. The 1870s and 1880s witnessed ongoing, virulent, and escalating levels of ethnoreligious tensions. Prohibition and parochial schools became the substantive and symbolic focal points of conflict.

Prohibition crusaders were driven by a zeal that was as inexhaustible as it seemed inextinguishable. They organized secular and church organizations to promote their cause; they lobbied local, state, and federal lawmakers; and they mobilized their supporters for statewide prohibition referenda and for countless local option and license elections. Never were they deterred or demoralized by defeat; for they believed that "right is right . . . [a]nd right the day must win."[37] Driven by religious enthusiasm, they pressed their crusade on all partisan fronts. They organized a separate party; they pressured Republican tacticians and officeholders; and they denounced Democrats. These public and unambiguous postures and acts kept the question alive in people's minds and provided reinforcement of the standing bases of party oppositions.

So, too, did the "school question." This multifaceted struggle was seen by those involved as a do-or-die battle for the minds of the next generation. Whose values would be passed on to the children of immigrants? Would they be "Americanized"—that is, would they become drink-abstaining, sabbath-observing, Catholic-fearing citizens? Or would they continue to be enslaved by "Lutheran formalism or Romish superstition"? If left to be educated in the church-supported parochial schools, if left without the correct Christian education that the public schools alone provided, "the children and grand-children of foreign-born parents are as foreign in their sympathies and loyalty to the churches of their fathers, as their parents were." Pietists saw public education as the great agency through which ultimately "to unify and make homogeneous the society." Their commitment to an ethic of ultimate responsibility entailed rejection of the behavioral implications of cultural pluralism. Thus what was at stake in the "school question," as they perceived it, was the future nature of the society.[38]

Battles over prohibition and the "school question" were not localized and isolated happenings. They raged repeatedly in most Northern states. Continuing conflict of this type reinforced psychological attachments to parties and solidified the social-group structure of partisanship.

That partisan identifications mirrored irreconcilable religious temperaments and were primarily rooted in ethnoreligious conflict had important systemic implications. Several of these need to be made explicit. First, the bases of partisanship help account for the longitudinal stability and high participation that characterized the third party system. To understand why that was so, we need to consider more precisely the concept of party identification.

To speak of a citizen's party identification is to refer to an affective orientation—either positive or negative—to a group object in the environment. Party, however, is a particular type of group. By definition, it is a group whose salience in any electoral situation is high and unidirectional. Moreover, citizens come to be members of this distinctive type of political group through the intermediary of their involvement in other social groups. In that sense, party links ostensibly nonpolitical groups to the political world.[39] However, the strength of its influence is not invariable. Some of the individual's other social group involvements may provide behavioral cues that crosscut the directional guides provided by party identification. The more of these crosscutting influences and the stronger they are, the weaker is the salience of party identification to the electoral decision. Conversely, when the cues that citizens receive from their involvement in nonpolitical groups overlap and reinforce that from their party involvement, then the salience of party identification may be expected to be quite strong.

For most social groups in the late nineteenth century, party identification was a means of asserting and defending the group's cultural values. Each member's sense of being a "Democrat" or a "Republican" was expressive of and anchored in group political culture. That meant that it was reinforced by continuing involvement and interaction with other group members. That type of interaction tended to induce a homogeneity of behavior within the group. Most late nineteenth century Americans were probably involved in an infrastructure of ethnoreligiously exclusive secondary groups.[40] The high levels of residential clustering that typified both urban and rural ethnoreligious groups and the high rates of religiously endogamous marriages suggest daily lives that were distinctly limited in their range of contacts and relations. Churches, church societies, parochial schools, ethnic clubs, and benevolent societies—all of these and more were ethnoreligiously exclusive secondary groups. These types of group involvements reinforced partisan identifications that were rooted in ethnoreligious group values. The cues that many of these groups provided were by no means vague and ambiguous; the churches and church-based organizations especially communicated group norms in direct and unequivocal ways.

A partisanship that was reinforced daily by secondary group involvements was likely to be strong and stable. The relevant empirical indicators demonstrate that it was. If they perceive that the election outcome is in doubt, intense partisans are particularly likely to vote.[41] Strong feelings of partisanship that were widely diffused among the electorate combined with expectations of close elections to produce the high turnout rates that marked the third electoral era.

There was a second systemic implication of some significance. Party not only cued the voting selections of most citizens, it also guided the roll call responses of most legislators. Whether in national or state legislatures, party was the single most important correlate of legislative voting behavior.[42] The levels of conflict between parties and of cohesive voting behavior within each typically were strongest on issues that overtly involved ethnoreligious values, but they were only insignificantly lower on a wide range of other questions—civil service reform, the regulation of private corporations, and tariff rates, for example.

A political party's capacity to shape legislative outcomes and to do so across issue clusters suggests that apparently nonrelated policy questions were in fact tied together in the thinking and voting of partisan legislators. Religious dispositions, which by their very nature addressed life in general, fostered the development of norms pertinent to all aspects of group life. Whether an individual's votes in the legislature resulted from the internalization of those norms, perceived constituency pressures, or the urgings of party caucuses and leaders, the fact remains that policy outputs simultaneously involved the allocation of tangible resources and the predominance of social-group values. In the world of the late nineteenth century, these were not separate but interrelated dimensions of thought and behavior.

The formative role that party played in determining legislative outcomes had another systemic implication. It considerably constricted the room for elite maneuver. Legislators who were bound by party "discipline"—in whichevever way that operated for a particular officeholder—were not wholly free to pick and choose among possible policy alternatives. The party's articulated position imposed constraints that narrowed the range of possibilities. The pressure on legislators to conform to that position was increased by the fact that it evoked "common meanings" among the party's support clientele in the electorate.[43] These strong partisans were not likely to reward betrayal.

Finally, these implications cumulate to another of broader systemic significance. They collectively point to late nineteenth century parties as strongholds of localist resistance to political centralization. The intense feelings of partisanship that marked election battles produced high turnout rates, stable coalitions, and close outcomes. They froze electoral and policy cleavages along ethnoreligious and sectional fault lines. Thus, the parties as constituted could not readily accommodate other types of demands. They could not, for example, integrate intersectional and cross-ethnic class demands. They could not aggregate anticorporate sentiment and shape that into policy outputs. Neither could they aggregate the demands of corporate elites and translate those into policy. Surely, the third party system provided policy that involved positive inducements to corporate growth—in the forms of land grants and favorable tariff rates. Furthermore, the party system's incapacity to aggregate anti-corporate demands and shape those into restrictive outputs created a policy climate in which corporate leaders enjoyed latitude in other areas—establishing wage rates and work conditions and settling strikes. But by the late 1870s modernizing corporate elites demanded more of the political system than inducements to growth and negative safeguards against restriction. They sought the capacity to intervene actively to consolidate and rationalize the corporate system. The prevailing party cleavage, by structuring outputs along other lines, was an impediment to the political centralization necessary to achieve that objective.

Indeed, by the final decades of the nineteenth century, modernizing elites came to see parties as inappropriate channels for aggregating their interests. Parties in their view were premodern institutions whose operation hampered "progress." Parties, as governments, were geographically fragmented, while corporate functions and jurisdictions cut across such arbitrary and artificial boundaries. Parties mobilized social coalitions and thus channeled mass opinion into policy directions; but by doing so, they minimized the impact of the efficiency and expertise that increasingly were becomng the hallmarks of corporate decision making. Besides, corporate elites remained wary of mass mobilization that might be diverted into anticorporate directions. Those elites thus came to view functionally organized and narrowly specialized interest groups as institutions better suited to aggregate their demands. But to increase the influence of such interest groups as shapers of policy, it was first necessary to reduce that of political parties. The assault on party organizations, the efforts to strip them of some of the functions they performed, and the exaltation of "independence of party" into a secular ethic were all aspects of the effort to rationalize and stabilize the public policymaking process by minimizing its susceptibility to organized mass public opinion.[44]

Given the widely diffused political-cultural expectations and positive evaluations of parties that characterized the third electoral era, these assaults on party went largely unheeded by a highly partisan mass public. But accumulating system tensions and the shock of a severe depression converged in the mid-1890s to shatter the prevailing coalitional arrangements and to inaugurate a new party system. And when they did, under these changed political-structural conditions, antiparty elites were well prepared to make sure that the new electoral system was one in which the very roles played by parties and electoral politics in the political system were drastically changed. They were prepared to impose upon the electorate their conception of "progress," a conception that involved the displacement of parties as instruments of mass mobilization and of popular government.

NOTES

1. The self-description and the articulation of the prevailing norm are in Carl Schurz to W. M. Grosvenor, July 16, 1875, in *Speeches, Correspondence and Political Papers of Carl Schurz*, ed. Frederick Bancroft, 6 vols. (New York, 1913), 3: 155-56. For other indications of adherence to the same norm, see ibid, Schurz to Grover Cleveland, December 10, 1884; [Neal Dow], *The Reminiscences of Neal Dow, Recollections of Eighty Years* (Portland, Me., 1898), p. 509; A[lexander] K. McClure, *Old Time Notes of Pennsylvania*, 2 vols. (Philadelphia, 1905), 2: 534-35, 545. For a general overview, see John G. Sproat, *"The Best Men": Liberal Reformers in the Gilded Age* (New York, 1968).

2. S. D. Warner to Nelson P. Wheeler, October 26, 1864, in W[illiam]

Reginald Wheller, *Pine Knots and Bark Peelers: The Story of Five Generations of American Lumbermen* (LaJolla, Calif., 1960), p. 66. For other supporting evidence, see [Dow], *Reminiscences*, p. 126; Edward W. Barber, "The Vermontville Colony: Its Genesis and History, With Personal Sketches of the Colonists," *Michigan Pioneer and Historical Collections* 28 (1900): 236-37; William Rufus Jackson, *Missouri Democracy: A History of the Party and Its Representative Members—Past and Present* 3 vols. (Chicago, 1935), 1: 589; and Clifford H. Moore, "Ohio in National Politics, 1865-1896," *Ohio Archaeological and Historical Publications* 37 (1928): 229-30.

3. The nonsouth in this and subsequent tables, unless otherwise indicated, is the nation minus the eleven states of the Confederacy. The data used here and throughout this chapter were obtained from the Inter-University Consortium for Political and Social Research. The Consortium bears no responsibility for the interpretations.

4. For additional data and detailed discussion and documentation of the voter movements in the 1850s and 1860s, see Paul Kleppner, *The Third Electoral System, 1853-1892: Parties, Voters, and Political Cultures* (Chapel Hill, 1979), chs. 3 and 4. And for a reconstruction of leadership perceptions and activities as these related to voter movements, see Joel H. Silbey, *A Respectable Minority: The Democratic Party in the Civil War Era, 1860-1868* (New York, 1977).

5. While my application of the term is broader than he intended, the quoted term is borrowed from Michael F. Holt, "The Politics of Impatience: The Origins of Know Nothingism," *Journal of American History* 60 (September 1973): 309-31.

6. My reconstruction of the behavioral impact of the revivalism of the 1820s and 1830s draws heavily on John Lockwood Hammond, Jr., "The Revivalist Political Ethos" (Ph.D. dissertation, University of Chicago, 1972), and "Revival Religion and Anti-Slavery Politics," *American Sociological Review* 39 (April 1974): 175-86. For supportive but more general overviews, see Timothy L. Smith, *Revivalism and Social Reform: American Protestantism on the Eve of the Civil War* (New York: Torchbook ed., 1965); and Clifford S. Griffin, *Their Brothers' Keepers: Moral Stewardship in the United States, 1860-1865* (New Brunswick, N.J., 1960).

7. On the disposition of the religious enthusiast, see Ronald Knox, *Enthusiasm: A Chapter in the History of Religion with Special Reference to the XVII and XVIII Centuries* (Oxford, 1950), pp. 17-19. Compare this temperament with that delineated by Max Weber, "Politics as a Vocation," in *From Max Weber: Essays in Sociology*, ed. H. H. Gerth and C. Wright Mills (New York: Galaxy Book ed., 1958), pp. 77-128, and especially with his distinction (pp. 120-21) between an "ethic of ultimate ends" and an "ethic of [political] responsibility."

8. For detailed studies of the realignment of the 1850s, see Ronald P. Formisano, *The Birth of Mass Political Parties: Michigan, 1827-1861* (Princeton, 1971); Michael Fitzgibbon Holt, *Forging a Majority: The Formation of the Republican Party in Pittsburgh, 1848-1860* (New Haven, 1969); Roger D. Petersen, "The Reaction to a Heterogeneous Society: A Behavioral and Quantitative Analysis of Northern Voting Behavior 1845-1870, Pennsylvania a Test Case" (Ph.D. dissertation, University of Pittsburgh, 1970); and Thomas Wesley Kremm,

"The Rise of the Republican Party in Cleveland, 1848-1860" (Ph.D. dissertation, Kent State University, 1974).

9. The Democrats reached only 50.8 percent in the 1852 presidential election. The high point of political antislavery voting was the 12.7 percent of the nonsouthern vote polled by the Free Soilers in 1848. For regression estimates of Free Soil recruitment from the ranks of the major parties, see Kevin Sweeney, "Rum, Romanism, Representation, and Reform: Coalition Politics in Massachusetts, 1847-1853," *Civil War History* 22 (June 1976): 188, Table I; and Hammond, "Revivalist Political Ethos," pp. 153, 156, 178, 180, 182.

10. On the political impact of anti-Southernism, see Formisano, *Birth of Mass Parties*, pp. 205-16; and for the diffusion of that outlook, see Merton L. Dillon, *The Abolitionists: The Growth of a Dissenting Minority* (DeKalb, Ill., 1974), pp. 87-88, 103, 106, 142-43, 199-202.

11. These matters are treated in detail in Kleppner, *Third Electoral System*, ch. 3. And on the growth of anti-Catholic sentiment, see Ray Allen Billington, *The Protestant Crusade, 1800-1860* (Chicago: Quadrangle ed., 1964). And for a detailed study of the Know-Nothings in a single state, see Jean H. Baker, *Ambivalent Americans: The Know-Nothing Party in Maryland* (Baltimore, 1977).

12. Ronald P. Formisano, "To the Editor," *Civil War History* 22 (June 1975): 188.

13. The expression was used by Neal Dow to describe the political impact of prohibition agitation in Maine: see [Dow], *Reminiscences*, p. 440.

14. Samuel J. Eldersveld, *Political Parties: A Behavioral Analysis* (Chicago, 1964), p. 7.

15. For regression estimates of the voter movement in Illinois, Indiana, Michigan, and Ohio, see Ray M. Shortridge, "The Voter Realignment in the Midwest during the 1850's," *American Politics Quarterly* 4 (April 1976): 193-222; and for New York and Ohio, see Hammond, "Revivalist Political Ethos," pp. 200-201.

16. *Boston Daily Advertiser*, November 11, 1844; [Dow], *Reminiscences*, pp. 446-49.

17. For examples of such sentiments, see New Jersey Methodist Episcopal Church, *Minutes of the Eighteenth Session of the New Jersey Annual Conference of the Methodist Episcopal Church, 1854* (Newark, N.J., 1854), pp. 18-19; Maine Baptist Church, *Minutes of the Thirty-Sixth Annual Meeting of the Maine Baptist Convention, 1860* (Portland, Me., 1860), p. 9; and Presbyterian Church, *Minutes of the General Assembly of the Presbyterian Church [New School] in the United States of America, 1852* (New York, 1852), pp. 181-82.

18. On the relation between proximate events and ultimate contexts, see Clifford Geertz, "Religion as a Cultural System," in *Anthropological Approaches to the Study of Religion*, ed. Michael Banton (London, 1966), p. 28.

19. Ronald P. Formisano, "Deferential-Participant Politics: The Early Republic's Political Culture, 1789-1840," *American Political Science Review* 68 (June 1974): 475; Frank J. Sorauf, "Political Parties and Political Analysis," in *The American Party Systems: Stages of Political Development*, ed. William Nisbet Chambers and Walter Dean Burnham, 2d ed. (New York, 1975), pp. 37-38.

20. For the details, see Kleppner, *Third Electoral System*, ch. 3.

21. Walter Dean Burnham, *Critical Elections and the Mainsprings of American Politics* (New York, 1970), pp. 27-31, discusses third parties as protorealignment phenomena. For a detailed discussion of the minor parties that characterized the 1876-1892 period, see Kleppner, *Third Electoral System*, ch. 7.

22. For the southern case in the 1880s, see J. Morgan Kousser, *The Shaping of Southern Politics: Suffrage Restriction and the Establishment of the One-Party South, 1880-1910* (New Haven, 1974), pp. 25-29.

23. James Edward Wright, *The Politics of Populism: Dissent in Colorado* (New Haven, 1974), is the best study available of the coalitional shifts in a Western state. Lawrence Goodwyn, *Democratic Promise: The Populist Movement in America* (New York, 1976), is especially strong on the southern conditions; and Michael Schwartz, *Radical Protest and Social Structure: The Southern Farmers' Alliance and Cotton Tenancy, 1880-1890* (New York, 1976), supplements Goodwyn.

24. Prohibition party activities can be followed in D. Leigh Colvin, *Prohibition in the United States: A History of the Prohibition Party and of the Prohibition Movement* (New York, 1926); and in *The Cyclopaedia of Temperance and Prohibition: A Reference Book of Facts, Statistics, and General Information on all Phases of the Drink Question, the Temperance Movement and the Prohibition Agitation* (New York, 1891).

25. That is, the linear trends were positive. The West was also something of an exception. But since absolute population change was greater and probably less uniform there than elsewhere and since the turnout calculations depend upon intercensus interpolations, the estimates for that region may be statistical artifacts.

26. M. Ostrogorski, *Democracy and the Organization of Political Parties* 2 vols. (Garden City, N.Y.: Anchor Books ed., 1964; originally published in 1902), 2: 165. For an insightful discussion of the role of campaigns and campaigning in the late nineteenth century, see Richard Jensen, "Armies, Admen and Crusaders," *History Teacher* 2 (January 1969): 33-50.

27. Party turnout is calculated, for example, by dividing the vote cast for a Democratic candidate by the total size of the eligible electorate, rather than by the more conventional denominator—the total vote cast. It measures a party's strength as a proportion of the total eligible electorate. The text describes only the bivariate case, and the real world is more complex than that. The estimates presented here were derived from regression equations that took into account the four real options open to voters at any election: Democratic voting, Republican voting, minor party voting, and nonvoting. For the technical details and assumptions of the technique, see Ray Myles Shortridge, "Voting Patterns in the American Midwest, 1840-1872" (Ph.D. dissertation, University of Michigan, 1974); and Laura Irwin Langbein and Allan J. Lichtman, *Ecological Inference*, Sage University Paper Series on Quantitative Applications in the Social Sciences (Beverly Hills and London, 1978).

28. In formal terms, an operationalized measure of the normal vote explains higher proportions of the variance of the vote distribution in a particular election than does any other variable. The normal vote measure used was a mean of the party's percentage in each of the four biennial elections immedi-

ately preceding the one in point. That measure explains a mean of 73.2 percent of the Democratic variance across all nonsouthern counties over the five presidential elections between 1876 and 1892; and it explains 74.2 percent of the Republican variance. For the measure and for a demonstration of its comparable impact in the nation's most highly mobilized state, see Melvyn Hammarberg, *The Indiana Voter: The Historical Dynamics of Party Allegiance During the 1870's* (Chicago, 1977), pp. 142-76.

29. Especially, Richard Jensen, *The Winning of the Midwest: Social and Political Conflict, 1888-96* (Chicago, 1971); Paul Kleppner, *The Cross of Culture: A Social Analysis of Midwestern Politics, 1850-1900* (New York, 1970); Kleppner, *Third Electoral System*; and Frederick C. Luebke, *Immigrants and Politics: The Germans of Nebraska, 1880-1900* (Lincoln, Nebr., 1969).

30. The estimates of group voting support are unweighted means calculated from data in Kousser, *Shaping of Southern Politics*, p. 15. Also see Gordon Bartlett McKinney, "Mountain Republicanism, 1876-1900" (Ph.D. dissertation, Northwestern University, 1971).

31. Clifford Geertz, "The Integrated Revolution," in *Old Societies and New States*, ed. Clifford Geertz (Glencoe, Ill., 1963), p. 109.

32. Jensen, *Winning the Midwest*, pp. 310-11.

33. The phrase is from Charles Grandison Finney, *Sermons on Important Subjects*, 3d ed., (New York, 1836), p. 62. In its general outline, Lenski's distinction between devotionalism and doctrinal orthodoxy parallels the one given here; see Gerhard Lenski, *The Religious Factor: A Sociologist's Inquiry*, rev. ed. (Garden City, N.Y.: Anchor, 1963). And for a superb and compelling analysis that integrates these distinctions into a modernization framework, see Richard Jensen, *Illinois: A History* (New York, 1978).

34. The label is from Samuel S. Hill, Jr., *Southern Churches in Crisis* (New York, 1966), p. 96.

35. Harry Eckstein, "A Perspective on Comparative Politics: Past and Present," in *Comparative Politics: A Reader*, ed. Harry Eckstein and David E. Apter (New York, 1963), p. 26.

36. For the concepts used here, see Walter Lippmann, *Public Opinion* (New York: Free Press, paperback, 1965; originally published in 1922), pp. 59-60; Robert E. Lane, *Political Life: Why and How People Get Involved in Politics* (New York: Free Press, paperback ed., 1965), pp. 299-300; "Secondary Groups, the Political Party, and the Influence Process," in Angus Campbell et al., *The American Voter* (New York, 1960), pp. 327-31.

37. Methodist Episcopal Church, *Minutes of the Eightieth Session of the New England Annual Conference of the Methodist Episcopal Church, 1879* (Boston, 1879), p. 22. The attitude recurred frequently and can be followed in the journals and minutes of the religious conferences and in *Cyclopaedia of Temperance*.

38. Maine Methodist Episcopal Church, *Minutes of the Thirty-Fourth Session of the East Maine Conference of the Methodist Episcopal Church, 1881* (Boston, 1881), pp. 24-25; Massachusetts General Association of Congregational Churches, *Minutes of the Ninetieth Annual Meeting of the General Association of the Congregational Churches of Massachusetts, 1892* (Boston, 1892), pp. 22-26; Na-

tional Council of Congregational Churches, *Minutes of the National Council of the Congregational Churches of the United States of America. Seventh Session, 1889* (Boston, 1889), pp. 44-45; American Baptist Home Mission Society, *Fifty-Fourth Annual Report of the American Baptist Home Mission Society, 1886* (New York, 1886), pp. 29-30. For analyses of the role of cultural conflict in shaping attitudes toward public education, see David B. Tyack, *The One Best System: A History of American Urban Education* (Cambridge, Mass., 1974), pp. 80-88 and 104-9; William A. Bullough, *Cities and Schools in the Gilded Age: The Evolution of an Urban Institution* (Port Washington, New York, 1974), pp. 3-14, 61-78; and Selwyn K. Troen, *The Public and the Schools: Shaping the St. Louis System, 1838-1920* (Columbia, Mo., 1975), pp. 31-78.

39. Campbell et al., *The American Voter*, pp. 327-31.

40. For evidence bearing on these observations, see Stanley Lieberson, *Ethnic Patterns in American Cities*, (New York, 1963); Josef J. Barton, *Peasants and Strangers: Italians, Rumanians, and Slovaks in an American City, 1890-1950* (Cambridge, Mass., 1975); Dean R. Esslinger, *Immigrants and the City: Ethnicity and Mobility in a Nineteenth-Century Midwestern Community*, (Port Washington, N.Y., 1975); Harold J. Abramson, "Inter-Ethnic Marriages among Catholic Americans and Changes in Religious Behavior," *Sociological Analysis* 32 (Spring 1971): 31-44; Lowry Nelson, "Intermarriage among Nationality Groups in a Rural Area of Minnesota," *American Journal of Sociology*, 48 (March 1943): 585-92; Jay Dolan, *The Immigrant Church: New York's Irish and German Catholics, 1815-1865* (Baltimore, 1975); and Silvano Tomasi, *Piety and Power: The Role of Italian Parishes in the New York Metropolitan Area* (New York, 1975).

41. Campbell et al., *The American Voter*, pp. 99-100.

42. Walter Dean Burnham, "Insulation and Responsiveness in Congressional Elections," *Political Science Quarterly* 90 (Fall 1975): 427; Jerome M. Clubb and Sandra Traugott, "Partisan Cleavage and Cohesion in the House of Representatives, 1861-1974," *Journal of Interidisciplinary History* 8 (Winter 1977): 375-402; William G. Shade et al., "Partisanship in the United States Senate: 1869-1901," *Journal of Interdisciplinary History* 4 (Autumn 1973): 185-205; and Ballard C. Campbell, Jr., "Political Parties, Cultural Groups and Contested Issues: Voting in the Illinois, Iowa and Wisconsin House of Representatives, 1886-1895" (Ph.D. dissertation, University of Wisconsin, 1970). For a brilliant analysis of the interrelations among party, cultural conflict, and policymaking in antebellum America, see William Gerald Shade, *Banks or No Banks: The Money Issue in Western Politics, 1832-1865* (Detroit, 1972).

43. Murray Edelman, *The Symbolic Uses of Politics* (Urbana, Ill., 1964), p. 188.

44. Paul Kleppner, "From Ethnoreligious Conflict to 'Social Harmony': Coalitional and Party Transformations in the 1890s," in *Emerging Coalitions in American Politics*, ed. Seymour Martin Lipset (San Francisco, 1978), pp. 41-60; and for an analogous argument, see Burnham, *Critical Elections*, pp. 71-90.

Walter Dean Burnham

THE SYSTEM OF 1896: AN ANALYSIS 5

The analysis of whole "party systems" necessarily presents the writer with many possible strategic choices. The emergence of an historic "party system" is in itself an enormously complicated sequence of events. So much more complex, then, must be an evaluation of the causes of these epochal transformations, or critical realignments, to say nothing of the problems of choice attendant on mapping the subsequent evolutionary dynamics of a "party system" across an entire generation. Thus, it is easy to understand why so much of the "new electoral history" of the past decade has been intensely monographic in orientation, or why so much of the literature has been preoccupied with establishing clear-cut temporal and spatial boundaries for realignments and the "party systems" lying chronologically between them.

Microscopic analysis is a highly justifiable activity in its own right, and has provided invaluable evidence about the nature of nineteenth century voters and the foundations of electoral stability and change. However, the danger always exists that preoccupation with the technical issues of microanalysis can lead to intellectual myopia. If one looks hard enough at a critical realignment at the level of the mass electorate, it can seem to disappear into a cloud of complex fragments. For example, the Democratic party was much stronger in northeastern congressional and state elections in the 1920s than it was at the presidential level. Similarly, 1928 was a "critical election" in areas with massive Catholic immigrant populations, but was not in cities like Akron or Duluth, or states like California or Michigan.[1] Work of this kind is very necessary, but it is also important that in the process of doing it we not lose sight of the forest for the trees.

What can we say about this "system of 1896"?

(1) It *was* a system, i.e., change occurred across a substantial number of arenas of politics, and conduced, broadly, to the same ends. Some of these changes occurred in mass voting behavior, both during the 1890s and later. Many others unfolded subsequently in policy and the characteristic behavior of institutions and the elites who ran them.

(2) This system was complex, both in its key components at any given time and in their evolution across time. It did not appear full-blown in 1896. That critical election represented the first confrontation (William Jennings Bryan's "The First Battle") among organized political forces over industrial capitalism. It was not the last, and in certain respects may not even have been the most important; but it opened the way for what followed during the long generation of the "system's" existence.

(3) The *cumulative* effects of electoral, institutional and rules-of-game changes from 1896 onwards were to entrench and intensify the system's leading characteristics in all parts of the country. By the mid-1920s, this fourth party system had acquired so many apparently conclusive stabilities in its workings that few if any knowledgeable observers assumed that it could be displaced by something else in the immediately foreseeable future.[2] Only a traumatic force such as that of the Great Depression could have dislodged it, and only leadership of the order provided by Franklin D. Roosevelt could have produced a relatively stable successor. And then not entirely: for the southern subsystem survived the New Deal intact—with fateful consequences for national policymaking in and after the 1940s.

(4) The system of 1896 can analytically be broken down into two longitudinal subunits separated midway between the realignment peaks of 1894–1896 and 1932–1934 by a period of electoral upheaval which fell—probably barely in this case—below the threshold of critical realignment. During this period of upheaval (1910–1916) much of the "second wave" of change in rules of the game and institutional behavior occurred, out of which grew the characteristic forms of party organization and of policy processes in Congress associated with modern American politics. These changes are often lumped together under the catchall phrase, "Progressive era reforms." Their cumulative practical effect, whatever the rhetoric may have been, was to paralyze or dismantle older forms of partisan linkage and to reinforce the protections which the organization of the electoral mass market provided to industrial-capitalist elites. It follows that the 1920s were not an era of "normalcy" in any sense: the second half of the fourth party system was significantly different from the first. They were linked together primarily by a national Republican ascendancy in

electoral politics and an equally pervasive national corporate ascendancy in the political economy.

THE ETIOLOGY OF THE SYSTEM OF 1896

Critical realignments owe their origin to certain primordial characteristics of the American polity. They are explosive, semi-revolutionary episodes which have occurred at remarkably regular intervals. The regularity of their occurrence and the relative ease with which American political history can be analytically periodized suggest the existence of some profoundly enduring set of relationships between civil society and the political economy on one hand and the network of governmental institutions and political elite behavior on the other. What are these relationships?

Certain aspects of the analytic problem were well-defined by Lee Benson twenty years ago.[3] The United States stands out as peculiar among advanced industrial societies in that the people have had high levels of personal aspirations; there has been overwhelming consensus over the nature of the political economy (i.e., the liberal-capitalist "tradition" explored by Louis Hartz and others); the state form has been one of decentralization (federalism and separation of powers), and there has been overwhelming consensus in favor of that too. In such a context a wide variety of factors (demographics, group relationships, and ethnoreligious and other cleavages) work to determine voting behavior. These factors display remarkable persistence over time. Thus, as Benson observes, "All American history is reflected in present and past voting behavior."[4]

But this is only part of the story. In a continental-sized country with a capitalist-individualist political culture protecting the dominant mode of production, the evolution of the political structure has involved a continuous process of power fragmentation. The United States has undergone a series of "democratic revolutions" against elites who came under broad political attack. Out of these attacks grew not only the classic nineteenth century party system, but also a democratized presidency (which in turn produced what Theodore Lowi has described as a *real* separation of powers at the federal level), and a wide proliferation of elective offices at the state level. Consider the Progressive era agitation over the place of the Senate in the political system. Had the Senate remained as it was, with Senators chosen by state legislatures, it might in the longer run have undergone a decline in relative influence in the legislative process—as has happened to most second chambers in the West since the onset of democratization. But the Seventeenth Amendment (1913) placed this unapportioned (and unapportionable) body on the same basis of democratic legitimacy enjoyed by the House. That guaranteed the Senate's enduring importance in national politics and solidified the complex fragmentation which dominates the legislative process.

Even in the America described by Hartz, Richard Hofstadter, and Benson, some mechanisms of coordination of institutions, behavior, and processes are required for minimally effective governmental performance. Not even in a laissez-faire utopia can pure fragmentation exist, since it denies to the state the essential capacity to perform its primordial functions. Party in the United States—particularly during the nineteenth century—was an integument which permitted both penetration and mobilization of non-elites by those who controlled the political/state apparatus at the "center." It acted as a constraining channel, not only simplifying the otherwise riotously pluralistic choices of the long ballot but providing for power accumulation across the formal chasms created by federalism and separation of powers.[5] V. O. Key, Jr., put the matter precisely when he observed that party is the solvent of federalism.[6] If the political culture and political systems of the late nineteenth century were anything at all, they were partisan—intensely, deeply, and structurally partisan.

It is probably well not to make too much of this partisan integument, or to sentimentalize the workings of American electoral and linkage politics in the late nineteenth century. The representative capacity and responsiveness of the major parties have been systematically limited by a number of interconnected realities. The first of these is the "liberal tradition" itself. This tradition not only corresponded to high levels of individuals' personal aspirations, but also was uniquely suited to be the least common denominator in a "nation of strangers" and extremely diverse subcultures. It was the lingua franca of politics, perhaps most purely represented by Daniel J. Elazar's "individualist political subculture," in which political organization and activity are undertaken for entrepreneurial gain and politics is assimilated to the norms of getting ahead in business.

The second constraining reality was the heterogeneity of the mass building blocks with which party entrepreneurs had to work. The larger the elective scale, the greater this heterogeneity was. Managing coalitions in such a way as to win elections was the raison d'être of politicians: as Mr. Dooley and others observed at the turn of the century, politics was a professional sport like playing ball or wheeling a truck. The best way for a party elite to do its basic job—getting itself or its candidates elected to office—was to reactivate traditional appeals to straddle emergent issues and demands for as long as possible and to concentrate on giving material and solidary incentives and benefits to the existing party subcoalitions and their leaders. This meant that there was every incentive for upholding the status quo and for restimulating traditional emotive appeals among major party elites. By the same token, there was no clear incentive for adapting programs and campaigns to new issues or for incorporating new dissenting groups into the already complex game of coalition-management. As Theodore Lowi observed, the majority party in a given area would have the least incentive of all to innovate, and for essentially the same reasons.[7] This organizational factor alone goes far toward explaining the tendency of American politics to be inert and non-developmental in the face of explosive and largely unconstrained changes in the political economy and society; hence the etiology of critical realignment can be traced.

The third reality of politics in the late nineteenth century was the intensity of the forces which worked to "freeze" electoral alignments under conditions of near total mobilization of the nonsouthern electorate. By the 1880s, this "freeezing" had created, along with demographic shifts documented by Paul Kleppner and others, a national party system where competition was balanced on a knife-edge.[8] Almost literally, handfuls of votes in key states (New York and Indiana alone were normally decisive) determined the winner of every presidential election from 1876 through 1888. Of the eighteen years from 1875 to 1893, Republicans controlled the Senate and the White House for fourteen years and the House for four. During the twenty-two years from 1875 to 1897, a single party controlled all three of these institutions at the same time for only six years (Republicans: 1881-1883, 1889-1891; Democrats: 1893-1895). The truth was that during the second half of the Civil War system, there was no majority party; or rather, there were two majority parties, depending on where the focus of analysis lay. Such a condition was optimal for producing policy deadlocks at the center. It also tended to constrain party elites to concentrate on managing existing coalitions so that they could eke out exiguous majorities.

Moreover, the traumas and stresses which froze these alignments were of a magnitude and intensity not seen again until the Great Depression and the New Deal, if then. The Civil War produced scars which took at least a century to heal. There was no town in the North without its memorial to the Union dead; no town in the South without its Confederate counterpart. An entire regional labor system and the culture of privilege that it supported were annihilated. The American polity in this era had its closest approximation to a revolution—in Barrington Moore's phrase, "the last capitalist revolution."[9] The revolution had to be financed, and it was—through greenbacks and a new form of taxation, the personal income tax. The inflation caused by the Civil War created a novel problem for a nascent industrial-capitalist empire, and it was "solved" by thirty-years of deflation, which recurrently convulsed electoral politics through 1896.

To the trauma of Civil War and Reconstruction must be added the intense ethnocultural conflict which permeated electoral coalitions. Conflicts over "right belief" and "right behavior" were of vital importance in shaping and then "fixing" major party electoral coalitions. This was an age in which far-reaching changes in the economy and society were for the most part evaluated not in terms of economic analysis or sociological categories, but in religious—or at least moralistic—terms. The influx of immigrants had produced nativist reactions in politics as early as the 1830s. Restoration of the ancient truths of American political and social culture was repeatedly sought by hard-pressed native-stock whites as a "solution" to this disruptive change. This influx overlay earlier cleavages between population groups supporting "positive" and "negative" liberalism in politics. Throughout the nineteenth century there were bitter, protracted local battles over the schools, the use of non-English languages outside the home, Prohibition, Sunday blue laws, and other points of acute conflict. They reinforced, and were reinforced by, the epic struggle over slavery and the Union.

The underlying transformation between the Civil War and the turn of the century was the creation of an integrated industrial-capitalist political economy. From its imperatives flowed the rapid influx of immigrants, urbanization and its manifold problems of social policy, and the regional differentiation of the country into a "Metropole" and a series of primary-sector internal "colonies" outside its borders. This tale has been too often and too well told to require documentation here. By the 1890s, this "Metropole" had even acquired a semiofficial boundary. Within an area extending from Minneapolis southward along the Mississippi past St. Louis (which was included) to the Ohio, thence along that river to West Virginia (including on its "colonial" bank the Louisville area), thence through the southern boundary of West Virginia and eastward across Virginia to Norfolk (the terminus of the coal-carrying Norfolk & Western railroad), the railroads had perfected a preferential rate scheme for hauling freight. Within the "scheduled territory," goods were shipped at between one-half and two-thirds as much per mile as they were outside of it, with vital long-term effects on the location of industry. By 1900 the territory northeast of the southern border contained 50.4 percent of the total population; but 79.5 percent of manufacturing employment, 81.2 percent of the national value-added by manufacturing, 62.1 percent of total personal income, 75.6 percent of all college and university endowment funds, and 71.2 percent of all bound volumes in college and university libraries. This large region's population was 56.8 percent urban by 1900, compared with 22.2 percent for the colonial regions outside. Put another way, the Metropole in 1900 contained 72.2 percent of the nation's urban population, but only 36.1 percent of its rural population. And economic modernization had stimulated a concentration of high income in the industrial states: by 1900, per capita personal income was $288 in the Middle Atlantic states, compared with $104 in the South Atlantic division and $100 in the East South Central states.

This "Metropole" was not only the industrial, financial, and educational heartland of the United States. Its agricultural sector—dairying, for example, or the corn-hog complex which fed into meatpacking for sale to the burgeoning populations of the cities—tended to weather the economic storms of the late nineteenth century relatively well, because of the markets for its products and because the relatively early settlement of the region implied a much more favorable financial balance for its farmers.

Confronting the Metropole were two or perhaps three "colonial" regions. Common to these were severe undercapitalization problems and heavy reliance on commodities which had to be sold according to the vagaries of international markets. The western "colonies" were broadly classifiable as involved in two primary-sector activities. In the Great Plains a debt-ridden cash crop agriculture developed in climatically marginal lands, with enormous oscillations in the prices received by farmers for their wheat, corn, and other crops. It was well said of Nebraska in the 1890s that it raised two crops: corn and mortgages. Further west, the primary-sector activities included a large and politically significant extractive element: mining, especially of silver, in the Mountain states and logging as well as mining in the Pacific Northwest.

The other major "colony" was the South, the classic underdeveloped region of the country. Devastated and impoverished by war, the South was overwhelmingly agricultural and was marked—and for long into the twentieth century—by extreme poverty at the mass base, both black and white, by the tiny size of the middle class, and by the presence of a hegemonic, even smaller, ruling class. To this mixture of "underdevelopment" was added the central problem of the South: the presence of a large black population which was in the numerical majority throughout the cotton belt from Virginia to Texas and formed an absolute majority of the population in Louisiana, Mississippi, and South Carolina in 1890.

From the end of the Civil War to the Gold Standard Act of 1900, the consistent fiscal policy of national political elites regardless of party was one of currency deflation.[10] The first stage of this process involved the retirement of the Greenbacks which had helped finance the war and the resumption of specie payments (or full convertibility) as of January 1, 1879. Coupled with the effects of the depression which began in 1873, this deflation produced a series of political explosions—most notably, the Greenbackers' uprising which peaked in 1878. In this movement we see for the first time—almost in embryo—the basic strategy of those who were suffering from the ascendancy of industrial capitalism: *the welding together of a farmer-labor coalition* devoted to a *political* overthrow of the "immutable economic laws" of laissez-faire capitalism. This thread was to link together the Greenback party with the Populists of the 1890s, the Socialists, a wing of the Bull Moose Progressives in 1912, La Follette's Progressive insurgency of 1924 and, finally, the successful consummation of this strategy in the New Deal of the 1930s. One could even extend the conflict far back into the American past, to the battles between Jacksonians and Whigs, Jefferson and Hamilton, and—so Charles Beard would have it—to the initial conflicts between federalists and antifederalists in 1787. In doing so, one need not assume that Lee Benson's theses about American voting behavior in and after the nineteenth century are wrong. In fact, they reflect the dominant reality of political alignments in normal times and in times of noneconomic crisis. But the struggle perceived by Beard, Vernon L. Parrington, and others—always latent as an axis of cleavage—comes clearly to the surface when the performance of the economy produces massive dislocations and suffering among the electorate.

So it was with the Greenback movement of 1878. There are two aspects of this movement's peak strength which are of particular interest in discussing the background for the construction of the system of 1896. The first of these is its geographical distribution. As Table 5.1 makes clear, there were significant territorial differences between the protest surges of 1878 and 1894.

In the first place, the South—still in the throes of immediate post-Reconstruction experience—was sterile ground for Greenbacker protest except in Texas and Arkansas. Apart from this, however, the striking thing about the 1878 vote is that it is much more widely dispersed sectionally than was the peak Populist vote of 1894. Greenbackism got almost nowhere in the states and territories of the Plains and Mountain areas. But it did conspicuously well in states within or bordering the Metropole—such as Iowa, Michigan, and Maine—where Populism was very weak half a generation later. Moreover, Greenback candidates made a much more significant dent into the electorates of urban and mining constituencies within the Metropole than Populism

Table 5.1 The Geographical Base of Political Dissent: Greenback (1878) and Populist (1894) Strength (in percentages)

Region	Total Vote		National Vote Cast in Region			
	Greenback 1878	*Populist 1894*	*Greenback 1878*	*Populist 1894*	*Total 1878*	*Total 1894*
New England	21.5	2.2	15.9	1.3	8.9	6.8
Middle Atlantic	10.6	2.0	21.4	3.7	24.2	21.8
Northeast	13.5	2.1	37.3	5.0	33.1	28.6
East North Central	12.2	6.5	28.2	13.9	27.8	25.4
Metropole	12.9	4.2	65.5	18.9	60.9	54.0
West North Central	11.2	26.0	7.1	24.8	7.7	11.4
Mountain	3.2	28.7	0.3	7.3	1.2	3.0
Pacific	22.2	23.0	5.3	7.3	2.9	3.8
Western States	13.0	25.8	12.8	39.4	11.8	18.2
Border	11.5	6.6	9.6	5.9	10.0	10.8
South	8.3	25.0	12.0	35.8	17.4	17.0
United States	12.0	11.9	100.0*	100.0*	100.0*	100.0*

*Sum of Metropole, Western States, Border, and South

was subsequently able to achieve (except in a few places like Chicago and Canton, Ohio, the home of Jacob Coxey).

The second leading fact about this upheaval of 1878 is that it was temporary. Save in a few states where the insurgents fused successfully with the minority party (usually but not always with Democrats) and a few others where the fires of protest kept burning throughout the 1880s, the movement simply evaporated. The old voting alignments essentially snapped back into place within two years of the peak. As early as 1880, the Greenback presidential candidate, James B. Weaver—who was also the Populist candidate in 1892—won a mere 3.3 percent of the vote.

That American third parties of the "movement" type have a "flash-in-the-pan" character is an obvious fact of our history. They arise only under conditions of quite exceptional crisis and conflict, and disappear with breathtaking speed as the crisis abates or is resolved. The Greenback movement not only disappeared, but also left few short-run traces on either electoral coalitions or public policy. A major reason for this is to be found in the generational and regional dynamics of American electoral alignment. In the first place, the full agenda of Civil War and Reconstruction issues remained unresolved until the repeal of most Reconstruction legislation by the Democrats in 1894. This is also true at the microlevel where ongoing and largely ethnoculturally fueled battles between "positive" and "negative" liberals continued and gradually escalated in intensity during the 1880s. The complex transformations affecting the whole of American society brought pain, loss, and anxiety in their wake. By no means all of these were, or were felt to be, directly economic in character. The 1880s, the 1920s, and 1960s all have this element in common: as the holding strength of the original alignment decays, and intense, complex pressures for change play over the society, communal tensions among Americans come to the surface. It is in such times, more than any others, that politics comes to be dominated by ethnocultural conflicts. In the period under review, it would be accurate to say that the resurgence of these "luxury" or "prosperity" issues—for such they are in the modern industrial state—worked both to reinforce the "freezing" of major party alignments and to promote the marginal success of the Democratic party nationally.

Finally, the generational impact must be cited. Greenbackism arose in response to serious economic dislocation, but only halfway through the long-term electoral cycle. For a very substantial proportion of the electorate—about two-fifths in 1878—the events of the Civil War were still living memories. Reconstruction had only ended the previous year. By the mid-1890s, on the other hand, about four-fifths of the electorate was made up of men who had come of age after the last great political realignment, and well over one-half were under voting age at the end of Reconstruction. In the meantime, (i.e., 1874-1892) the gross national product had risen from $23.4 billion (1958 dollars) to $61.2 billion; the industrial production index had risen from 13.9 to 38.8; and the population had climbed from 44 million to 66 million. The regional/spatial definition of the national political economy was now well on its way to completion.

The general economic crisis of the mid-1890s was preceded by a worsening of the farmer's lot. This appears to have had partly climatological origins in the Great Plains after 1885. But in much of the rest of the cash crop agrarian world—notably in the South—the persistent deflationary deterioration in the farmer's terms of trade had finally reached the level where a political flash point was ignited. The realignment sequence began, in 1890, with the raising of the Populist banner at Ocala, Florida, and continued with the Populist Omaha platform and campaigns of 1892, when its presidential candidate James B. Weaver won twenty-two electoral votes in the Plains and Mountain states.

To this point in the sequence, traditional major party alignments remained virtually unaffected outside the peripheral areas of primary agrarian distress and silver mining interest. The old Civil War alignment and the complex political games employed to sustain it continued to predominate in most of the country. In the years since the late 1880s, evidently fueled by the surfacing of pietistic "cultural issues" among a number of Midwestern state Republican parties (Ohio, Wisconsin, Illinois, Iowa) and by the long-term demographics of immigration, the Democrats appeared to be moving into ascendancy and the long post-1874 political deadlock seemed to be coming to an end.[11] The national leaderships of both political parties were hostile to the demands being made by the Populist-agrarian rebels of the periphery. These latter were still isolated, their support confined to the areas hardest hit by economic pressure and most interested in maximizing silver production. But they were the vanguard of a much larger potential clientele among farmers and others in the "colonies" who still remained loyal to their traditional party indentifications.

Critical realignments in American political history have occurred only under quite special conditions affecting the polity or the economy. Put at its simplest, they have occurred only when enough time has passed so that for the vast majority of voters the "heroic age" of the preceding major cleavage has receded into the historic past. Then, a sudden sharp blow can "ignite" a volatilized electoral mixture.[12] What is involved in such complex events is a drastic and sudden realignment followed by a durable substitution of a new cleavage for the old. This entails a redefinition of the "power bloc" at the center of politics, the agenda and chief actors of public policy formation, and a reorientation of primary symbolic codes which sustain and reinforce mass political allegiances and expectations.

The sudden, sharp blow of the 1890s was the catastrophic collapse of the economy in and after the spring of 1893. A detailed exploration of the events which produced the "critical election" of 1896 cannot be attempted in the confines of this essay; a few observations must suffice. First, it is interesting and significant that national "gold bug" Democratic leadership was much more inflexibly committed to conservative, monometallic finance than were their Republican rivals. As it was under Benjamin Harrison that the Sherman Silver Purchase Act of 1890 was adopted as a palliative, so Grover Cleveland expended a very large part of his political capital in securing its repeal in 1893. Moreover, Cleveland's temperament—rigid and dogmatically Calvinist—contributed, in the classic style of "repudiated presidents" from James Buchanan to Lyndon Johnson, to the intensification of the crisis within the Democratic party which resulted in Bryan's nomination and the subsequent fusion with the Populists. The Republicans, on the other hand, continued throughout to advocate a supposedly "moderate" position: currency inflation (i.e., bimetallism), but by international agreement only—an agreement that the party's elites had excellent reason to suppose could never be obtained since Great Britain had been on the gold standard since 1816.

The Democratic party was thus to labor under two exceptional stresses which were to thrust it decisively into a minority position for the next thirty-five years. The first was that there was an acute dialectical strain between its "Bourbon" leadership and its rank-and-file supporters over these now overwhelming issues. The party's mass base was intrinsically much more susceptible to inflationist, anticorporate, and egalitarian-democratic appeals than was the mass base of its Republican opponents. The votes in the two conventions of 1896 sensitively reflected this reality (Table 5.2).

By the time of the Democratic convention in 1896, the Northeastern party elites—who had been in control of the party nationally during the previous party era—were isolated and defeated. In the Republican case, however, the only substantial isolates were among the Far Western state parties; the regional elites of this area had not been at the center of power within the party. With less than 10 percent of the convention vote, their defection produced only minor tremors within the GOP as a whole. The disruption of the Democratic party was incomparably greater; it produced enduring effects at the elite level. Its

Table 5.2 Votes on Financial Planks: 1896 Democratic and Republican Conventions

Region	Dem. Substitute Minority Plank			Rep. Table Minority Plank		
	N	*Yea* (in percentages)	*Nay*	*N*	*Yea* (in percentages)	*Nay*
Northeast plus Maryland	256	96.1	3.9	256	100.0	0
East North Central	176	13.6	86.4	176	98.9	1.1
Metropole	432	62.5	37.5	432	99.5	0.5
West North Central	93	20.4	79.6	94	93.6	6.4
Mountain and Pacific	84	3.6	96.4	84	26.2	73.8
West	177	12.4	87.6	178	61.8	38.2
Border	84	0	100.0	83	92.8	7.2
South	224	1.3	98.7	224	85.0	15.0
Periphery	485	5.2	94.8	485	77.8	22.2
Total	917	32.2	67.8	917	88.1	11.9

Richard C. Bain and Judith Parris, *Convention Decisions and Voting Records*, 2nd ed. (Washington, D.C.: Brookings Institution, 1973), unpaginated appendix of convention roll-calls.

cosmopolitan elites gone, the national leadership of the party fell into the hands of parochial leaders of the South and West. In the Northeast a power vacuum was created which tended to be filled over time with "urban parochials" centered on immigrants and their political machines. The ground was thus paved far in advance not only for the fortuitous rise and startling collapse of the Wilson administration, but for the "politics of provincialism" which dominated the party in the 1920s and led to the fiasco of the 1924 convention.[13]

The second major stress, which interacted throughout the fourth party system with the first, stemmed from the fact that the Democrats had controlled all branches of the federal government when the economic roof caved in in 1893-1894. Surveys and other evidence of mass attitudes in the 1940s and early 1950s have demonstrated the staying power of this association of a major party with economic hard times in the minds of the mass electorate. It was not until after Dwight D. Eisenhower had been elected and had served a term that the association of Republicanism with hard times faded away.[14] As the Democrats after 1932 ran again and again against Herbert Hoover, so the Republicans after 1896 had the double pleasure of running against both Cleveland's administration and the new parochialism which Bryan represented. After 1918, this was reinforced (so far as platform denunciations of Democratic "incompetence" in running the political affairs of a modern industrial state were concerned) by the collapse of Wilson's administration into inchoate fragments.

It may be profitable to ask what strategies were potentially available to the counter-elites who led the forces of protest against industrial-capitalist laissez-faire and what strategies their "cosmopolitan," pro-capitalist opponents had at their disposal during and after this crucial decade of the 1890s. This in turn requires an assessment of what proved to be organizable in American political coalitions at that time and what was not. Clearly the optimal strategy for Populist insurgents was to fashion a farmer-labor coalition, a coalition of those who were most severely affected by the emergence and operation of concentrated corporate power. Intellectuals like Henry Demarest Lloyd and Clarence Darrow saw that this would require the development of a comprehensive critique of this concentrated and democratically irresponsible power structure, a critique which would incorporate but go far beyond the demands of any given sectoral group. The basic struggle between fusionists and stay-outers among Populists in 1896 turned over such issues. Yet it is easy to demonstrate that even in 1894—at the height of the depression—Populist electoral support had proportionately vastly smaller working-class and Metropole-area support than the Greenbackers of 1878 had had or the La Follette candidacy of 1924 was to have.

Despite the voluminous literature on this subject, it remains less than wholly clear why this was so . That the effort was made to produce such a comprehensive critique and to secure broad support among both urban and rural victims of "development" is clear both from the contemporary work of Lloyd and from Lawrence Goodwyn's recent study.[15] That it failed in its purpose was evident from the electoral data as early as 1894; this failure was conclusively confirmed in 1896.

The coup de grace was given by the fusion of the Populists with the "reorganized" Democratic party in that year, and the extreme narrowing and "sectionalization" of the protest agenda which this fusion entailed. This point was not lost on contemporaries. As McKinley's campaign manager Mark Hanna perceptively noted of Bryan's campaign as early as midsummer, "He's talking silver all the time, and that's where we've got him." This was obviously true tactically as the election returns showed. Not only did workers not move into the Bryanite coalition, significant minorities of them throughout the Metropole defected to the Republicans. Despite the pathos evoked by subsequent pro-Populist historians, this movement cannot be understood as just the result of uninhibited employer pressure on their workers. For while the Democrats were to make significant local recoveries during the subsequent electoral history of the 1896-1932 era, the urban defection at the presidential level persisted in some cities until 1928 and in others until 1932 or later. A more extensive discussion of these and related issues occurs below. It is enough to say here that while electoral behavior became vastly more volatile on all dimensions after 1896 than it had been before, this volatility pivoted around a decisive Republican ascendancy within the active electorate.

Similar considerations may apply to the argument that currency inflation through the coinage of free silver was a "colonial," regionalist, and sectoral issue which could not appeal effectively to working-class and lower-middle-class voters attached to the mushrooming industrial economy. From the perspective of the urban voter *committed to the network of urban-industrial social and economic relationships that now existed,* currency inflation could only be regarded as irrelevant at best and disruptive at worst. It is patent that the Democratic campaign of 1896 could not effectively rebut this charge.

It is worth remembering that inflationist appeals had made a notable penetration into the urban-industrial electorate in the late 1870s, and that Henry George had moved his own protest movement, despite its apparent radicalism, very close to success in the New York City mayoral election of 1886. Moreover, currency inflation disappeared as a leading national political issue immediately after 1896, and was not to be on the elite agenda seriously until the Great Depression of the 1930s. Yet the reorganization of mass electoral forces which abruptly surfaced in the 1894-1896 period very largely defined the American electoral universe for the next generation.

The deeper answers to the question of why it was that the 1896 election was followed by a "system" must be located in the analysis of what kinds of cleavages were *organizable* in the American political context during the first third of the twentieth century. Perhaps the most important single characteristic of American politics in the age of industrialization is that it was a mobilized democratic-participatory system before, during, and to some extent after the transition occurred. In all other political systems of any consequence, industrializing elites have been insulated from opposition arising from below. Industrialization adds immensely to national power, and may also promote the long-term betterment of the material conditions of the mass of the population. But this is bought at a price: for it not only involves a new system of economic exchanges, it involves the creation of structures of power and, indeed, conquest. This in turn requires the economic and cultural subordination of the mass of the population and the redefinition of the terms of their social and cultural existence. Bitter resistances to the brutalities of this process quite naturally develop. Everywhere else in the world, the elites responsible for "modernization" could rely either upon traditional autocratic or oligarchic political defenses against mass uprisings (e.g., the *régime censitaire*) as in Communist and many third-world countries, upon the dictatorship of the single party, the army, and the secret police.

But in the United States there was no clean-cut way by which the threat of mass political movements directed against the "cosmopolitan elite" could be *legitimately* repressed and the elites insulated from the demands of the subaltern classes. Democracy was already in place, and indeed reached its maximum levels of mass mobilization in the period just before and during the convulsion of the 1890s. This vulnerability goes far to explain the mood of panic among the "comfortable classes" which was so striking a feature of the political climate in the 1890s.[16] In 1913, Justice Oliver Wendell Holmes alluded to this mood, and to the decisive political consequences which that panic produced among judicial power-holders: "When twenty years ago a vague terror went over the earth and the word socialism began to be heard, I thought and still think that fear was translated into doctrines that had no proper place in the Consitution or the common law."[17] This was by no means the last occasion on which elite panics produced such results. These panics surface in periods of transitional stress because basic to the American condition is a lack of defined social space linked to an essentially uncontested hegemony in the ideological sphere.[18]

Nor was this panic entirely ill founded. For the great debate of the 1890s was much more fundamental and far-reaching in its implications for the future of the social and economic order than any debate resulting from subsequent crises, the New Deal not excepted.[19] The Populists came very close to a comprehensive critique of the emergent industrial-capitalist order and to a program for displacement, if not overthrow, of the power bloc and its public policies. The danger this represented to the established order was most extreme in the South, because the underdeveloped social structure left its elites much more exposed to a devastating attack at the polls than in any other region of the country.

As the challenge was extreme, so elite response was extreme. It ranged from intimidation to wholesale electoral fraud and even to minor coups d'etat such as that which Josephus Daniels and others were to engineer in the Wilmington race riot of 1898. As this event indicates, the chief trump which both the old Bourbon leaders and the new generation of southern Progressives played in this period was the racist card. There were many ways to play this card. Race conflict was utilized to break up the Republican-Populist coalition in North Carolina in 1898, and blacks were marched en masse to the polls in Alabama to defeat the Populist challenge in 1892-1894, and then to vote overwhelmingly for their own disfranchisement in 1901. Throughout the ex-Confederate states, the specter of a dangerous and overwhelmingly numerous mass electorate was exorcised by the disfranchisements of 1890-1908 and the replacement of a meaningless general election by a personalized direct primary alternative for the remaining white voters.[20]

What eventually turned out to be politically organizable in this southern context? An electoral regime based on racial and economic disfranchisement, on the destruction of interparty competition, and on the replacement of this partisan competition by the personalized choices offered by the white Democratic primary to the survivors of the electoral purge carried out by the 1890-1908 "counterrevolution." This electoral regime proved exceptionally stable once it was created. It lasted some seventy years—a very long time in politics. This stability reflected the realities of social power in the region, concentrated in a tiny educated elite of planters, businessmen, and county-seat lawyers and sustained by the pervasiveness of racism and anti-Yankeeism in the region's political culture.

But it is probably best for analytic purposes to treat the South not as a deviant case, but as an extreme example of more general tendencies in the America of the 1890s and after. Racism was by no means confined to the South, and by no means were blacks its only targets. The same elite fears of overthrow from below were widespread in the North: a perusal of remarks by members of the majority at the New York Constitutional Convention of 1894 repays reading. These fears were very similar to those expressed by the Convention's president, Joseph H. Choate, in his argument before the Supreme Court the same year on the iniquities of the 1894 income tax.[21] They were, however, more specific: Emma Goldman and her lower-East-Side Socialists formed the perfect class-racial negative reference group for the Convention's native-stock majority as they set out deliberately to malapportion the state legislature to keep it out of the hands of New York City.

Yet a substantial majority of those voting on these constitutional changes (to be sure, only 41 percent of the potential electorate) voted in favor of them. Moreover, 55.5 percent of New York City's voters approved them, insignificantly different from the 55.7 percent approval of upstate New York. This, no less than the national result of the 1896 election and the "maintaining" elections which followed, suggests a point of cardinal importance to the understanding of organizable politics in this period. Simply put, *the quest by class-conscious elites for insulation from the potential dangers of a mass electorate was essentially supported by a majority of that same mass electorate.*

In the specific political and socioeconomic context of the 1890s, the overwhelmingly "organizable" component of mass electoral politics turned on a broad popular acceptance—even at the height of the crisis—of the industrial-corporate path to economic development. This acceptance was to broaden still more as prosperity returned. To be sure, the consensus was never complete, as the rise of socialism in the years before World War I demonstrated. Moreover, severe intra-elite conflict over redefinition of the consensus erupted on several occasions, most notably in the Bull Moose uprising within the Republican party in 1912. Nevertheless the consensus was overwhelming, and it was associated from beginning to end with the Republican party as the one organized electoral force which was the political agent of the new industrial-capitalist dispensation.

Closely associated with this dominant consensus and the post-1896 "political settlement" which naturally flowed from it, was the impact of what has broadly been labeled as "sectionalism" on the politics of this period. This sectionalism involved the virtual destruction of the Republicans as an organized political force in the ex-Confederate states and a parallel and almost as complete a destruction of the Democrats throughout large areas of the North and West. It intensified across the entire period through 1930. Its effects will be analyzed more fully below, but two points may be noted here about this sectional polarization. First, it reflected the great diversity of regional political subcultures and of regional economies in an era of extreme regional division of labor. Second, its emergence marked a decisive shift from the cellular "island-community" political medley of nineteenth century electoral politics toward the beginnings of genuine nationalization of American electoral politics.

At the same time, ethnocultural and racial cleavages continued to play crucial roles in American politics. Racism was of obvious and fundamental importance in the politics of the Southern states before, during, and for long after the system of 1896. Moreover, it is clear that racist doctrines reached the height of acceptability among "scientific" academic elites, political and business leaders, and the white Anglo-Saxon component of the mass electorate in this period between the depressions of the 1890s and the 1930s. These doctrines not only paved the way for Republican abandonment of the blacks and the "Southern question" in the 1890s, but were actively used for economic, social, and political discrimination against immigrant whites in the North. They performed an important fixative function for mass electoral alignments, particularly within the Metropole. Even there, the history of the system of 1896 is one of progressive nationalization of conflicts along these lines, peaking in the 1920s with the spread of the Ku Klux Klan to states like Indiana and Oregon, the head-on clash between urban-cockney and Bible Belt delegates in the 1924 Democratic convention, and the Al Smith electoral upheaval of 1928 in the Metropole's polyglot cities. This partial nationalization of ethnocultural conflict accompanied the transition to a mass consumption economy and the liquidation of the older "island communities."[22]

THE ANATOMY OF THE SYSTEM OF 1896: RULES CHANGES

The period 1896-1932 is primarily marked by an ideological hegemony which moves over time from being only ineffectively and sectorally contested to one which is not seriously contested at all. Several implications arise from this striking—and, from a comparative point of view, unique—political fact. One of these is that politically effective or mobilizable class consciousness existed only within a very limited upper-and upper-middle-class sector. This became increasingly evident as time went on and the socialism of the first years of the century was eliminated (partly by force) during and just after World War I. As both major parties were significantly controlled by elites who shared this class consciousness—especially during the second half of the "system's" lifetime—certain implications for mass involvement in the political system unfolded. We shall return to these below. A second major implication of relatively uncontested hegemony is to be found in another domain of consciousness. As Louis Hartz has insisted, the absence of organizable opposition to the foundations of the state and the political economy produces a situation in which issues and the conflicts centering on them can and do recede below the level of explicit consciousness. It also implies critically important ambiguities. Chief among these (except, partially, in the South) is the ambiguous tension between industrial capitalism and electoral democracy, one which can never be "cleanly" resolved in favor of either.

The Progressive impulse, concentrated in the years 1905-1915, strikingly reflects the accuracy of both components in Hartz's argument. Taken as a whole, this movement is a remarkable mixture of contradictory elements: a striving for mass democracy on one hand and corporatist-technocratic elitism on the other. The exponents of each element, though for different reasons, shared a strong desire to overthrow the hold of the traditional party organizations over electoral decisions. Purifying the electoral process and bringing it into line with the emergent corporate ideal as extended to political life were important values which were to be realized in legislation changing the rules of the political game. Out of all these pressures for "reform," i.e., bringing the political system into line with the dominant political and economic realities, came the following changes in the rules of the game:

(1) *The direct primary*. Initiated in Mississippi in 1903 and Wisconsin in 1904, the direct primary became an essential substitute for the general election in areas where no effective party competition had survived realignment or disfranchisement. Evoking as it did democratic-participatory symbolisms which remained essential ingredients of the political culture, the direct primary spread to most states before the end of World War I. Its appeal was hard to resist, even in states where party competition had survived. As V. O. Key, Jr. has shown, it had a variety of deleterious long-term effects on the integrity of party structure and almost certainly worked to reinforce one-partyism.[23] The primary was a new kind of democratic instrument, replacing the durable collective structures of party with ad hoc personal electoral choice. The elite-insulating implications of this change are especially conspicuous and documented in the South—again, an extreme but not a unique case.[24]

(2) *Initiative, referendum, recall*. About these "direct democracy" innovations, little will be said except to note that their enactment

issued from the same kinds of dissatisfactions with the workings of traditional representative structures which fueled the introduction of the direct primary.

(3) *Direct election of U.S. Senators*. This was a procedurally oriented reform which was undertaken with the hope (and resisted by the fear) that removing the choice of U.S. Senators from the state legislatures and placing it in the hands of the people would eliminate massive corruption arising from the play of party organization or the concentrated power of money on a legislative body, and would also make the Senate a more representative body. This change appears to have had very limited effects, though perhaps more than woman suffrage produced. It consolidated the legitimacy of this nonapportioned second chamber, and ensured its status as the most important second chamber to be found in any Western legislature. It therefore bypassed (without any organized debate on the subject) the possibility of reducing the power of this nonpopularly elected (and unapportioned) second chamber in the political process, as was done in Britain with the House of Lords during this period.

(4) *Personal registration laws*. In the overwhelming majority of cases, these laws were initially enacted to apply to the populations of large cities, and to them alone. They reflected the absence of any system of keeping track of potential voters in anonymous urban environments and a hostility to urban machines as sources of corruption of the political process. It seems reasonable to suspect that one motivation of the lawmakers was to reduce as much as possible the impact of urban immigrants on statewide elections. One remarkable feature of such laws must be noted. They reflect an "individualist" legislative solution to the problem of identifying eligible voters rather than a state bureaucracy-oriented solution.

Everywhere else in the West (including neighboring Canada), it was early accepted that it was the state's task to compile and update electoral registers. This presupposed the existence of a bureaucracy for administering such enrollment laws or a consensus that such a bureaucracy should be created. Conversely, in the United States it was a traditional, unquestioned practice to require that an individual assume the burden of demonstrating his legal qualifications to vote. In the South, of course, this—along with a network of devices such as poll taxes, literacy tests, and the like—served a specific purpose: by giving electoral officials maximum discretion in determining the qualified voters, it kept undesirables (especially blacks) away from the polls. But the universal character of such laws, no less than the nearly complete absence for many decades of any academic or other analysis of their effects on different classes of potential voters, suggests their compatibility with the "inarticulate major premises" of American political culture as a whole.

Perhaps the classic case in this respect is Massachusetts, where since the turn of the century the police have compiled lists of residents pursuant to another state law and where compilations of "legal voters" have been conducted. It would be very simple to convert these lists into something approximating the Canadian electoral roll, compiled by the chief electoral officer and his assistants, but nothing of the sort has ever been done: standard personal registration is required for voting. Moreover, only within the past decade or so has serious professional analysis of these laws and their impact been undertaken.[25] Altogether, the history of registration requirements in America is a peculiarly good example of the effects of uncontested hegemony and its concomitant lack of organizable political alternatives on the shaping of the American political process.

(5) *Anitpartisan legislation*. A chief feature of Progressive era activity was the effort to rationalize politics and bring it into harmony with procedural electoral democracy and with the imperatives of the "corporate ideal" in the management of complex social entities. As Samuel Hays has persuasively demonstrated, this process of adaptation was carried to its conclusion most fully in reshaping the structures of city governments.[26] The urban reformers' ideal appears to have included the elimination of party, a shift in representational base from the ward level to at-large elections, and the establishment and insulation from popular control of expert-dominated islands of decision making. The remarkable career of Robert Moses provides an excellent, concrete example of this.[27] The ultimate purpose of these changes that eliminated partisan "corruption" and "parochialism" was to pave the way for urban statesmanship by adopting the corporate model as the ideal for urban government. In reshaping city governments, the corporatist-elitist aspect of Progressivism is perhaps most decisive. Recasting the structures of democracy so as to break the hold of the plebeians and the party organizations associated with them is most clearly on the reformers' agenda.

Basic to the corporate ideal is the replacement of politics by administration and of lateral conflicts and bargaining among equals by technocratic (and implicitly hierarchical) modes of conflict adjustment. The elimination, where possible, of the "political" was a key component of the system of 1896. Until very recently, it achieved its most complete success in that era. But antipartisan legislation was also fueled, particularly in the "colonial" areas of the country, by radical-democratic rebellion against traditional party organizations. C. B. Macpherson has described a very similar process at work in Alberta: in "the colonies," economically dominated by a remote but apparently all-powerful Metropole, *both* major parties take on the character of local agents for an alien imperialism.[28] Much of the work of people like Robert La Follette in Wisconsin, Hiram Johnson in California, and the organizers of the Nonpartisan League and other such western colonial protest movements is better understood in Macpherson's terms than in terms of a quest for assimilation to the corporate model of political life. For that matter, socialism at its peak in 1912 contained significant western colonial protest components.[29] The cumulative effect of these two currents—the urban reform and western protest movements— on the vitality and integrity of existing party organization was devastating.

What were the total effects of these rules changes on electoral behavior? First, they worked to "cure the ills of democracy by more democracy" through an unevenly distributed but profound destruction of party organization. One of many consequences of this was the emergence of unprecedented heterogeneity of nominally partisan outcomes at different levels of election within the same jurisdiction. This was to give electoral politics, especially in the "era of normalcy," its strikingly volatile, complex, and heteroclite character. Second, these changes contributed to the growing exclusion of the lower classes from participation in the active electorate: by 1926, less than 31 percent of the national potential electorate voted for members of Congress. Finally, by the 1920s, it had appeared that the elites' continuing "search for order"[30] had been successfully concluded: by then, the insulation of "modernizing elites" had apparently been perfected. The rules changes discussed here made their contribution to that end. It is important to recall that they were not merely imposed by class-conscious elites: they were accepted by the active electorate at large. Most of them remain with us still, mute testimony to the power of uncontested hegemony to define in advance the stuff of which organizable politics can be made.

THE ANATOMY OF THE SYSTEM OF 1896: STATIONARY COMPONENTS

Much or most realignment theory is based on the argument that American electoral politics are intrinsically nonevolutionary or nondevelopmental in character. Electoral alignments tend in such a context to move rather abruptly, in response to the political effects of the collusion between this static tendency in the political superstructure and rapid, untrammeled evolution of the socioeconomic base. Cyclical change processes reflect this underlying historical tendency toward stasis in political representation and electoral alignments.

But if there are large cycles, why should there not also be lesser ones? These would arise from the same generic (or systemic) causes, but would lack for various reasons (chiefly, it is suspected, chronological and generational) the explosive system-transforming permanence of full-blown critical realignments. As one explores the range of voting, elite turnover, and other data of American electoral politics across time, the evidence for such "subcritical realignment" episodes seems to become rather strong. Surely there was a "mini-realignment" episode from 1873 to 1880, coinciding with the severe economic dislocations of the 1870s and peaking in the Greenback party's remarkable showing in the congressional elections of 1878. Similarly, the period 1910-1916 was one of notable upheaval in the history of the system of 1896, accompanied by the Progressive-Standpat rupture within the Republican party and the rise of the Socialist movement to temporary significance as a third (or fourth) party phenomenon. In a variety of important ways, a "mini-realignment" occurred within the New Deal system between about 1948 and 1952, particularly but not exclusively in the Southern states. Common to all these episodes is that they appeared halfway between the chronological beginning and end of the larger "party system" within which they occurred; that they constituted major temporary or locally concentrated upheavals; that they were associated with marginal but rather durable reorganizations of electoral coalitions; but also that they did not lead to a replacement of the system as a whole.

What we suggest here is that each historical "party system" may be subdivided into two parts, "maintaining" and "decaying" phases. The specific identity and behavioral characteristics of these phases must be clarified on empirical grounds if they are to be deemed to exist at all. And, at every step, the pure cyclical-stationary component is likely to be contaminated by the effects of long-term or secular trends. At no period in our history, at least down to the very recent past, was this contamination more extensive than during the system of 1896, particularly so far as the effects of rules-of-the-game changes and the decline in electoral participation are concerned.

Moreover, a very large part of critical realignment theory has been worked out by using presidential election data only. It does not take very much work on the data for other offices—and conspicuously in gubernatorial contests during the "normalcy" era—to conclude that this provides a seriously misleading picture of twentieth century American electoral politics.[31] For such data will reveal that the Democratic party was significantly weaker as an electoral force at the presidential level than at most others. This concentration on presidential elections has been criticized for giving a misleading picture of the total situation. This criticism has force, and must be explicitly addressed. In doing so, we shall also shed some light on the two "stable" phases of the system of 1896, the original "maintaining" phase extending from about 1896 to about 1908, and the "normalcy" phase extending from 1918 to 1930 or 1931.

It is very clear that the velocity of electoral movement after 1900 was far greater at the presidential level than elsewhere. This implies that the Democratic party (or, perhaps one should say, Democratic candidates) fared much better overall during the system of 1896 than Democratic presidential candidates did. Conversely, Republican candidates performed much more successfully in the aggregate after 1932 than did the Republican presidential candidates opposing Franklin Roosevelt or Harry Truman. What happened electorally after 1900 was that a diversity of coalitions opened up at different levels of elections which would have been unimaginable during the nineteenth century. This, of course, was of the essence of the system of 1896. We may even attempt to pinpoint the beginning of this "new" ticket-splitting with the election of two Democratic governors, William L. Douglas of Massachusetts and John A. Johnson of Minnesota in 1904, in the teeth of the first modern presidential landslide for Republican President Theodore Roosevelt.

There are many ways by which this problem can be explored. For the sake of brevity, analysis is confined at this point to two data files. The first (Table 5.3) is based on the state level popular vote for president, governor, and U.S. congressmen. The second (Table 5.4) is a similar analysis based on the partisan composition of the lower house of each state legislature. Tables 5.3 and 5.4 are divided into four chronological periods: 1874-1892 (the second half of the Civil War alignment); 1894-1910 and 1914-1930 (approximately corresponding to the two halves of the system of 1896); and 1934-1950 (the first half of the New Deal alignment era). Each state is classified by its central-tendency partisan lead in each era, with these derived from the median percentage for each party and each office. The percentages in the body of Table 5.3 are of the total regional number of representatives elected to Congress in 1890, 1910-1911, 1920, and 1940; a measure chosen as a politically useful approximation of the relative population size of each state.

Thus, states with 7.0 percent of all nonsouthern representatives in 1890 had an average Republican lead in the presidential popular vote of 20 percent or more in the period 1874-1892, while by the period 1914-1930 this percentage had risen to 57.7 percent. Arguably, a lead of

Table 5.3 Nonsouthern and Southern States Stratified by Party Lead and Major Office, 1874-1950* (in percentages)

PARTISAN	LEAD	1874-1892 Pres.	1874-1892 Gov.	1874-1892 H.R.	1894-1910 Pres.	1894-1910 Gov.	1894-1910 H.R.	1914-1930 Pres.	1914-1930 Gov.	1914-1930 H.R.	1934-1950 Pres.	1934-1950 Gov.	1934-1950 H.R.
Nonsouthern States													
30+	R	0.8	0.8	0.8	2.1	0.7	4.4	22.4	6.9	28.4	0	0.3	0.9
20-29	R	6.2	2.0	5.3	31.4	2.0	13.9	35.3	9.7	5.4	0	5.5	4.2
10-19	R	12.4	8.1	9.8	35.0	31.2	38.0	26.6	28.1	27.5	3.3	14.2	9.1
0-9	R	41.7	48.0	45.9	18.4	50.2	31.2	13.3	21.5	25.7	7.9	38.5	42.7
0-9	D	28.1	37.0	25.6	12.7	15.3	10.2	2.4	29.6	10.3	60.0	38.2	27.0
10-19	D	10.7	4.1	12.6	0.4	0.7	2.4	0	4.2	2.4	25.2	2.7	12.4
20-29	D	0	0	0	0	0	0	0	0	0	3.6	0	0.6
30+	D	0	0	0	0	0	0	0	0	0.3	0	0.6	3.0
Southern States													
30+	R	0	0	0	0	0	0	0	0	0	0	0	0
20-29	R	0	0	0	0	0	0	0	0	0	0	0	0
10-19	R	0	0	0	0	0	0	0	0	0	0	0	0
0-9	R	0	0	0	0	0	0	0	0	0	0	0	0
0-9	D	24.7	12.9	10.6	20.4	10.2	0	9.6	0	0	0	0	0
10-19	D	17.6	23.5	25.9	10.2	10.2	20.4	9.6	19.2	9.6	0	0	0
20-29	D	16.5	5.9	0	7.1	10.2	0	20.2	0	9.6	9.5	0	0
30+	D	41.2	57.6	63.5	62.2	69.4	79.6	60.6	80.8	80.8	90.5	100.0	100.0

Source: Congressional Quarterly's Guide to U.S. Elections, Washington, D.C., 1975.

*Percentages are of the total number of representatives in each region following the censuses of 1880, 1900, 1910 and 1940.

more than 20 percent in the popular vote for either party reflects a noncompetitive situation: it would translate under roughly normal distribution conditions into an ascendancy of nearly five to one in legislative seats and other outcomes. Similarly, a lead of less than 10 percent for either party may be considered as closely competitive.

The Southern states in this array are in their usual class by themselves. There is a long-term tendency toward ever more extreme one-party conditions, with the two middle chronological periods also lying between the less extreme conditions of the late nineteenth century and the solidified one-partyism of the New Deal era. During the system of 1896, considerable two-party competition survived in parts of the southern region, notably in North Carolina and Tennessee. Throughout, presidential elections show considerably less Democratic hegemony than do the races for governor and the U.S. House of Representatives. Without question, not only the widespread regional disfranchisements but also the substitution of the direct (Democratic) primary for a meaningful general election after 1903 contributed heavily to the long-term erosion of Republicanism below the presidential level.

The nonsouthern states present a contrasting picture. The first point of departure is that there is a remarkable symmetry in the distribution for the three offices during the 1874-1892 period. To only a limited extent does this reflect the existence of the party-created ballot.[32] For, then as later, gubernatorial elections only occasionally coincided with presidential elections. Indeed, in some cases, they fell in odd-numbered years and thus coincided neither with presidential nor congressional elections at any time during this period. Rather, this symmetry of distributions reflects—even at so aggregate a level—the underlying density, stability, and tenacity of party attachments within the electorate.

The pattern changes dramatically during both phases of the system of 1896. The presidential—and to a lesser but notable extent, the congressional—distribution is massively displaced toward the noncompetitive-Republican end, while the gubernatorial distribution is affected to a much smaller extent. Indeed, there is a noteworthy resurgence of Democratic support at the gubernatorial level during the second phase of this partisan era (1914-1930). This reflects not only the local semi-realignment associated with Al Smith's rise to power in New York (1918-1928), but frequent victories for Democratic gubernatorial candidates in populous states like Ohio and New Jersey. Similarly, in the first phase (1894-1910), Democratic gubernatorial victories were common in states like Minnesota, Oregon, and North Dakota—all rock-solid bastions of Republican strength at all other levels of election in this period. Finally, in the New Deal era, Republicans did much better in gubernatorial than in presidential contests. Indeed, were we to concentrate on aggregate gubernatorial distributions alone, we would be hard put to find any convincing evidence of national critical realignment after 1932!

The implications of this analysis are clear. First, the nineteenth century symmetry breaks up during the system of 1896 and is not restored after the rise of the New Deal. Thus, to take the 1894-1910 period, only 31.1 percent of the congressmen came from states with competitive presidential outcomes, and 41.4 percent came from states with aggregate competitive congressional outcomes. But fully 65.5 percent came from states with competitive gubernatorial outcomes. While the competitive dimension is restored in the 1934-1950 period, the distributions retain considerably more asymmetry than in the late nineteenth century, though also somewhat more than in either phase of the system of 1896. Second, it seems fair to say that the Democratic party was stronger in its parts than as a whole (or as a national coalition). Conversely, after 1932, the Republican party was considerably stronger in its parts than it was in presidential election competition.

But it would be unfortunate if all these diverse trees should cause us to lose sight of the forest. A fundamental characteristic of the system of 1896 was the fragmentation of politics which unfolded during it. This fragmentation took many forms, from the detailed statutory regulation of political parties, the institution of the direct primary, and, at the local level, nonpartisan elections as cures for the "ills of democracy," to the mushrooming of split-ticket voting, the dismantling of the Speaker's powers over the business of the House of Representatives, and the ascendancy of the Supreme Court over legislation affecting corporate capitalism.

Viewed at the macro level, it can be observed that corporate hegemony over polity, society, and economy did not depend on large, stable, and uniform *partisan* majorities either in the electorate or in terms of officials elected. Business primarily wants to be let alone by government, since if it is let alone, it will win most or all of what it wants to win. Large, stable, and uniform *partisan* majorities are needed by those whose political objectives include basic changes in the existing order. The laissez-faire which business sought and largely achieved during the system of 1896 was politically anchored in Republican control of the presidency throughout all but eight of these thirty-six years—and with this went control over appointments to the Supreme Court.

Republican control of Congress was much less completely secure during the system of 1896 than Democratic control was to be after 1932. During the thirty-eight years from 1894 to 1932, Republicans had clear majority control of both houses only 63.2 percent of the time, while Democrats enjoyed clear majorities in both houses in the four years

1913-1917 (10.5 percent of the time). Moreover, Republican control of the Senate was considerably less solid after World War I than it had been during the first phase of the system of 1896, with a mean absolute majority of 18.5 seats in the 1894-1908 period and of only 8.0 seats in the 1918-1930 period. Without doubt, this change reflected the same sort of fragmentation effects already mentioned in our discussion of gubernatorial outcomes.

This insecure Republican control over the legislative process might have constituted a problem for a party which had a unified, comprehensive, and permanent set of objectives requiring public sector action for their realization. Except during the initial years after 1897, when the agendas of the new majority coalition were developed by legislation (and overall Republican control of the political branches of the federal government was most secure), the dominant Republican party did not have any such set of objectives. Fragmentation, policy drift, and the dominance of the political process over economic issues by the negative veto of the Supreme Court were compatible, in the most fundamental sense, with the whole point of the system of 1896.

Thus, even at the most aggregate level, the data of the post-1896 period indicate that a contemporary kind of electorate had come into being. Very shortly after 1900—clearly, Theodore Roosevelt's presidency and his unprecedented landslide victory of 1904 represent the turning point—the presidency assumed the *independently* visible, "charismatic," and "focusing" role in the national political process with which we are familiar today. The tensions between Bryan and his conservative, largely eastern opponents within the Democratic party prior to World War I were paralleled even more dramatically after it by the collapse of the Wilson administration into fragmented ruins and the epic collision of 1924 between the party's cockney and Bible Belt factions. Similarly, after 1932 Franklin Roosevelt was much stronger than his party throughout much of the North and the West. Indeed, it was not until after World War II that the "mature" New Deal coalition fully developed at other elective levels, particularly in areas like the upper Midwest.[33]

The obvious growth of personalism in voting coalitions at the presidential level during the system of 1896 was paralleled by personalist elements in gubernatorial elections. If the presidential level favored Republicans, the gubernatorial often favored Democrats. How strong —and confined to particular candidates—this personalism was can be sensed in examining the career of Governor John A. Johnson of Minnesota before World War I and of Governor Vic Donahey of Ohio after it. While Johnson's median share of the vote in his three contests (1904-1908) was 52.2 percent, the comparable Democratic showings in the same period were far less: for President, 26.0 percent; for Congress, 25.7 percent; while Democrats won only 11.8 percent of the seats in the lower house of the state legislature, suggesting a Democratic vote share of about 34 percent. The case was similar with Donahey's four races in Ohio (1920-1926). While he won a median share of 50.5 percent, the Democratic presidential value was 31.2 percent, and 42.4 percent in the congressional races. The median Democratic share of the lower house of the state legislature was only 17.7 percent suggesting a Democratic share of the vote cast of about 37.5 percent. Overall, Johnson had to run more than 25 percentage points ahead of his party in order to win, while Donahey ran 8 percent ahead of Democratic congressional candidates, probably about 13 percent ahead of the party's state legislative candidates, and 19 percent ahead of the party's presidential candidates. There is something which is very modern indeed about all this, as there is about the drastically shrunken turnout rates in these contests compared with those of the nineteenth century.

When all is said and done, however, it cannot be forgotten that the system of 1896 was preeminently characterized by the growth of massive one-partyism in crucial areas of the North and West. The state legislative data is particularly useful here, since these are genuinely grass roots elections with very low visibility and no personalist-charismatic overtones. They, if anything, should cast light on the aggregate state of competition before, during, and after the system of 1896. Because of a number of factors relating to the nature of the data here—percentages of seats won in the lower houses of the state legislatures rather than of votes cast—simple dichotomizations have been used here.[34] The assumption is that a median lead of 40 percent or more for either party (a 70-30 or more extreme two-party imbalance) is indicative of one-party hegemony at the grass roots level.[35] While other measures could be used, depending on the purposes of the investigation, our aim here is simply to identify places where no generally effective competition between the two parties exists at the grass roots, as aggregated to the level of the state legislature. Tables 5.4 and 5.5 define these areas for the periods 1874-1892, 1894-1910, 1914-1930, and 1934-1950. Ten of the eleven ex-Confederate states are wholly noncompetitive throughout, and North Carolina joins them at the state legislature level during the first phase of the system of 1896. The movements which are nationally decisive are concentrated outside this region.

During the last phase of the preceding Civil War alignment system (1874-1892), the overwhelmingly Republican states are found in New England and in the "new" states of the West. The overwhelmingly

Table 5.4 Nonsouthern and Southern States Stratified by Partisan Lead, Lower House of State Legislature, 1874-1950*

CATEGORY OF LEAD		1874-1892 N	1874-1892 %	1894-1910 N	1894-1910 %	1914-1930 N	1914-1930 %	1934-1950 N	1934-1950 %
United States									
40+	R	24	7.2	155	39.3	195	45.9	50	11.8
0-39	R	160	48.2	97	24.6	100	23.5	202	47.9
0-39	D	40	12.0	27	6.9	17	4.0	30	7.1
40+	D	108	32.5	115	29.2	113	26.6	140	33.2
Nonsouthern States									
40+	R	24	9.7	155	52.4	195	60.7	50	15.8
0-39	R	160	64.8	97	32.8	100	31.2	202	63.7
0-39	D	31	12.6	27	9.1	17	5.3	30	9.5
40+	D	32	13.0	17	5.7	9	2.8	35	11.0

*Minnesota nonpartisan from 1914, excluded from third and fourth columns; Nebraska nonpartisan from 1937, excluded from fourth column.

Because of factors specific to the representational history of both states, elections for the state senate have been substituted for those of the state house of representatives in Connecticut and Illinois.

N=absolute number of cases

Table 5.5 Location of Individual States on State-Legislative Partisan Lead Continuum, 1874-1950

Republican Leads							
1874-1892		*1894-1910*		*1914-1930*		*1934-1950*	
40% & over	*0 to 39%*	*40% & over*	*0 to 39%*	*40% & over*	*0 to 39%*	*40% & over*	*0 to 39%*
Me.	Conn.	Conn.	N.H.	Conn.	N.H.	Vt.	Mass.
R.I.	Mass.	Me.	Del.	Me.	R.I.	N.J.	N.H.
Vt.	N.H.	Mass.	N.J.	Mass.	Del.	Wis.	Del.
Kans.	N.Y.	R.I.	N.Y.	Vt.	N.Y.	Iowa	N.Y.
Neb.	Pa.	Vt.	Ind.	N.J.	Ind.	Kans.	Pa.
S.D.	Ill.	Pa.	Ohio	Pa.	Neb.	N.D.	Ill.
Colo.	Mich.	Ill.	Neb.	Ill.	Colo.	S.D.	Ind.
Ida.	Ohio.	Mich.	N.M.	Mich.	Mont.		Mich.
Nev.	Wis.	Wis.	W. Va.	Ohio	Nev.		Ohio
Wash.	Iowa	Iowa		Wis.	N.M.		Colo.
	Minn.	Kans.		Iowa	Utah		Ida.
	N.D.	Minn.		Kans.	Mo.		Wyo.
	Wyo.	N.D.		N.D.	W. Va.		Calif.
	Ore.	S.D.		S.D.			
		Idaho		Idaho			
		Utah		Wyo.			
		Wyo.		Calif.			
		Calif.		Ore.			
		Ore.		Wash.			
		Wash.					

Democratic Leads			
Del. Ky. Md. Mo. 10 Southern States N.J. Ind. Mont. Calif. W. Va. N.C.	Ariz. Ky. Okla. 11 Southern States Colo. Mont. Nev. Md. Mo.	Ariz. Okla. 11 Southern States Ky. Md.	Ariz. N.M. Utah Ky. Md. Okla. W. Va. 11 Southern States Conn. R.I. Mont. Nev. Wash. Mo.

Democratic states outside the South are confined to Delaware (then a Border state in electoral behavior) and to the other Border states of Maryland, Kentucky, and Missouri. Otherwise, there is relatively-to-very-close competition, especially in the emergent Metropole. Of course, it should also be noted that normal Republican majorities existed in the North and West during this period, except in New Jersey and Indiana.

Both phases of the system of 1896 of course resemble each other more than they resemble either the eras preceding or following them. There is an enormous increase in noncompetitive Republican bulwarks at the grass roots level. The pattern is not monolithic as in the South. But among the most industrially and socially developed states in the Union, we find one-party Republican hegemony throughout lower New England, Pennsylvania, Illinois, Michigan, Wisconsin, and California. By the second or "normalcy" phase of the era, these states are joined by Ohio and New Jersey. Of the fourteen states of the Metropole, three were one-party Republican bastions in the 1874-1892 period, nine in the 1894-1910 period, eleven in the 1914-1930 period, and four in the 1932-1950 period.

Of the most economically advanced states inside and outside the Metropole, *the only one which preserved competition throughout at this level of analysis was New York*. To it can only be added New Jersey in the pre-World War I phase of this partisan era and Rhode Island in the "normalcy" phase. Apart from the Empire State, the only areas which remained or became competitive were the Border states, perennially competitive Indiana and Delaware, New Hampshire, and areas in the Mountain and far Plains states where the sectional realignment of the 1890s had long-term pro-Democratic effects. In the late nineteenth century, about three-fifths of the nation's population lived in states with roughly competitive political systems at the state legislature level. This proportion fell to less than one-third in the first phase of the system of 1896 and to little more than one-quarter by the second; it increased to about 55 percent during the New Deal era. By this latter period, the Metropole as well as much of the West had returned to broadly competitive status.

What does this extensive survey tell us? Very broadly, the data at other levels of election than the presidential reinforce, but make more nuanced, our prior understanding of this partisan era and its place in American electoral history. They highlight the extent to which this system displayed many more signs of electoral fragmentation—of growing diversity of electoral coalitions at different levels of election—than had existed in the nineteenth century. This fragmentation was reduced somewhat with the arrival of the New Deal, but only somewhat. It was to resume its forward march with great vigor during the second half of the twentieth century. This and other characteristics of behavior—notably trends in electoral participation—reflect the creation of a "new" electorate out of the old, an electorate essentially similar to that described in the major academic voting studies of recent years.

But the other side of the coin was the fact that this fragmentation pivoted on a bifurcated, increasingly entrenched structure of one-party hegemony: Democratic throughout the ex-Confederate states and some nearby areas, Republican in a diverse range of states from the most highly developed (like Pennsylvania, Michigan, or California) to primary-sector-dependent areas in the western "colonies." This fragmentation formed an essential part of the decomposition of political parties which was so fundamental a characteristic of this system. The Republican grass roots hegemony throughout most of the Metropole, and many of its western tributaries, testified to the futility of the many opposition movements which were locally or nationally launched against it. The strength of Democratic showings at other than the presidential level reflected the extreme difficulty which that party's leadership continually faced in attempting to weld together a credible national coalition to control the national political system on more than an episodic—indeed, almost accidental—basis as it did during the ill-fated Wilson administration.

Overall, the system of 1896 performed admirably as a system. Despite the occasional complexity of relationships among its component parts, it provided effective political resources for the interests that more fully dominated the nation's political economy than ever before or since. Those interests were primarily concerned with insulating themselves from pressures arising from below. Stable control of key parts of the political system—the presidency and above all the Supreme Court—was sufficient for that purpose. If this system was successful, it was because the vision of economic development, affluence, and "modernization" of society which prevailed in Republican and corporate circles was not only itself relatively coherent and integrated, but it was also persuasive to the public—at least to a majority of those still voting—until the great smashup of 1929.[36] Particularly was it persuasive when the alternative "establishment" and its competing voices and claims were considered. The Democrats were necessarily involved, as David Burner argues, with "the politics of provincialism," and remained so until the great "social issues" of the 1920s were finally swept away in the economic holocaust.[37] It was after all in this period that Will Rogers put the matter most succinctly: "I belong to no organized political party: I am a Democrat."

When we return to the presidential data, the fact of Republican hegemony in the major urban areas of the country looms large as a permanent characteristic of this system. This hegemony was, of course, mediated by major regional differences and in the relative ethnocultural balances to be found in American urban areas. Table 5.6 provides the basic information, couched for brevity in terms of major party leads in the total vote, stratified by metropolitan and nonmetropolitan status.[38] In 1896, during the initial shock of realignment, the metropolitan areas showed heavy marginal shifts toward the Republicans. For the country as a whole, the 1892-1896 swing in partisan lead was 23.3 percent pro-Republican in the metropolitan areas, compared with only 2.9 percent in the nonmetropolitan areas. At no time thereafter until 1932, not even in 1916, did these urbanized areas aggregately show a Democratic lead. Overall, during the entire system of 1896, the mean Republican presidential lead in urban areas was 16.6 percent compared with 11.2 percent for the nonmetropolitan areas.

There are many examples of regional differences, even if one excludes the South from analysis. One of the most striking of these is the outcome of the 1904 election (and the 1900-1904 swing). Theodore Roosevelt's landslide was particularly concentrated in the Midwest and the West, while the South showed a countercyclical pro-Democratic movement and the Northeast remained relatively stable. The huge Democratic rout of 1920, on the other hand, was quite uniform everywhere outside the South and Border states. But probably the most striking regional disparity came in 1928. While Al Smith won a bare plurality of the vote in the Northeast's cities, he trailed Hoover by 30 percentage points in western cities, and suffered the only loss ever registered in the South's cities by a Democrat from the end of Reconstruction until well after World War II. By 1940, excluding the South, these regional differentials in metropolitan partisan lead had been remarkably smoothed out, varying from a low of 12.9 in the Northeast to a high of 17.3 in the Pacific region.

When one excludes the South—and to a lesser degree the Border states—the most striking feature of this stratified array is *not*, as one might expect, a large difference between the aggregate voting data in metropolitan and nonmetropolitan jurisdictions. Rather, it is a shrinkage of the preexisting differential by which Democratic candidates enjoyed a larger urban than nonurban percentage of the vote in the nonsouthern states. In the states of the Metropole the mean pro-Democratic urban differential was 9.5 percent in the 1876-1892 period, and 1.2 percent in the 1896-1924 period. As the entire Metropole moved more or less solidly into the Republican column from 1896 on, this of course meant that its cities produced consistent Republican majorities throughout the era. Indeed, only in 1916 and 1928 were these majorities small.

In 1928 the "Al Smith revolution," described by Samuel Lubell and others, occurred, but this "revolution" was confined quite narrowly within the Metropole to some of its largest cities; elsewhere it was hardly, if at all, visible.[39] It is important to stress just how narrowly based this Smith-related shift was and how ephemeral it might have proved. For analysis of the 1930 gubernatorial and other elections in such vital urbanized states as California, Michigan, and Pennsylvania reveals that the electoral alignments of the system of 1896 in its "normalcy" phase were still firmly entrenched. Who knows what would have happened had the Great Depression not supervened?

As it was, Republican presidential ascendancy even in the conurbations was shattered not by Al Smith but by the economic collapse of 1929. It was only temporarily impaired by the rupture of the Republican party in 1912 and the special circumstances surrounding the deviating election of 1916. It was left almost entirely unaffected by the La Follette uprising of 1924. Protest was plentiful during the lifetime of the system of 1896; this protest was clearly concentrated in some urban working-class areas (for example, in Pittsburgh and Cleveland) and especially in the "colonies" of the Northwest in a great arc extending from Wisconsin to California. Only in retrospect does it appear as part of a step-by-step process by which the New Deal coalition was built. In the high noon of the mid-1920s the protest seemed remarkably ineffective, as did the Democratic party.

THE ANATOMY OF THE SYSTEM OF 1896: SECULAR TRENDS

Parts of the previous discussion have already touched upon some of the more important secular trends which marked the course of the system of 1896. For example, the discussion of periodization below the presidential level has stressed that the proportion of geographical areas in which there was relatively close two-party competition showed a strong tendency to decline across the 1896-1930 era. In particular, the near Midwest became much more solidly Republican at most levels of election after World War I than it had been before. By 1924 close Republican-Democratic competiton at the presidential level had come to be confined almost exclusively to the Border states and counties immediately adjacent to them, the Appalachian uplands of the South, and the two southernmost Mountain states, Arizona and New Mexico.

An examination of the internal distribution of congressional election outcomes suggests even more forcefully the extraordinary change in competitiveness which occurred as the system of 1896 grew more

Table 5.6 Major Party Leads by Selected Region and Metropolitan Status: Presidential Elections, 1876-1940*

			Metropolitan				
Year	*Northeast*	*East North Central*	*Pacific*	*West*	*Border*	*South*	*United States*
1876	5.3	2.0	–3.2	–5.2	18.2	23.0	5.8
1880	–0.1	–7.5	0.6	–4.2	11.3	42.6	–0.5
1884	1.1	–2.9	–11.2	–12.1	6.0	28.8	–0.1
1888	2.0	–0.7	–4.0	–4.9	2.1	30.8	0.9
1892	5.1	5.8	2.8	–13.4	10.9	47.8	4.9
1896	–26.2	–14.8	–5.4	14.0	–14.7	40.8	–18.4
1900	–13.2	–7.2	–19.7	–8.2	–3.2	60.0	–8.8
1904	–18.3	–31.2	–41.6	–31.8	–4.5	81.9	–21.5
1908	–16.8	–14.4	–26.6	–14.3	–3.9	76.6	–13.9
1912	–15.8	–16.9	–2.9	–3.3	–3.5	62.0	–13.0
1916	–7.7	–0.7	–0.3	4.6	3.7	52.5	–0.1
1920	–37.1	–36.1	–41.1	–36.8	–13.0	27.3	–32.0
1924	–29.2	–41.8	–49.2	–45.5	–11.4	33.3	–32.2
1928	0.2	–14.7	–32.2	–30.0	–9.3	–3.2	–9.3
1932	14.7	12.8	20.2	19.5	27.0	62.0	17.5
1936	36.5	30.0	36.8	36.0	33.4	68.8	35.4
1940	12.9	13.6	17.3	16.5	15.0	55.2	15.4

			Nonmetropolitan				
1876	–6.3	–3.0	–1.6	–16.8	17.6	19.2	2.3
1880	–12.8	–6.7	–0.6	–17.9	13.4	20.4	–1.5
1884	–8.0	–2.5	–4.1	–16.0	8.4	18.9	0.6
1888	–9.5	–3.5	–4.6	–16.1	5.6	23.7	0.8
1892	–6.8	–0.8	–8.9	–6.9	7.7	33.0	2.5
1896	–26.5	–8.4	4.2	17.9	5.4	27.4	–0.4
1900	–20.0	–11.6	–11.2	–4.7	1.8	25.5	–5.0
1904	–25.1	–26.4	–40.7	–36.7	–2.4	36.6	–17.2
1908	–20.7	–11.8	–22.1	–13.1	1.1	31.8	–8.5
1912	–21.0	–15.1	–13.4	–13.5	1.4	37.2	–7.2
1916	–8.8	–5.8	1.9	8.2	6.5	45.4	5.0
1920	–38.0	–31.9	–34.6	–33.1	–6.2	25.3	–23.0
1924	–41.3	–31.2	–38.5	–31.4	0	39.9	–21.0
1928	–30.0	–29.7	–30.3	–29.1	–20.0	5.6	–23.1
1932	–9.4	10.6	22.9	22.2	25.4	62.4	18.0
1936	–2.0	11.2	33.5	24.5	19.7	60.1	18.4
1940	–5.7	–8.3	12.9	3.1	10.3	57.0	6.0

West=Pacific (Calif., Ore., Wash.,) plus Mountain states (Ariz., Colo., Ida., Mont., Nev., N.M., Utah, Wyo.).

* Minus sign signifies Republican lead.

entrenched. Taking as our benchmark the percentage Democratic of the total vote in each congressional district, we then aggregate the number of districts in the North and West which fall into each of four categories of competitiveness, from the most solidly one-party to the most marginal. These numbers are then converted into percentages and presented in the following two tables (Tables 5.7 and 5.8). The first covers the whole history of congressional elections by broad periods from 1834 to 1978, and the second provides a more detailed year-by-year measurement from 1880 to 1940.

Table 5.7 A Summary History of Competitiveness in Congressional Elections: North and West by Period, 1834-1978*

	Percentage Democratic of Total District Vote (Mean for Period)			
PERIOD	0-29.9; 70.0-100.0	30.0-39.9; 60.0-69.9	40.0-44.9; 55.0-59.9	45.0-54.9;
1834-1852	8.9	15.0	22.2	53.8
1854-1860	16.7	20.6	24.6	38.1
1862-1876	7.7	19.2	26.2	47.0
1880-1892	7.6	19.0	25.8	47.6
1896-1908	15.3	30.3	25.3	29.1
1910-1916	16.6	28.3	25.2	30.0
1918-1930	34.6	29.2	18.4	17.8
1932-1940	14.6	24.0	25.2	36.1
1942-1960	14.2	34.4	24.7	26.7
1962-1970	20.2	36.8	21.9	21.2
1972-1978	33.9	31.7	16.5	17.9

*The percentages within the table are means, based ultimately on the total number of congressional outcomes in the North and West which were decided in each year within each of the four categories into which the table is divided. The North and West consists of the United States minus the eleven ex-Confederate (Southern) states and the Border states of Kentucky, Maryland, Missouri, Oklahoma and West Virginia.

Virtually all of the nineteenth century displays very high levels of competitiveness with half of the seats being decided by quite close margins and typically less than a tenth being solid one-party bastions. This pattern was only temporarily interrupted during the critical realignment of the 1850s. In this era, a large number of seats were poised at the razor's edge of competitiveness. The swing ratios were extremely high, i.e., it required but a very small swing in votes to produce a hugely amplified partisan change in seats, exactly as happened in such elections as 1874, 1882, and especially 1890. The aggregate distribution was steeply unimodal.

This pattern was decisively broken by the realignment dynamics of the 1890s. The break was at first relatively marginal following "re-

Table 5.8 Aggregate Competitiveness in Congressional Elections, North and West, 1880-1940*

	Percentage Democratic of Total District Vote			
YEAR	0-29.9; 70.0-100.0	30.0-39.9; 60.0-69.9	40.0-44.9; 55.0-59.9	45.0-54.9;
1880	7.4	21.3	24.5	46.8
1882	11.7	16.1	19.0	53.2
1884	4.4	21.0	27.8	46.8
1886	9.3	18.5	26.8	45.4
1888	4.7	16.5	34.9	43.9
1890	8.0	17.9	21.7	52.4
1892	7.4	21.7	26.1	44.8
1894	27.8	35.7	24.3	12.2
1896	14.7	28.1	20.8	36.4
1898	7.4	23.4	29.9	39.4
1900	8.7	27.3	32.0	32.0
1902	12.8	31.2	28.0	28.0
1904	28.0	40.8	15.6	15.6
1906	21.6	29.6	24.0	24.8
1908	14.0	31.6	26.8	27.6
1910	12.6	18.6	26.1	42.7
1912	17.6	33.8	23.6	25.0
1914	21.5	31.7	24.3	22.5
1916	14.8	28.9	26.8	29.6
1918	26.4	29.2	21.1	23.2
1920	47.5	29.6	13.7	9.2
1922	25.0	24.6	22.2	28.2
1924	40.1	28.5	16.2	15.1
1926	37.3	35.9	15.1	11.6
1928	29.9	35.6	20.4	14.1
1930	35.9	20.8	20.4	22.9
1932	12.8	20.0	27.2	40.0
1934	14.8	22.1	23.8	39.3
1936	15.2	23.4	26.6	34.8
1938	14.8	30.0	20.7	34.5
1940	15.5	24.5	27.9	32.1

*The percentages within the table are based on the total number of congressional outcomes in the North and West which were decided each year within each of the four categories into which the table is divided. The North and West consists of the United States minus the eleven ex-Confederate (southern) states and the Border states of Kentucky, Maryland, Missouri, Oklahoma and West Virginia.

covery'' from the abnormal results of 1894, but it was substantial enough to be closely associated with a steep increase in the mean tenure of incumbents during the 1890s. This was associated with a strong overall pro-Republican thrust. What these tables do not show is that the mean percentage of districts in the North and West which Democratic candidates won by an absolute majority of the votes cast declined from 29.2 in the 1880-1892 period to 15.4 in the 1896-1908 period—thereafter, 18.7 (1910-1916), 18.4 (1918-1930), and 51.8 (1932-1940).

This aggregate structure of competitiveness remained largely unchanged during the 1910-1916 ''deviation.'' This again suggests the extent to which the Democratic ascendancy during that decade of this century was largely the artifact of divisions within the majority party. Equally clearly, the 1918-1930 period is one in which there is a vast increase in noncompetitive congressional elections in the North and West. At more than one-third of the total, the solidly one-party seats (the overwhelming majority of which were Republican) were now 4.5 times more numerous in relative terms than they had been in 1880-1892, while the seats falling in the most competitive category declined from just under one-half to under one-fifth of the total. Swing ratios fell to remarkably low levels, comparable only with those of the post-1965 period; i.e., even a relatively large aggregate vote swing tended to ''underproduce'' corresponding partisan shifts of seats.

An extremely similar distribution was achieved in the 1972-1978 period, long after the New Deal had come and gone. The two eras have in common the overriding fact of party decomposition, but these aggregate similarities are founded on important divergences. In the 1920s, the noncompetitiveness tended to be generic, e.g., Michigan was solidly one-party Republican from top to bottom. Party decomposition in the 1970s, so far as congressional elections were concerned, was reflected in the emergence of marked incumbent-insulation effects resulting in a *bimodal* distribution, with a trough between the modes located in the most competitive zone. This latter phenomenon is now quite well documented.[40] Incumbent-insulation effects in the 1920s were extremely limited by current standards, though of course larger by far than in the late nineteenth century. Finally, the extreme noncompetitiveness which characterized the ''normalcy'' era was abruptly reversed during the New Deal realignment. This reversal was both limited and itself subject to subsequent erosion—one more reflection of the limited, ambiguous, but still real redemocratization of American politics which the New Deal brought in its wake.

This tendency for organizable general election alternatives to disappear as one-party dominance grew was associated with another systemic property, the growing heterogeneity of electoral outcomes at different levels of elections. This phenomenon was partly a byproduct of a media-assisted change in the relative visibility of presidents, and perhaps governors and senators as well. It mostly reflected the break-up of political parties as relatively organized, relatively coherent collective forces. In this context, the probable role of the direct primary is worth recalling. Twenty-five years ago, the late V. O. Key, Jr., stressed that the creation of the direct primary brought in its train some *possibly* unintended antiparty consequences. Chief among these was the tendency to shift competiton among ambitious political entrepreneurs from the general election to the primary of the majority party. This not only sapped the pool of talent on which the minority party could draw, but, along with other rules changes, fatally undermined comprehensive third-party activity as well.[41]

Two peculiarities of the system of 1896 are worth noting in this regard. First, the direct primary was established in almost all states between 1903 and 1915. It seems plausible that the "normalcy" sequence, which begins with the congressional election of 1918, owes some of its noncompetitive peculiarities (compared with the aggregate shape of outcomes in the 1896-1908 phase) to the institutional factors which Key analyzed. Second, the rise and fall of Progressivism and socialism in the period extending from 1910 to 1918 represent the "last hurrah" of the old-style third party movements as organized structures of collective action. Prior to this turning point, these parties fielded candidates at most or all levels of election, and not solely at one of extremely high individual visibility (e.g., especially the presidency). Thus, Socialist congressional candidates in 1912 received 5 percent or more of the total vote in 169 congressional districts and contested many more. The Roosevelt Progressives of 1912 constituted in large part a personalistic faction within the Republican party. Yet Progressive candidates also won 5 percent or more of the vote in 214 congressional districts.

All of this activity abruptly disappears during and just after World War I, except in a very few special cases like Minnesota and New York.[42] It was characteristic of the new order that the La Follette Progressive insurgency of 1924 was limited to the presidential contest. So were subsequent dissident movements like the Dixiecrats of 1948 or the Wallace/American Independent "party" of 1968. Insurgent candidacies have come and gone since World War I, but they have lacked organizational penetration across many levels of election. Coupled with the harsh measures taken by state legislatures in the 1920s and

1930s to keep third parties off the ballot altogether, the rise of the direct primary mode of major party nomination almost certainly had a great deal to do with these changes.

What we have described so far is a structure of electoral politics marked by a continuous narrowing of organizable general election alternatives. It is, or should be, axiomatic that close relationships exist between the cohesiveness and competitiveness of parties as structures of collective action and the willingness or even the ability of the public to participate in general elections. To the extent that party disintegrates, to that extent participation will deteriorate. This relationship can be seen from the earliest days of American electoral politics. For example, the New Hampshire gubernatorial election of 1814, fought in the midst of the War of 1812, was hotly contested by Jeffersonian Republicans and Federalists. The turnout rate reached 81 percent of the estimated potential electorate. By 1820, after the Federalists had disappeared from the scene, the turnout had fallen to 47 percent. It was not again to reach its 1814 level until 1838—precisely when the party-building of the so-called second party system was at its height. This party-building was associated everywhere with a hitherto unprecedented mobilization of voters. In the late 1970s, at the other end of the historical track, party decomposition and mass public disaffection with politics and politicians have been closely associated with steep declines in voting participation from the mediocre levels of the 1960s. Indeed, turnout in the nonsouthern states in the 1978 congressional election finally reached the lowest point since the series begins in 1826—lower even than it was in 1926, the all-time low until this past year.

Detailed analyses of electoral participation in the history of American politics have been presented by myself and others in recent years.[43] We must confine ourselves here to a brief summary of the issues involved.

(1) There is no question that a decrease in turnout was intended by those who fashioned the rules-of-the-game changes affecting access to the ballot after 1890. The case of the South is straightforward. Granted the region's primitive, colonial socioeconomic structure, its elites felt an overpowering need to curb a fickle and dangerous mass electorate and to ensure that episodes like the Populist uprising of the 1890s would never happen again. Racist and regional home rule symbols helped to provide the political resources to carry out this counterrevolution. But the South should be read as an extreme rather than a unique case. Those in control of politics in New York state, for example, not only required a literacy qualification for voting but also after 1908 imposed a periodic personal registration requirement on New

York City alone, while requiring no registration in the small towns and rural areas of upstate New York.

(2) Personal registration requirements have depressing effects on electoral participation.[44] Moreover, these requirements discriminate on class grounds: they are more onerous for the poor than for the middle class. The lack of any serious political or analytical challenge to such requirements for well over a half-century after their enactment is best explained by their congruence with the dominant liberal-individualist value system of the country. They admirably reflect, and have helped to reinforce, uncontested hegemony in American politics.

(3) There was not only a very large decline in electoral participation prior to the enfranchisement of women, but much less than one-half the variance in this decline can be explained by the introduction of registration statutes.[45] Most of it can be accounted for on other grounds. The narrowing of organizable general election alternatives and the disintegration of party organization during the system of 1896 are certainly crucial intervening variables which account for some of the aggregate evidence not only of behavior, but also nonbehavior (i.e., growing and increasingly class-skewed nonvoting) as well.

(4) The introduction of woman suffrage accelerated the turnout decline. Data from Philadelphia and Chicago suggest that the pre-1928 sex-related participation differential was about 30 percent. Comparative studies by H. L. A. Tingsten make it clear that sex-related participation differentials are always most marked just after female enfranchisement.[46] In the United States the differential was at least four times as large as in any comparative case—be it Austria, New Zealand, or Sweden—which Tingsten examines. The whole history of the system of 1896 leaves the strong impression that, even before woman suffrage, it was marked by a cumulative lack of integration of new (male) voters. The sex differentials of the 1920s suggest at least as strongly that electoral politics was not organized to stimulate entry of this large, weakly socialized group into the political process.

(5) The most striking feature of electoral participation in the 1970s is its extremely class-skewed character. Thus, the Census Bureau survey for the 1976 election reveals an aggregate turnout of 59.2 percent (nearly 5 percent higher than actual presidential turnout). But turnout among the top occupational classes (professional, managerial, and farm owners) was 76.9 percent compared with 46.7 percent among semiskilled and unskilled manual workers. By contrast, Swedish turnouts in these two categories in 1960 were 89.6 percent and 87.0 percent, a differential of only 2.6 percent in a national turnout of 86.5 percent.

The data for the 1920s is of extremely fragmentary character. Tingsten does report one class stratification from the small town of Delaware, Ohio, in 1924.[47] This found a turnout rate of 86 percent among the local upper class (corporate and banking people), compared with 63 percent among the "mass of industrial workers." This gap of 23 percent was found in a town for which personal registration requirements for voting did not exist until 1965. There seems little doubt that, at some point in the second decade of the system of 1896, a very large class skew in participation opened up and that it tended to grow across the lifetime of that system. Similarly, turnout rates in the late nineteenth century—particularly in the most advanced, densely populated states —do not substantiate the existence of any such class gap. The mean congressional turnout throughout the North and West in presidential years was as high as 84.8 percent of the estimated potential electorate (1880-1892). With so full an aggegate mobilization of voters, the class gap in participation was close to what it is in Sweden today. The overall turnout picture for the period 1880-1940 is presented in Table 5.9.

Finally, the remobilizations of the New Deal era were particularly heavily concentrated among urban-industrial, working-class populations. These populations entered the electoral politics universe overwhelmingly on the Democratic side during the New Deal realignment. We may take two parts of the Pittsburgh area as examples. The first, Ward 6 of Pittsburgh, was largely populated by steelworkers, many of East European origin. In 1940, 16.0 percent of its male labor force worked in white-collar occupations. The second is the suburb of Edgewood just east of the city, largely populated by native-stock professional and executive people (71.3 percent of its 1940 male labor force worked in white-collar occupations, and well over 40 percent in professional-managerial occupations). As Table 5.10 reveals, the 1920-1948 electoral evolution of these two areas is a study in contrasts.

This table graphically illustrates certain basic propositions about the nature of the electorate on which the system of 1896—at least in its "normalcy" phase—was based. Although there is considerable stability in the Republican share of the vote in Ward 6 from 1920 through 1928, it is small in size, one-fifth of the total potential electorate. The opposition vote was volatile in the extreme, with the Democrats forging ahead in 1928 on the well-known "Smith tide," but even then getting less than 30 percent of the potential electorate. The ambiguous character of 1932—in many respects, it was the last of the sequence beginning in 1896, and not only the beginning of the New Deal sequence—is also revealed as the Republican share of the vote is halved while turnout declines to about the usual levels for the 1920s. Then comes the extraordinary Democratic mobilization from 1936 on. It is

Table 5.9 Turnout in Congressional Elections, by Region, 1880-1940

Year	North & West	Border	South	United States
	PRESIDENTIAL YEARS			
1880	86.8	73.3	63.7	79.7
1884	84.2	74.4	61.8	77.8
1888	87.7	82.3	61.6	81.1
1892	80.3	75.5	57.8	74.7
1896	83.5	87.4	57.0	77.9
1900	81.0	85.9	41.9	72.4
1904	74.6	75.0	27.9	63.9
1908	73.6	76.4	28.7	63.6
1912	63.8	66.9	25.4	55.7
1916	65.3	76.4	29.9	58.8
1920	53.5	61.1	20.1	46.7
1924	52.4	54.3	17.9	44.9
1928	61.6	63.3	21.3	52.9
1932	61.5	63.5	23.6	53.3
1936	67.6	65.4	23.2	57.4
1940	69.0	63.9	23.3	58.2
	NONPRESIDENTIAL (OFF) YEARS			
1882	71.4	61.8	51.9	65.7
1886	71.6	64.1	42.0	63.9
1890	71.3	64.2	44.7	64.6
1894	75.0	72.0	47.2	67.4
1898	68.1	66.3	33.6	60.1
1902	65.7	60.7	23.8	55.6
1906	60.6	72.7	18.6	52.0
1910	60.4	63.7	20.6	51.6
1914	58.4	59.5	18.6	50.1
1918	45.2	51.0	14.8	39.9
1922	42.8	41.5	11.8	35.7
1926	39.7	40.9	8.5	32.9
1930	43.7	43.8	12.2	36.7
1934	54.3	47.8	13.1	44.5
1938	58.6	44.6	11.3	46.6

Table 5.10 Turnout and Partisan Distribution of the Presidential Vote in Ward 6 (Pittsburgh) and Edgewood, 1920-1948

Year	Percentage Voting	Percentage Non-Voting	Partisan Percentage of Potential Electorate			
			D	*R*	*OTHER*	
		Ward 6 (ethnic industrial working class)				
1920	36.0	64.0	11.5	21.4	3.2	(2.8 Soc.)
1924	38.5	61.5	1.8	19.1	17.7	(17.5 Prog.)
1928	49.1	50.9	28.2	20.8	0.1	
1932	41.6	58.4	29.7	11.3	0.6	
1936	62.9	37.1	50.3	9.4	3.1	(2.5 Union)
1940	72.5	27.5	61.1	11.2	0.1	
1944	62.4	37.6	52.3	10.0	0.1	
1948	66.8	33.2	54.8	10.7	1.2	
		Edgewood (upper-middle to upper class)				
1920	55.8	44.2	10.0	43.4	2.4	
1924	61.8	38.2	6.8	48.0	7.0	(6.7 Prog.)
1928	75.4	24.6	13.8	61.3	0.3	
1932	68.8	31.2	19.1	47.0	2.7	
1936	84.9	15.1	31.1	52.5	1.3	
1940	80.2	19.8	19.6	60.4	0.2	
1944	70.8	29.2	17.8	52.6	0.4	
1948	69.2	30.8	12.8	55.4	1.0	

very clear that Republican ascendancy in an area like Ward 6 had been predicated on a huge pool of nonvoters rather than on widespread Republican support among the electorate. Equally clearly, while mobilization after 1932 accounts very largely for Democratic gains in the New Deal period, almost one-half of Ward 6's Republican electorate of the 1920s deserted the GOP in 1932 never to return.

The picture in Edgewood reveals that in some areas, 1928 was a year of voter surge not to Al Smith but to Herbert Hoover.[48] It also reveals much higher participation rates from 1920 through 1936 than those in Ward 6, and overwhelming Republican strength, modally just under one-half of the town's potential electorate. Finally, if there was a well-known Democratic mobilization among the steelworkers during the New Deal sequence, there was also a distinct, if much less dramatic, pro-Republican mobilization in this town as class antagonisms intensified.

What conclusions can we draw from all this? Overall, electoral participation was intimately related to the organization of "real" political alternatives available to voters during and after the system of 1896. As that system aged, turnout continuously fell until it achieved its low point around 1926. The class gap grew as the turnout declined. An electorate had come into being which had strikingly contemporary characteristics to an observer writing in the late 1970s. It was, in short, an electorate heavily skewed toward the middle classes *in the absence of an organizable socialist mass movement capable of mobilizing or representing the collective interests of lower-class voters.* As the case of Ward 6 reveals, the Democratic coalition forged in the crucible of depression and New Deal provided a mobilizing substitute. This substitute was to prove temporary and increasingly amorphous as the years passed so that by the 1970s less than one-half of Ward 6's electorate participated in presidential elections. But it represented in the shorter term a remarkably sharp contrast with the system of 1896, which had been implicitly based on a demobilization of the potential electorate—particularly its lower half—and had reached the point where oligarchy was a plausible way of describing it. By the 1920s, the structure of electoral politics had been recast to bring it into admirable harmony with an ascendant industrial capitalism.

CONCLUSION

Long ago, the late E. E. Schattschneider observed that there was no reason to assume from our past that Americans would not or did not get approximately the kinds of parties they wanted.[49] This, like so many other of his insights, strikes me as a perfectly sound observation. The knotty question is how those wants are shaped by ideas, events, men, and the socioeconomic base of human action so that they develop one way and not another. As our argument has stressed and as the entire history of the system of 1896 bears witness, the range of effective, organizable political oppositions in the United States falls far short of possibilities that exist in the histories of other electoral systems.

What kinds of oppositions were durably organizable in this period, and what structures of alternatives did they present the American voter then? The answer to this question may well be found in what happened to the dreams of the more cosmopolitan Populist leaders when fusion with the Democrats occurred in 1896, and in what happened to socialism as an electoral movement after 1912. The Populist vision at its broadest was not a narrowly sectoral, hayseed-reactionary affair clothed in radical rhetoric. It amounted to nothing less than the last significant American challenge to industrial capitalism as a system of social, economic, and political power. While it was not Socialist—still less was it Marxist—this alternative vision demanded the active use of "the people's power" (i.e., the state) to limit and if necessary to take over concentrations of corporate power in strategic sectors of the economy, and to manage the financial structure in the interests of what Populists perceived to be the well-being of the population as a whole.

This effort to construct a broadly based anticapitalist coalition in the cities as well as on the farms, in the Metropole as well as in the colonies, foundered. Bryan's fusion campaign of 1896 was both culturally and programmatically narrowed to the point where it could appeal with any marginal effectiveness only to primary-sector producers in the colonial regions of the country who were in serious economic straits. Neither then nor later, at least until 1932, was a general farmer-labor coalition against big business a feasible electoral enterprise. Instead, what emerged was a trisectional cleavage pattern which broadly reflected the regionally concentrated division of labor in industrial America before World War II. This consisted of a largely Republican Metropole, including solid urban majorities for Republican presidential candidates and some solid GOP industrial bastions; a colonial West with highly volatile oscillations in party support, a region dominated at various times by Republicans, protest parties, and antiparty politics based on the assessment that parties were tools of alien finance-industrial capital; and an even more colonial Solid South, giving the Democrats their permanent regional bastion and predicated on racial exclusion, the lowest and most fragmented possible electoral participation, and rule by a kind of comprador oligarchy.

The Socialist party's problem casts more important light on these issues. This party's maximum penetration of the electorate, achieved in 1912, was concentrated geographically in the colonial peripheries from Florida to Washington. It also had considerable local importance among Jewish immigrants in New York, Germans in Milwaukee, and other urban-industrial populations. These patterns were to appear again in the La Follette insurgency of 1924 and especially—enormously magnified—during such post-realignment New Deal electoral campaigns as 1940 and 1944. But socialism as such virtually disappeared. Some recent detailed analysis suggests that a prime cause of this disappearance was the problem of retaining a Marxist ideology while coping with ethnic heterogeneity within the Socialist electoral coalition.[50] It appears that the native-stock "colonial" wing of the Socialist party was far more radical both in domestic and in foreign policy matters during World War I than were the Germans of Milwaukee or even the Jewish Socialists of the lower East Side. These tensions appeared to have multiplied during and after the war.

Moreover, socialism was not able to penetrate working-class Catholic populations.[51] And the industrial working classes of the Metropole were heavily populated by Catholic immigrants whose immigrant experience caused them to cleave to the church and to the political and social leadership which their priests gave them. Later, La Follette as a Progressive rather than as a Socialist made a considerably deeper penetration into Catholic industrial working-class populations than did Debs in 1912 or 1920. And still later, the New Deal—which was not Socialist at all and which was channeled through an existing major party—won over Catholics, Jews, Scandinavians, German ex-Socialists, and native-stock radicals from Oklahoma to Washington in the first, and so far only, successful working-class coalition in American history. But it was able to do this precisely because it was *not* Socialist and did not present a fundamentally alternative challenge to individualist liberalism and the private ownership of productive property.

What we have been describing, then, is the emergence of the kind of electorate and the kind of electoral politics which best fit the requirements of an uncontested hegemony in the ideological domain. Within a specific historical context in which that hegemony was couched in the language of the upward march toward individual affluence under corporate-capitalist auspices, the Republican party was its political vehicle. The Republican position was propped by the fact that the rival Democratic coalition, with the Solid South as a permanent nondisplaceable anchor, could be truncated but not displaced. The fact that the Democratic party was not a nationally acceptable alternative but was also indestructible virtually guaranteed that organizable political alternatives would be limited to sectional and ethnocultural oppositions. It was also to be expected that as long as these conditions survived, both the sectionalism and the ethnoculturalism would become increasingly entrenched. With this kind of systemic overdetermination, the collapse in mass electoral participation and the increasing fragmentation of electoral outcomes would have followed as a matter of course even if insulation-minded elites had not changed the rules governing access to the ballot box.

But of course, they did change them, and many other things besides, in their quest for protection from a large, mobilized, potentially dangerous mass electorate. They were outstandingly successful in their quest for order but only because—granted the basic value system of the American electorate, and the record of corporate and Republican success in the march toward industrial affluence—they were the only game in town. It is an interesting but insoluble question as to whether the political system which these elites and the voters built after 1896 could ever have been destroyed by anything less overwhelming than the collapse of the economic order after 1929.

In any event, the history of American electoral politics before the New Deal and after about 1950 suggests that the structures of concentrated economic power are not compatible with older agrarian-era party organizations. Nor is the kind of society which these structures dominate conducive to the creation of more modern organizations of mass mobilization and representation. The system of 1896 presents us with one concrete, if highly complex, example in support of this proposition. The current era of American electoral politics presents us with another. But one can, after all, get to a destination by more than one route. The destination is likely to remain the same in the long run, until or unless hegemony ceases to be uncontested.

NOTES

1. See John L. Shover, "Was 1928 a Critical Election in California?" and Jerome M. Clubb and Howard W. Allen, "The Cities and the Election of 1928," in *Electoral Change and Stability in American Political History*, ed. Jerome M. Clubb and Howard W. Allen (New York, 1971), pp. 215-34 and 235-54.

2. For examples, see Frank R. Kent, *The Democratic Party: A History* (New York, 1928); and Arthur N. Holcombe, *The Political Parties of Today: A Study in Republican and Democratic Politics* (New York, 1924). For a presentiment of the future, see Felix Frankfurter, "Why I Shall Vote for La Follette," in *Law and Politics: Occasional Papers of Felix Frankfurter 1913-1938*, ed. Archibald MacLeish and E. F. Prichard, Jr. (New York, 1939), pp. 314-19.

3. Lee Benson, *The Concept of Jacksonian Democracy: New York as a Test Case* (Princeton, 1961), especially pp. 270-87.

4. Ibid., p. 276.

5. See the important analysis of the urban machine by Robert K. Merton in *Social Theory and Social Structure*, 2d ed. (New York, 1957), pp. 71-82. Daniel Elazar also stresses that the individualist subculture could readily lead to uninhibited aggrandizements by individual political actors were it not for the norms and sanctions of "party regularity" which one historically finds in this modal American subculture. See Daniel J. Elazar, *American Federalism: A View from the States* (New York, 1966), pp. 86-89.

6. V. O. Key, Jr., *American State Politics: An Introduction* (New York, 1956), pp. 34-41.

7. Theodore Lowi, "Toward Functionalism in Political Science: The Case of Innovation in Party Systems," *American Political Science Review* 57 (September 1963): 570-83.

8. Cf. Paul Kleppner, *The Cross of Culture: A Social Analysis of Midwestern Politics, 1850-1900* (New York, 1970), especially pp. 93-100.

9. Barrington Moore, Jr., *Social Origins of Dictatorship and Democracy: Lord and Peasant in the Making of the Modern World* (Boston, 1966), pp. 111-55 ("The American Civil War: The Last Capitalist Revolution").

10. For an expert discussion from the monetarist point of view, see Milton Friedman and Anna J. Schwartz, *A Monetary History of the United States, 1867-1960* (Princeton, 1963). Few things are ever absolutely clear-cut in politics, and the currency issue of the late nineteenth century is no exception. The generalization is valid, but one has on the other side the adoption of the Sherman Silver Purchase Act of 1890 by a Republican Congress. Repeal of this act was a major political issue for Grover Cleveland's second administration, and contributed in no small measure to his repudiation by the Democratic convention in 1896.

11. See particularly J. Rogers Hollingsworth, *The Whirligig of Politics* (Chicago, 1967).

12. These sequences have been described and analyzed in, inter alia, Walter Dean Burnham, *Critical Elections and the Mainsprings of American Politics* (New York, 1970); and James A. Sundquist, *Dynamics of the Party System* (Washington, D.C., 1973).

13. For a general review of Democratic coalitional problems, see David Burner, *The Politics of Provincialism* (New York, 1968); and, for a blow-by-blow account of the 1924 Democratic presidential convention, see Robert K. Murray, *The 103rd Ballot: Democrats and the Disaster in Madison Square Garden* (New York, 1976).

14. See the data and discussion in Angus Campbell et al., *The American Voter* (New York, 1960), pp. 44-47.

15. Lawrence Goodwyn, *Democratic Promise: The Populist Movement in America* (New York, 1976).

16. This is particularly well documented in the work of certain legal and constitutional historians; for example, see Arnold Paul, *Conservative Crisis and the Rule of Law: Attitudes of Bar and Bench, 1887-1895* (Ithaca, 1960), for an exceptionally thorough discussion. See also Alan F. Westin, "The Supreme Court, the Populist Movement, and the Campaign of 1896," *Journal of Politics* 15 (February 1953): 3-41.

17. "Law and the Court," reprinted in *The Mind and Faith of Justice Holmes*, ed. Max Lerner (Boston, 1943), p. 390.

18. The definitive analysis of this underlying reality is still Louis Hartz, *The Liberal Tradition in America* (New York, 1955).

19. Goodwyn, *Democratic Promise*; using content analysis of business, agricultural, and other publications, Louis Galambos provides important documentation for the relative depth of the 1890s crisis in *The Public Image of Big Business in America, 1880-1940: A Quantitative Study in Social Change* (Baltimore, 1975).

20. The best and most comprehensive recent treatment is J. Morgan Kousser, *The Shaping of Southern Politics: Suffrage Restriction and the Establishment of the One-Party South, 1880-1910* (New Haven, 1974). See also Sheldon Hackney, *Populism to Progressivism in Alabama* (Princeton, 1969); and William I. Hair, *Bourbonism and Agrarian Protest: Louisiana Politics, 1877-1900* (Baton Rouge, 1969).

21. Paul, *Conservative Crisis*, pp 192-95.

22. The term "island communities" is from Robert Wiebe, *The Search for Order* (New York, 1969). The classic sociological studies of the processes

involved in the small town of Muncie, Indiana, are by Robert S. Lynd and Helen Merrill Lynd, *Middletown: A Study in American Culture* (New York, 1929), and *Middletown in Transition* (New York, 1937).

23. Key, *American State Politics*, pp. 169-96.

24. The classic analysis is the magisterial study by V. O. Key, Jr., *Southern Politics in State and Nation* (New York, 1949).

25. See, e.g., Stanley Kelley, Jr., Richard E. Ayres, and William G. Bowen, "Registration and Voting: Putting First Things First," *American Political Science Review* 61 (June 1967): 359-79; Walter Dean Burnham, "A Political Scientist and Voting-Rights Litigation: The Case of the 1966 Texas Registration Statute," *Washington University Law Quarterly* (1971): 335-58; Steven J. Rosenstone and Raymond E. Wolfinger, "The Effect of Registration Laws on Voter Turnout," *American Political Science Review* 72 (March 1978): 22-45.

26. Samuel P. Hays, "Political Parties and the Community-Society Continuum," in *The American Party Systems: Stages of Political Development*, ed. William N. Chambers and Walter Dean Burnham, 2d ed. (New York, 1975), pp. 152-81.

27. Robert Caro, *The Power Broker: Robert Moses and the Fall of New York* (New York, 1975).

28. C. B. Macpherson, *Democracy in Alberta* (Toronto, 1953). See also Seymour M. Lipset, *Agrarian Socialism* (Berkeley, 1950).

29. The nine states with the largest vote for Eugene V. Debs in 1912 were, in order, Nevada (16.5 percent), Oklahoma (16.4 percent), Montana (13.5 percent), Arizona (13.4 percent), Washington (12.4 percent), California (11.7 percent), Idaho (11.3 percent), Oregon (9.7 percent), and Florida (9.5 percent).

30. Wiebe, *Search for Order*.

31. See Shover, "Was 1928 a Critical Election?" and Clubb and Allen, "The Cities and the Election of 1928." Lee Benson and Joel Silbey are working on a manuscript with the tentative title, "American Political Eras, 1788-1984." Much of their argument is that the sharp, durable, and systemwide electoral adjustments posited by critical realignment theory only appear to "work" empirically for the 1890s and perhaps the 1850s, and that the whole notion of "party systems" disappears into thin air when analysis is applied to nonpresidential electoral levels, especially in the twentieth century. A professional controversy over this argument seems certain to ensue.

32. For a discussion of this issue of state-printed ballots and split-ticket voting, see Jerrold G. Rusk, "The Effect of the Australian Ballot Reform on Split-Ticket Voting: 1876-1908," *American Political Science Review* 64 (December 1970): 1220-38. A rejoinder to this and other arguments of the "Michigan school" is found in Walter Dean Burnham, "Theory and Voting Research: Some Reflections on Philip E. Converse's 'Change in the American Electorate,' " *American Political Science Review* 68 (September 1974): 1002-23, especially pp. 1015-17. The discussion continues in separate "Comments" by Professors Rusk and Converse, with final remarks by the original author; see ibid., pp. 1028-57.

33. For examples, see Leon D. Epstein, *Politics in Wisconsin* (Madison, 1958); and John H. Fenton, *Midwest Politics* (New York, 1966). Fenton's description of

the Democratic party prior to the mid-1940s as a "hollow shell" and an "empty vessel" seems quite apt.

34. The exceptions are Connecticut and Illinois, where partisan data for the state senators have been substituted; in the first case because of the extreme nonapportionment scheme of 1818 in the lower house, in the second because of the severe damping effects associated with the cumulative vote system used for the lower house but not the upper house. It should also be noted that Minnesota eliminated partisan elections to its legislature effective with the 1914 elections, and Nebraska effective with the 1938 elections. Accordingly, Minnesota is included for the first two periods but not the last two; and Nebraska for the first three but not the last one.

35. The median value for each party and for each period has been used here rather than the arithmetic mean. The median is a more "robust" measure than the mean, i.e., it is insensitive to extreme values while the mean is not. This is of some importance, since, for example, Democratic legislative representation was virtually, but temporarily, wiped out in most of the nonsouthern states by the Republican landslide of 1920. Overall, the substitution of the median for the mean in Tables 5.4 and 5.5 produced considerably closer two-party margins —especially for the 1918-1930 period—than would otherwise be derived. It, therefore, involves a conservative estimate of the extent of Republican one-party legislative hegemony.

36. This point is argued forcefully, particularly so far as Herbert Hoover's vision is concerned, by William Appleman Williams, *Contours of American History* (Cleveland, 1961), pp. 413-38. For an extensive analysis of the corporate ideology at a somewhat later period, see Francis X. Sutton, Seymour E. Harris, Carl Kaysen, and James Tobin, *The American Business Creed* (Cambridge, 1956).

37. Burner, *The Politics of Provincialism*.

38. For the purposes of Table 5.6, counties (towns in New England) with a census population of 100,000 or more in 1920 were separated out and their presidential data analyzed after being summed to the regional level; the residue falls into the "nonmetropolitan" category. The data are presented in terms of subtracting the Republican from the Democratic percentage of the total presidential vote in each election; in 1912, Republican and Progressive votes are treated as a single Republican vote. This procedure results in the loss of much important detail. But—at the broad brush level to which it is appropriate —it conveys the "bottom line" of competition at the presidential level from 1876 to 1940 quite accurately.

39. Samuel Lubell, *The Future of American Politics* (New York, 1952); see also V. O. Key, Jr., "A Theory of Critical Elections," *Journal of Politics* 17 (February 1955): 3-18.

40. See, for example, David R. Mayhew, *Congress: The Electoral Connection* (New Haven, 1974). Morris P. Fiorina, *Congress: Keystone of the Washington Establishment* (New Haven, 1976); and Walter Dean Burnham, "The 1976 Election: Has the Crisis Been Adjourned?" in *American Politics and Public Policy*, ed. Burnham and Martha Wagner Weinberg (Cambridge, 1978), pp. 1-25, and especially pp. 14-20; and Walter Dean Burnham, "Insulation and Responsive-

ness in Congressional Elections," *Political Science Quarterly* 90 (Fall 1975): 411-35.

41. See Key, *American State Politics*, pp. 85-196; idem, "The Direct Primary and Party Structure: A Study of State Legislative Nominations," *American Politican Science Review* 48 (March 1954): 1-26.

42. Minnesota had a two and one-half party system from about 1916 to 1944 (Republicans and Farmer-Laborites, with Democrats a distant—largely Irish-Catholic—third). In New York, electoral law was changed in the 1930s to accommodate the fact that the electorate was too polyglot to be contained readily within a two-party framework. Thus arose multiple "lines" on the ballot, a succession of well-known and apparently durable third parties such as the American Labor party (1936-1954), the Liberal party (1944 to date), and the Conservative party (1962 to date), and multiple party nominations of the same candidate.

43. Burnham, "Theory and Voting Research"; and idem, "The Appearance and Disappearance of the American Voter" (paper presented to a conference of the American Bar Association on voting participation, June 1978).

44. Rosenstone and Wolfinger, "The Effect of Registration Laws on Voter Turnout."

45. Burnham, "Theory and Voting Research," especially pp. 1004-12.

46. H.L.A. Tingsten, *Political Behavior* (London, 1937), pp. 10-78.

47. Ibid., pp. 157-58.

48. Efforts to reconstruct the partisan preferences of the American electorate prior to the New Deal should not overlook that this "Hoover surge" was also evident in 1928 in cities with large but primarily native-stock working-class populations like Flint, Michigan and Akron, Ohio. Did such surges reflect the "real" underlying distribution of (mobilized) partisan preference prior to the Great Crash of 1929, or was this merely a "deviating election" in such areas? The counterfactual problems here are very considerable. For example, see Kristi Andersen, "Generation, Partisan Shift, and Realignment: A Glance Back to the New Deal," in *The Changing American Voter* by Norman H. Nie, Sidney Verba, and John R. Petrocik, (Cambridge, 1976), pp. 74-95.

49. E. E. Schattschneider, "United States: The Functional Approach to Party Government," in *Modern Political Parties*, ed. Sigmund Neumann (Chicago, 1956), pp. 194-215.

50. Even before World War I, the ethnicity problem which Socialists faced seems to have been formidable; Arthur Goren, "A Portrait of Ethnic Politics: The Socialists and the 1908 and 1910 Congressional Elections on the East Side," in *Voters, Parties and Elections*, ed. Joel H. Silbey and Samuel T. McSeveney (Lexington, Mass., 1972), pp. 235-59.

51. This Catholic antagonism to socialism seems to have been of exceptional importance as a limiting factor. See Marc Karson, "Catholic Anti-Socialism," reprinted in *Failure of a Dream? Essays in the History of American Socialism*, ed. John H. M. Laslett and Seymour Martin Lipset (Garden City, N.Y., 1974), pp. 164-84.

Richard Jensen

THE LAST PARTY SYSTEM: DECAY OF CONSENSUS, 1932-1980

6

A consensus on three fundamental political values united Americans in the first two-thirds of the twentieth century. First, the country was committed to a capitalist system and a program of steady economic modernization, based on the spread of technology and education. Second, Americans embraced a pluralism, affirming that every ethnic and socioeconomic group was to share in the benefits of modernization (not necessarily equally), and no white group was to be proscribed. Third, continuous progress toward a single modern standard of universal morality was called for. William McKinley led the way for acceptance of the first two points, the Progressives, the third. The American consensus stood in sharp contrast to the fundamental disagreement over ultimate values that characterized the major continental countries; unlike Germany, Russia, France, Spain, and Italy, the United States did not come close to civil war or major political violence during the century. As a result, American politics was dull—all the major changes were no more than minor variations on basic themes.[1]

During the first thirty years of the century, the acceptance of economic modernization was unchallenged by vast majorities of voters, politicians, and elites. In sharp contrast to Europe, the Socialist movement in the United States was small, static, and peripheral. The pluralist conception of society held up fairly well, once it was agreed (in the 1890s) that blacks could share economic and social benefits in segregated and inferior forms only, and could have no share whatever of political power. The anti-German sentiment during World War I briefly threatened the pluralist consensus. Fortunately, the Anglo-Saxon majority quickly dropped its anti-German crusade by 1919, though the German-Americans themselves remained embittered and cynical through 1924. The Ku Klux Klan, with its platform that moral progress was incompatible with pluralism, flashed on and off the scene too quickly to challenge the consensus effectively. In 1928 the issue for many Protestans was whether a Catholic president, particularly one tied to machine politics and opposition to Prohibition, could lead a society committed to moral progress. It is important to note that this sort of anti-Catholicism appeared only at the presidential level, and did not infect contests at lower levels.

THE NEW DEAL ERA

Did the Great Depression have the potential to undermine the consensus regarding continued modernization in a capitalist framework? Historians, well aware of the emergence of autarky and dictatorships throughout the world in the 1930s, have searched for indications of a permanent loss of faith in America. They have found few examples. The Unemployment Councils were one candidate, but they were so clearly controlled by Socialists and Communists who rejected the whole consensus that they cannot be taken as representative. At the time, Midwestern farmer unrest was considered an indicator of violent rejection of the consensus. Careful recent studies have undercut this argument, showing that a limited number of farmers were engaged in strictly limited actions to protect their own property interests. Dumping milk in the milksheds around small cities, for example, served to raise prices, not to challenge the economic order. The type of agrarian socialism that caught hold in Saskatchewan was not reflected south of the border; even in Canada the agrarians preached a much watered version of socialism.[2]

The Democrats challenged the Republicans in 1932 on the grounds of failure to produce the prosperity called for by the consensus. Throughout the 1930s and beyond, the Democrats argued that they could do a better job of producing prosperity. The 1932 contest showed a surge of middle class votes into the Democratic column. One national survey indicated that 18 percent of the middle class voters who supported Herbert Hoover in 1928 switched to Franklin D. Roosevelt.[3] A 1936 Gallup poll indicated that businessmen split 50-50 in 1932, and professionals gave Roosevelt a slight edge (53-47).[4]

This is not to argue that there was no clear differential in 1932. To the contrary, skilled workers (in terms of their *1936* jobs) voted 65 percent for Roosevelt in 1932; those who were unskilled or employed by the Works Progress Administration (WPA) in 1936 had voted 82 percent for Roosevelt in 1932; farmers were 67 percent behind FDR the first time around. (These figures are probably inflated from 4 to 6 points because too many people recalled voting for the winner.)[5]

The first New Deal reflected a slightly revised version of the three consensual themes. Historians now mostly agree that Roosevelt's reform programs, though more dramatic and far-reaching than Hoover's, in essence represented a continuation rather than a divergence from Hoover's philosophy. The consensual style of the first New Deal was perfectly captured by the mass enthusiasm—parades, speeches, banners, posters everywhere—stirred up for the NRA.

Above all the New Deal in 1933-1934 was pluralistic. It had a program for everyone; farmer and consumer, worker and industrialist, banker and depositor, importer and exporter, old and young, rich and poor, economizer and spendthrift. Everyone, that is, who was represented by an organized group. Only the Socialists were left out (but brought in later through FDR's ties to third parties, like the Farmer-Labor party in Minnesota or the American Labor Party in New York City). Special recognition, through highly visible patronage, was accorded Catholics and Jews. Blacks were not recognized at first, and Orientals, especially Japanese, continued to be ostracized. On the other hand, there was a special New Deal for Indians.

Roosevelt's recovery programs and his all-embracing pluralism occasioned surprisingly little criticism in 1933-1934. More pointed was the reaction to his new version of moralism. Prohibition was abandoned and, much more controversial, Roosevelt's programs helped rebuild the big city Democratic machines, even the most corrupt. (He fought Tammany Hall in Manhattan, using the machines in other boroughs as counterweights.) Staunch New Dealers like Harold Ickes (Secretary of the Interior) and Senator George Norris (Republican, Nebraska) protested to no avail. In 1934 the machines produced enormous Democratic majorities, washing away the last of the Republican middle class urban reformers. (New York City, with "Republican" Mayor Fiorello La Guardia, again represented the major exception.)

The New Deal relief program became increasingly heavily politicized. The WPA, in particular, tied to state politicians, was a major factor in politics, much to the dismay of good-government moralists. In March 1938, for example, 53 percent of the population—and 47 percent of those on WPA—claimed that politics entered "quite a bit" into "giving relief in this community."[6] Econometric analysis of state-by-state relief expenditures shows that political considerations (like closeness of the vote) far overshadowed poverty in explaining the distribution of billions of dollars of relief money. Historians examining the situation by states and cities concur that politicized relief, especially as channeled through Democratic organizations, played a major role in rebuilding the Democratic coalition.[7] At one time or another during the decade, somewhere between 40 and 45 percent of all American families received federal relief.[8] Gallup polls show that families receiving politicized relief (WPA, CCC, NYA, and related programs) voted much more heavily Democratic than did poor people not on relief. In August 1936, for example, reliefers were 82 percent for Roosevelt; the lowest one-third income group was 70 percent; and the highest third, only 41 percent. On the other hand, persons receiving nonpoliticized relief, such as the veterans' bonus or old age assistance, voted only slightly more Democratic.[9]

It would be crass to say that the New Deal was buying votes. (People said it anyway, and Congress passed the Hatch Act in 1939 after the exposure of some nasty scandals.) The New Deal was building a new coalition, based largely on the votes of poor people who needed relief and a sense that society cared about them. Relief recipients hailed Roosevelt as a savior, but their traditionally low turnout rates posed a serious obstacle to mobilizing their latent strength. The deep strategy of the New Deal was to build mechanisms for turning loyalty into votes. The Democratic machines were available for the modest cost of being allowed to distribute relief. The inefficiency and corruption that ensued troubled only a few New Dealers (Ickes and Norris, again). The blacks, who suffered severely in the depression, received relief not in proportion to their needs—far from it—but in proportion to what was needed to switch their votes. By 1934, or 1936 at the latest, blacks had deserted the GOP.[10]

Labor unions were a second factor in the new coalition. McKinley's consensus politics allowed cooperative labor unions to flourish, particularly unions in the building and printing trades, and in the coal mines. The unions had rid themselves of most Socialist elements, and were enthusiastic supporters of consensus politics. Many top leaders were Republicans. Roosevelt was never enthusiastic about unions, but the New Deal did foster a legal climate favorable to their rapid growth in the mid and late 1930s. In return, the unions swung their new members toward the Democratic party. Equally important, they worked hard to increase the turnout in labor districts. In 1936 and 1940, union members voted 8 points more Democratic than blue-collar workers who did not belong to unions. The importance of unions became even more apparent in 1944 and 1948, when members voted far more Democratic than nonunion labor (see Table 6.1).[11]

The split between the American Federation of Labor (AF of L) and the Congress of Industrial Organizations (CIO) had little direct consequence on the vote, for members of both federations supported Roosevelt unreservedly. Indirectly, the split generated offsetting poli-

Table 6.1 Labor Vote, 1936-1948, Democratic Percentage

	1932	1936	1940	1944	1948
Nonunion Labor	—	72	64	56	60
AF of L Members	—	80	71	69	73
CIO Members	—	85	79	78	76
Union—Nonunion Differential	—	8	8	16	14
Union Members as percentage of total labor force*	6.0	7.4	15.5	21.4	23.1

Source: George Gallup, *The Political Almanac: 1952* (New York, 1952), p. 37; Bureau of the Census, *Historical Statistics of the United States* Washington, D.C., 1976), p. 178.

*The percentage of voters in union families was about the same as that of union members in the total labor force.

tical consequences. The AF of L roused itself to enlarging its membership, and actually grew more than the CIO. On the other hand, the two federations opposed each other bitterly in internal Democratic politics. The AF of L, siding with big city machines and occasionally with Republicans (as in New York), largely blocked the CIO from access to power. The CIO leaders—younger and more militant than AF of L counterparts—for a while contemplated the formation of a labor party. The fiasco of Henry Wallace in 1948 convinced Walter Reuther and other CIO stalwarts of the folly of third partyism. Furthermore, the CIO was never large enough to win, even in strongholds like Detroit. The CIO membership was younger and poorer than the AF of L's, factors conducive to formation of a third party. However, the CIO's concentration in the largest Eastern and Midwestern states meant a third party would collide head-on with the better established party organizations. By the 1950s the CIO leadership itself was beginning to age. Realizing that the legitimacy of unions had long been accepted by large corporations and that memories of the militant days of the 1930s were receding, the CIO merged with the AF of L in the mid-1950s. Thereafter, with the exception of defensive reactions to occasional antiunion GOP campaigns (1958, 1964), the unions played a modest role in elections. The membership, concerned more with wages than power, had accepted consensus politics and could no longer be rallied. On the other hand, the membership had little control over union leaders and was unable to prevent the leadership from supporting causes (for example, stop-Wallace in 1968, pro-integration throughout the 1960s) that were unpopular with the rank and file.[12]

Within the union movement itself, social, ethnic, economic, and ideological divisions existed. Indeed, the voting patterns *within* the unions mirrored those in society at large, though with a shift to the left. Thus, in 1944, *among union members*, religion, ethnicity, socioeconomic status, occupation, and size of city were all strong predictors of the vote.[13] The obvious explanation is that American unions, unlike their European counterparts, had never sought a homogeneous worker culture (with separate cooperative stores, clubs, sports, entertainment, newspapers, and so forth), and operated instead as another interest group within a complex, pluralistic society. Consequently, unions could mobilize members only when issues directly relevant to job security and pay were at stake.

The pluralistic character of American society in the 1930s and 1940s can be underscored by examining a major group, the Catholics, that superficially appeared quite homogeneous. It is true that Catholics far more than Protestants supported the Democratic party and comprised an imporant core group in Roosevelt's coalition. In 1944, for example, Catholics provided one-fourth of Roosevelt's total vote. However, they also provided one-tenth of Thomas Dewey's vote. Although the Catholics voted 70 to 80 percent Democract in the 1930s and 1940s, the variations in their vote over time exactly paralleled the national totals (see Table 6.2). More impressive is the fact that the same personal and

Table 6.2 Correlates of the Vote, 1940-1944: Catholics and Total Population*

	1940		1944	
	ALL	*CATHOLICS*	*ALL*	*CATHOLICS*
Denomination	.21	—	.25	—
Father's Birthplace	.15	.17	.19	.20
Occupation	.15	.16	.14	.11
Socioeconomic Status	.16	.13	.15	.04
Region	.11	.06	.11	.08
Age	.02	.10	.05	.05
Sex	.04	.03	.01	.05
Union Membership	.16	.17	.17	.16
Size of Place	.12	.15	.11	.11

Source: American Institute for Public Opinion (AIPO) no. 335 (October 1944); N=2453 total, 440 Catholics

*Entries are eta coefficients. In most cases, the partial beta coefficients, measuring the effect of a variable after controlling for other variables, are slightly lower than the reported etas.

community characteristics that were linked to voting behavior among Protestants were also linked among Catholics. Because of the role of southern Protestants, regionalism was more important for the entire electorate than for Catholics alone. Socioeconomic status was also less important among Catholics in 1944, but that may have been an ephemeral effect.[14] Ethnicity was as important among Catholics as it was in the electorate at large. (This was caused by the lukewarm reception Roosevelt received among Italian and German Catholics.) In general, the correlations are strikingly similar for Catholics and all voters. The implication is that, apart from specific denominational effects, exactly the same social forces affected Catholics and Protestants. Detailed tables (not shown here) indicate that the specific social effects were almost exactly parallel among Catholics and among Protestants.

Religious denominational effects were strong throughout the 1930s and 1940s. The religious effects observed in the New Deal era (see Table 6.3) resembled those of the late nineteenth century.[15] Whether the linkage was continuous or primarily shaped by intervening events requires analysis of voting patterns between 1900 and 1936. My opinion is that the effects were continuous. These religious denominational effects only began to fade after 1960, and by the 1970s they were reduced to minor importance.

Table 6.3 Denominational Effects, 1940-1944

	Deviation from National Average*			
	1940		*1944*	
	Observed	*Controlled*+	*Observed*	*Controlled*+
Catholic	22.7	17.1	24.8	21.5
Jewish	48.6	36.2	72.1	61.0
Baptist	6.3	6.7	5.4	4.9
Methodist	–10.6	–8.5	–12.8	–11.6
Lutheran	2.6	1.0	–1.6	–2.3
High Status Protestant**	–15.2	–12.4	–12.3	–9.6
Other Protestant	–15.3	–11.1	–17.4	–14.2
None	9.1	3.2	9.4	5.3
eta/beta	.21	.15	.25	.21

Source: American Institute for Public Opinion (AIPO), no. 335 (October 1944).

*The entries are vote scores, with a Roosevelt vote = 100, a Republican vote = –100, and nonvote = 0. The national average was 2.2 in 1944, 8.8 in 1940. Thus, Catholics scored 2.2 + 24.8 = 27.0 in 1944. To convert to vote shares, divide by 2 and add 50. This makes the Catholics 63.5 percent Democratic in 1944 (counting a nonvote as 50 percent).

+Controlled for father's birthplace, union membership, sex, and socioeconomic status.

**Presbyterians, Congregationalists, and Episcopalians.

The size of place effect in the politics of the 1930s and 1940s was striking, and calls for more explanation than it usually receives (see Table 6.4). Consider the 1940 election. One-third of the voters lived in the 106 cities with more than 100,000 population; they gave Roosevelt 61 percent of their ballots.[16] One-sixth of the voters lived in the South, where FDR swept 73 percent of the vote. The remaining half of the electorate, the rural and small town North, favored Wendell Willkie by 53 percent. Roosevelt carried 71 of the 80 largest northern cities (mean share of 59 percent). There was little variation, as every type of city went Democratic. Of course, Roosevelt did best in ethnic mill towns (77 percent in Camden, 71 percent in Fall River and New Bedford, 70 percent in Youngstown), and worst in old stock nonindustrial trade centers and suburbs (47 percent in Berkeley, 43 percent in Pasadena, 44 percent in Tulsa, 46 percent in Yonkers, 50 percent in Indianapolis). Nevertheless the uniformity of his urban support is striking. The standard deviation of his city vote share was only 6.6 percent, despite the heterogeneity of the cities, while the standard deviation of his vote share in nonmetropolitan northern counties was a much higher 9.9 percent.

Table 6.4 Democratic Vote by Size of Place, 1932-1948

	1932	1936	1940	1944	1946*	1948+
Total vote	59	63	55	54	43	55
106 large cities	62	70	61	61	48	60
Rest of the United States	58	59	52	50	40	52

Source: George Gallup, *Political Almanac, 1952* (New York, 1952), pp. 32, 65; *Newsweek* (November 18, 1946), p.34.

*North only.

+Includes Wallace and Thurmond vote.

The class structure of cities does not help explain their behavior. In the presuburban era, the central cities had a large middle class population. In fact, the ratio of white-collar to blue-collar workers was almost exactly the same inside and outside large cities. Other compositional effects were somewhat stronger. The large cities held 28 percent of the entire population (1940), 33 percent of the voters in 1944, 49 percent of union members, and 44 percent of Catholics. (The Jewish population, though heavily urban, was not significant outside New York; the northern black population was also urban, but still small in 1940.) About one-half of Roosevelt's extra votes in northern cities can be attributed to compositional factors. The other half came from *inside* the groups. Union members were 12 points more Democratic in 1944 if they lived in big cities, Catholics were 16 points more Democratic, Protestants were 12 points higher.

The historian naturally fastens on the machine as the only distinctive urban feature that could cause effects of this magnitude. Recent scholarship has clearly shown that the New Deal, far from rendering the machine obsolete, reinvigorated it for at least another decade.[17] By channeling relief money through the machines and by an unabashed return to a heavy-handed use of patronage on a scale unknown since the 1880s, the New Deal more than satisfied the local bosses. In return, the machines assumed a new role in politics. Traditionally they were primarily concerned with local patronage and local elections. Majorities in key wards and in citywide contests had been their prime electoral goal. Now they were called upon to generate huge vote totals that could swing statewide, and, indeed, national elections. Winning the city was no longer enough if the machines were to fulfill their end of the bargain. The machines responded enthusiastically by enrolling new voters. Total turnout soared in the cities, as ethnics, especially women, came to the polls in unprecedented numbers. To a large degree, the success of the New Deal coalition resulted not from the conversion of former Republicans but from the mobilization of former nonvoters. The chief weakness of the new strategy was its heavy reliance on the symbolization of Franklin Roosevelt. It proved possible to idolize the president and turn out millions when his name appeared on the ballot. In nonpresidential contests, however, the new electorate was difficult to mobilize. The unions tried to help, but the AF of L versus CIO tensions undercut the unanimity needed to mobilize the full Democratic vote. Thus the off-year contests of the 1938, 1942 and 1946 produced an average Democratic congressional vote of 48.2 percent nationwide and 46.1 percent in the key urban states, while the corresponding Democratic presidential vote in 1936, 1940, 1944, and 1948 was 55.3 percent nationwide and 52.9 percent in the urban states.[18] The Democratic vote plunged 6 or 7 points when Roosevelt was not on the ballot, thereby allowing Republicans to capture the major states in off-year contests. Turnout was the key factor, with congressional turnout averaging 52.2 percent of the electorate in presidential election years (1936-1948), but only 38.0 percent in off years (1938-1946). Despite machine and union efforts, class strongly affected turnout. Nationally in 1940, for example, among adults who had not attended college, 83 percent of the wealthiest one-fourth reported a vote, compared to only 54 percent of the poorest one-fourth.[19] In off-year contests, the class differential in turnout was even stronger (see Table 6.5), thereby neutralizing the Republican deficit in loyal supporters.

Table 6.5 Turnout in 1940 and 1942 by Socioeconomic Status

	Reported Turnout*	
	1940	*1942*
Very High (top seventh)	93	79
Above Average (next third)	87	72
Below Average (bottom half)	75	47
All	82	62

Source: AIPO, no. 294 (April 1943).

*People typically overreport turnout in polls; the relative patterns are probably accurate.

Patronage and turnout, while decisive in controlling the outcome of elections after 1936, are of less intrinsic interest to the historian than the ideological structures of politics. Historians still debate the New Deal's relationship to the prime element in the American consensus, economic modernization under capitalism. The New Dealers and their programs were a diverse lot. They never attempted to overthrow capitalism, but their programs gave sharply conflicting signals regarding the desirability of further economic modernization. Democratic rhetoric was posited upon a return of 1929 levels of prosperity, and, in the case of TVA and other southern-oriented programs, of pulling backward areas up to the national standard. On the other hand, the New Dealers rarely thought in terms of permanent continuous growth. Roosevelt at several points, including key campaign statements in 1932 and 1936, suggested that the economy was fully built, if not overbuilt, and that his task was to remove power from the hands of the growth-oriented entrepreneurs who were no longer socially useful. They had become "economic royalists." The New Deal vision was of a no-growth economy, with a permanent class of unemployed for whom elaborate welfare programs were required.[20]

Whether or not this was the true goal of the New Deal, it certainly seemed that way to friend and foe alike. A large cadre of party leaders and early New Dealers bolted Roosevelt and supported Alfred Landon in 1936 on these grounds. When Wendell Willkie emerged as a fresh spokesman for sustained economic growth, he became a hero in the GOP, won the nomination (despite his recent Tammany Hall affiliation), and crusaded for a return to the growth society.

By 1935 or 1936 politics began to pivot on class and ideological lines. Class effects were not new, as we have seen, but they grew in importance reaching a climax in 1948. The ideological debate was a new development in recent American politics. Growth-oriented Americans, largely from the middle class, switched to the conservative opposition. Security-oriented Americans, largely from the working classes, became politicized on behalf of the liberal party. Farmers, a mix of the two types, veered first toward the Democrats for security; when farm prices firmed, they moved toward the GOP.

Inter-election vote switching underscores the pattern. Businessmen switched to Landon while workers went the other way between 1932 and 1936. Even stronger patterns followed ideological issues. Social Security was a major issue in 1936, and of ex-Hoover voters who supported the new program, 30 percent switched to Roosevelt (versus only 7 percent of those opposed). Conversely, 40 percent of the 1932 Roosevelt voters who disliked Social Security switched to Landon, compared to only 12 percent of the supporters of the plan. Previous nonvoters who liked Social Security preferred Roosevelt by 74 percent, while 59 percent of its opponents favored Landon (see Table 6.6).

Political liberalism in 1936 correlated with class; the poor were more liberal, the better off more conservative. Controlling for the vote, however, the relationship was weak. Roosevelt supporters, rich or

Table 6.6 1936 Roosevelt Vote by 1932 Vote and Opinion of Social Security

	Favor		Oppose	
1932 Vote	*% FDR*	*N*	*% FDR*	*N*
FDR	88.3	1630	60.0	482
Landon	29.7	643	6.8	635
No Vote	74.3	303	40.9	127
Total	72.0	2576	30.9	1244

Source: AIPO, no. 53 (October 1936); cf. V.O. Key, *The Responsible Electorate* (Cambridge, 1966), pp. 41-43.

Note: Socialist 1932 voters heavily favored the plan, and two-thirds deserted Norman Thomas, nearly all going to Roosevelt. Lemke voters, largely drawn from FDR's earlier supporters, also favored the plan.

Table 6.7 Liberalism in 1936, by Socioeconomic Status and Vote

Socioeconomic Status	**Liberalism scores***			
	All	*FDR*	*Landon*	*No Vote*
High	–.31	.34	–.78	–.13
Average	–.03	.52	–.72	–.06
Poor	.18	.44	–.56	–.02
Relief	.24	.38	–.38	–.05
Unknown	–.02	.49	–.77	–.21
Black	–.15	.06	–.62	–.06
ALL	0.0	.44	–.71	–.07

Source: AIPO, no. 57 (November 1936); N=2720.

*Based on opposition to the gold standard, to the Supreme Court's overturning the New Deal and Congress, or to a balanced budget; plus preference for Borah, Farley, Lewis, Wagner, or Wallace in 1940. Entries are Z scores, with mean = 0 and standard deviation = 1.00.

poor, were about equally liberal. A class-based tension did exist inside the GOP, however, with higher income Republicans more conservative than poor Republicans (see Table 6.7). The implication is that the Roosevelt coalition in 1936 was more viable than Landon's opposition. The deep split among Republicans over Social Security underscored this phenomenon. The Republicans in 1936 had already lost many of their poorer supporters, and would lose more if they could not develop a more united front against the New Deal. After 1936 they were saved by the Supreme Court fight, labor unrest, and the depression of 1937-1938, which tended to create tensions in the Roosevelt coalition while reducing them inside the GOP.

In the four presidential contests after 1936, the Democrats lost their wealthiest voters to the GOP and gained few poor switchers in return. Such a pattern may seem paradoxical, but the evidence is consistent. By 1948 the Democrats had ridiculously little support among the top one-fourth of the socioeconomic structure, whether measured by wealth, occupation, or education.[21] The party's overall support slid steadily, as the Democrats lost one percent of the electorate every year. That is, the *net* loss was one percent, comprised of offsetting trends. Defections were high but the Democrats gained among young voters entering the system, while old voters who died were heavily Republican. The polarization along class lines increased after 1936 (possibly after 1934, but we lack poll data), reaching a climax in 1948, when European-style divisions between the working class and the middle class almost became paramount in American politics.

Americans were polarized not only along class lines but also on ideological points. The two effects united to influence partisanship. Thus the consensus within the GOP became diametrically opposed, on many issues, to the consensus within the Democratic party. Public opinion polls revealed vast gulfs between partisans on issues like Supreme Court reform, responsibility for continued depression, and the threat of domestic dictatorship. The differences between Republicans and Democrats on foreign policy, however, were quite small. By the late 1930s Americans were snarling at each other, with economic hardship exacerbating the tension and the aura of violence around sit-down strikes threatening to touch off political violence in the streets.

Businessmen (and professionals) had lost confidence in the ability of the government to restore prosperity. The loss of confidence carried over into economic decision making. Major investments were postponed, with large quantities of corporate reserves and private savings going into unproductive government notes instead of expansion capital. Everyone agreed the situation was bad. Republicans built their campaigns in 1936, 1938 and, especially, 1940 around the theme of restoring a favorable investment climate. Roosevelt was livid, denouncing the tailspin depression of 1937-1938 as a deliberate attempt by business to discredit the New Deal (by going bankrupt!). He charged that it was capital striking against the government, while businessmen angrily shouted it was just the reverse. American businessmen, particularly corporate executives and bankers, have always been suspicious of the federal government; and have felt that they, not the government, had built the economy. Worse, the democratic system risked having the government controlled by enemies of permanent growth. The solution, business felt, was to keep government out of the economy. The alternative was socialism.[22]

Liberals (that is, supporters of the New Deal) were convinced that business was plotting to seize control of the government, through the agency of the GOP and use it to recover lost profits by exploiting the poor. Fascism was the threat, and this fear animated all the presidential campaigns from 1936 through 1948. Willkie was savaged as a little Hitler by leading New Dealers. Dewey was, in Truman's impassioned rhetoric, a front man for the selfish big interests, particularly Wall Street. Comity no longer softened rhetoric; only good and evil were on the ballot.

The war years saw the underlying crises of political economy resolved, while the partisans carried on angrily as if nothing had changed. Rapid growth replaced economic stagnation, as the munitions-induced climate for investment suddenly turned highly favorable for business. Furthermore, it was patriotic to push for all-out production. The New Deal welfare programs, posited on permanent stagnation, were dismantled. (Except for Social Security—in terms of welfare, it was a minor program in the 1940s, and it reflected as well a broad consensus that old people should be retired to give youth a chance.) The wise New Dealers turned their antifascism to foreign policy, where they worked in harmony with the corporate executives called in to direct wartime mobilization. Those New Dealers who continued to focus on domestic dangers, like Henry Wallace and Chester Bowles of the Office of Price Administration (OPA), were systematically defeated. Indeed, the strongest Republican arguments during the war and early postwar era attacked price controls and rationing as vestiges of New Deal bureaucratic interference. "Free enterprise," the conservatives insisted, would win the war and generate permanent prosperity. Licking their wounds after the 1942 elections, Democratic leaders across the country attributed their defeat first, to resentment of the OPA; second, lethargic conduct of the war; third, hostility to federal bureaucracy. (In New York, Pennsylvania, and several other states, Democratic party leaders complained that the Hatch Act prohibiting politicking by government employees had ruined their campaign techniques.)[23]

PROLONGING THE NEW DEAL: 1948

The 1948 election returns not only dumbfounded everyone at the time, they have also left historians speechless. The basic facts are that Harry Truman enjoyed a modest lead in the polls early in 1948, fell far behind in the summer, and caught up rapidly in October to surge ahead of Dewey by a small margin (52-48) at the last minute. Such a scenario never occurred to pollsters and commentators in 1948, because they knew that little shifting took place in the late stages of the 1936, 1940, and 1944 elections. A little history can be dangerous. Our knowledge of the dramatic catchup campaigns of Hubert Humphrey in 1968, Gerald Ford in 1976, and Jimmy Carter (against Edward Kennedy) in 1979-1980 puts 1948 in clearer perspective.[24]

Truman's strategy in 1948 was to emphasize long-term forces, such as party loyalty and the New Deal heritage. Democrats outnumbered Republicans by a wide margin. Furthermore, even the Deweyites had friendly memories of the New Deal: 54 percent felt it had done more good than harm, and 92 percent of the Trumanites, and 87 percent of the undecided agreed.[25] Dewey's challenge, conversely, was to emphasize short-term factors, especially personality and concern over inflation. The bitter infighting within the Democratic ranks in 1948, leading to schisms left and right and machine efforts to dump Truman, accentuated short-term factors. There was grave doubt whether Truman could govern.

Until the very eve of the election Truman was unable fully to mobilize such key elements of the New Deal coalition as Catholics, union members, and the urban poor generally. He ran well behind the state and congressional tickets throughout the summer and early fall. Truman's tactic was a "give 'em hell" campaign that was designed to revive historic loyalties. It may have done that, in the end, but for most of the campaign Truman's raucous tone, contrasted to Dewey's presidential demeanor, only further highlighted the personalities of the candidates.[26]

The cities were the key battleground in 1948. The suburban trend had just begun to escalate, so millions of middle class voters, newly prosperous after the war years, still lived inside the city limits. Regardless of partisanship they were hostile to machine politics. The effects of the Hatch Act and the termination of discretionary federal relief programs left the machines depleted in patronage. Bipartisan or nonpartisan reform movements put the machines on the defensive in most large cities. Boston, Jersey City, Memphis, and even Chicago were threatened with reform. The only remaining Republican machine, in Philadelphia, verged on collapse. Catholics, who comprised one-third of the big city population, seemed vulnerable to nonpartisanship for the first time. Catholics in cities over 500,000 were 10 points *less* Democratic in party affiliation in 1948 than Catholics in other places, controlling for age, education, and socioeconomic status (see Table 6.8). Somehow, the remnants of the machines, aided enormously by the unions, managed to achieve victory in 1948. They were attempting to salvage state and congressional candidates, but in the process they pulled Truman back into the New Deal long-term coalition. It was the last hurrah—except for Chicago, all the machines were in rapid decline. Not until the emergence of black ward machines in the 1960s would old-style politics again play a significant role.[27]

The Democrats in 1948, leaders and rank and file alike, had little confidence in Truman. They reelected him anyway, as part of their reaffirmation of long-term loyalties, hoping that short-term disasters

Table 6.8 Party Identification in 1948

	Northern Protestants		Catholics	
	OBSERVED[1]	*ADJUSTED*[2]	*OBSERVED*[1]	*ADJUSTED*[2]
Overall Mean[3]	45.6	45.6	67.2	67.2
Education: Eta/Beta	+ .15	+ .11	+ .15	+ .07
Grade school	+ 8	+ 6	+ 7	+ 3
High school	− 2	− 3	− 3	− 2
College	−11	− 4	−11	− 4
Age: Eta/Beta	+ .12	+ .09	+ .06	+ .04
SES: Eta/Beta	+ .23	+ .19	+ .19	+ .17
Top 1/6	−19	−16	−17	−15
Next 1/3	− 7	− 5	− 9	− 8
Bottom 1/2	+ 8	+ 7	+ 5	+ 4
Size of Place: Eta/Beta	+ .04	+ .04	+ .11	+ .11
Rural, farm	0	0	+ 1	+ 2
Town, city (2500-100,000)	+ 1	+ 1	+ 3	+ 2
Large city (100-500,000)	0	+ 1	+ 3	+ 4
Metropolis (500,000 plus)	+ 4	+ 3	− 7	− 7

Source: AIPO, no. 429 (October 1948), weighted N=3307 northern Protestants, 1395 Catholics, and 257 Jews.

[1]Scale values: 100 = Democratic or Progressive; 50 = Independent; 0 = Republican. The standard deviation was 43.5 for northern Protestants, 36.0 for Catholics.

[2]Controlling for the other three variables.

[3]For Jews, mean = 69.3, st. dev. = 27.6; eta and beta were .18, .26 for education; .05, .16 for age; .13, .03 for SES; .15 and .14 for size of place. Jewish detailed patterns were parallel to those of northern Protestants, but about twice as large in each category.

could be avoided. Their hopes were frustrated, as the second-term president continued to anger foes and bewilder friends. The issue of communism was a case in point. Public and elite opinion turned sharply against the Soviet Union shortly after the war, almost entirely as a result of American reactions to foreign events. The Republicans had raised the issue of domestic communism during the war, but had gained little from it. By 1948 liberals had turned anti-Communist, as unions and party organizations deposed entrenched left-wing elements in their ranks. The Truman administration embraced domestic anti-communism in an effort to establish its leadership of the morality dimension of the American consensus. A series of spectacular spy cases, however, shifted the initiative to Republicans like Richard Nixon and Joe McCarthy.[28]

The failure to resolve the Korean War eroded what was left of Truman's popularity, and he bowed out of the 1952 race as a new Republican leader, Dwight Eisenhower, crusaded for a restoration of the moral consensus. A long series of scandals, reaching into the White House, further tarnished the Democratic image. The selection of an outsider, Governor Adlai Stevenson, as the Democratic presidential candidate did little to blunt the onslaught against communism, Korea, and corruption. The most successful issues for GOP candidates in 1952 were "Trumanism," inflation and waste, municipal corruption and crime, communism in government, the Korean war, and creeping socialism. Ingeniously, the Republicans were silent on the New Deal, attributing all its defects to Trumanism.[29] The best argument the hapless Democrats could muster was that Eisenhower was a dangerous "man on horseback"—a military figure who did not understand the consensus around which American politics revolved. Their response to his crusade was a countercrusade, which failed because of Eisenhower's secure control of the morality issue.[30]

Liberal Democrats in 1952 feared that the Republicans would undo the New Deal. They were surprised by Eisenhower's first term—indeed, by 1956, Democratic leaders in Congress claimed they were giving the popular president more support than the Republicans. This tactic left Stevenson isolated in his second presidential bid, but it did signal a return to comity in American politics. By 1956 epithets like "Communist," "Fascist," and "traitor" had disappeared from political rhetoric. The liberals, however, were mistaken about Republican acceptance of the New Deal. Party leaders, including Eisenhower, were as conservative as ever. Most of the New Deal programs obnoxious to the conservatives had been dismantled or radically redone during the 1940s. The Republicans accepted and expanded Social Security and minimum wage coverage primarily to head off liberal demands for new welfare programs. They were successful throughout the 1950s and early 1960s.[31]

The period from 1950 through 1962 saw a stalemate in national and state politics. Although the Democrats had more adherents, the wealthier and better-educated Republicans turned out to vote more often. Short-term forces, revolving around personality and morality issues, tended to favor the GOP. Foreign policy, essentially a short-term factor, also favored the Republicans, as did their reputation for superior management. The chief weakness of the GOP was its unfavorable reputation for maintaining prosperity (a major liability in 1958) and its negative image in terms of group benefits. Polls from 1944 to the present show that farmers, blue-collar and clerical workers believed that the Democrats best represented their interests, while the GOP remained saddled with the onus of being the party of big business. Consensus politics, as personified by Eisenhower, neutralized most of this poor image. Conflict politics, as practiced by Senator Barry

Goldwater (Republican presidential nominee in 1964), however, brought the Republican weaknesses to the fore, allowing Lyndon Johnson to score a spectacular landslide through consensus appeals to everyone on the full range of the spectrum from Left to Right.[32]

THE DECLENSION OF PARTIES

The history of party politics and partisanship after 1960 was a story of declension. Three forms of decline can be identified: the progressive weakening of party organizations; the decay of partisan loyalties among the people; and a general loss of faith in the entire political system. We will examine the symptoms of each facet, consider the causes, and speculate on the implications.

Historically, party organizations served primarily to select candidates for office, to elect them, and to bond together the fate of officeholders, thereby assuring some degree of accountability to the electorate. Antiparty reformers in the Progressive era attempted to strip parties of the selection function by instituting the direct primary. On the whole, however, the organizations controlled the selection function of major candidates through 1960. By then, the big city Democratic machines had either collapsed or fallen into petty factionalism; thus the mainstay of organizational activity was eliminated. Routine reliance on labor union campaign support eroded the functions of Democratic party organs in most states, and in the South, apart from Virginia, state units were of minor importance. After two decades of Democratic control of federal patronage, the GOP was reduced to a handful of suburban machines around New York City, Philadelphia, and Chicago. State GOP organizations slowly decayed as well, leaving only skeleton operations in most states.

Candidates for office selected themselves. They were successful to the extent to which they could achieve name recognition, organize a personal campaign staff, mobilize a network of friends and allies, and find their own money. The media, increasingly important to achieve these goals, rarely was used by party organizations after 1936. (Before then, however, the GOP had often run major advertising campaigns.) The laggard states, Indiana and New York, finally abandoned the state convention, leaving control of party leadership in the hands of primary voters. In presidential politics, as late as 1968 there were only fifteen primaries, in which less then 40 percent of the delegates were chosen. This permitted Democratic local leaders, in their last hurrah, to force through Hubert Humphrey's nomination over violent opposition. In 1980, there were thirty-seven primaries selecting 71 percent of the Democratic delegates and 75 percent of the Republican delegates.[33]

Candidates now have to sell themselves to the public. They rely for advice—indeed, all phases of campaign management—not on seasoned party leaders, but on market researchers and professional organizers, drawn largely from the advertising industry. There is nothing new in the business of selling candidates; the methods and techniques were all in place by 1920 (when movie ads served the place of TV commercials). The major difference is that campaign management became wholly separate from party organization. The extreme example was Nixon's ill-fated Committee to Reelect the President, which deliberately distanced itself from the GOP in order to attract more Democratic votes.[34]

The Republican National Committee regularly planned to provide campaign services for state and local candidates, but only in 1978 did it become effective, giving a million dollars to local candidates and spending an equal amount in staff support, publicity, and advisory services. The RNC thus acted as a supercampaign management firm, in competition with scores of private organizations. Its activity underscored the collapse of state and local party organizations. "We've let the local base erode," warned the RNC campaign director. "You can't have a healthy party unless you have that training ground."[35] The GOP did score modest gains in the legislatures in 1978, controlling 36 percent of all the seats in the fifty states. But the trend was clear (see Table 6.9). From 1948 through 1956, the GOP held 46 percent of legislative seats. From 1958 through 1978, the proportion was only 37 percent.[36]

Accountability to the citizenry is a function that was assumed by the party-in-the-legislature in the 1950s. Congressional powers, notably Senators Robert Taft and Lyndon Johnson, took on a leadership role that President Eisenhower downplayed. There has been no tendency since then for party cohesion in Congress to diminish. Indeed, the reforms in the 1960s that weakened committee chairmen and enhanced the caucuses increased the level of party responsibility. Since 1953, all presidents save perhaps John Kennedy and Gerald Ford have worked as closely with opposition leaders on major legislation as with their own party.[37] Little recent information is available about party cohesion and self-identity in state legislatures, though they probably remain steady at reasonably high levels.[38]

The decay of partisan loyalties became apparent about 1965. From 1952 through 1964, 36 percent of all Americans, give or take a point, identified themselves as "strong" partisans. In 1966, the total dropped to 28 percent, and since has slipped to 24 percent. The proportion of Independents crept up slowly from 9 or 10 percent in the 1920s, to 15 percent in the 1940s, 24 percent in 1952-1964, then surged rapidly,

Table 6.9 Republican Share of Elected Officers, 1948-1980

	Governors	Senators	U.S. House	State Legislatures
1948-1956	47.5	48.2	45.7	45.7
1958-1964	24.5	33.5	36.9	36.5
1966-1978	37.9	41.9	40.0	37.5
1948-1980	39.2	41.7	40.8	39.7

Source: John F. Bibby and Robert J. Huckshorn, "The Republican Party in American Politics," in *Parties and Elections in an Anti-Party Age*, ed. Jeff Fishel (Bloomington, Ind., 1978), p. 56; *Public Opinion* 3 (December/January 1981): 25.

approaching 40 percent in 1974. Younger voters first developed the trend, but all age groups joined in a grand escape from partisanship.[39] Voters showed their new independence by splitting their tickets. In 1940, one-fourth of the voters were splitters; in the 1950s, one-third; in the 1970s, two-thirds. Of course, this produced split outcomes, with each party winning some races in the same constituency. Split wins in senatorial and gubernatorial contests occurred 20 percent of the time in the 1920s, rose slightly thereafter, and routinely exceeded 50 percent beginning in 1964.[40] The concept of party responsibility through unified control of government clearly had evaporated.

The decline in partisanship was not uniform around the country. The groups most alienated by federal policy showed the greatest abandonment of partisanship, notably the white South and the younger generation, but all groups participated. Only one countercurrent existed—blacks moved from apolitical or split loyalties to staunch support of the Democratic party.[41]

The GOP suffered most from the decline of partisanship. From 1940 to 1960, it slipped from 43 percent of the population to only 28 percent, while the Democrats held steady at 50 percent plus or minus four.[42] Republicans could still win, but it became harder and harder. The long-term demographic trends produced a downward ratchet effect. Losses were harder and harder to recoup. Districts that switched parties after Democratic landslides (1958, 1964, 1974), seldom switched back, even when the top of the ticket ran well. Table 6.9 shows the progressive shrinkage of the GOP share of important offices from 1948 through 1978.

The decline in Republican partisanship was, surprisingly, *not* due to an excessive leakage of former partisans becoming Democrats or Independents. The GOP held its own in this regard. Nor was it due to intergenerational switches; the sons and daughters of Republican parents were just as likely to stay with the family allegiance as were Democratic children. What happened was a curious interaction of demographic effects. The main trend (excluding the white South and blacks) was for a steady slow drift into the Independent column by *both* Democratic and Republican partisans. There was little or no movement from an Independent to a partisan status after 1964, so the number of Independents grew rapidly, drawn from *both* parties in about equal numbers. Then why did not the number of northern Democrats also decline? Birth rates. Before 1970, most Democrats were poor, Catholic, black, or southern, and therefore had high birth rates. The Republicans reflected a middle class, Protestant population with lower birth rates. A 1936 Gallup poll signaled the phenomenon: Democrats desired 10 percent more children than Republicans. Half a century of this sort of "political" behavior, and the Democrats could replenish their losses while the GOP could not.[43]

The combination of growing government and declining parties forced interest groups to mobilize their resources in more systematic fashion. They formed new lobbies, refunded old ones, and stepped up their cash contributions to candidates. The creation of Common Cause hinted at the possibility of a citizens' lobby that represented only the public interest. Common Cause, however, discovered that it had to hew the line favored by its liberal supporters; it soon became just one of many special interest groups. More fascinating was the emergence in the 1970s of lobbies funded by and acting on behalf of government bodies. Colleges and universities, their budgets so heavily dependent on federal aid and their policies determined by administrative decisions, headquartered their efforts at One DuPont Circle in Washington. Cities and towns discovered that their collective interests transcended the localized services of their own congressmen. The National Governors' Association, itself a growing power, wanted to mediate between local government and the feds, taking their cut in the process, as they do in education grants. But direct activity was needed to inform local government of the available benefits and to lobby for new rules and laws. The National League of Cities, U.S. Conference of Mayors, and the National Association of Counties worked for their biggest constituents. Realizing this, the National Association of Towns and Townships (formed only in 1963) set up shop in Washington in 1976. The American Association of Small Cities, begun in 1976, concentrated on lobbying and services to its 1,300 members. The National Association of Smaller Communities, with 190 members, became a feisty advocate of federal community development aid. The National Conference of Black Mayors, mostly representing 170 small, poor southern towns plus a few giant cities, organized itself in 1974. "Sometimes small cities get lost in the shuffle," one senator noted; "Clearly, what the federal government thinks about is the problem of big cities."[44]

Not only did local governments organize as political actors in the state and national arena, but so did government employees. Laws and customs prohibiting unionization among civil servants broke down, and strikes in essential and nonessential services became commonplace. With the decline in voter participation, public service unions realized they could become potent electoral forces. By 1980, the state affiliates of the National Education Association had become the most powerful single lobby in a majority of state capitals, and the NEA could take considerable credit for Jimmy Carter's election in 1976. The public was losing confidence in education, so the teachers united their numbers and salaries in a direct effort to enlarge their slice of the pie.

What hope for democracy will remain when government policy is in the hands not of the people at large but of civil servants acting either on behalf of other levels of government or explicitly on their own personal behalf? Tax revolts will continue to restrain the fiscal growth of government, but nothing will stop, revise, or reevaluate the steady accretion of administrative powers. The inner-directed sense of a common good, the essential dynamic of the Progressive era, has been discredited as "merely" a cover for selfish interests. American society will tolerate only explicit self-interest, thereby freeing established interest groups from old restraints and encouraging the formation of new groups. Is there anyone not represented by a lobbyist today? Probably not.

Organized interest groups, representing business, professions, labor, veterans, conservationists, agriculture, and fixed-boundary social groupings (like women, Jews, blacks, the elderly, and the handicapped), filled some of the vacuum left by the decline of parties. Their lobbyists worked directly with bureaucrats and with legislators regardless of party. A main function was to explain the needs of their groups, to watch out for unfavorable legislation and rulings, and to explain the complexity of government to their constituents. To guarantee access to lawmakers, the groups contributed heavily to campaigns. In 1976, 1,166 Political Action Committees, most newly formed, contributed $23 million to congressional candidates. Two years later PAC's gave $28 million, three-fourths of it to incumbents.[45] There is no point in seeking access to losers.

With the decline of the parties, the role of legislators changed. Congressmen began to emphasize their role as ombudsmen. Elaborate and effective constituency service, in terms of helping individuals with bureaucratic red tape, paid off handsomely at the polls. From 1960 through 1978, 94 percent of House incumbents and 83 percent of Senate incumbents running in the general election were reelected. Although public opinion consistently rated Congress as doing a very poor job—even worse than the president—the same pollees usually gave their local congressmen a highly favorable rating.[46]

The negative rating given to Congress as a whole reflected the failure of government to resolve the painful social and economic problems of the 1960s and 1970s and the inability of Congress as an institution to project a positive role of its activities. People might speculate that society would be better off if some spectacular computer malfunction would reverse the election returns and turn the losers into winners. Unfortunately, even a programming bug of this magnitude would not make any difference. Analysis of the positions on issues of the winners and losers in 1966 House races demonstrates that a great reversal would have produced *exactly the same* distribution of congressional votes on foreign and domestic issues.[47]

As popular confidence in government eroded in the mid-1960s, significant changes occurred in public administration. Absence of long-term planning, weak budgetary controls, patronage-oriented administration, confused chains of command, and weak administrative authority had always characterized American government at all levels. The Progressive era (up through the early 1920s) saw important reforms (city managers, reorganization of state agencies, the federal Bureau of the Budget), but little had been accomplished in the next forty years to cope with the rapid expansion of functions. Beginning in the mid-1960s a series of reforms quietly swept through most of the states and the federal government. Their genesis can be attributed to the revolution in managerial skills in large banks and corporations fostered by the MBA's fresh from business schools. The computer revolution, by giving top executives exact and frequent reports on all phases of business operations and statistical projections that facilitated long-term planning, set standards of administrative achievement that could be applied to government.

Robert McNamara, ex-whiz kid at Ford, revolutionized the Defense Department in the early 1960s. Soon the slogan of PPB—planning, programming, budgeting—began to work its way through the federal agencies. Congress mandated the creation of area planning agencies by the states in 1966, and soon "urban planning" and "regional planning" became hot growth fields. The striking Republican surge in governorships in 1966 and 1968 brought in men attuned to business more in the new spirit of managerial efficiency than in the old anti-labor, low-tax, low-welfare mold. State spending tripled during the 1960s, welfare and education budgets quadrupled, and civil service ranks doubled. Republican governors Nelson Rockefeller (New York), Richard Ogilvie (Illinois), George Romney (Michigan), William Scranton (Pennsylvania), Claude Kirk (Florida), and Ronald Reagan (California) took the lead in reorganizing state governments, with the help of brilliant young aides borrowed from business. In the smaller states the need seemed less pressing, but "little Hoover Commissions" sprang up to point the way to managerial improvements.[48] An example of the change was the creation of state boards of higher education. Reporting to the governor, they coordinated planning for universities, colleges, and community colleges that previously had grown without regard for statewide priorities and capabilities. Richard Nixon made reorganization a high priority, giving extensive power to his Office of Management and Budget. Had it not been for Watergate, Nixon would have succeeded in radically restructuring the executive departments, especially by reducing the policymaking powers of the bureaucracy.[49]

Reorganization did not prove popular. The new taxes that were involved cost the reelection of several governors. Jimmy Carter promised to extend his Georgia reforms to Washington but in so doing, he brought in Bert Lance who caused no end of embarrassment. Popular reaction, on the whole, seems to have been negative. The sentiment that "government is too powerful" climbed steadily from 44 percent in 1964 to 69 percent in 1976. Although voters measured gubernatorial candidates in terms of administrative skills, they had grave doubts about the efficacy of reforms. In 1978, 70 percent blamed extensive "overhead and administration" costs for rising local taxes. People simply felt they were not getting their tax dollar's worth from government at any level. Frustrated taxpayers revolted in 1978, and California's Proposition 13 movement was copied around the country. A federal constitutional amendment to freeze spending rates nearly succeeded in 1979.[50]

The decline in partisanship, coupled with the brief resurgence of the GOP in the late 1960s, facilitated governmental reorganization. Without it the system would be in real trouble by now. But with it, the people were more unhappy than ever. The nominal nonpartisanship of this reorganization, however, prevented the electorate from identifying the GOP as the responsible party. Hence they expressed their grievances in shotgun fashion, hitting the closest taxes and eroding confidence in all levels of government.[51]

LOSING CONFIDENCE IN THE CONSENSUS: 1963-1980

America's self-confidence was shattered in the 1960s, and still has not recovered, if it ever will. The symptoms showed up in attitudinal surveys. In 1964, 22 percent trusted the national government "to do what is right" only some of the time. In steady increments the distrusting minority grew to 44 percent in 1970, then leaped to 63 percent in 1974. The Watergate scandal accelerated the downward trend, but did not cause it; the lack of trust was so transparent in 1976 that Jimmy Carter made it a central campaign theme. Even more important, however, was the collapse of confidence in all established institutions whose functioning had become central to the society—medicine, finance, science, the military, the FBI, education, religion, retail stores, the Supreme Court, unions, Congress, the press, advertising, and business generally. An age of anomie had begun.

We will not find the roots of the malaise in economic hardship. The United States was remarkably prosperous in the 1960s. Real income grew steadily, unemployment was low, the stock market was high. Inflation began bothering people when it began to gallop ahead at the outrageous rate of three percent per year! Taxes, always considered high, did not increase. Strikes were infrequent, and public services expanded rapidly. Overall inequality, while it became more noticed, declined somewhat, as welfare programs extended to a much larger proportion of needy families. The proportion of Americans below the poverty line dropped steadily.

The dissatisfaction was not, however, directed at personal concerns. However rotten people thought their society had become, they remained happy with themselves, their families, their neighborhoods, and their friends. Indeed, Americans were far more satisfied within their personal domain than were Europeans. It must be noted, however, that dissatisfaction with public institutions increased in Europe, both East and West, at about the same time. The cause of the American malaise must be traced to value shifts that were paralleled in Europe, and not simply unique to the United States.[52]

A clue to the upsurge of dissatisfaction was that it occurred uniformly across all the socioeconomic groupings that had structured politics during the New Deal era. Blacks and whites, young and old, rich and poor, Northerners and Southerners all lost faith. As a result, some of the effects of the malaise were uniformly distributed. The loss of faith in politics produced sharp declines in party loyalty among every population group except one (the blacks became more loyal to the Democratic party). Since older people still remembered the days when parties meant something, they were slower to cast off their loyalties. Young people, on the other hand, while still inheriting partisan predispositions from their parents, had fewer favorable recollections of party and abandoned partisanship more rapidly.

The first response to the malaise, in the middle 1960s, was to interpret the nation's ills in ideological terms. Liberals moved left and became agitated, as conservatives moved right and became agitated. Ideological polarization, dormant during the Eisenhower years, pulled people away from the middle. The chief victim of the polarization was Lyndon Johnson, who had posited his presidency on his ability to bring everyone together by brokering policy packages that gave every group what it wanted. The Great Society worked for a while, then fell apart, as Johnson discovered that hawks and doves, conservatives and liberals (and, of course, radicals), bitterly rejected any compromise with the opposition. Johnson quit. Hubert Humphrey, trying the same strategy with more charm, saw his party ripped apart in the summer of 1968. Consensus failed because in a society polarized by conflicting values, compromise cannot satisfy a majority. The politician who tried to take a middle ground, in the spirit of Eisenhower, was attacked from both directions.

Just what were the causes of polarization? It is easy to point to two overriding issues, racial integration and the war in Vietnam. But other issues existed too—changing standards of morality, sharply rising crime, annual summer riots in black ghettoes, and an unpleasant awareness of political corruption pervasive at every level of government, from city hall up to and including the federal courts and the White House.

At a deeper level than the specific issues was a growing cleavage in basic values, not only in America but Western Europe as well.[53] Faith in modernization and the goodness of all its manifestations had become almost completely dominant, if not universal, in Eisenhower's America. The crisis of the 1960s consisted of an ideological conflict between the conservatives who still believed in modern values and the postmodern radicals who rejected those values. Liberals were forced to choose sides; the young, professional, and best educated (including academics) tended to adopt postmodern values. Older and less educated liberals, typified by "hard hat" workers, union leaders, and old line politicians (like Chicago's Mayor Richard Daley), emphasized their commitment to modernity and were labeled, much to their surprise, as conservatives. (A band of liberal intellectuals, opting for modernity, became known as neo-conservatives.)

The postmoderns were the children of the most modern families—you "had to grow up in Scarsdale to know how bad it was." They sought complete freedom for self-awareness using drugs, sex, rock music, distinctive dress and, for a while, militant confrontation politics. They rejected the faith in science, technology, rationality, organizational complexity, and very strict psychological self-control that typified the modern personality. Politically, they sympathized with the victims of modernity—ghetto blacks, the Third World peasants, the poor, Indians, even prisoners. Some formed self-sufficient communes to break completely with modern America; a few went underground to destroy the corrupt society by force (e.g., the Weathermen).

Vietnam, seen by the postmoderns as the ultimate violence inflicted by an imperialist modernity on a helpless peasantry because it sought its own national independence, was the catalyst for political involvement. But cultural events, notably Woodstock (1969), also helped create the postmodern ethos. Demonstrations and confrontation on hundreds of college campuses made the polarization of values obvious to everyone. Not nearly so well known were the thousands of smaller-scale confrontations that affected high schools throughout the country, including those in the inner cities and affluent suburbs.

In political terms the postmodern revolution fueled the crusade for Eugene McCarthy in 1968, the confrontations at the Democratic convention that year, and George McGovern's campaign in 1972. Assassinations of the heroes of postmodern politics (John Kennedy, 1963; Martin Luther King, Jr. and Robert Kennedy, 1968; Kent State and Jackson State demonstrators, 1970) created martyrdoms that "proved" modern society would stop at nothing to crush dissent at home.

Conservatives responded to the crisis of values in two phases. Barry Goldwater articulated the theme that interference from big government was stifling the modern values that made the country great—a mirror image of the postmodern concerns. Southern whites, fearful for decades that a liberal president beholden to northern pressure groups would destroy the fabric of white supremacy in the South, switched the Deep South to Goldwater. Loosened from their loyalties to their historic party, they fed the George Wallace crusade in 1968. The first phase of conservative distrust of government resurfaced in 1978, as the Proposition 13 movement blazed out of California, with strong impact on the spending habits of government at all levels.

The second phase of conservative reaffirmation of modern values involved a reaction against the postmoderns. Disrespect for the flag, for the code of peaceful assembly, heavy drug usage, and apparent alliance with the nation's foreign enemies fueled conservative reactions into the early 1970s. The climax came as Nixon rallied modernists to destroy the McGovern crusade in 1972. Shortly after, conservative women clinging to the modernist ideal of separate spheres for men and women rallied to block passage of the Equal Rights Amendment. Although cloaked in modern terminology, ERA came to symbolize the postmodern effort to dissolve the ideology of separate spheres (women dominant inside the home, men outside the home). Likewise a delayed conservative-modern reaction against abortion, led by Catholics and Mormons, raised that issue to high saliency beginning in the mid-1970s.

The clash of values forced Americans to rethink their most basic beliefs. Among moderns, this led to a heightened sense of public propriety and moral standards. Postmoderns, particularly journalists, concentrated on finding evidence for the hypocrisies of the establishment. They exposed the CIA, FBI, and, stunningly, the White House itself. The sharpened moral standards of the conservatives—typified by Judge John Sirica—could not tolerate the corruption thus exposed. Impeachment was, in a sense, a triumph for both modern and postmodern ethics, but it eroded trust in government. Even apart from Watergate, a long series of legal episodes between 1964 and 1980 underscored the breakup of the old consensus on morality. The moral opprobrium once suffered by felons and delinquents gave way to societal self-guilt and new rights for prisoners and inmates of all institutions. The assumption that businessmen and professionals were basically good and honest was upset by criminal charges, malpractice suits, and stupendous damage claims. Politicians had never been fully trusted, but the "Abscam" sting operation conducted by the FBI in 1979 suggested universally low resistance to bribery. The moral consensus that emerged in the 1970s involved a heightened modern sense of absolute rectitude for public officials; new postmodern standards of strict accountability for businesses, professionals, and individuals dealing with the public; and, increasingly, a new postmodern principle of absolute freedom for consenting adults to behave any way they wished, so long as the public interest was not directly involved.

The historic consensus regarding the wisdom of steady economic modernization under capitalist auspices came under sharp attack by postmoderns. Concern for environmental damage, or psychic and physical harm to people, fueled most of the concern. The most aggressive postmoderns attacked nuclear energy programs as inherently evil, and after the Three Mile Island incident in 1979, won support from leading Democratic politicians. Big business was on the defensive throughout the 1970s, as its historic claim to baking a bigger pie for everyone to share (unequally) no longer was reflected by a stagnant GNP. By 1980, however, the transparent failure of demand-(i.e., consumer-) oriented economic policy was encouraging growth-oriented politicians like Jack Kemp and Ronald Reagan to emphasize supply-oriented policies, like heavy tax and spending cuts designed to reverse the downtrend in business productivity. The old consensus had been shattered, and the ways the economy should be reshaped to reflect new values had become a central political issue.

The historic consensus on pluralism was transformed drastically in the 1960s and 1970s. The civil rights movement advanced the claim that blacks deserved an equal share in the power structures of society. Success was not immediate, but the disfranchisement of southern blacks ended in 1964; black politicians started winning major and minor offices; and universities and large corporations, somewhat grudgingly, began recruiting and advancing blacks. Inspired by this record, other minorities that had been excluded or left on the fringes by the old pluralist system made their demands known. By the mid-1970s so much pressure had built up against the old consensus that postmoderns began arguing for the ideal of equality of results rather than equality of opportunity. The storm over the Bakke case (1978) showed that Americans divided bitterly over what the new standard of pluralism should be like.

Ideological conflicts softened in the 1970s. Younger cohorts holding postmodern values became numerically more important, while the bitter confrontations on campuses and the streets died out. Thanks to postmodern media influences and the apparent failure of modern institutions to cope with new crises, the postmodern ethic became more broadly diffused throughout the population. Marijuana took on the status of beer in the 1920s—illegal but widely used and tolerated. Long hair and jeans, freer attitudes toward sex (including homosexuality), routine divorce, the presence of blacks and women in positions formerly reserved for white males, and the enhanced emphasis on leisure (rather than productivity) signaled the rapid diffusion of postmodern values. The chasm that had opened in the mid-1960s seemed to be narrowing, though age and educational differentials continued to determine attitudes and values.

America was tired of the across-the-board confrontations of the 1960s. Individuals concerned with particular ideological points (gay rights, abortion, ERA, gun control) set up organizations that worked outside the party system to achieve these goals. The failures of McGovern in 1972 and Agnew and Nixon in 1973-1974 meant that the old parties would not be realigned to accommodate the new modern-postmodern cleavage. For that reason, the parties had become irrelevant.

Have ethnocultural effects finally disappeared? Not quite. The 1968 election showed that national origins, religion, and race, of course, still made a difference. Table 6.10 shows that in six of eight Northern states ethnocultural factors were more important than socioeconomic status or perceived class. (This was also true among whites only.) Curiously, in highly ethnic Minnesota national origins were uncorrelated with party identification. Only in California, where origins are forgotten, did class exceed ethnocultural factors. In the East, religion remained especially potent, while class effects were small. (Well-to-do

Table 6.10 Ethnocultural and Socioeconomic Correlates of Party Identification by State, 1968*

	Religion[1]	Ethnicity[2]	Perceived Class[3]	Education	Income	Occupation[4]
Massachusetts	.530	.401	.257	.195	.151	.194
New York	.475	.414	.147	.129	.117	.072
Pennsylvania	.367	.375	.202	.267	.115	.261
Average *East*	.457	.397	.202	.197	.128	.176
Illinois	.365	.372	.226	.252	.264	.293
Minnesota	.151	.186	.299	.281	.256	.308
Ohio	.308	.340	.275	.288	.187	.232
South Dakota	.263	.207	.209	.107	.116	.161
Average *Midwest*	.272	.276	.252	.232	.206	.249
California	.311	.322	.349	.294	.189	.348
Average *North*	.346	.327	.246	.227	.175	.234

Source: David M. Kovenock, *et al.*, *Explaining the Vote: Presidential Choices in the Nation and the States, 1968* (Chapel Hill, 1973), 6-7, 44-45, 84-85, 130-31, 172-73, 210-11, 248-49, 297-98.

*The entry is eta, which resembles the Pearson *r* correlation coefficient.
[1]Categorized as white Protestant, black Protestant, Catholic, Jewish
[2]Blacks, Jews, 8 categories of white Gentiles
[3]Average working, upper working, average middle, upper middle
[4]Six census groupings

Catholics and Jews were heavily Democratic.) In the older industrial states of Ohio and Illinois class was more important than back East, and religion less so. It remained true that after a century the best indicators of a person's partisanship were race, religion, and ethnic origins, rather than perceived class, education, income, or occupation.[54]

However, most people simply stopped voting; turnout in 1978 bottomed out at 34 percent. Those who still voted paid more attention to the particular appeals of individual candidates (including personality, service to constituents, and ideology). Voters packaged their own tickets, picking and choosing as if party hardly mattered. Partisanship had not completely disappeared but statisticians were hard pressed to find a strong party component in voting after nonpartisan and ideological effects were considered. In 1972, the conclusion that the party coalitions created by the New Deal were dissolving was inescapable. Worse, the entire fabric of partisan politics was unraveling; the old consensus had disappeared. The fifth party system had lost the confidence of the people and by 1980 was ready to be interred as the last party system.

POSTSCRIPT: A REAGAN REVOLUTION?

Did the 1980 Republican landslide mark the end of the fifth party system and open a new political era? Three questions are involved: Did a new alignment of voters, with permanent potential, emerge? Could the GOP make a comeback to full parity, or even superiority? Had a new consensus on deep values emerged? Historians are notoriously fallible futurologists, and the opening phase of a new administration provides meager perspective, but I would hazard a "no" to each question.

Presidential voting patterns in 1980 revealed a softening of the New Deal era cleavages. Education, class, Southernness, union membership, and religion were sharply less divisive than ever before. Age differentials continued to be important, as did race. Indeed, not only were blacks as supportive of Carter in 1980 as in 1976 (84 percent), but early 1981 polls showed them more hostile to Reagan than any group has been toward an incumbent president since at least the First World War.[55]

One cleavage emerged for the first time in American politics: sex. Women voted 46 percent for Reagan, 45 percent for Carter, while men gave the Californian his landslide, 54-37 percent. Younger women, ERA supporters, and those especially concerned with war and peace gave heavy majorities to Carter. In 1976 and previous elections, the sex differential was trivial. The women's fear of Reagan partly reflected Carter's counter-crusading campaign tactics. By February of 1981, however, women were still much more worried by Reagan's bellicosity than men. In terms of permanent realignments, however, it is hard to visualize how sex could become the basis of electoral politics, particularly since Carter failed to win a majority of the female vote.

Short-term forces increasingly dominate presidential politics. Pocketbook voting, by which incumbents are punished when times are hard, may have begun to overshadow partisanship and ideology. In 1976, Democrats who felt their family economic situation was worse than the year before voted 94-6 for Carter. In 1980, however, such Democrats (different people) split 47 for Carter, 39 for Reagan. Democrats who felt better off in 1980 stayed with Carter 77-16, a difference of 30 points. For Independents, Carter won 45 percent of those better off and 21 percent of those worse off, a 24-point differential. Even among Republicans, there was a 12-point differential.

The emphasis on pocketbook voting may reflect the narcissistic culture of our time. That is, what happens to the entire economy, or people in the neighborhood, is not important—only what happens to me. Broader values, and partisanship itself, can easily fade in such an environment. Long-term realignment is hardly likely if short-term economic fluctuations dominate voters' behavior.[56]

The stunning Republican capture of the Senate in 1980, even more than Reagan's victory, pointed to the possibility of a GOP resurgence to parity or even superiority. A slight upturn in early 1981 in the proportion of Republican identifiers gave the GOP a glimmer of hope that its downward progress among the people had at last been reversed. A closer look at the patterns that year suggests that the visibility of specific candidates was the critical factor. Reagan carried 88 percent of the states; Republicans won 67 percent of Senate contests; 54 percent of governorships, 44 percent of House districts, and 39 percent of state legislative seats. There is no doubt that the GOP has a vastly superior national organization. In an age of PACs, computers, mass mailings, and expensive television ads, the centralized Republican operations have been more effective than their flimsy Democratic counterparts, even when union activity is added. The Republicans succeeded in 1980 (and 1978) by targeting highly visible Democrats. More committee chairmen were defeated in 1980 than in the last ten elections combined! Republicans had far less success with opponents who could not be charged with a share of the responsibility for economic malaise. With the GOP in power nationally, the party will not be able to castigate the Democrats in 1982 and 1984. The Democrats, meanwhile, have a good model to copy in their efforts to fund, train, and sell candidates.

Finally, will the Reagan era involve a restructuring of deep values? The 1981 Stockman budget proposals—the most dramatic fiscal package since the Lloyd George/Asquith budget of 1909—did rest on a fundamental restructuring of priorities. The federal share of GNP was to fall from 23 percent to 19 percent, with a much larger portion to military and "safety net" programs, and a severe slashing of subsidies. Combined with extensive deregulation and large tax cuts, the budget certainly marked a new direction for the government. Hardest hit were narrowly targeted programs that had emerged since the mid-1960s, fostered by an army of lobbyists in Washington. Return of programs to state capitals meant a return to an arena where the national pressure groups were weaker. Apart from the teachers, few groups can afford to support fifty sets of lobbyists when, until 1981, one set sufficed.

Reagan, however, articulated his programs in terms of the basic consensus points of twentieth century American politics. The goal he emphasized was a renewal of the ideal of steady economic modernization. Pluralism was a goal he also reaffirmed, but with a new definition. The federal government had to provide a "safety net" of income support programs so that poor people outside the modernized economy (e.g. the retired, the unemployed, those on welfare) would still be protected. There would no longer be subsidies for persons or groups, including the near-poor, who were inside the modernized sector.

Postmoderns feared that Reagan would seize on morality issues—the third component of the historical consensus—to declare them outside the pale. Indeed, the highly visible activities of the "Moral Majority" and its allies in 1980 fueled such fears.[57] In foreign policy, a new hard line against Communism *per se* and terrorism, grounded on modern moral values, quickly emerged in the new Administration. In domestic politics, however, only Antiabortion proposals, pushed by a nationwide network of grass roots committees, represented the sort of attack on postmodern morality that had been feared. In general, the new morality would continue, allowing everyone to do his or her own thing (except congressmen).

The death throes of the fifth electoral system continued in 1980, yet a new realignment is not upon us. Instead the steady depoliticization of the electorate continues. Reagan may repulse the interest groups that took advantage of the vacuum of partisanship, and he might even reverse the erosion of America's worldwide prestige. But nobody is going to restore party politics to the central role it once played in American history.

NOTES

1. Was a commitment to democracy inherent in the system? Possibly not. Pluralism guaranteed representation of all white groups, but did not inhibit increasingly severe restrictions on voting or the belief that voting was a privilege, not a right. No serious effort was made to enfranchise southern blacks until the 1950s. Free speech did not enter the consensus until the 1930s or 1940s. When people spoke of economic democracy, they referred to the first point of the consensus. Most discussion of democracy, I believe, concentrated on the problem of bringing about moral progress; the arguments for woman suffrage were a case in point. The Great War, as a crusade for universal democracy, likewise incorporated only the three points of domestic consensus.

2. The locus classicus of the loss of faith argument is Arthur Schlesinger, Jr., *The Age of Roosevelt* 3 vols. (Boston, 1957), vol. 1, "The Crisis of the Old Order, 1919-1933." I have relied chiefly on William Leuchtenberg, *Franklin D. Roosevelt and the New Deal, 1932-1940* (New York, 1963). See John Shover, *Cornbelt Rebellion: The Farmers' Holiday Association* (Urbana, Ill.: 1965); Seymour Martin Lipset, *Agrarian Socialism* (Garden City, N.Y.: Anchor Books, 1968).

3. Samuel P. Hays, Jr., "Voters' Attitudes Toward Men and Issues," *Journal of Social Psychology* 7 (1936): 157. The *Literary Digest* reported that 41 percent of Hoover's 1928 supporters switched to FDR. Even taking the South into account, this figure is far too high, suggesting that too many people incorrectly recalled their 1928 vote. *Literary Digest*, Nov. 5, 1932, p. 8.

4. American Institute for Public Opinion (AIPO), poll no. 53 (October 1936); original cards furnished by the Roper Center.

5. AIPO no. 53. See J. Morgan Kousser, *The Shaping of Southern Politics: Suffrage Restriction and the Establishment of the One-Party South, 1880-1910* (New Haven, 1974), pp. 250-57.

6. George Gallup, *The Gallup Poll, 1937-1971* (New York, 1972), p. 102.

7. Gavin Wright, "The Political Economy of New Deal Spending: An Econometric Analysis," *Review of Economics and Statistics* 56 (1974): 30-38. The WPA needs more study. See the essays in John Braeman, Robert Bremner and David Brody, eds., *The New Deal: The State and Local Levels* (Columbus, 1975); also James T. Patterson, *The New Deal and the States* (Princeton, 1969); Searle F. Charles, *Minister of Relief: Harry Hopkins and the Depression* (Syracuse, 1963); Harold F. Gosnell, *Machine Politics: Chicago Model* (Chicago, 1968).

8. National Resources Planning Board, *Security, Work, and Relief Policies* (Washington, 1942), pp. 100, 107-9.

9. According to a 1938 recall, Roosevelt in 1936 won 80 percent of the reliefers, 73 percent of recipients of home or land loans, 68 percent of the recipients of AAA payments, 62 percent of the recipients of soldiers' bonuses, and 57 percent of those who received no government money. Gallup, *Gallup Poll*, pp. 32, 103.

10. Fillmore H. Sanford, "Public Orientation to Roosevelt," *Public Opinion Quarterly* 15 (1951): 189-216. Harvard Sitkoff, *A New Deal for Blacks* (New York, 1978); National Resources Planning Board, *Security*, pp. 116-17, 159-60; John M. Allswang, *The New Deal and American Politics* (New York, 1978), pp. 39, 52-57.

11. See Irving Bernstein, *The Lean Years: A History of the American Worker, 1920-1933* (Boston, 1960), and idem, *The Turbulent Years: A History of the American Worker, 1933-1941* (Boston, 1970); Milton Derber and Erwin Young, eds., *Labor and the New Deal* (Madison, 1957).

12. Seymour Martin Lipset, *The First New Nation* (New York, 1979), pp. 168-204; Juanita Kreps, "Developments in the Political and Legislative Policies of Organized Labor: 1920-1947" (Ph.D. dissertation, Duke University, 1947); J. David Greenstone, *Labor in American Politics* (New York, 1969); Jack Barbush, ed., *Unions and Union Leadership* (New York, 1959); Richard A. Lester, *As Unions Mature* (Princeton, 1958).

13. Religion and the 1944 vote correlated at .24 (controlling for ethnicity), ethnicity at .24 (controlling for religion), status at .10, occupation at .10, size of place at .14, age at .04, region at .05, sex at .01 (Based on AIPO 335 [October 1944], with 425 cases.) Similar patterns held in 1940, except ethnicity was weaker that year.

14. For details on the role of class within ethnic groups, see Richard Jensen, "The Cities Reelect Roosevelt: Ethnicity, Religion and Class in 1940," *Ethnicity* (1981).

15. Richard Jensen, *The Winning of the Midwest: Social and Political Conflict, 1888-1896* (Chicago, 1971); Paul Kleppner, *The Third Electoral System, 1853-1892* (Chapel Hill, 1979).

16. George Gallup, *The Political Almanac, 1952* (New York, 1952), pp. 30-32, and retabulations of original polls provide most of the data used here.

17. Lyle W. Dorsett, *Franklin D. Roosevelt and the City Bosses* (Port Washington, N.Y., 1977) is a good synthesis. Also see idem, *The Prendergast Machine* (New York, 1968); Gosnell, *Machine Politics*; Arthur F. Mann, *LaGuardia Comes to Power, 1933* (New York, 1965); Edgar Litt, *The Political Cultures of Massachusetts* (Amherst, 1965); and Alexander B. Callow, ed., *The City Boss in America* (New York, 1976).

18. On the importance of mobilizing previous nonvoters in big cities, see Kristi Anderson, *The Creation of a Democratic Majority, 1928-1936* (Chicago, 1979). The Democrats received about one point less of the Congressional vote than the presidential vote in 1936-1940, 1944 and 1948. The key urban states were Massachusetts, Rhode Island, Connecticut, New York, New Jersey, Pennsylvania, Ohio, Michigan, and Illinois. States were weighted by vote cast. Gallup, *Political Almanac*, p. 65 and Richard Scammon, *America at the Polls* (Pittsburgh, 1965), provide the data.

19. G. M. Connelly and H. H. Field, "The Non-Voter," *Public Opinion Quarterly* 8 (1944): 178-79.

20. Jerold S. Auerbach, "New Deal, Old Deal, or Raw Deal: Some Thoughts on New Left Historiography," *Journal of Southern History* 35 (1969): 18-30; Paul Conkin, *The New Deal* (New York, 1967); Ellis W. Hawley, *The New Deal and the Problem of Monopoly: A Study of Economic Ambivalence* (Princeton, 1966), is the best study of New Deal economic policy. John Braeman, Robert Bremner and David Brody, eds., *The New Deal: The National Level* (Columbus, 1975) is the most recent overview. See also Allswang, *New Deal*; and, especially, Richard S. Kirkendall, "The Great Depression," in *Change and Continuity in Twentieth-Century America*, ed. John Braeman, Robert Bremner and Everett Walters (Columbus, 1964), pp. 145-90.

21. Everett Carll Ladd and Charles Hadley, *Transformations of the American Party System* (New York, 1978), pp. 101, 240, 243.

22. Kenneth Roose, *The Economics of Depression and Revival* (New Haven, 1954); Leuchtenberg, *Roosevelt*, pp. 231-84; Joseph Boskin, *Opposition Politics: The Anti-New Deal Tradition* (Beverly Hills, 1968); Donald Bruce Johnson, *The Republican Party and Wendell Willkie* (Marquette, Mich., 1966); Donald McCoy, *Landon of Kansas* (Lincoln, 1966); Herbert S. Parmet and Marie B. Hecht, *Never Again: A President Runs for a Third Term* (New York, 1968); Francis X. Sutton et al., *The American Business Creed* (New York, 1956); David Vogel, "Why Businessmen Distrust Their State: The Political Consciousness of American Corporate Executives," *British Journal of Political Science* 8 (1978): 45-78.

23. "Campaign of 1942—Post Mortems," in Records of the Democratic National Committee, Franklin D. Roosevelt Library, box 1156. On wartime politics, the best study is John W. Jeffries, *Testing the Roosevelt Coalition: Connecticut Society and Politics in the Era of World War II* (Knoxville, 1979); see also James McGregor Burns, *Roosevelt: Soldier of Freedom* (New York, 1970); Donald R. McCoy, "Republican Opposition during Wartime, 1941-1945," *Mid-America* 49 (1967): 174-89; James T. Patterson, *Mr. Republican: A Biography of Robert A. Taft* (Boston, 1972); Robert Garson, *The Democratic Party and the*

Politics of Sectionalism, 1941-1948 (Baton Rouge, 1974); Norman D. Markowitz, *The Rise and Fall of the People's Century: Henry A. Wallace and American Liberalism, 1941-1948* (New York, 1973); James Boylan, *The New Deal Coalition and the Election of 1946* (New York, 1981), and Alonzo L. Hamby, *Beyond the New Deal: Harry S. Truman and American Liberalism* (New York, 1973).

24. Were the polls wrong in 1948? The quota sampling technique in use overrepresented the better educated, a serious flaw when education was so highly correlated with the vote. Gallup, however, corrected for this bias, and his October polls showed a narrow lead of only 3 points for Dewey and his November post-election poll was accurate (infra p. 212). Furthermore, Gallup's early October poll showed the Democrats were well ahead in congressional races; indeed, the poll predicted the outcome exactly (but with media attention focused on the presidential contest, Gallup did not publish his findings!). My conclusion is that *the Gallup polls were quite accurate*, and that Truman won because of a last-minute switch of voters, especially undecided groups. See Frederick Mosteller et al., *The Pre-Election Polls of 1948* (New York, 1949) for a contrasting view.

25. After adjusting for the Gallup polls' biases regarding education and city size, the proportion of Democrats, Independents, and Republicans was 49-22-30 in 1948 (AIPO, no. 429). See also Ladd and Hadley, *Transformations*, pp. 123, 321, and Mosteller, *The Pre-Election Polls*, p. 276.

26. On 1948, see Richard Kirkendall, "The Election of 1948," in *History of American Presidential Elections*, ed. Arthur Schlesinger, 4 vols. (New York, 1971), 4: 3099-211; Jules Abel, *Out of the Jaws of Victory* (New York, 1959); Irwin Ross, *The Loneliest Campaign: The Truman Victory of 1948* (New York, 1968); Allen Yarnell, *Democrats and Progressives: The 1948 Election as a Test of Postwar Liberalism* (Berkeley, 1974); Bernard Berelson et al., *Voting* (Chicago, 1954); Samuel Lubell, *The Future of American Politics* (New York, 1965); Hamby, *Beyond the New Deal*.

27. On labor in 1948, see also Arthur M. McClure, *The Truman Administration and the Problems of Postwar Labor, 1945-1948* (Rutherford, N.J., 1969); R. Alton Lee, *Truman and Taft-Hartley* (Lexington, 1966); and James Foster, *The Union Politic: The CIO Political Action Committee* (Columbia, Mo., 1975). For later labor activity, see Jong Oh Ra, *Labor at the Polls: Union Voting in Presidential Elections, 1952-1976* (Amherst, 1978); Greenstone, *Labor in American Politics*; Fay Calkins, *The CIO and the Democratic Party* (Chicago, 1952); Charles Rehmus and Doris McLaughlin, eds., *Labor and American Politics* (Ann Arbor, 1977); Graham K. Wilson, *Unions in American National Politics* (New York, 1979); and Harry Holloway, "Interest Groups in the Post-Partisan Era: The Political Machine of the AFL-CIO," *Political Science Quarterly* 94 (1979): 117-33. There is no good treatment of the big city machines in the 1940s.

28. On the Communist issue, see Earl Latham, *The Communist Controversy in Washington: From the New Deal to McCarthy* (Cambridge, 1966); Athan Theoharis, *Seeds of Repression: Harry S. Truman and the Origins of McCarthyism* (Chicago, 1971); Alan D. Harper, *The Politics of Loyalty: The White House and the Communist Issue, 1946-1952* (Westport, Conn., 1969).

29. The best account of the nonpresidential campaigns of 1952 is Gary W.

Reichard, *The Reaffirmation of Republicanism: Eisenhower and the Eighty-Third Congress* (Knoxville, 1975), ch. 1. See also Robert A. Divine, *Foreign Policy and U.S. Presidential Elections: 1952-1960* (New York, 1974), chs. 1 and 2; Louis Harris, *Is There a Republican Majority? Political Trends, 1952-1956* (New York, 1954); Herbert S. Parmet, *Eisenhower and the American Crusades* (New York, 1972); Angus Campbell, Gerald Gurin, and Warren Miller, *The Voter Decides* (Evanston, Ill., 1954).

30. Angus Campbell et al., *The American Voter* (New York, 1960), pp. 44-59. In 1956 this issue was dead; Eisenhower was allegedly now too old and sick to lead.

31. Reichard, *Reaffirmation*, is especially insightful on Republican policy. See also James Sundquist, *Politics and Policy: The Eisenhower, Kennedy, and Johnson Years* (Washington, 1968); Herbert McCloskey et al., "Issues Conflict and Consensus Among Party Leaders and Followers," *American Political Science Review* 54 (1960): 406-27; Norman Nie, Sidney Verba, and John Petrocik, *The Changing American Voter* (Cambridge, 1976), pp. 200-209.

32. On party image, see Campbell et al., *American Voter*, p. 47; Nie, Verba and Petrocik, *Changing American Voter*, pp. 68-70; Gerald Pomper, *Voters' Choice: Varieties of American Electoral Behavior* (New York, 1979), ch. 6, 7: and, generally, Richard J. Trilling, *Party Image and Electoral Behavior* (New York, 1976). On the ability of politicians to blunt unfavorable images, see Benjamin I. Page, *Choices and Echoes in Presidential Politics* (Chicago, 1978).

33. *The New York Times*, September 30, 1979; *Congressional Quarterly* (CQ) *Weekly Report* (August 16, 1975), pp. 1807-17; William R. Keech and Donald R. Matthews, *The Party's Choice* (Washington, 1976).

34. Robert Agranoff, ed., *The New Style in Election Campaigns* (Rockleigh, N.J., 1972); *CQ Weekly Report* (May 1, 1970), pp. 1183-91; Dan D. Nimmo, *The Political Persuaders* (Englewood Cliffs, 1970). For earlier developments see Stanley Kelley, Jr., *Professional Public Relations and Political Power* (Baltimore, 1956); Richard Jensen, *The Grass-Roots Voter* (Westport, Conn., 1981).

35. *CQ Weekly Report* (November 18, 1978), p. 3301. See Cornelius P. Cotter and John F. Bibby, "Institutional Development of Parties and the Thesis of Party Decline," *Political Science Quarterly* 95 (1980): 1-27.

36. John Bibby and Robert J. Huckshorn, "The Republican Party in American Politics," in *Parties and Elections in an Anti-Party Age*, ed. Jeff Fishel (Bloomington, 1978), p. 56. See also Jerome M. Clubb, William H. Flanigan, and Nancy H. Zingale, *Partisan Realignment: Voters, Parties, and Government in American History* (Beverly Hill, 1980), Ch. 6.

37. Aage Clausen, *How Congressmen Decide* (New York, 1972).

38. On state and local legislatures, see Jack Van Der Slik, *American Legislative Processes* (New York, 1977); L. Harmon Zeigler and Harvey J. Tucker, *The Quest for Responsive Government* (Belmont Cal., 1978). *CQ Weekly Report* (August 25, 1979), pp. 1747-1819, tells about the Mama Lucy Gang in New Mexico, the Dirty Dozen in Illinois, and the Killer Bees in Texas—signs of party splintering at the state level.

39. Nie, Verba, and Petrocik, *Changing American Voter*, p. 83; Ladd and Hadley, *Transformations*, p. 321; Paul R. Abramson, *Generational Change in*

American Politics (Lexington, Mass., 1975), pp. 51-70; John Kessel, *Presidential Campaign Politics: Coalition Strategies and Citizen Response* (Homewood, Ill., 1980), pp. 222-41. The slippage is, however, not apparent in the 1968 data in Merle Black, *Political Attitudes in the Nation and the States* (Chapel Hill, 1974), pp. 50-52.

40. Ladd and Hadley, *Transformations*, p. 325; Walter De Vries and V. Lance Tarrance, *The Ticket Splitter* (Grand Rapids, 1972); Hadley Cantril and Mildred Strunk, *Public Opinion, 1935-1946* (Princeton, 1951), p. 199.

41. Nie, Verba, and Petrocik, *Changing American Voter*, ch. 13; Ladd and Hadley, *Transformations*, p. 112.

42. Ladd and Hadley, *Transformations*, p. 321.

43. For a good collection of studies on partisan behavior, see Richard G. Niemi and Herbert F. Weisberg, eds., *Controversies in American Voting Behavior* (San Francisco, 1976). The structure of departisanship is clearly explained in Nie, Verba, and Petrocik, *Changing American Voter*, ch. 3 and passim.

44. Rochelle L. Stanfield, "Small Cities Are on the Prowl for Help from Washington," *National Journal* (October 7, 1978), pp. 1597-1601; *CQ Weekly Report* (February 5, 1971), p. 337.

45. *National Journal* (March 19, 1977), p. 416; *CQ Weekly Report* (July 7, 1979), p. 1354. See Michael J. Malbin, ed. *Parties, Interest Groups and Campaign Finance Laws* (Washington, D.C., 1980) and Gary C. Jacobson, *Money in Congressional Elections* (New Haven, 1980).

46. On incumbency, see *National Journal* (September 25, 1978), pp. 1509-13; *CQ Weekly Report* (July 7, 1979), p. 1351; David R. Mayhew, "Congressional Elections: The Case of the Vanishing Marginals," *Polity* 6 (1974): 295-317. On the ombudsman role, see Richard F. Fenno, *Home Style: House Members in Their Districts* (New York, 1978), and Morris Fiorina, *Congress: Keystone of the Washington Establishment* (New Haven, 1977).

47. John L. Sullivan and Robert E. O'Connor, "Electoral Choice and Popular Control of Public Policy: The Case of the 1966 House Elections," *American Political Science Review* 66 (1972): 1256-68.

48. For an overview, see Larry Sabato, *Goodbye to Good-Time Charlie: The American Governor Transformed, 1950-1975* (Lexington, Mass., 1978). The best specific coverage is by Robert H. Connery and Gerald Benjamin, *Rockefeller of New York, Executive Power in the Statehouse* (Ithaca, 1979), pp. 153-88. For the other states, see the perceptive reporting in Neil R. Peirce's surveys of the American states, e.g., *The Megastates of America* (New York, 1972), pp. 255-61, 306-9, 390-91, 425-26, 576, 595; *The Great Plains States of America* (New York, 1973), pp. 44, 102-3, 168, 207-8, 235-36, 262; *The Border South States* (New York, 1975), pp. 69-80, 141, 144, 307, 311-12; *The New England States* (New York, 1976), pp. 82-83, 161, 206-7, 273, 326, 387; *The Deep South States of America* (New York, 1974), pp. 140, 323-25, 456. Charles E. Jacob, "The Governor, the Bureaucracy, and State Policy Making," in *Politics in New Jersey*, ed. Alan Rosenthal and John Blydenburgh, (New Brunswick, 1975); Deil S. Wright, "Executive Leadership in State Administration," in *The American Governor in Behavioral Perspective*, ed. Thad Boyle and Oliver Williams (New York, 1972), pp. 275-92.

49. Otis L. Graham, *Toward a Planned Society: From Roosevelt to Nixon* (New York, 1976); Richard P. Nathan, *The Plot That Failed: Nixon and the Administrative Presidency* (New York, 1975); Ronald Randall, "Presidential Power Versus Bureaucratic Intransigence: The Influence of the Nixon Administration on Welfare Policy," *American Political Science Review*, 73 (1979): 795-810; Richard Rose, *Managing Presidential Objectives* (New York, 1976).

50. *Newsweek* (July 19, 1978), p. 22; *Public Opinion* 1 (July 1978): 3-14, 29-33; Gerald Wright, *Electoral Choice in America* (Chapel Hill, 1974), p. 63; Stephen Salmore, "Public Opinion," in *Politics in New Jersey*, ed. Rosenthal and Blydenburgh, pp. 58-77.

51. On the tax cutting mood, see Seymour Martin Lipset and Earl Raab, "The Message of Proposition 13," *Commentary* 66 (September 1978): 42-46. See also James L. Sundquist, "The Crisis of Competence in Our National Government," *Political Science Quarterly* 95 (Summer 1980): 183-208.

52. For details on the decline of trust see Arthur H. Miller, "Political Issues and Trust in Government: 1964-1970," *American Political Science Review* 68 (1974): 951-72; Seymour Martin Lipset and William Schneider, *The Evaluation of Basic American Institutions* (New York, 1981); James D. Wright, *The Dissent of the Governed: Alienation and Democracy in America* (New York, 1976); Vivien Hart, *Distrust and Democracy* (Cambridge, England, 1978); Francis E. Rourke, Lloyd Free, and William Watts, *Trust and Confidence in the American System* (Washington, 1976); Patrick H. Caddell, "Crisis of Confidence: Trapped in a Downward Spiral," *Public Opinion* 2 (October/November 1979): 2-7; Warren Miller, "Crisis of Confidence: Misreading the Public Pulse," ibid., pp. 9-15; Everett Ladd, "A Nation's Trust," ibid., pp. 27-37; Louis Harris and Associates, *The Harris Survey Yearbook of Public Opinion: 1973* (New York, 1976), pp. 51-70; Arthur H. Miller, "The Institutional Focus of Political Distrust," (unpublished paper, U. of Michigan, 1979); James S. House and William M. Mason, "Political Alienation in America, 1952-1968," *American Sociological Review* 40 (1975): 123-47; and U.S. Senate Subcommittee on Intergovernment Operations, *Confidence and Concern: Citizens View American Government* (Washington, 1973); Ann Statham Macke, "Trends in Aggregate-Level Political Alienation," *Sociological Quarterly* 20 (Winter 1979): 77-87; and David B. Hill and Norman R. Luttbeg, *Trends in American Electoral Behavior* (Itaska, Ill., 1980), ch. 4.

53. The best discussion of postmodern values in comparative perspective (though marred by a poor index of postmodernism) is Ronald Inglehart, *The Silent Revolution: Changing Values and Political Styles among Western Publics* (Princeton, 1977). See also Daniel Bell, *The Coming of Post-Industrial Society* (New York, 1973); Louis Harris, *The Anguish of Change* (New York, 1973); Warren E. Miller and Teresa E. Levitin, *Leadership and Change: The New Politics and the American Electorate* (Cambridge, 1976); Theodore Roszak, *The Making of a Counter Culture*, (Garden City, N.Y., 1969); Daniel Yankelovich, *The New Morality: A Profile of American Youth in the 1970's* (New York, 1974); and Everett Ladd, "The New Lines Are Drawn: Class and Ideology in America," *Public Opinion* 1 (July/August 1978): 48-53; and *Public Opinion* (September/October 1978): 14-20. For the historical context, see Godfrey Hodgson, *America in Our Time* (Garden City, N.Y., 1976).

54. For national patterns in the 1970s, see Everett Ladd, "American Ethnic and Religious Groups," *Public Opinion* 1 (November/December 1978): 35. For another analysis of the 1968 data, see Mark Schneider, "Migration, Ethnicity, and Politics: A Comparative State Analysis," *Journal of Politics* 38 (1976): 938-62. Voting data also appears in Mark R. Levy and Michael Kramer, *The Ethnic Factor* (New York, 1972).

55. For election results and exit polls, see *National Journal* 12 (Nov. 8, 1980): 1876-95; *Public Opinion* 3 (December/January 1981): 21-44; also, *New York Times* November 8, 1980, February 3, 1981, and March 1, 1981.

56. On the importance of economic issues, see Ricardo Klorman, "Trends in Personal Finances and the Vote," *Public Opinion Quarterly* 42 (Spring 1978): 31-48; Howard S. Bloom and H. Douglas Price, "Voter Response to Short-Run Economic Conditions: The Asymmetric Effect of Prosperity and Depression," *American Political Science Review* 69 (1975): 1240-54; Arthur H. Miller, "Partisanship Reinstated? A Comparison of the 1972 and 1976 U.S. Presidential Elections," *British Journal of Political Science* 8 (1978): 129-52; and Arthur H. Miller and Richard Glass, "Economic Dissatisfaction and Electoral Choice," (unpublished paper, Center for Political Studies, University of Michigan, 1976).

57. Seymour Martin Lipset and Earl Raab, "The Election and the Evangelicals," *Commentary* 71 (March 1981) 3:25-31.

Samuel P. Hays

POLITICS AND SOCIETY: BEYOND THE POLITICAL PARTY

7

Since the mid-1950s political historians have made extensive use of quantitative data to analyze popular and legislative voting and political leadership. From this effort a new dimension has been brought to the more traditional focus on political leaders, political ideologies, and political strategies. The research has covered the full sweep of American electoral history, and it has brought together the more contemporary analyses of political scientists with those of historians.

The essays in this book bring together the results of this new work. Each is written by a specialist in a particular time period and hence focuses on a particular era. Together they provide a sense of ebb and flow in long-term evolution and an opportunity to reflect on the larger role of parties in American history and their ramifications. What does this stage-by-stage, system-by-system reconstruction of American political parties over almost two hundred years imply? What perspective does it provide? How can it help to formulate ideas which can shed light on American political history as a whole?

It is appropriate at this juncture to pose the question of the relationship between political parties and the larger society. The detailed quantitative analysis, especially that involving electoral behavior, and the observation of patterns of voting to identify trends and classify types of electoral patterns, inevitably entices one to emphasize the intrinsic importance of the party system itself, divorced from its larger social context. Yet at several points that larger context is clearly evident. Electoral analysis suggests the social roots of voting behavior, the identification of specified social characteristics of voters who made particular choices and who, over the years, developed or modified party loyalties. Such characteristics can be regarded simply as statistical variables associated with voting. But one can also go beyond that to examine the social context itself, its patterns and changes, and use electoral analysis primarily as a point of departure for an examination of the society of which party is only one factor.

The larger social setting is especially evident in the concept of realignment. Realignment assumes an unusual juxtaposition of public attitudes as shaped by the context of voters and party loyalty; such disjuncture in either the situation of voters or the symbolism and meaning of party identifications effects long-term changes in voting preferences. One might hypothesize that such realignments reflect major changes in the social order and that there is some connection between stages in party development, as displayed by electoral patterns, and changes in the larger society. Some time ago we were warned by V. O. Key, Jr. to distinguish between "realigning elections" and "realigning periods," to broaden our vision of the realignment process from specific elections to longer periods of time. The implication was that fundamental social changes were working their way through the formal system of parties and that their meaning would be missed if our attention was confined only to the dramatic impact of a single electoral contest.[1] In any event, the realignments of the early 1850s, the early 1890s, and the early 1930s all can be understood as reflecting extensive changes in the wider society.

One can readily visualize the early "preparty" stages of development, that period which is covered in these essays by Formisano and Shade, as integrally related to the wider social context. Parties did not always exist, and now that we have some sense of their relative decline in more recent years as well as their rise in the late eighteenth and early nineteenth centuries, we can avoid the temptation to speak of inevitability and concentrate instead on the analysis of gradual development. What was the social setting within which parties played a significant role by 1840 when that was not the case several decades earlier? Political life was rich and vibrant even without parties, as the issues debated in Massachusetts in the years between 1776 and 1780 make abundantly clear.[2] Varied devices evolved to express the political impulses which emerged in the wider society. But why did parties arise?

The vigorous political life after World War II sharpens the argument further. It is not that the society has become any less political; in fact, the opposite is alleged, that society has made too many demands. It is too highly charged with political drive, and the weight of political impulses has become far too varied and intense for parties to contain and discipline them. Too many values are in collision, too many "interest groups" are in the fray, and too many political leaders seek to capitalize on this intensity of political interest directly rather than to work through party institutions. So the argument goes. This also suggests the more fundamental context of the wider society. Social change, the relationship of individuals and institutions to the social order and the options available to them for expressing their political concerns must be studied if we are to understand the recent role of parties.

Consider political parties, for a moment, as a form of private, voluntary association in which individuals join together in order to act in ways which they could not do separately. Perhaps it is not altogether accidental that parties in their "classic form" arose in the 1830s and 1840s at a time when it appears that rapid increases also took place in the formation of a wide range of voluntary associations. How were parties different from or similar to other types of voluntary associations? For one thing their base of recruitment and loyalty was territorial, which brought together all people in a given geographical area for action, whether it ended in victory or defeat. The larger strategies of parties were built upon smaller strategies heavily bounded by the need to win in small electoral units. This can be contrasted with voluntary associations based upon similarities of function, either work or recreation or specialized civic interest, which joined people in different or dispersed geographical areas and organized them for action on a level above and beyond the local community. In such a distinction we can visualize the larger social setting within which parties function, within which they rise, flourish and fall.

We can emphasize three types of linkages between society and party. First are the voters themselves. Social changes in daily life affecting work and family, religion and education, home and community, leisure and recreation, provide the starting point from which to observe connections between social values and social institutions, on the one hand, and political mechanisms including political parties on the other. It is no wonder that detailed analyses of voting behavior have brought this relationship to the fore. And this is especially the case with the strong emphasis on ethnic and cultural factors. What this connection with voting demonstrates is not simply an explanatory variable, but a social context which has a life of its own and within which changes must be observed in order to understand shifts in voting behavior. Society is the larger context within which party is rooted.

The second link involves party leaders who seek to organize it as an institution for action. In the preparty years we often observe the maneuverings of political leaders, those elected and those who sought to be elected. At times they felt comfortable with little contact with the voting public. At other times when the stakes of legislative or executive victory were greater, they reached out to mobilize voters and draw them into the arena of political combat. The social context within which we understand party leadership differs markedly from that of voters. It is far more closely related to the hierarchies of networks which constitute the organizational processes in the economy, education, religion, and government. Those at the upper levels of these hierarchies relate to each other far more closely than they relate to the broader public in daily affairs, institutional contacts, and a wide range of social involvements from youth to adulthood. In this case the links between society and party are found in the evolution of institutions, their development from small to large scale, the upward flow of authority and decision making, and the resulting networks of human relationships. It is no wonder that a considerable body of historical research indicates that political leaders within a given community, city, region, state, or the nation, came from the upper levels of the social order in which they sought leadership.

Party ideologies constitute a third link between society and party. Leaders of each party sought to identify their institution in ideological terms, to place it within the context of statements of national and personal aspiration, to distinguish their party from others, all in an effort to gain the support of the voting public. These were not superficial activities; they constituted the major links between voters of many different personal and collective views dispersed throughout the land and the necessities of action at the larger levels of state and federal decision making. Party leaders could not manipulate voters directly, but they could hope to sway them by appealing to their values, hopes, and fears. In the classic period of party development in the nineteenth century, newspaper editors, partisan to the core, repeated and elaborated without compromise the party views on banks and tariffs, blacks and whites, natives and immigrants, economic growth and economic security; one of the most crucial elements of the political party, they played a major role in defining party ideology.

In each of these major facets of political parties—voters, leaders and ideologies—we could well look upon society as merely the independent variable by which to understand party phenomena. But we need to go further, to shift our vantage point, to start with varied sectors of society, and then to visualize the varied forms in which people reached out to the larger world of public choice. If voting behavior were rooted in the immediate world of the voter, then what changes took place in that social context to make political parties more meaningful at one time and less so at another? If political leadership was rooted in the hierarchical networks which linked institutional leaders, then what changes in those networks and institutions occurred to make these leaders emphasize parties at one time and other avenues of political expression at another? And if political ideologies, those larger links between the public and the wider political world, at one time were peculiarly shaped by political parties and at other times not, then what changes took place in social ideology, either the larger society that needed to be interpreted and explained on the one hand or the public desires for explanation on the other, which caused the rise and fall of party ideology?

Thus, we are driven back to the social context of political life, which not only contributes the variable by which a given twist in political behavior can be examined but also provides the broader setting for understanding the varied fates of political parties. People and institutions related to the wider political order at times through parties and at other times through other institutions. Unless we can remove ourselves from the confines of party and define social change, with its varied twists and turns, in a more comprehensive way, we will not have the conceptual apparatus capable of understanding the political party in American history.

This larger perspective underlines a pitfall in analysis which the previous essays might well foster. It is easy to consider the years from the early 1850s to the early 1890s as a classic era of the political party. Here all the rudiments of party flourished: intense popular commitment, vigorous leadership, and sharply focused ideologies, all of which dominated the realm of broad public involvement in the political order. We tend to regard this as the golden era of political parties and to use it as a point of departure for defining what went before and after. We speak of the preparty era, as if we have difficulty defining what the politics of that era was all about save as a forerunner to the party politics of later years. We know that in the first and second party systems, parties were still ill-formed and rudimentary. Our vantage point is not the society and politics of the era itself, but party as a precursor to the fully formed institutions of the halcyon years of the third system.

We can also look upon the decades since World War II as a period of aftermath. The golden years have come to an end; the integrative institutions of previous years have now waned. As a result political society has come apart at the seams. There is a sense of romanticism about the role of those political parties and the cohesive function they served, a romanticism which is all the more heightened by the fears of today. Perhaps the medicine we need for clearer perspective is the same set of concepts about long run social change appropriate for the analysis of earlier stages of party development. It might well lead to the conclusion that it is not the decline of the political party which we have witnessed but the emergence of the new individual and institutional relationships to the larger world for which parties are far less appropriate than are other mechanisms.

Let us then go beyond the political party to the relationship between society and politics, make forays from the world of each party system back into the social order from which it sprang, and construct ideas about politics independent of ideas about parties. Let us use the various essays as the springboard for establishing the changes in society from which we might obtain more perspective on the "rise and decline" of political parties and party systems as recounted by the five authors, from the preparty focus of Ronald P. Formisano and William G. Shade and the golden years outlined by Paul Kleppner to the system's weakening and collapse according to Walter Dean Burnham and Richard Jensen.

"Parties, yes—system, no." This is Ronald Formisano's answer to the perennial question posed since Joseph Charles and William Chambers argued that parties existed from the time of the Constitution. Formisano describes the fitful appearance of electoral competition, in some states rather than in others, at some times rather than at other times, and its ebb and flow, which prevents one from arguing that a full-fledged system of parties had emerged by 1824. His point of departure, therefore, is the simple descriptive task of classification based on the question, Were there parties in those years? He goes on to identify the peculiar demographic roots of voting when party competition did occur. The Federalists rallied pro-English groups, and the anti-Federalists, anti-English groups; and the two parties enjoyed different loyalties from dominant and dissenter religious adherents.

What insight does all this provide about the political relationship of people to their larger world? That focus is not implicit in Formisano's essay. His view is limited to party, the description of its rudimentary elements and its voting base. While this gives some sense of the nature of party, it does not help to answer the larger question of the relationship between party and society. We still have to make some very large guesses about the question of why a particular society at a particular time gave rise to political parties. From Fromisano's treatment we are led to believe that this evolution was inevitable, that parties would come with time, and that during the years from 1789 to 1824 their growing pains could be witnessed. Yet if looked at from the vantage point of 1820, one might well have concluded that this experiment with a divisive institution was over, that party was nothing more than a temporary faction, and that it had been superseded by new political unanimity. The Federalists were right; faction was a temporary device utilized by the discontented. They were also wrong, for the "Era of

Good Feelings" was not on their terms but on that of their opponents. Once the pressure of the Anglo-French Wars had been removed from American politics, the controversy over the connection with England seemed to be anachronistic in the midst of an outburst of energy to subdue a continent.

Suppose that we begin at the other end of the analysis, not with party but with society. We can visualize people evolving new ways of life rapidly after the Revolution: shaping new worlds and institutions, developing cities, clearing and planting new farms, producing, buying and selling. Between 1790 and 1820 the nation's population increased 145 percent, a larger rate of increase than in the next 30 years; the population of urban areas increased by 243 percent.[3] What diverse aspirations did all this engender? What was new and what was old? While some were in the forefront of these changes, did others tend to lag behind? And what of the relationship between this vitality of individual and institutional action on the one hand and government and politics on the other? How did people who were caught up in the maelstrom of change, either to their benefit of detriment, understand that wider world and seek to reach out for positive aid or protection? In other words, what was the relationship between society and politics?

One cannot sensibly argue that this vigorous change was carried on relatively independent of the formal institutions of government and that Americans saw no need to call upon public authorities for help, and hence were "a-political." The treatment of this relationship by Oscar and Mary Handlin in *Commonwealth* makes clear that even in the late 1770s a vigorous political life was very much the order of the day,[4] arising from the Revolution's impact on a wide range of economic opportunities and conditions. Although little of this relationship between society and politics after 1789 has been charted in monographic studies, it would seem logical to assume that the vigor of social and economic change was matched by an equal vigor in the demands of people upon their government. Those changes and demands shaped relationships between society and politics in the absence of well developed parties, as Van Beck Hall has shown in his work on Massachusetts in the 1780s entitled, instructively, *Politics Without Parties.*[5] At the same time it seems sensible to argue that only from the vantage point of understanding the general relationship between society and politics can one understand the peculiar sort of relationship mediated through the institution known as the political party.

The available research, as Formisano has summarized it, gives rise to a curious twist. On the one hand, the role of the external relationships of the young nation, the problem of being buffeted about amid the struggles of the French and the English, and the difficulty of remaining independent with a significant number of people sympathetic to the English exercised an overwhelming influence on party activity. More than any other factor, these disputes brought forth vigorous party competition, which ebbed and flowed as the impact of the external struggle did and led to the collapse of the entire "quasi-system" of party politics once those external pressures were removed. Of this the reader is very much aware in Formisano's treatment. But what of the internal evolution of American society and the rapid changes which took place? Of these the reader is not much aware. There are ethnic voters who reflect the distribution of population throughout the states and their attitudes toward the English; and there are the patterns of religious differentiation. Ethnic and religious patterns are made clear by the social analysis of voting preferences, but these are not sufficient to give meaning to the vitality of the social, economic, personal, and institutional changes which took place. Because the parties apparently did not reflect these changes in their strategies, neither does the historian observe them readily.

Parties, in fact, were somewhat irrelevant to much of the times; individuals could carry out their demands upon government rather effectively without them. Parties were useful to help contest the options in the face of the impact of foreign wars, but not to help contest options arising out of domestic affairs. Because Formisano's essay confines itself to party and its electoral support, it does not provide a sense of this political vitality "without parties" which accompanied social and economic change. This, in turn, only reflects the state of the art; historians have become so immersed in the phenomenon of party that they have failed to recapture the larger world of society in its relationship to politics.

Formisano's essay contains one glimmer of linkage between the broader aspects of society and party—his mention of the phenomenon of "deference."[6] The low level of participation in parties, so the assumption goes, must be explained, and this can best be done by assuming a positive attitude of popular deference toward one's "betters." It is not clear if Formisano really wishes to use this explanation for the lack of popular protest, or whether it is only a gesture of recognition of the problem. In either case, it seems inadequate. If by deference Formisano means the belief that one should give way to those thought to be one's social superiors in a deliberate act of submission to their authority, it appears to be too formal a political attitude. More convincing is something akin to "indifference," the attitude that for the most part what happens in the larger realm of state and nation is beyond one's experience, interest, or concern. One might well believe that the larger world of decision making is irrelevant or cannot be influenced, or perhaps it is relatively unknown. Indifference then prevails. The lack of a clear idea about one's relationship to politics, is a more satisfactory key for understanding the low participation than is studied deference.

But there is more to it than that. One has difficulty in describing the world of Americans in the nation's early years as a matter of either deference or indifference. There was much in the economy, social relations, and government which affected people favorably or adversely, and it seems safe to assume that looking outward from one's own personal affairs to the larger society activated a considerable number of people. Yet this activity was not reflected in vigorous party participation. Other forms of political involvement prevailed, and parties did not seem relevant. If we are to undertand the lack of parties in these years, therefore, it seems that we should look to the positive impulses emerging in the new nation's society and economy and understand their relationship to the wider political world. The relative weakness of parties can be understood only by contrasting them with alternative methods of political expression, as individuals established links with each other to use the government—local, county, state, and national—to realize their aims.

William Shade's account of the "creation of a modern party system" between 1815 and 1832 reflects the more extensive development of parties and the more abundant historical data. Benefiting from the intercorrelation of votes between successive elections, the similarities in patterns between state and national elections, and the determination of degrees of party cohesion in legislative voting, Shade is able to sort out stages of development of "constituent parties" and to focus on the transition years in the last half of the 1830s. By the 1850s fairly well disciplined parties had evolved with consistent patterns of popular and legislative voting over time and with nationwide similarities which superseded state and regional variations. Shade's essay provides a useful summary and interpretation of recent work.

At the same time Shade recognizes that it is desirable to place all this in the context of a larger society. At the start of his essay he emphasizes the "dizzying pace of social and economic change."[7] To make his general statement a bit more precise, while the nation's population grew by 145 percent between 1790 and 1820, it grew by 141 percent in the next thirty years; the rate of increase in urbanization was 410 percent as contrasted with the 243 percent between 1790 and 1820.[8] Shade mentions the "rapidly expanding society on the move," that "economic growth and geographic mobility reached unprecedented levels" and that "increasing religious fragmentation and ethnic heterogeneity forced a widespread acceptance of cultural pluralism." After an extensive analysis of party phenomena he comes back to this theme in the essay's final paragraph, reiterating the broader economic and social changes, but concluding that a lack of systematic study of the relationship between socioeconomic change and political development and a similar lack of "rudimentary theoretical tools" preclude a successful attempt to "explain the genesis of modern political parties."

This is true enough but perhaps we should strike out and chart a sense of direction about this social context of politics. Shade's essay displays as firmly as does Formisano's the problem that arises when historians turn inward into the detailed analysis of political parties. His brief foray into the wider socioeconomic scene suggests his own frustration at not being able to provide the larger meaning which he fully recognizes is required, that while historians have worked over party history in the period in far greater detail than in earlier years, they have not been able to tackle the more significant question of the relationship between society and politics. Yet the analytical field is not all barren. One can outline some forays which focus on the manner in which those deeply involved in change reached out into the wider realm of politics.

Some of these attempt to outline categories of change and the people who were involved. There were individuals who created new modes of commerce and production and organized a wide range of ventures created by the expansion of market opportunities; in these instances we focus on the entrepreneurs who promoted ventures and the way in which they established relationships with that wider world. There were people who moved to new farming areas, cleared land, and began to produce for the market; they were new actors reaching out to influence market forces as well as their governments. There were those caught up in the new evangelical and Arminian religious forces, seeking to reshape human values by emphasizing the capacity of people to undergo internal moral transformation and, in turn, to transform the world around them. The most visible institutional expressions of most of these forces were the growing towns and cities where social, economic, cultural and ideological innovation seemed to thrive. Here is the starting point of analysis. In each of these four sets of impulses we can focus on individuals and institutions generating change.

In this approach we soon recognize how inadequate is the inherited notion of Jacksonian Democracy to describe the relationship between this society in motion and its politics. It is one thing to describe the breakdown of constraints on political action through the extension of suffrage and eligibility for holding office; it is another to describe the positive political impulses which accompanied that change. The egalitarian impulses present from 1815 to 1852 appear to be holdovers from the steady erosion of privilege set in motion earlier rather than products of the dynamism of change after the War of 1812. If those decades convey any meaning at all, it is one of vast differentiation with centers of vigorous and active innovation flourishing in the midst of a wider world of more limited change and established ways. It is correct to argue that the breakdown of privilege gave rise to extensive opportunity for initiative, but it is even more correct to emphasize the wide variation in participation in those opportunities.[9]

Shade's description of all this as "pluralism" and "fragmentation" implies that there was little order to the variety of impulses. It would be more useful to speak of "differentiation," a concept which injects some notion of pattern into the social context. We can visualize the years from 1815 to 1852 in terms of specific types of differentiation that took place with rapid change. There was differentiation between those who organized economic ventures in industry and commerce and those who were organized by them, between those who spearheaded more intensive and commercial agriculture and those who did not, between those who fashioned new religious impulses and those who hung on to the old, and between the growing towns and their peculiar institutions and activities and the surrounding countryside and theirs. To reconstruct history amid a sense of patterned differentiation would enable one to bring more order and meaning to the rather generalized and not very useful concepts of "pluralism" and "fragmentation." The first connotes variety without identifying types of variety; the second connotes a "breakdown" in the social order when in fact the process of change involved the creation of a new and restructured one.

The most critical question in all of this is that of relative inequality. The fundamental social context for these years accepted by most historians is egalitarianism. Yet the quantitative data developed over the past two decades, in extraordinary abundance for a single problem of historical analysis, demonstrate a pattern of pervasive and persistent inequality. True, there was abundance, but there was "inequality amid abundance," not equality.[10] Edward Pessen's valiant effort to persuade historians to accept this evidence is slowly succeeding.[11] Rapid change generated new patterns of inequality, replacing those patterns which had evolved in farming and mercantile activities with those shaped by the new industrial economy. Equal opportunity to become unequal was the order of the day; a pattern of differentiation continued which can be described only as economic inequality.

This was only a part of the larger context of these decades, a rapidly differentiating society under the impact of rapid social change, which in turn gave rise to patterns of variation among people more involved in the substantive activites of change and those less so. Some were more mobile, geographically and vertically, and others less so; some organized enterprises and others did not; some shaped new religious impulses and others held to the old; some developed new urban areas and others defended the more traditional rural life. If we could shift the description of all this from the more generalized concepts of pluralism and fragmentation into more patterned categories of social structure and social change, then we would be in a better position to ask larger questions about the relationship between society and politics and, specifically, about the role of the party as one form of political expression in the larger social order.

This rich and varied set of individual and institutional impulses gave rise to equally rich and varied political impulses. There were several connections between them. One is the degree to which persistent economic inequality was reflected in leadership rather than in popular voting. Leadership came from the upper levels of the social order, a consequence for party which flowed from the persistence of economic inequality in the wider society. Another is the degree to which the nationalization of "constituent parties," that is the creation of a sense of ideological identity which enabled party adherents in one geographical area to obtain a sense of belonging with those in another, rested largely on ethnocultural identity.[12] This contrast between the characteristics of party leadership and those of the party electorate emphasizes the different linkages between society and party at distinct levels, one emphasizing hierarchical institutional networks and the other ideologically identified and communicated values.

Amid the vigor of social and economic development, associational activity emerged in varied forms to link people in diverse ways. The political party constituted one form of such activity, with a high degree of commitment.[13] Can one obtain clues to the relationship between society and party politics by exploring this line of inquiry? Certainly it makes sense if our point of departure is the individual, caught up in social and economic change, reaching out to establish contacts, relationships and meaning with others in the larger world. For their peculiar time and place political parties constituted a massive federation of associational activity to bring people together and translated the community of ethnicity and religion into larger institutions of meaning and action at a time when alternative larger social relationships had not emerged.

The last half of the nineteeth century was the golden age of the political party. During these years two well-organized parties squared off in persistent combat. Both mobilized voters extensively and persistently; turnout rates were higher than in previous or later periods and consistent as between local, state, and national races. Both parties were relatively equal in support nationwide and neither, save for the Civil War years, could muster a clear and sustained majority as did the Republicans, for example, between 1894 and 1910. In his essay Paul Kleppner details that persistence of constituency involvement which Formisano finds absent and Shade recounts in only an embryonic stage. Party leaders, with their well-developed institutions such as conventions and party newspapers, vigorously mobilized voters to help elect a president, Congress, governors, and state legislators. What had been rudimentary in earlier years now was fully developed, and historians are tempted to take this golden age as the point of departure from which to think about parties and their role in American society.

All this has come from one type of venture into historical research—the analysis of voting patterns. The extent and consistency of voting from the very start of the "new political history," has attracted historians of a quantitative bent. Voting realignments in the early 1850s and the early 1890s are dramatic enough to elicit attention, and the long slow, secular changes from the 1870s to the 1890s are almost as intriguing. Here is a unit of historical time, with a clearly defined beginning and end. Here also are clear demographic distinctions in partisan electoral differences obvious to the eyeballing historian making a quick foray into the data. Hence the ethnic and religious dimension of voting has been probed more deeply in one study after another, of which Kleppner's work has been the most extensive. What is particularly striking about his analysis is the degree to which he has gone beyond simply identifying the demographic variables associated with voting patterns and has reconstructed the social context itself. The distinction between pietistic and ritualistic or liturgical sets of religious values involves an attempt to find pattern and order in social phenomona independent of party and a recognition of the degree to which party takes on meaning only within that larger context.

What analysis can be made of the links of leadership and ideology, those two types of interaction between society and politics other than voting? These have received far less attention, a limitation which Kleppner's essay reflects. While some legislative voting analyses focus on the "party in legislature" and enable one to deal with such questions as the relative role of constituency and party, few have probed beyond to the interaction between leadership in the larger society and leadership in the party. Party ideology has been dealt with less; but if we are to view parties as institutions which link masses of people to the larger world, ideology becomes a critical element in bridging the gap between the smaller context of daily life within which the attitudes and values of voters are formed and the larger strategies of political leaders in state and national affairs. What ideologies, playing a similar linkage role, competed with party ideologies? Did explanations of the larger social and political reality offered by parties preempt the field; if not, what was the relationship among alternative systems of explanation?

Analysis of political leadership usually emphasizes social demography —age, occupation, religion, ethnicity, status of parents, education, and other factors. In these respects party leaders were strikingly similar, the overwhelming number drawn from the upper levels of the social order. There were some ethnic differences, like those in popular voting. And some leadership distinctions were associated with stages of economic development; Republican leaders, for example, tended to come from industry to replace older Whigs associated more with commerce.[14] More significantly, however, leaders were linked with evolving hierarchies of human networks in social, economic, and institutional life.

Just as Kleppner has made clear that the social context of voting in which the society-politics link must be analyzed is the spectrum of ethnocultural values relating to family, religion, education, and community, so it would seem sensible to argue that the social context in which the linkage among leaders should be analyzed must include the web of network relationships within which leaders function. Leadership studies thus far suggest a spectrum of networks ranged on a dimension of scale from smaller to larger units, including smaller to larger geographical areas, institutions, and communication links, and perceptions of them. Within the larger society a pattern of such networks evolved rapidly amid nineteenth century growth, with layers and hierarchies of leadership within each context of community, city, state, and nation. The character of political leadership followed this evolution rather closely, with leaders at given levels in social and economic networks playing similar roles as leaders at corresponding levels in politics. This would seem to be the most profitable set of concepts through which to examine the links between society and politics in the realm of leadership.

What of the social context of ideologies? Party leaders sought to mobilize voters by explaining to them what America was, where it was going and what action was appropriate to head in the right direction. Republican and Democratic ideologies were not party "principles" in the traditional meaning of the term but explanations which drew people together and linked voters at the grass roots level with national leaders. It makes sense, as Kleppner has suggested, to join the Arminian and moralistic thrust of evangelical religion with an emphasis on economic development and achievement to arrive at the Republican world view. It also makes sense to join the historical and traditional stance of liturgical religion with a more protective economic response, emphasizing action to guard against the adverse impact of rapid growth, as characterizing the Democratic party. Ideological choice lay between Republican affirmations of the positive state amid economic development and a civilizing morality, on the one hand, and Democratic affirmations of both economic freedom and personal liberty on the other. Each set of ideals drew together large numbers of people with distinctively, similar values. But what of the perspective of the American people amid rapid social and economic change independent of party. That perspective involved both varieties of ethnocultural outlooks and varieties of perceptions about the meaning of work and achievement. The most crucial aspect of ideological description, however, is to capture the narrowness or breadth of the world view of different people, and the varied range of choice or habitual and customary thought and behavior which their world views entailed. For those whose vision of analysis is more universal than parochial, it is easy to impute a similar range of perspective to others and to suggest that workers in the midst of adversity were imbued with a larger vision of an alternative society rather than simply with sustaining family life; that farmers sought to transform society rather than merely make a day-to-day living; or that Americans generally were impelled by a well-thought-out ideology of rapid advancement and "success" rather than being immersed in more limited day-to-day routines. Ideological analysis requires a distinction between those who sought to arouse people with alternative explanations of the larger world, and those who responded with varying degrees of affirmation or indifference to such entreaties. What is known about parties in this golden era and especially about voters suggests that the meaning of ideology was rooted overwhelmingly within the smaller context of family, community, the daily round of work, religion, and personal networks rather than in the larger realm of abstractions. Idea makers had to make sense not within their own logic but within the concrete experience of personal lives. At this task political party ideologues seem to have been more successful than those in social movements outside the party.

One further thought about the third party system. Toward the end of his essay, Kleppner suggests that by the end of the nineteenth century modernizing elites were dissatisfied with the parties which had come to full flower in the golden age. Parties were more of a hindrance than a help, and thus elites sought to construct other modes of political action while limiting party roles. If this be true, what were the roots of dissatisfaction? If elites found parties to be appropriate in the mid-nineteenth century and far less so by 1900, then one ought to be able to outline the process of change, and the evolution of new institutions outside the party which competed with the established parties in the public arena. As of yet this is only dimly perceived. We have been told often that private corporate leaders controlled parties. And tradition tells us that in the mid-1890s, in the nomination of William McKinley, this control reached a high point. Yet Kleppner's argument pinpoints a growing interest in alternatives to political parties on the part of those seeking to shape society and the need for historians to focus on the evolution of these new modes of public action.

Much of the third party system carried over into the fourth. The stage of development reached between 1852 and 1896, including party conventions, high levels of turnout, and close relationships between voting patterns at different political levels, persisted between 1896 and 1934 to a far greater extent than in the years prior to 1852. Yet there were cracks in this edifice and Walter Dean Burnham recounts these in considerable detail: party fragmentation, the emergence of differences in party "behavior" in different races and different sections, and the decline in voting turnout and party loyalty. The political party was no longer what it had been. Although the magnitude of change by 1894 should not be overstressed, there is clear evidence of erosion of party strength.

Our interest in this essay lies in the relationship between society and party, not simply the decline of party from within, but also the challenge from without. In the late nineteenth and early twentieth centuries many attacks on party arose from objections to its mode of operation and its results for public affairs. Two aspects of this criticism appear in Burham's work. One involves reforms in the formal mechanisms of party which were intended to limit its action, such as the direct primary, the initiative, referendum, recall, and formal registration. But he also describes, while corroborating the concluding ideas of Kleppner's essay, dissatisfaction over parties on the part of "corporate elites," and attributes much of the revision in political mechanisms to their objectives. Using this thought as a point of departure, we can explore more fully the way in which social and economic changes give rise to competing institutions of political action.

The most obvious of these new political phenomena was the "pressure group." The very term reflects the complexities of its historical development, both the evolution of a new institution and the degree to which it was met with mixed response. The pressure group which appeared in business, agriculture, and labor constituted a form of action markedly different from the political party. While the party was organized geographically, drawing into its units of activity all the people who lived in a given area, the pressure group brought together those with common functional interests in public affairs growing out of similar economic occupations. Grocers organized into trade associations, carpenters into one trade union and bricklayers into another, farmers into organizations of grain, meat, and milk producers and citrus, potato, and walnut growers. The rise of such functional groups occurred fitfully before the mid-1890s but steadily thereafter; they reflected a stage in the organization of an increasingly complex society and especially an effort to shape action at a level above and beyond that of community. Their role is to be found, therefore, in the evolution of human networks, the hierarchical patterns of organization from smaller to larger which grew up as modern industrial society moved on apace. These linkages are most elusive because little evidence reflects them directly; yet the resulting networks of human relationships and the organizational forms to which they gave rise constitute one of the most important developments in twentieth century American society.[15]

Equally significant as a new mode of political action were the large-scale systems of organization that were centrally directed and managed. While the private corporation is first to come to mind as the typical large-scale system, similar types of institutions appeared in government, education, and religion, as described by W. Lloyd Warner et al. in their book on "emergent American systems."[16] In each case when a new system emerged, the crucial element of change was the shift of control from smaller to larger units so that the geographical range over which control was exercised increased as did the number of factors brought under central direction. These large-scale systems came to be one of the overriding institutional conditions of American society. Their emergence created the new context within which individuals worked out their daily lives, institutions evolved and interconnected, and relationships between private and public affairs developed. These large-scale systems gave rise to a hierarchical order, shaped and directed centrally, and brought together a battery of scientific and technical professionals, who found the centralized power and authority inherent in those institutions congenial to their pretensions of applied knowledge.[17]

Those involved in shaping both functional organizations and large-scale systems found the political party inadequate to their objectives. The party was organized on the basis of geography, encompassing all voters within a given area. Those who organized functional groups and large-scale systems sought to divorce themselves from such limited influences. Their scope of action differed from that of the party, involving attempts to shape large-scale events rather than local affairs. They were geared not to mass action with its ideological elements but to the operation of institutions needing continuous, day-to-day control and influence at a higher level in the hierarchy of organization. Labor unions and farm cooperatives, for example, warned their members against entanglement in party politics; they urged "nonpartisanship," with support for candidates who agreed with their objectives independent of party. Leaders of large-scale systems had only contempt for parties and legislatures which responded more to public currents from the grass roots than to the imperatives of applied knowledge from the top. They contrasted the system and efficiency of the corporate model with the chaos and confusion of party politics. The work of institution builders in both functional groups and large-scale systems was a direct challenge to the primacy of the political party as an instrument of public action.

Parties were not eroded by these new institutions alone; they were also undermined by social changes at the grass roots level which in the third party system had constituted the cohesive base of party life. The changes were gradual. Much of the firm nineteenth century ethnocultural roots to political parties continued into the fourth party system. If the old Irish and German communities of that era faded they were followed by the newer eastern and southern European communities whose members injected more diverse party loyalties into the political world at the same time that they perpetuated the party system. The central role of family, within which values evolved and were sustained, for which stable and continuous livelihood was sought, and from which community activities were ordered and developed, continued to shape political party attachments through the depression of 1929 and the elections of 1934 and 1936. These particular ethnocultural loyalties even in 1936 were strong and did not fully erode until the fifth party system.

Evolving alternatives in the manner in which individuals reached out to the wider world undermined the influence of family and community. These alternatives could be observed in the claims for the "independent voter," who made up his own mind about issues and candidates and did not blindly follow party policies or candidates. The demand for reforms in party affairs which were reflected in the direct primary, the initiative, referendum, and recall came not only from the capitalist "elites" as Burnham describes them but also from individuals, largely in the upper half of the social order, who expressed their personal resentment over party discipline. This, in turn, gave way to a form of personal emancipation from party which came to be thought of not as "independence" but "indifference," the nonvoting which as time went on increased and was related inversely to socioeconomic levels. Those at the lower end of the occupational and educational scale tended to be "nonvoters" far more than those at the upper end. While nonvoting became more obvious after the 1930s, its origins could be observed during the fourth party system. The world of public affairs was moving beyond the imaginative bounds of many Americans; it seemed remote and beyond their capacity to understand, let alone to control. This was due partially to the construction of new institutions of decision making above and beyond community but it also arose from the gradual erosion of community itself, the loosening of ties to the primary group through which political values and loyalties had been mediated in the halcyon days of party in the last half of the nineeenth century.

In the first four decades of the twentieth century, the political party became only one of several types of institutions through which people sought to relate to the world of the government and politics. This idea sharpens our analysis. It emphasizes types of distinctions between society and politics which are often difficult to discern in the third party system but which are clearly delineated in the first and second when politics was carried on with vigor but without fully developed parties. Party did not preempt the field of institutions of action in public affairs; the historian, in turn, must develop some scheme for sorting out the two realms of society and politics. As new institutions began to compete with party in the late nineteenth and early twentieth centuries, we can observe alternative social and economic impulses which turned into alternative political impulses, gave rise to parallel and competing institutions of political action, and established new ways in which individuals related themselves to the wider political order. These tendencies which emerged in the early twentieth century set the tone for the evolution of relationships between society and politics in the years to come.

Observers of recent politics frequently have emphasized the erosion of party. Voting turnout, which stabilized and increased slightly in the 1930s, declined thereafter and reached new lows in the 1970s. The percentage of voters who identified themselves with party dropped to 25 percent, while those who considered themselves Independents increased to over 40 percent in the late 1970s. The influence of party on elected officeholders decreased: candidates ran more on their own and less as party nominees, developed financial resources independent of the party, and sought to approach voters directly to build personal support. Finally, organized interest groups reached a new high in numbers and activity, battering governmental institutions with demands which the machinery of party could not contain. While in previous years, the argument went, party was sufficiently strong to be the dominant agency for reconciling conflicting political impulses, it could no longer do so. The political system was flying apart.[18]

Richard Jensen discusses this erosion in his description of the "last party system," emphasizing the decline in party identification and the growth of Independents. There are warnings about nuances within the system, about stages of evolution before and after 1960. Prior to that time party history went through traditional types of development. The realignment of 1934-1936 was much akin to earlier realignments. In this case, however, the depression of 1929, accelerating long-term demographic changes, reordered voting patterns and firmed up the social and economic differences between the two major parties. Contrary to the case of the 1893 depression, ethnocultural patterns did not return to their former strength in the late 1930s. While working-class groups shifted strongly Democratic in 1932 and retained those loyalties, voters at upper-class levels veered back to the Republicans in 1934 and 1936; thus was launched the socioeconomic basis of voting which persisted for many years. From such beginnings arose the New Deal coalition, a pattern of politics which had considerable staying power.

By 1960, so Jensen argues, this new alignment gave way to a decay in the party itself. These were long-term changes, the beginnings of which, observed in the fourth party system, were retarded for several decades by the political intensity of the depression years. The change, according to Jensen, did not merely continue the erosion of party; it involved a decline in faith in government as a whole. Public opinion polls which measured "trust" in public institutions revealed a steady decline. The demands for reduction in government spending reflected this, but the full dimensions of such a major change Jensen does not develop. He seems to rest his explanation primarily upon the value conflicts which emerged in the 1960s, summarized by the terms "modern" and "postmodern," with special emphasis on the elections of 1968 and 1972.

The fate of political parties in this fifth system brings home forcefully the larger problem of the relationship between society and politics. To observe parties in decay during a period of vigorous institutional evolution and massive changes in human circumstance only emphasizes the degree to which there is a larger world beyond party which continues to be influential as political parties rise and wane. It calls for a vantage point similar to that which I took in discussing the first and second party systems, observation of the political impulses arising from social changes independent of party so as to define that larger context.

It is useful to observe these changes at three levels in the social and political order, the top, the middle, and the grass roots. Stages in the evolution of centrally managed systems which I observed in the fourth party system continued to be succeeded by even more elaborate stages after World War II. Hardly a phase of human life was immune—the economy, government, education, religion. Almost every period of human life, from birth to death, involved extensive participation in large-scale systems from medical to educational and occupational institutions to those providing security for older citizens. As these developed, administration, both private and public, became the central political phenomenon, the context within which individual lives were ordered and within which the potential for human influence was defined. The loss of faith in government was paralleled by an equally significant loss of faith in private corporations, a belief that the world of massive institutional systems had become far too remote for individual choice to make a difference. This was the most significant context for the evolution of public life after World War II.

The emerging political world also involved changes at the grass roots, in family, community, work, and leisure. Party loyalty and high turnout rates in earlier years were mediated through the primary social ties of family, sustained by work, reaching out to community. These patterns of life, undergoing slow change prior to World War II, went through massive transformations in succeeding years. The family changed from a context dominated by the need to cooperate and pool work in order to sustain all within it, characteristic of the ethnic communities, to one of caring for the separate creative development of its individual members. Leisure and recreation, along with family, became increasingly more important in contrast with work, for absorbing time and energy. Within this new world of nonwork activities one could exercise far more individual choice than in the disciplined work setting managed by others; one could adopt this or that avocation or recreational activity, become an expert in nonwork skills, and devote energies to the physical and amenity activities of house and home. Finally, cheap automobile transportation made it possible to separate the physical location of work and home so as to sharpen the distinction between these two realms of personal life.

These changes gave rise to a new relationship of individuals to their political world. On the one hand, patterns of life through which party loyalty had been mediated were weakened. On the other, new human preoccupations arose which made much of the larger world of public affairs seem secondary and irrelevant. Diverse human activities and ideas gave rise to intense human preoccupation with personal affairs to such a degree that the world of public life seemed remote and often fanciful. The incessant penetration of the larger world into human experience by means of the communication media often generated an experience of overload on one's senses which, in turn, gave rise to preferences for vicarious media experiences rather than for the information that would enable one to participate actively in the wider world of public affairs. Self-conscious efforts at political decentralization, to bring control closer to the grass roots—the enthusiasm for direct use of solar energy was one of these—captured some of this preoccupation, but simple apathy was often as important as self-conscious construction of alternatives.

While the evolution of technical and managerial systems and the increasing interest in personal development tended to erode human involvement in the wider political system, political participation also grew rapidly in the form of "interest groups." The relative rise of recreational, leisure, and civic activities, as contrasted with work, generated a host of new organizations which proliferated far beyond those associated with occupation. There was no avocation which did not result in individuals reaching out to others with similar interests. They were brought together through their own delight in sharing creative activities such as hiking, stamp collecting, science fiction, or bonsai gardens and through commercial groups which found that these activities provided markets from new products and services. At the same time each group which specialized in civic affairs—education, the handicapped, the elderly, the urban community, consumer and environmental problems—also grew rapidly, and sought public support for public action. Because the benefits of these political drives were not simply personal and extended to a very large portion of the social order, the new organizations were known as public interest groups. As was the case in earlier years, these new functional groups served to expand interest in public affairs and shaped new institutional devices which enhanced political development. Neither technical system nor party proved as attractive for linking individuals with the wider political order.

Many observers have been unwilling to accept this new set of political demands. They view them as a threat to party and hence the entire society. But in taking a larger approach, we can recognize that impulses other than party (which can be described as alternative political institutions) have always related individuals to the political world. To understand the relationship of society and politics in the fifth party system, moreover, we must recognize that it was not the New Deal, which set this new political world in motion, but World War II, with its rapid pace of social and economic development. The evolution of technical systems; changes in family, work, and leisure; the growth of new types of functional groups—all are far more closely related to those changes than to the 1930s which, by way of contrast, appear to be a more conservative pause amid the massive modernizing forces of the mid-twentieth century.

Each of the authors of the preceding essays has recognized, in one way or another, the significance of the larger social and economic context of political parties. Formisano asserted briefly that politics did exist without parties; Shade, that the major factor in the second party system was rapid social and economic change; Kleppner, that ethnocultural values underlay the partisan loyalties of the third system; Burnham, that corporate elites sought to restrain the influence of parties by means of reform; and Jensen, that modern and postmodern values in conflict constituted the major setting for the decline in the party system. While giving primary emphasis in their essays to the work on political parties, each author conveys a sense of the limitations of that work because of the failure of historians to sharpen the relationship between society and party.

The concern for the social and economic framework of parties has, for the most part, been dominated by the search for independent or explanatory variables with which to associate the evidence of primary concern, the behavior of voters, legislators, and party leaders.This search has turned historians to standard demographic variables, often transferred directly from contemporary social research onto the historical scene. Thus, the very task of thinking about appropriate independent variables and the reconstruction of the larger historical setting have been pursued with rather limited vision. Kleppner's exploration of the spectrum of ethnocultural values as rooted in the ethnic and religious life of a large number of Americans is the most extensive effort to go beyond the limited notion of an explanatory variable in order to reconstruct the underlying social and economic context in its own right. His approach constitutes an effort to translate an independent into a dependent variable and to emphasize it as a major problem for analysis in the first place, a phenomenon which itself must be described, ordered, and explained. These essays suggest the importance of making this translation, i.e., taking independent demographic variables and reconstructing how they are conceived so that they become dependent social and economic variables.

Patterns of social and economic development out of which political impulses spring cannot be understood more than dimly if subordinated as explanatory features of the more dominant political party. From the latter vantage point one can only take party as given and then explain its course narrowly. A more satisfactory treatment requires that society be reconstructed on its own terms, independent of its confined context as an explanatory variable, so that one can observe the impulses which reach out from individual and institutional endeavor into the wider political world. Those social and economic processes take place independent of party; political impulses in the eras of both preparty years and the years of party decline were no less intense and real than in periods of high levels of party development.

Historians have done much recently to develop greater understanding of political parties in America's past. They have defined stages in party history that are far more appropriate than are the four-year terms of presidential history, and they have established nuances of change and development within each of the five systems. At the same time, the evidence has helped to identify the relative degree of development in a party system by focusing on election intercorrelations over time and similarities of party support in elections at different levels and in legislative voting. All this has sharpened the description of historical units of party analysis.

Our understanding of the social roots of popular voting has also advanced considerably. Each of the essays contains abundant evidence about the social characteristics of voters. This is particularly striking in the essays on the first three party systems in which considerable time is devoted to the demographics of voting as well as the pervasiveness and consistency in partisanship. This search for the roots of electoral support is a common theme in contemporary political analysis, having been popularized by public opinion polling and election night and postelection analyses. One might well argue that in this fashion the perspective of historians has been shaped heavily by the perspective of contemporary political sociology.

Yet all this has emphasized the limitations as well as the possibilities of party analysis as an integral part of political history. It has enabled us to know more precisely a number of elements of party history. But it has also brought more sharply into focus the larger question of the relationship between society and politics as the more important task for historical inquiry. To understand the internal elements of parties is not enough. The long sweep of historical perspective which these essays provide makes clear that party is a somewhat delimited phenomenon of political history, that the rise and decline of party is very much a function of the larger political world which arises from the ebb and flow of social and economic development.

These essays, therefore, represent a description of the "state of the art" and, at the same time, suggest the outlines of research "beyond the political party" which needs to be done. To conceptualize, then specify, then explore the ways in which society is related to politics and the ways varied social and economic impulses, individual and institutional, reach out to shape the larger world, seem to be high on the unfinished agenda for American political history. The relationship between society and politics is the next order of business which the enormous expansion of both social and political history has now set for American historians.

NOTES

1. V.O. Key, Jr. "Secular Realignment and the Party System," *Journal of Politics* 21 (May 1959): 198-210; and idem, "A Theory of Critical Elections," ibid., 17 (February 1955): 3-18.

2. See, as an example, Oscar and Mary F. Handlin, *Commonwealth: A Study of the Role of Government in American Economy, Massachusetts, 1774-1861* (New York, 1947), in the opening chapters.

3. Data are from U. S. Bureau of the Census, *Historical Statistics of the United States, Colonial Times to 1970* (Washington, D. C., 1975), Series A 1-5 and Series A 57-72.

4. Oscar and Mary F. Handlin, *Commonwealth*.

5. Van Beck Hall, *Politics Without Parties; Massachusetts, 1780-1791* (Pittsburgh, 1972).

6. Formisano, supra, refers to the period as a "deferential-participant" phase in party history.

7. Shade, supra, for this and the following quotations in this paragraph.

8. See *Historical Statistics*.

9. This distinction is made effectively in Oscar and Mary F. Handlin, *Dimensions of Liberty* (Cambridge, Mass., 1961), pp. 9-22.

10. See, for example, Lee Soltow, "Inequality Amidst Abundance: Land Ownership in Early Nineteenth Century Ohio," in *Ohio History* 88 (Spring 1979): 133-51.

11. Edward Pessen, "On a Recent Cliometric Attempt to Resurrect the Myth of Antebellum Egalitarianism," *Social Science History* 3 (Winter 1979): 208-27.

12. Robert Kelley, "Ideology and Political Culture from Jefferson to Nixon," *American Historical Review* 82 (June 1977): 531-82; idem, *The Cultural Pattern in American Politics* (New York, 1979).

13. The popularity of naming children for mid-nineteenth century political figures—Jackson, Harrison, Clay, Taylor—is one reflection of this attachment.

14. Ari Hoogenboom, "An Analysis of Civil Service Reformers," *The Historian* 23 (November 1960): 54-78.

15. Kenneth Boulding, *The Organizational Revolution* (New York, 1953).

16. W. Lloyd Warner, Darab B. Unwalla, and John H. Trimm, *The Emergent American Society*, vol. 1, *Large-Scale Organizations* (New Haven, 1967).

17. See, further, Samuel P. Hays, "Political Parties and the Community-Society Continuum," in *The American Party Systems: Stages of Political Development*, ed. William Nisbet Chambers and Walter Dean Burnham (New York, 1967); idem, "The New Organizational Society," in *Building the Organizational Society: Essays on Associational Activities in Modern America*, ed. Jerry Israel (New York, 1972).

18. *The New American Political System*, ed. Anthony King (Washington, 1978), as one example.

INDEX

Abolitionist movement, 118, 119
"Abscam," 229
Adams, Henry, 58
Adams, John, 33, 37, 40, 41, 56, 58, 84
Agnew, Spiro, 230
Agrarian socialism, 204
Agriculture, 153, 154, 157, 252, 253
Alabama, 101, 163
  voting behavior in, 88, 103
Albany Regency, 88, 101
Alberta, Canada, 169
Alexander, Thomas, 94
Alien and Sedition Acts, 38
Alien Law, 64
"Amalgamation party," 88
American Association of Small Cities, 222
American Federation of Labor (AF of L), 206-7
American Independent party, 189
American Labor party, 202 n.42, 205
American Revolution, 37, 105, 249
Anti-Catholicism, 105, 120-22, 123, 204
Anti-Masons, 80, 81, 85, 88, 101
Anti-Nebraska Democrats, 121
Anti-Northernism, 116, 131, 163
Antipartyism, 68, 79, 81, 113, 122, 127, 130, 189, 196, 219
Antislavery, 119, 120, 136, 143 n.9
Anti-Southernism, 120, 122
Arizona, voting behavior in, 183, 200 n.29
Arkansas, voting behavior in, 103, 154
Asquith, Herbert Henry, 233
Austria, voter turnout in, 191

Bakke, Allan, 230
Baltimore, 57
Bank of the United States, 95
Bank of England, 62
Baptists, 63, 103, 132, 136
Beard, Charles, 154
Benson, Lee, 149, 150, 154
Blacks, 131-32, 153, 163, 164, 165, 167, 203, 205, 206, 210, 216, 221, 222, 223, 226, 227, 230, 232, 234 n.1, 246
  disfranchisement of, 230
Bleeding Kansas, 120
Bloch, Mark, 33
Boardman, Elijah, 49
Bowles, Chester, 215
Brant, Irving, 40
Brethern, 102
British, 132
Bryan, William Jennings, 148, 158, 160, 161, 175, 196
Buchanan, James, 158
Buel, Richard, 62
Bull Moose party, 164
Bull Moose Progressives, 154
Bureau of the Budget, 224
Burke, Edmund, 106 n.8
Burner, David, 181
Burnham, Walter Dean, 7, 8, 9, 14, 15, 16, 104

Calhoun, John, 81
California, 147, 169, 183, 225, 228, 230
  voting behavior in, 180, 181, 200 n.29

Calvinists, 158
Campaign management, 220
Campaigns, 129, 223, 226
Canada, 167, 168, 204
Canadians, English, 132
Canadians, French, 132, 133
Candidate selection process, 8
Carter, Jimmy, 215, 223, 225, 226, 232
Catholics, 102, 103, 132, 133, 147, 197, 204, 205, 208-9, 210, 216, 222, 228, 230
Central Intelligence Agency (CIA), 229
Chambers, William, N., 34, 248
Charles, Joseph, 34, 248
Choate, Joseph H., 164
Civil rights movement, 229-30
Civil service, 98
Civil War, 8, 15, 17, 104, 114, 122, 123, 124, 131, 137, 151, 152, 153, 156, 157, 171, 176, 255
Civilian Conservation Corps (CCC), 206
Clay, Henry, 80, 84, 95
Cleveland, Grover, 17, 158, 160, 199 n.10
Clinton, DeWitt, 41
Clinton, George, 40, 41
Coalition management, 4
Committee to Reelect the President, 220
Common Cause, 222
Communications, growth of, 105
Communism, 204, 217, 218, 234
Competitive politics, 65, 68-69, 77, 93, 100-101, 118, 174, 176, 183, 186, 188, 248, 250. *See also* State elections
Confederacy, 20, 131
Confederation, 36
Conflict politics, 218
Confrontation politics, 227, 228
Congregationalists, 46, 48, 63, 132, 136
Congress, 93, 94, 97, 99, 148, 169, 174, 199 n.10, 206, 218, 220, 223-24, 226
  speakership contests in, 94
Congress of Industrial Organizations (CIO), 206
Congressional parties, 93-94, 95, 103, 104
Connecticut, 63, 81
  voting behavior in, 236 n.18
Consensus politics, 218, 227
Conservative party, 202 n.42
Constitution (1787), 37, 38, 103, 162, 248
Convention system, 67, 79-80, 99
conventions, 74 n.65, 81, 158, 160, 255, 258
  congressional, 93
  Democratic, 165, 199 n.10, 228
  regional development of, 88
  state, 79
Copperheads, 123
Core voter, 26, 27, 28; defined, 26
Court of St. James, 95
Coxey, Jacob, 156
Crawford, William, 80, 86
Critical election, 6, 7; defined, 5
Critical realignment, 1-32, 30 n.31, 93, 103, 104, 114, 116, 118, 147-51, 157, 174, 186
Cross-party movement, 129-30
Currency inflation, 158, 161, 162
Customhouse Service, 98

Daley, Richard, 227
Daniels, Josephus, 163
Darrow, Clarence, 160
Debs, Eugene V., 197, 200 n.29
Decentralization, 149, 264
Defense Department, 224
Delaware, 55, 58, 63, 64
  conventions in, 93
  voting behavior in, 180
Democratic party, 14, 15, 16, 17, 20, 22, 30 n.31, 31 n.33, 34, 35, 66, 68, 80, 81, 82, 84, 85, 86, 88, 89, 93, 94, 96, 97, 99, 102, 103, 113, 114, 116, 118, 119, 120, 121, 122, 123, 124, 126, 129, 130, 131, 132, 133, 136, 137, 139, 143 n.9, 144 n.27, 147, 151, 156, 157, 158, 160, 161, 163, 164, 165, 170-71, 173, 174, 175, 176, 180, 181, 182, 183, 186, 188, 192, 194, 195, 196, 197, 202 n.42, 204, 205, 206, 207, 208, 209, 210, 211, 212, 213, 214, 215, 216, 218, 219, 220, 221, 222, 226, 229, 230, 232, 233, 256, 257, 262
"Democratic Republicans," 81
Depression (1819), 101
Depression (1870s), 114, 137, 154, 170
Depression (1890s), 116, 141, 262
Depression (1930s), 17, 18, 148, 151, 162, 165, 183, 195, 204, 206, 213, 214, 260, 262
Deutsch, Karl, 105
Dewey, Thomas, 208, 214-16
Direct primary, 166, 174, 189, 190, 219, 258, 260
  Democratic, 173

Disciples of Christ, 133
Disfranchisement, 163, 173
Dixiecrats, 189
Donahey, Vic, 175-76
Dooley, Mr., 150
Douglas, William L., 171
Dutch, 65, 121, 123
Dutch Calvinists, 136

East, 230, 231
East South Central states, 153
Economic class. *See* Economics and politics
Economic growth, 246
Economic modernization, 203-4, 229, 233
Economics and politics, 98-103, 104-5, 149-65, 169, 174-75, 190, 195-96, 198, 204-7, 208, 210-15, 216, 226, 230-31, 232, 243-67
Economy, political, 152-66, 181, 211-15
Edwards Ninian, 89
Eisenhower, Dwight D., 160, 217, 220, 226, 227
Elazar, Daniel J., 150
Election, congressional, 14, 93, 119, 147, 170, 171-75, 183, 186, 188, 189, 211, 255
  North, 192
  West, 192
  (1804), 57-58
  (1936), 236 n.18
  (1940), 236 n.18
  (1944), 236 n.18
  (1948), 236 n.18
Election, gubernatorial, 55, 67, 170, 171-75, 221
  Alabama, 89
  California, 183
  Illinois, 89, 91
  Michigan, 183
  Minnesota, 173,
  Mississippi, 89, 91
  Missouri, 89
  New Hampshire, 91, 190
  New Jersey, 173
  New York, 89
  Ohio, 173
  Oregon, 173
  Pennsylvania, 88, 89, 91, 183
  South Dakota, 173
  Virginia, 89, 91
Election, House of Representatives, 173, 224, 233
Election, legislative, 220
Election, off-year, 16, 24, 128-29, 211
Election, presidential, 128-29, 171-75, 180-81, 255
  (1800), 33, 38-39, 42, 70 n.9, 104
  (1804), 40, 41, 58
  (1808), 40, 41, 59
  (1812), 41, 52, 54, 59, 104
  (1816), 41, 42
  (1820), 42
  (1824), 84, 86, 87
  (1832), 79, 80, 85, 86, 87, 99, 104
  (1836), 80, 81, 82, 84, 86, 87, 91
  (1840), 86, 87, 91
  (1842), 84
  (1844), 91, 100
  (1852), 16, 91, 143 n.9
  (1854), 14, 114, 121
  (1856), 114
  (1860), 114, 121
  (1864), 114
  (1868), 114
  (1872), 114
  (1876), 114, 145 n.28, 151
  (1880), 145 n.28, 151, 156
  (1884), 145 n.28, 151
  (1888), 145 n.28, 151
  (1890), 17
  (1892), 17, 145 n.28, 156-57, 182
  (1894), 14, 30 n.31
  (1896), 161-62, 164, 182, 196
  (1900), 182
  (1904), 175, 182
  (1912), 200 n.29
  (1916), 182-83
  (1920), 182
  (1924), 161, 189
  (1928), 31 n.31, 147, 165, 182-83, 194
  (1930), 14, 30 n.31
  (1932), 182, 204, 212
  (1936), 17, 206, 211, 212, 213, 214, 236 n.18
  (1940), 182, 196, 206, 209-10, 211, 213-14, 235 n.13, 236 n.18
  (1944), 196, 206, 207, 208, 210, 211, 213-214, 235 n.13, 236 n.18
  (1948), 189, 206, 211, 213-14, 215-17, 236 n.18
  (1952), 213-14, 217-18
  (1956), 218
  (1960), 17
  (1964), 219

(1968), 189, 215, 228, 230
(1972), 228
(1976), 191, 215, 223, 226, 232
(1980), 215, 232-33
Election, primary, 22
Election, senatorial, 221, 233
Election, state legislature, 15, 171, 179-80, 233, 255
California, 180
Connecticut, 20 n.34
Delaware, 180
Illinois, 180, 201 n.34
Indiana, 180
Kentucky, 180
Maryland, 180
Michigan, 180
Minnesota, 176, 201 n.34
Missouri, 180
Nebraska, 201 n.34
New Hampshire, 180
New Jersey, 180
New York, 180
North Carolina, 176
Ohio, 176
Pennsylvania, 180
Rhode Island, 180
Virginia, 89
Wisconsin, 180
Election, state. *See* State elections
Election, types
deviating, 7
maintaining, 6, 164, 199, 218-19, 271-72, 310
realigning, 7, 8, 9, 10, 13, 244
reinstating, 7
system-sustaining, 6
Election era. *See* Electoral system
Election returns, 4
Electoral behavior, 97, 161, 169
Electoral competition, 53, 126
Electoral era. *See* Electoral system
Electoral participation, 22, 170, 181, 190-92 194-95
Electoral reorganization, 8, 9
Electoral stability, 8, 17, 103, 147
Illinois, 91
Mississippi, 91
Pennsylvania, 91
Electoral system, 1-32, 82-88, 266
defined, 10
partisan nature of, 150
first, 67-68, 247, 261, 262, 266
second, 18, 20, 22, 24, 27, 67-68, 77-111, 114, 118, 190, 247, 261, 262, 265, 266
third, 17, 18, 22, 24, 27, 31 n.35, 104, 113-46, 247, 261, 265, 266
fourth, 17, 18, 27, 147-202, 258-61, 262, 263
fifth, 17, 18, 22, 203-41, 160, 261-64
Electorate, size, 20
Ellmaker, Amos, 80
Embargo (1808), 45-46, 53, 57, 59, 74 n.64
England, 62, 158, 167, 249
English, 102, 248, 249, 250
Episcopalians, 49, 63, 64, 103, 132
Equal Rights Amendment, 228, 230, 232
"Era of Good Feelings," 53, 248-49
Ethnicity and politics, 60-61, 64-65, 99, 101, 102, 153, 163, 182, 196-97, 205, 207, 208, 209, 210-11, 230-31, 232, 235 n.13, 245, 250, 251-52, 254, 256, 265

"Family party," 88, 101
Far West, 158
Farmer-Labor party, 202 n.42, 205
Fascism, 214
Federal Bureau of Investigation, 226, 229
Federalists, 33-76, 149, 150, 154, 190, 248
Fee, Walter R., 55
Finney, Charles Grandison, 118
Fischer, David H., 61, 65
Florida, 58
voting behavior in, 200 n.29
Floyd, John, 81
Ford, Gerald, 215, 220
Foreign policy, 214, 215, 218, 234
France, 62, 203
Free Soil party, 116, 119, 120, 121, 143 n.9
Free Will Baptists, 132
French, 65, 249
French Revolution, 36
Friends of Peace, 54
Fusion party, 16, 121

George, Henry, 161
George, Lloyd, 233
"Georgia Machine," 101
Georgia, 59
voting behavior in, 103
German-Americans, 203
German Catholics, 208

German Lutherans, 65, 132, 133
German Reformed church, 102, 132
German Sectarians, 132
Germans, 64, 65, 102, 103, 196, 197, 260
Germany, 203
Gold standard, 158
Gold Standard Act, 153
Goldman, Emma, 164
Goldwater, Barry, 218-19, 228
Goodman, Paul, 65
Goodwin, Lawrence, 161
Great Plains, 153, 157
Greenback party, 127, 128, 154-57, 160-61, 170
Griswold, Roger, 48, 49
Gwin, Samuel, 95

Hall, Van Beck, 249
Hamilton, Alexander, 33, 154
Handlin, Mary, 249
Handlin, Oscar, 249
Hanna, Mark, 161
Harrison, Benjamin, 158
Harrison, William Henry, 81
Hartz, Louis, 149, 150, 166
Hatch Act, 206, 215, 216
Hays, Samuel, 168
Hofstadter, Richard, 150
Holmes, Oliver Wendell, 162
Home rule, 190
Hoover, Herbert, 160, 182, 194, 204, 205
House of Lords, 167
House of Representatives, 14, 93, 94, 99, 150, 151, 173, 174, 223
Humphrey, Hubert, 215, 219, 227

Ickes, Harold, 205, 206
Idaho, voting behavior in, 200 n.29
Ideological polarization, 226-30
Illinois, 157, 231
  voting behavior in, 86, 88, 134, 180, 236 n.18
"Immigrant vote." *See* Voting behavior, immigrant
Immigrants, 105, 136, 147, 152, 160, 165, 167, 196, 197, 246
Income tax, personal, 152, 164
Incumbent-insulation effects, 188
Independent party, 16
Independents, 220-22, 232, 262
Indiana, 151, [illegible], 219
  voting behavior in, 180
Indians, 205, 227
Industrialization, 162
Inflation, 216, 226
Ingersoll, Jonathan, 49
Initiative, 166-67, 258, 260
Interest groups, 264
Iowa, 157
  voting behavior in, 154
Irish, 98, 260
Irish Catholics, 17, 31 n.31, 65, 102, 133, 202 n.42
Irish Protestants, 102
Italian Catholics, 208
Italy, 203

Jackson, Andrew, 41, 67, 78, 80, 81, 82, 84, 85, 86, 93, 95, 97, 98, 99, 102
Japanese, 205
Jay Treaty, 37
Jefferson, Thomas, 33, 37, 40, 47, 54, 58, 59, 98, 154
Jews, 65, 196, 197, 205, 210, 223, 230
Johnson, Hiram, 169
Johnson, John A., 171, 175-76
Johnson, Lyndon, 158, 219, 220, 227
Johnson, Richard M., 80, 81

Kelley, Robert, 62, 65
Kemp, Jack, 229
Kennedy, Edward, 215
Kennedy, John F., 17, 220, 228
Kennedy, Robert, 228
Kentucky, 60, 101
  voting behavior in, 180
Key, V. O., Jr., 4, 5, 6, 7, 8, 93, 166, 244
King, Martin Luther, Jr., 228
King, Rufus, 41
Kirk, Claude, 224
Kleppner, Paul, 151
Know-Nothing party, 15, 16, 116, 121
Korean War, 217, 218
Ku Klux Klan, 165, 204

Labor parties, 127, 128
Labor unions, 206-8, 210-11, 216, 217, 219, 226, 259, 260
Lance, Bert, 225
Landon, Alfred, 212, 213

La Follette, Robert M., 154, 161, 169, 183, 197
La Guardia, Fiorello, 205
Lee, Henry, 81
Lee, Robert E., 137
Legislative parties, state, 95-97
Levine, Peter, 96
Liberty party, 116, 119, 120, 121, 202 n.42
Literacy test, 167, 190
Lloyd, Henry Demarest, 160, 161
Lobbies, 222-23, 233, 261-62
Louisiana, 153
  voting behavior in, 103
Lowi, Theodore, 149, 151
Lubell, Samuel, 183
Lutherans, 102

McCarthy, Eugene, 228
McCarthy, Joe, 217
McCormick, Richard, 79, 82, 91
McGovern, George, 228, 230
McKinley, William, 161, 203, 206, 258
McNamara, Robert, 224
Macpherson, C. B. 169
Madison, James, 37, 40, 58
Maine, 64, 75 n.79
  voting behavior in, 154
Marxism, 196
Maryland, 55, 58, 62, 63, 98
  voting behavior in, 40, 132, 180
Masons, 99
Massachusetts, 42, 63, 64, 76 n.95, 81, 168, 171, 244, 249
  voting behavior in, 43-45, 65, 133, 236 n.18
Media, 226, 230, 233, 246, 264; importance of, 219
Methodists, 63, 64, 103, 132, 135, 136
Metropole, 152, 153, 160, 161, 165, 169, 180, 181, 182-83, 196, 197
Michigan, 147
  voting behavior in, 154, 180, 181, 188, 236 n.18
Michigan Survey Research Center, 5, 6, 7, 8
Middle Atlantic states, 153
Midwest, 175
Minimum wage, 218
Mining, 153, 157
Minnesota, 171, 175, 189, 202 n.42, 205, 230
  voting behavior in, 30 n.31
Minor parties, 16, 17, 101, 116, 119-21, 126, 127, 128, 137, 154-57, 189, 196-97, 202 n.42. *See also individual parties*
Mississippi, 153, 166
  voting behavior in, 84, 85, 88, 103
Missouri, voting behavior in, 88, 103, 180
Monroe, James, 42, 93
Montana, voting behavior in, 200 n.29
Moore, Barrington, 151
"Moral Majority," 234
Moralism, 203, 205
Moravians, 102
Morison, Samuel E., 44
Mormons, 228
Moses, Robert, 168
Mountain states, 153

Napoleonic Wars, 105
National Association of Counties, 222
National Association of Smaller Communities, 222
National Association of Towns and Townships, 222
National Conference of Black Mayors, 222
National Education Association, 223
National Governors' Association, 222
National League of Cities, 222
National Recovery Administration (NRA), 205
National Youth Administration (NYA), 206
Native American party. *See* Know-Nothing party
Nebraska, 153
Nevada, voting behavior in, 200 n.20
"New Court" party, 101
New Deal, 17, 24, 28, 148, 151, 154, 163, 170, 171, 173, 174, 175, 180, 183, 188, 192, 195, 197, 198, 205, 206, 210, 211, 212, 213, 214, 215, 216, 218, 226, 231, 264
New England, 63, 64
New Hampshire, 63
  voting behavior in, 65, 84, 85
New Jersey, 55, 59, 63, 64
  conventions in, 93
  voting behavior in, 85, 88, 133, 180, 236 n.18
New Mexico, voting behavior in, 183
New York, 55, 58, 63, 64, 79, 80, 101, 151, 173, 189, 190-91, 196, 215, 219

voting behavior in, 88, 102, 119, 132, 133, 180, 263 n.18
New York Constitutional Convention, (1894), 164
New Zealand, voter turnout in, 191
Nichols, Roy, 80
Nixon, Richard, 17, 217, 220, 225, 228, 230
Nominating conventions, 41, 66
Nominating process, 8, 10, 15, 38, 67, 79-80, 81, 99, 128, 190, 212
Nonvoters, 26, 27, 28, 116, 130, 137, 191, 194, 211, 212, 231, 260-61
defined, 26
Norris, George, 205, 206
North Carolina, 64, 163
voting behavior in, 40
North, 164, 175, 176, 222, 226, 230
Northeast, 158
Norwegian Lutherans, 132, 133, 136
Norwegians, 121, 123

Office of Management and Budget, 225
Office of Price Administration (OPA), 215
Ogilvie, Richard, 224
Ohio, 63, 64, 80, 157, 175, 231
conventions in, 93
voting behavior in, 132, 180, 236 n.18
Oklahoma, voting behavior in, 200 n.29
"Old Court" party, 101
Oregon, 165
voting behavior in, 200 n.29
Orientals, 205

Pacific Northwest states, 153
Panic of 1819, 100
Panic of 1837, 84, 101, 104
Parrington, Vernon L., 154
Partisan stability, 9, 10, 12, 17, 22, 24-26, 57, 85, 86, 87, 96-97, 104, 126, 129, 131, 134, 137, 138, 140, 163, 173
Democratic, 130
Illinois, 89
Mississippi, 89
New Hampshire, 88-89
Virginia, 89
Party coherence, 55, 56-57, 87, 95, 103, 190, 220
legislative, 71 n.37
Party committees, 82
Party competition, 17-26, 35, 42, 43, 82, 96, 104, 129, 166, 190, 250
Party decline, 266
Party decomposition, 188, 190, 262
Party development, 58, 95, 97, 98, 103, 104
Party disintegration, 191
Party identification, 131, 136, 138, 139, 244, 262
Party ideology, 256-57
Party instability, 114, 119
Party loyalty, 5-6, 7, 10, 129, 137, 215-16, 243, 244, 258, 260, 263
decline in, 219-26, 231
Party organization, 169
weakening of, 219-20
Party participation, 250-51
Party system. *See* Electoral system
Party unity, 94, 96
lack of, 57
Patronage, 42-43, 205, 210-11, 216, 219, 224
Maryland, 56
Massachusetts, 44
New Hampshire, 44
New Jersey, 55
Rhode Island, 44
Vermont, 45
Pennsylvania, 55, 58, 63, 64, 80, 81, 101, 215
voting behavior in, 85, 88, 102, 119, 133, 180, 181, 236 n.18
"People's party," 16; (New York), 101
Peripheral voter, 26, 27, 28; defined, 26
Personal registration, 190, 191, 192, 258
Personal registration laws, 167-68
Personalism, 175, 189, 216, 218, 231
Pessen, Edward, 253
Pierce, Benjamin, 88
Pluralism, 203, 205, 208, 229-30, 233-34, 234 n.1, 252, 253, 254
Political Action Committees (PACs), 223, 233
Political elites, 98, 99, 113, 118, 127, 149, 150, 151, 158, 162-63, 165, 166, 169, 190, 197, 198, 217, 257-58
Political parties
coalitional nature of, 3-4
homogeneity of, 3, 4
social bases of, 61-66
state
New Hampshire, 88
Pennsylvania, 88
Political platforms, 38, 81
Political symbolism, 122-23, 126, 130, 136, 166, 190, 211

Politics, mass, coalitional bases of, 7
Politics, preparty, 13, 34, 244, 245, 247, 266
Polk, James, 67
Poll tax, 167
Population growth, 65, 105, 249, 251
Populism, 128, 154, 156, 157, 158, 160, 161, 163, 190, 195-96
Presbyterians, 64, 102, 103, 132, 135, 136
Pressure groups, 258
Price controls, 215
Prince, Carl, 55
Progressive era, 148, 149, 168, 219, 223, 224
Progressive movement, 166, 189, 203
Progressive party, 170, 197
Progressive party (La Follette's), 154, 189, 196
Prohibition, 114, 127, 128, 136, 137, 152, 204, 205
Prohibition party, 127-28
Proposition 13, 225, 228
Public service unions, 223

Quakers, 53, 64, 132

Racism, 163-65, 196, 227
Rationing, 215
Reagan, Ronald, 224, 229, 232-34
Realignment theory, 11, 12, 169, 170
Recall, 166-67, 258, 260
Reconstruction, 17, 78, 114, 126, 131
Referendum, 166-67, 258, 260
Regional loyalty, 42
Regionalism, 100-101, 103, 104, 116, 118, 119, 208
Relief, 205, 206, 216
"Relief" parties, 101
Religion and politics, 60-61, 63-65, 101-3, 152, 208-9, 230-31, 232, 235 n.13, 250, 251-52, 254, 255, 256-57, 263, 265
Republican National Committee, 220
Republican party, 16, 17, 20, 30 n.31, 33-76, 80, 113, 124, 126, 128, 130, 131, 132, 133, 134, 137, 139, 148, 151, 157, 158, 160, 161, 163, 164, 165, 170, 171, 173, 174, 175, 176, 180, 181, 182, 183, 188, 189, 190, 192, 194, 196, 197, 199 n.10, 202 n.42, 204, 205, 206, 207, 211, 212, 213, 214, 215, 216, 217, 218, 219, 220, 221, 224, 225, 232, 233, 255, 256, 257, 262
  development of, 121-24
Reuther, Walter, 207
Revolutionary War, 35, 38
Rhode Island, 81
  voting behavior in, 40, 180, 236 n.18
Richmond Junto, 88
Ridgway, Whitman H., 56
Risjord, Norman, 41
Ritner, Joseph, 88
Rockefeller, Nelson, 224
Rogers, Will, 181
Roll call voting, 42, 59, 94, 95, 96-97, 104, 109 n.32, 139
Romney, George, 224
Roosevelt Progressives, 189
Roosevelt, Franklin D., 148, 171, 175, 204, 205, 206-7, 208, 209, 210, 211, 212, 214, 235 n.9
Roosevelt, Theodore, 171, 175, 182
Russia, 203, 217

Sargent, John, 80
Saskatchewan, 204
Scandinavians, 197
Schattschneider, E. E., 195
Schlesinger, Arthur, Jr., 100
Scots, 102
Scots-Irish, 64, 65
Scots-Irish Presbyterians, 65
Scranton, William, 224
Secession, 15, 17, 122, 131, 137
Sectionalism, 93, 94, 164-65
Sectionalization, 161
Senate, 93, 95, 99, 149, 150, 151, 167, 175, 223
Separation of powers, 149, 150
Seventeenth Amendment, 149
Sherman Silver Purchase Act, 158, 199 n.10
Silbey, Joel, 94
Silver, 153, 157, 161
Sirica, John, 229
Slavery, 101, 118, 119, 122, 152, 166
Smith, Al, 165, 173, 182-83, 192, 194
Smith, John Cotton, 49, 50
Smith, William, 81
Snyder, Simon, 52
Social Security, 212, 213, 215, 218
Social status, 75 n.83
Social tension, 9-10, 116-21, 127, 128, 137, 152, 156, 214
Socialism, 154, 164, 165, 169, 170, 189, 195-97, 206, 214, 218

Socialist party, 197, 203, 204, 205
Socioeconomic class. *See* Economics and politics
South, 122, 153, 157, 160, 163-65, 166, 167, 170, 196, 197, 219, 221, 226
South Atlantic states, 153
South Carolina, 59, 63, 81, 153
Southern Baptists, 132, 135
Spain, 203
"Stand Up" law, 46, 48, 50
Standing committees, 93
Standing Order, 48, 49, 63, 71 n.28
Standpat party, 170
State elections, 43, 67, 88, 89, 91, 93, 101, 147, 167, 251
  Connecticut, 46-50
  Delaware, 55-56, 66, 180
  Georgia, 59
  Indiana, 180
  Kentucky, 60
  Maryland, 56-57, 66
  Massachusetts, 43-45, 51, 66, 75 n.79
  New Hampshire, 43-44, 51, 89, 180
  New Jersey, 53-54, 66, 180
  New York, 51-52, 65, 180
  North Carolina, 59, 173
  Ohio, 60
  Pennsylvania, 52, 65
  Rhode Island, 43-44, 51, 72 n.40, 180
  South Carolina, 59, 84
  Tennessee, 60, 75 n.76, 173
  Vermont, 45, 66
  Virginia, 59
State legislatures, 167
  Illinois, 96-97
  New Jersey, 96-97
  Virginia, 96-97
State parties, 100
State politics, 101 104
Stevenson, Adlai, 218
Stockman, David, 233
Strong, Josiah, 113
Suffrage, 252
  Connecticut, 78
  Illinois, 78
  Kentucky, 78, 79
  Louisiana, 78
  New Jersey, 78
  North Carolina, 79
  Pennsylvania, 78
  Rhode Island, 78, 134
  South, 78, 79
  South Carolina, 78
  Virginia, 78, 79
  women's, 167, 234 n.1
Sunday blue laws, 152
Supreme Court, 164, 174, 175, 181, 213, 214, 226
Sweden, voter turnout in, 191, 192
Swedish Lutherans, 132

Taft, Robert, 220
Tammany societies, 60
Tammany Hall, 205, 212
Tax revolts, 223, 225
Taxes, 226
Taylor, Zachary, 79
Tennessee, 60
Tennessee Valley Authority (TVA), 212
Texas, 153
  voting behavior in, 154
Third-party movements, 189, 190, 207, 256-58, 260
Three Mile Island, 229
Ticket-splitting, 171, 174, 221
Tingsten, H.L.A., 191
Tolerationists, 49-50, 64, 76 n.96
Transportation, growth of, 105
Truman, Harry, 171, 214, 215-17
Trumbull, Jonathan, 47, 49
Turner, Frederick Jackson, 77, 93
Turnout. *See* Voter turnout
Tyler, John, 81

Unemployment Councils, 204
Unionists, 64
Unitarians, 63
Universalists, 63
U.S. Conference of Mayors, 222
Urban reform, 168
Urbanization, 152, 249, 251, 252, 253

Van Buren, Martin, 67, 80, 81, 82, 85, 95
Vermont, 81
  voting behavior in, 45-46
Vietnam War, 227, 228
Virginia, 42, 59, 63, 64, 81, 109 n.32, 152, 153, 219
  voting behavior in, 86, 103
Voter turnout, 10, 12, 17-18, 22, 24, 26-28, 31 n.38, 32 n.40, 34-35, 43, 51, 58, 66, 67-68, 82, 84, 114, 116, 124, 126,

127, 128-29, 130, 137, 138, 139, 140, 141, 150-51, 176, 190-92, 194-95, 198, 204, 206, 208, 210-11, 216, 223, 231, 246, 255, 256, 258, 261, 263
Connecticut, 49
Delaware, 55
Democratic, 129, 144 n.27, 192, 194
Illinois, 87
Maryland, 56, 57, 74 n.61
Massachusetts, 49
New Hampshire, 86, 89
New Jersey, 86
North, 192
Pennsylvania, 55, 88
Republican, 194
South, 32 n.40, 128, 190
South Carolina, 84
Virginia, 86-87
West, 144 n.25, 192
Voting behavior, 6, 9, 12, 13, 26-28, 82, 87-88, 91, 93, 99-100, 129, 131, 148, 149, 154, 243-46, 255, 265
congressional, 93-95, 97
Democratic, 16, 18
economic effects on, 133-34
ethnic, 113-46, 132-33
immigrant, 102-3, 123, 132
in state legislatures, 96-97
legislative, 139-140
regional, 11, 40. *See also individual states and regions*
Border states, 18-20, 31 n.31, 31 n.33, 55, 62, 65, 114, 124, 131, 132, 180, 182, 183
East, 133
East North Central, 18, 124
Midatlantic, 18, 51-55, 62, 65, 121, 124, 133
Middle states, 37, 38, 62, 82, 102
Midwest, 102, 119, 121, 130, 133, 136, 182, 183
Mountain states, 18, 154, 157, 180, 183
New England, 16, 18, 37-38, 43-51, 55, 62-63, 65, 82, 118, 119, 124, 136, 176, 180
North, 17, 102, 121, 130, 131, 132, 180, 186, 188, 209
Northeast, 147, 182
Northwest, 183
Pacific, 18, 182
Plains states, 154, 157, 180
South, 16, 17, 18-20, 31 n.31, 31 n.33, 37, 38, 58-60, 62, 82, 102-3, 114, 116, 118, 121, 124, 126, 130, 131, 132, 154, 173, 180, 182, 183, 209, 228
West, 17, 60, 62, 126, 176, 180, 182, 186, 188
West North Central, 18, 126
religious, 113-46, 132-33
Republican, 20
rural, 209-10
urban, 209-10, 216
Voting patterns, 232
Voting stability, 5-6

Wallace, George, 189, 207, 228
Wallace, Henry, 207, 215
War of 1812, 35, 41, 44, 45, 46, 49, 53, 56, 59, 60, 68, 77, 103, 190, 253
Warner, W. Lloyd, 259
Washington, George, 37, 42, 62
Washington, voting behavior in, 200 n.29
Washington Benevolent Societies, 45, 54, 58, 60
Watergate, 226, 229
Weathermen, 228
Weaver, James B., 156, 157
Welsh, 102
West, 160, 164, 175, 176, 196
West Virginia, 152
Whig party, 15, 16, 18, 34, 35, 66, 67, 68, 79, 81, 82, 88, 93, 94, 97, 98, 99, 102, 103, 114, 118, 119, 120, 121, 123, 124, 133, 136, 137, 154, 256
Wilkins, William, 81
Willkie, Wendell, 209, 212, 214
Wilson, Woodrow, 160, 175, 181
Wirt, William, 80, 85
Wisconsin, 157, 166, 169, 183
voting behavior in, 180
Wolcott, Oliver, 49, 50
Wolf, George, 88
Women, 211, 223, 228, 230, 232
enfranchisement of, 24, 191
Woodbury, Levi, 88
Woodstock, 228
Workingmen party, 101
Works Progress Administration (WPA), 204, 205, 206

World War I, 164, 165, 166, 175, 180, 183, 189, 196, 203, 234 n.1
World War II, 175, 182, 196, 215, 217, 244, 247, 263, 264

Yale University, 48

About The Authors

PAUL KLEPPNER is Professor of History, Professor of Political Science, and Director for the Office for Social Science Research at Northern Illinois University in DeKalb. He is the author of *The Cross of Culture* and *The Third Electoral System: 1853-1892*.

WALTER DEAN BURNHAM is Professor of Political Science at Massachusetts Institute of Technology. He is the author of *Critical Elections and the Mainsprings of American Politics, Presidential Ballots, 1836-1892* and co-author of *The American Party Systems*.

RONALD P. FORMISANO is Professor of History at Clark University and is the author of *The Birth of Mass Political Parties: Michigan 1827-1861*, and of articles in *The American Political Science Review, The Journal of American History, American Quarterly*, and other journals.

SAMUEL P. HAYS is Distinguished Service Professor of History at the University of Pittsburgh. He is the author of *Conservation and the Gospel of Efficiency, The Response to Industrialism*, and *American Political History as Social Analysis*.

RICHARD JENSEN is Professor of History and Sociology at the University of Illinois at Chicago Circle and Director of the Family and Community History Center at the Newberry Library. He is the author of *The Winning of the Midwest* and *Illinois: A Bicentennial History*.

WILLIAM G. SHADE is Professor of History and Director of American Studies at Lehigh University. He is the author of *Banks or No Banks: The Money Issue in Western Politics, 1837-1865*, and co-author of *Our American Sisters: Women in American Life and Thought* (revised edition), and *Before the Molly Maguires: The Emergence of the Ethno-Religious Factor in the Politics of the Anthracite Region, 1844-1972*, and other publications.